Putnam County Tennessee

Circuit Court Minutes

1842-1856

By:
Work Projects Administration

Copyright 1941
By: Works Projects Administration

New Material Copyright: 2018
By: Southern Historical Press, Inc.

All rights reserved. No part of this publication may be reproduced, stored in a retrieval system, transmitted in any form, posted on to the web in any form or by any means without the prior written permission of the publisher.

Please direct all correspondence and orders to:
www.southernhistoricalpress.com
or
SOUTHERN HISTORICAL PRESS, Inc.
PO BOX 1267
375 West Broad Street
Greenville, SC   29601
southernhistoricalpress@gmail.com

ISBN #0-89308-874-9

Printed in the United States of America

PUTNAM COUNTY

CIRCUIT COURT MINUTES
1842-1856

March Term 1842

P-1 Be it remembered that at a Circuit Court began and held at White Plains in and for the County of Putnam in the State of Tennessee on the Second Monday it being the 14th day of March in the year of our Lord one thousand Eight Hundred and Forty Two - Present the Honorable Abraham Caruthers Judge of the 4th Judicial Circuit in said State presiding who ordered said court to be opened and proceeded to dispatch the business thereof.

It appearing to the court from the certificate of Joseph Hyder here produced by William H. Carr that at a popular Election opened and held at the places of holding elections in all the Civil Districts for the County of Putnam and State of Tennessee on the First Saturday it being the 5th day of March 1842 that the said Carr was duly and constitutionally elected Clerk of the Circuit Court for the said County of Putnam for four years then next ensuing and it also appearing that said Joseph D. Hyder was returning officer for said County appointed by the County Court; therefore came the said William H. Carr together with Elijah Carr, John Brown, David Patton, Carr Terry, John Terry, John L. H. Huddleston Isaac A. Huddleston, John L. Huddleston, Andrew Wassum, Henry Davis, William H. Barnes, Alexander Madden and John West, and Entered into three several Bonds, one for Ten Thousand one for five thousand and one for one thousand Dollars and all conditioned as the law Directs and which Bonds are in the word and figures following to wit,

"Know all men by these presents that we William H. Carr, Elijah Carr, John Brown, David Patton, Carr Terry, John Terry, John L. H. Huddleston, Isaac A. Huddleston, John L. Huddleston, Andrew Wassum, Henry Davis, William H. Barnes, Alexander Madden and John West are held and formerly bound unto James C. Jones Govenor of the State of Tennessee and his successors in office the sum of ten thousand dollars for the payment of which will and truly to be made and done we bind ourselfs our heirs, Executors and administrators _____ these sealed with our seals and dated this the 14th day of (p-2) March Anno Domini 1842.

The condition of the above obligatoon is such that whereas the above bound William H. Carr at a popular election opened and held at the place of holding elections in the several Civil Districts in the County of Putnam in said State on the first Saturday in March 1842 was duly and constitutionaly elected Clerk of Circuit Court for said County of Putnam for four years then next ensuing. Now if the said William H. Carr shall safely keep the records of said court and faithfully discharge the duties of his office as Clerk as aforesaid during his continuance in office, then this obligation to be void otherwise to remain in full force .

William H. Carr (Seal) Elijah Carr (Seal) John X Brown (Seal) David
                                His   His   Mark
Patton (Seal) Carr X Terry (Seal) John Terry (Seal) John L. H. Huddles-
                         Mark
ton (Seal) Isaac A. Huddleston (Seal) John L. Huddleston (Seal) Andrew

Wassum (Seal) Henry Davis (Seal) W. H. Barnes (Seal) John West (seal)
    His
Alexander X Madden (Seal), Duly acknowledge in open court at the White
       Mark
Plains in Putnam County.

                              Ab. Caruthers - Judge presiding.

    Know all men by these presents that we, William H. Carr, Elijah Carr,
John Brown, David Patton, Carr Terry, John Terry, John L. Huddleston,
Andrew Wassom, Henry Davis, William H. Barnes, John West and Alexander
Madden are held and firmly bound unto James C. Jones, Governor of the
State of Tennessee and his successors in office in the penal sum of Five
thousand Dollars for the payment of which well and truly to be made we
bind ourselves, our heirs administrators and in testimony whereof we have
hereunto subscribed our names and affixed our seals this the 14th day of
March in the year 1842. The condition of the above obligation is such
that whereas the above bound William H. Carr has heretofore on the First
Saturday of March 1842 at a popular election opened and held in the Civil
Districts in Putnam County in said State duly and constitutionally elected
Clerk of the Circuit Court for said County of Putnam now if the said William H. Carr shall well and truly account for and pay over all monies that
shall arise from taxes on suits in said   (p-3)   Circuit Court to such
persons as shall be by law authorized to receive the same then this obligation to be void otherwise to remain in full forse and effect William
H. Carr (Seal) Elijah Carr (Seal) John X his mark, Terry (Seal)
David Patton (Seal) Carr X his mark, Terry (Seal) John L. H. Huddleston (Seal) Isaac A. Huddleston (Seal) John L. Huddleston (Seal)
John West (Seal) W. H. Barnes (Seal) Alexander X his mark, Madden
(seal) .

"Attest A. B. Caruthers - Judge presiding in open court at White Plains
in Putnam County ".

    Know all men by these presents that we William H. Carr, Elijah Carr,
John X his mark, Brown, David Patton, Carr X his mark, Terry, John Terry,
John L. H. Huddleston, Isaac A. Huddleston, John L. Huddleston, Andrew
Wassum, Henry Davis, William H. Barnes, John West and Alexander Madden,
are held and firmly bound unto James C. Jones Governor of State of Tennessee and his successors in office in the sum of one thousand Dollars for
the payment of which well and truly to be made we bind ourselfs or heirs
administrators and etc. In testimony whereof we have hereunto subscribed
our names and affixed our seals this the 14th day of March A. D. 1842.

    The condition of the above obligation is such that whereas the above
bound William H. Carr was therefore on the first Saturday of March 1842
at a popular election opened and held at the places of holding elections
in all the Civil Districts in the County of Putnam and State aforsaid
duly and constitutionally elected Clerk of Circuit Court of said County
for the four years then next ensuing now if the said Clerk shall well and
truly collect and pay over all fines and forfietures that shall be adjudged by said Court to the person authorized by law to demand and receive the same then this obligation to be void otherwise to remain in full
force and effect William H. Carr (Seal) Elijah Carr (Seal) John X his
mark, Brown (Seal) David Patton (Seal) Carr X his mark, Terry (Seal)
John Terry (Seal) John L. H. Huddleston (Seal) Isaac A. Huddleston
(Seal) John L. Huddleston (Seal) Andrew Wossum (Seal) Henry Davis

(Seal) John West (Seal) W. H. Barnes (Seal) Alexander X his mark, Madden (Seal).

Duly acknowledged in open court at the White Plains in Putnam County. A. B. Caruthers Judge presiding " Which said several bonds having been acknowledged in open court by all of said securities are duly attested were ordered to (p-4) be spread upon the minutes of said court and then came the said William H. Carr and the several oaths of office prescribed by law having been duly administered to him to him he is permitted to enter upon the duties of his office.

Court adjourned to the court in course.

A. B. Caruthers

P-5   July Term 1842

Be it remembered that at a Court of Pleas began and held at the White Plains in and for the County of Putnam in the State of Tennessee on the Second Monday it being the Eleventh day of July in the year of Our Lord One thousand Eight hundred and forty two - present the Honorable Abraham Caruthers one of the Judges of Circuit Court of the State of Tennessee and assigned to hold the courts of 4th Judicial Circuit in said State: Who took his seat, ordered said court to be opened and proceeded to dispatch the business thereof: -

T. James Bartlett the Sherriff of Putnam County returns into court the State Writ of Venire facias to him directed, executed upon Henry W. Sadler, Lawrence Byrne, McClellan Jones, Elijah Carr, David Patton, Abraham Ditty, John B. Pointer, John Shoat, John Terry, Robert Peak, Rufus Tinsley, Augustin Lee, Robert Officer, John Bohannon, Benjamin F. Wroe, William K. Bradford, Henry L. McDaniel, William R. Vance, Garland Anderson, and John Rogers all good and lawful men of said County of Putnam and also returnes the he has by intree of said Writ summoned Isaac A. Huddleston and John L. H. Huddleston to attend this court as constables and thereupon from the jurors summoned as aforesaid, the court proceeded as a Statute in such case made and provided directs to select and empanel a grand jury for the County of Putnam for this Term where are elected Abraham Ditty, Robert Officer, Henry L. McDaniel, Lawrence Byrne, Benjamin F. Wroe, John Shoat, Henry W. Sadler, Rufus Tinsley, John Rogers, John Bohannon, Augustin Lee, Robert Peak and Elijah Car of whom the court appointed Henry L. McDaniel foreman, who together with the rest of the said grand jurors having been empanelled sworn and charged according to law to enquire for the body of the County of Putnam retired to consider of presentments and indictments and Isaac A. Huddleston a constable summoned as aforesaid was sworn to attend the Grand Jury - John A. Minnis Esqr., Lee Gardinhire Esqr., (p-6) George M. McWhorter Esqr., William B. Richardson Esqr., Richard Nelson Esqr., James T. Quarles Esqr., Alvin Cullom Esqr., Samuel Tinny Esqr., and William McClain Esqr., counsellors and attornies at Law, were admitted to the Bar, ordered to be placed upon the roll and are permitted to practice as counsellor and attornies as aforesaid in all the court of said County of Putnam:

It appearing to the court that the regular Atty. Gen. did not attend. It is ordered that James T. Quarles Esqr. be appointed Attorney General for this term pro tem for the County of Putnam who came here into open court and was duly sworn as the law directs and entered upon the duties of his said office.

Herald D. Marchbanks summoned as a juror for reasons appearing to the satisfaction of the court from further attendance as such is excused.

It is ordered by the court that tomorrow be set as States day in the Court; and that the second day after Term of said Court thereafter shall be States day.

Simon Hagin, Admr. of F. B. McKinley Decd.) Debt Cert.
Vs) Came the parties by
Lawson Clark) their Attornies and
) the pltff enters his
appearance and moves the court to Dismiss Defts. Petition - Whereupon it is considered by the court that said petition be dismissed - that the plaintiff have his judgment for the sum of Forty seven Dollars and forty two cents confirmed together with 12½ per cent damage from the 3rd day of November 1841 up to this day for the detention of the same and that execution issue against John Rogers Security for the prosecu Cirtiviari jointly with the said Defendants for said sum of $47.42 the debt aforesaid and the further sum of three Dollars and seventy nine cents the damage aforesaid and also his cost by him about his suit in this behalf expended.

P-7 Shadrach Price) Came the parties by their attor-
Vs) neys and on motion of the plaintiff
Joseph Terry, Isaac Crook) the Defendants petition for a cer-
and Charles Crook) tiorari in this case is dismissed
) it is therefore considered by the
court that the plaintiff recover against the Defendants his cost in this court expended and that a procedendo issued to the Justice of Peace who tried this cause below directing him to issue execution etc.

Thomas Nicholas Admr.) Petition to sell slave - Be it remembered
Vs) that on this 11th day of July 1842 the
Expartee) above cause came on to be heard before
) the Hon. Ab. Caruthers Judge presiding
upon petition - When it appeared to the court that John Ellison late of this County departed this life intestate leaving his widow and ten distributees and possessed of one negro slave named Ann - that petitioner is administrator of estate of said Ellison and that it would be manifestly for the advantage of said distributees that said negro be sold for the purpose of division as distribution can not other wise be made. It is therefore ordered that petitioner sell said negro woman at publick sale upon a credit of 12 months giving 20 days previous notice of the time and place of sale by advertisement at White Plains and Kinslow in the County and Sparta and Milledgeville in the County of White and make report to next term.

Simon Hagin Admr of F. B. McKinley Decr.) Debt Cert.
Vs) Came the parties by their
Lawson Clark) Attorneys and the plain-
) tiff enters his appearance
and moved the court to dismiss Defendants petition whereupon it is considered

by the court that said petition be dismissed (p-8) and that the plaintiff recover costs in this court expended of said Deft. and it is further ordered that a procedendo issued directed to the Justice of peace _____ the _____ he issue Execution against Defendant.

Ordered that Court adjourn until tomorrow morning at 9 oclock.

Ab. Caruthers

Tuesday 12th July 1842

Court met according to adjournment.

James Snodgrass) Motion to condemn land Robert Buckhannon
Vs) Justice of Peace filed here in court the
William Scarborough &) following papers to wit:
William Kinnaird)

State of Tennessee) To any lawful Officer to Execute and return
) you are hereby commanded to summons William
Putnam) Scarbourrough to appear before same Acting
) Justice of Peace for said County to answer
the complaint of James Snodgrass in a Debt due by note given under my hand and sealed.

March 26 - 1842) Edmnd Stamps
) Justice of Peace
) (Seal)

Executed and set for trial on 2nd day of April 1842 Before Edmond Stamps Esqr.

T. S. Elms Const.

Judgment for the Plaintiff for Eighty two Dollars and Eighty four cents Debt and all Lawful cost.

This given under my hand and seal this the 2nd of April.

Edmond Stamps J. P.

State of Tennessee) To the sherriff or any constable in said County
) to Execute and return, you are hereby commanded
Putnam County) that of the Goods and chattles, lands and tene-
) ments of William Scarborough and William Kin-
naird if to be found in your county as will make the sum Eighty Two Dollars and Eighty two cents Debt and all lawful Interest and cost of a Judgment that James Snodgrass obtained against the said William Scarborough before Edmond Stamps Esqr. on 2nd day of April 1842, in this fail not and make due (p-9) Return of this Writ given under my hand and seal May 31st 1842.

Robert Buckahhon (Seal)
Justice of the peace

Come to hand 31st of May 1842 $101.31
Judgement 2 day of April 1842   .50
Constable survey warrant
Justice Edmond Stamps rendering Judgment   .25
Fi Fa   .12½

                                Robert Buckhannan   (Seal)
                                Justice of the peace

    No personal property of any discription to be found in my County Levied on one tract of land in Putnam County belonging to William Scarborough defendant, lying in the round cove where he now lives in district No. 11 containing 150 acres held by deed from John Henry beginning at a <u>steake</u> in the round Cove runing thence south 125 poles to a small sugartree, walnut and pointers on the side mountain thence west 200 poles to a dog wood thence north 120 poles to a maple thence East 200 poles to the beginning 150 acres this the 1st day of June 1842.

                                   T. S. Elms Cost.

    On motion of the plaintiff it is ordered by the court that said land bee condemed and sold to satisfy said Execution and the costs of this motion and that on order of sale issue to the sherriff of Putnam County for that purpose.

James Snodgrass   )   Warrants
    Vs   ) On motion to condemn land Robert Buckhannon
Harrison Whitson   ) Justice of the peace filed herein in court the
) the following papers to wit:

State of Tennessee   ) To any Lawful Officer to Execute and return
) you are hereby commanded to sums Harrison Whit-
Putnam County   ) son to appear before me as same a Justice of
) peace for said County to answer the complaint
of James Snodgrass in a plea of:

    By note given under my hand this 20th May 1842.

                                   George McCarmack   (Seal)
                                   J. P.

P-10   Executed and set for trial on 21st day May 1842 before Robert Buckhannan Esqr. T. S. Elms Csl. Judgement for the plaintiff for Twenty four dollars and Thirty Two and Three fourth cents and all lawful cost May 20 1842.

                                   Robert Buckhannon
                                   Justice of Peace

State of Tennessee   ) To the sheriff or any constable in said
) County to Execute and return - I command
Putnam County   ) you that of the goods and chattles lands
) and Tenements of Harrison Whitson if to be
found in your County you make the sum of twenty four dollars and thirty

two and three fourth cents debt and all lawful intruse and cost of a a Judgement that James Snodgrass obtained against the said Harrison Whitson before me on 20th day of May 1842 and made return of the same as the law directs this given under my hand and seal June 22" 1842.

       Robert Buckhannon J. P.

 Came to hand June 22" 1842 - Judgment May 20th 1842 for - - $24.32 3/4
 Constable Elms services warrent   .50
 J. P. Judgment   .25
 Fi Fa   .25

       Robert Buckhannon J. P.

No personal property of any discription to be found in my County Levied on Two tracts of land in Putnam County belonging to the defendant one where he now lives and the other one where Jerimiah Whitson lives lying in the Board Valley in Dist. No. 6 called and bounded as follows - Beginning at a sugartree and Beech standing near each other runing, thence west 126½ poles to a Beech an white walnut and pointers, Thence East 126½ poles to a large chesnut on a mountain thence north 126 poles to the Beginning Containing 100 acres be the same more or less - the other one beginning at a white hickory and sugartree the northwest corner of a tract of land formerly owned by John _____ and purchased by him of Joseph B. Dibrell running thence north 39 poles to a dogwood on a hill side. Thence west to the conditioned line - Thence with the conditional line to the old line, Thence south East thence with (p-11) line to the beginning corner containing 125 acres, the same more or less.

        July 1, 1842
        T. S. Elms Const.

James Snodgrass)   Warrant
  Vs   ) Motion to condemn land Robert Bohannon, Justice
James Scarborough) of peace filed here in court the following papers
) to wit,

State of Tennessee) To any lawful Officer in said County to execute
) and return you are hereby commanded to summons
Putnam County   ) James Scarborough to appear before some acting
) Justice of the peace for said County to answer
the complaint of James Snodgrass in a plea of debt due by note given under my hand and seal March 26th 1842.

        Edmond Stamps   (Seal)
        Justice of the peace

Executed and set for trial before Edmond Stamps Esqr. on the 31st March 1842.
        T. S. Elms Const.

Judgment for plaintiff for thirty nine dollars and ten cents debt and all lawful costs.

        Edmond Stamps   (Seal)
        Justice of the Peace

State of Tennessee) To any lawful Officer in said County to exe-
) cute and return you are hereby commanded that
Putnam County) of the goods and chattle lands and Tenements
) of James Scarborough If to be found in your
County you cause to be made the sum of thirty nine dollars and Ten cents
debt and all lawful cost to satisfy a Judgment that James Snodgrass obtained against the said Scarborough before me on the 31st March 1842 in
this fail not and make due return of this to wit, this given under my
hand and seal this 5th of April 1842.

                                                        Edmond Stamps   (Seal)
                                                        Justice of the peace

P-12   Judgement 31st of March 1842 $39.10
        T. S. Elms Serving warrant   .50
        Justice for Judgement fi fa   .37½

No personal property of any discription to be found in my County, levied
on a tract of land in Putnam County belonging to defendant in district
No. 6 lying on the south side of Mill Creek adjoining the lands of William
Gammons on the East and the widow Shirley on the west _____ Beginning on
a beech Tree running north Sixty poles to a chestnut thence west one hundred and twenty poles to a cherry tree thence south sixty poles to the beginning containing 50 acres be the same more or less.

                                                   April 6th 1842
                                                 T. S. Elms Const.

    All of which being seen and heard by the court it is considered by the
court that said land be condemned and sold to satisfy the plaintiffs debt,
cost aforesaid and also the costs herein accrued and that a vendition ex-
ponai issue &c.

The State   )   Indictment for assault Battery - Jesse B. Terry
  Vs   )   and Stephen D. Burton was this day sworn in
Daniel Bartlett &   )   open court to give evidence on this Bill of In-
Joseph Bartlet   )   dictment in behalf of the State and retained
)   under charge of the proper officer and after
wards the Grand jury came into court and return a Bill of Indictment
against Daniel Bartlet and Joseph Bartlet for assault and Battery endorsed
by Henry L. McDaniel thier foreman a "True Bill" and retind.

    The Grand jury presented Harden Chitty for retailing spirits, Robert G.
Hughs for nuisance, Asa Herald and James Haynes for Affray and Hugh Owen
and Nicolas McDonald for affray and retired, and said Grand jury having
no further business before them they are discharged.

State   )   Indictment for Assault and Battery - This day
  Vs   )   came the attorney General for the State and
Daniel Bartlet &   )   the defendant in proper person and said de-
Joseph Bartlet   )   fendant being charged upon the Bill of indict-
                       ment say they are guilty in manner and form
as charged it is therefore considered by the court that   (p-13)   said
defendant pay a fine of two dollars and fifty cents each also cost of this

prosecution and Benjamin F. Wroe came into court acknowledge himself security for said defendants for said fines and costs and agree that the execution for same may issue against him jointly with said defendants.

Abraham Buck)
Vs)
Gideon Anderson)
and)
Peter Anderson)
and)
John Welsh)
)
trial at next term.

Certiorari
Upon petition of John Welch one of Defendants It is ordered by the court that certiorari and supersidias issue as to John Welch returnable to next term upon his giving bond and security according to law for the prosecution of the same - and the plaintiff enters his appearance and it is ordered that this cause be set for

Benjamin Mackie)
Vs)
John L. H. Huddleston)
)

Appeal from J. P. On affidavit of Defendant this cause is continued until next term and it is condemned by the court that the plaintiff recover against said defendant the cost of this.

William Carland for the use)
of Hugh Wallace)
Vs)
Jesse Pollard)
)
neither is said suit prosecuted - It is therefore considered by court that said plaintiff be non suited and that he the defendant go hence without day and recover against Hugh Wallace for whose use this suit is brought the cost of this suit.

Appeal from J. P. - This cause being called for the trial the defendant came by attorney and plaintiff being solemnly called to come into court and prosecute this suit came not,

Mathew England)
Vs)
John Johnson)
)
and recover against the plaintiff the cost of this suit.

Certis
This day came the plaintiff by attorney and dismissed this suit - It is there considered by the court that the Defendant go hence without day

Elizabeth Glover)
Vs)
Henry Glover)
)
ordinary process of law cannot be served on him (p-14) on motion it is ordered by the court that publication be made in the central Gazette a news paper published in McMinnville for three successive weeks for the defendant to appear at the next term of the Circuit Court of the County of Putnam at White plains on the 2nd Monday of November next and then and there answer complainants Bill or the same will be taken for confessed and set down for hearing expartee.

Bill of divorce
This day came complainant by solicitor and it appearing to the court affidavit that the defendant is not an inhabitant of this state so that the

Jesse Conway)
To)
Charles Phillips and)
David Phillips)

Warrant
Motion to condemn land John Welch Justice of the Peace filed herein court the following papers to wit -

10

State of Tennessee) To any lawful Officer to Execute and Return
) you are hereby commanded to summons Charles
Jackson County   ) Phillips and David Phillips to appear be-
) fore me or some Justice of peace to answer
Jesse Conway in a plea of Debt due by a note Ten dollars herein fail not
given under my hand and seal this 6th January 1842.

                 John Welch (Seal)
                 Justice of Peace

 Executed and set for trial on 29th of January 1842 - before John Welch Esqr. J. L. H. Huddleston Cost.

                 January 29th 1842

 Jesse Conway Vs Charles and David Phillips by note of hand therefore it considered by me that the Defendant pay ten Dollars principle and lawful Interest until paid on cost of suit given under my hand the date above.

                 John Welch (Seal)
                 Justice of the peace

 Execution Stayed by James and Stephen Phillips - Execution spent the 6th June 1842.

State of Tennessee) To any lawful officer to Execute and return
) Greeting - You are hereby commanded that of
Putnam County   ) the Goods and Chattles lands and tenements
) Charles Phillips and David Phillips and Stephen
and James Phillips there security for stay of Execution you cause to be
made the sum of ten dollars principle and lawful interest until paid and
cost of suit to satisfy Judgment (p-15) that Jesse Conway recovered
against said Charles and David Phillips before me on the 29th of January
1842 - fail not given under my hand and seal this 6th of June 1842.

                 John Welch (Seal)
                 Justice of the peace

 Judgement Rend 29th January 1842 and a note due 25 of December 1841
for ten dollars Interest up to this date June 6th 1842 A .26½
Warrant Executed by John L. H. Huddleston .50
Justice fees for Judgement and this fi fa .37¼
 Returned not satisfied no property found in my county.

June 27th 1842   J. L. H. Huddleston

State of Tennessee) To any lawful officer to execute and return
) you are by commanded as heretofore that of
Putnam County   ) the Goods and chattles, Lands and tenements
) of Charles Phillips and David Phillips and
Stephen Phillips and James Phillips their security for stay of Execution
You cause the sum of Ten Dollars principal and lawful Interest until paid
and cost of suit to satisfy a Judgement that Jesse Conway recovered a-
gainst the said Charles Philip and David Philips before me on the 29
January 1842 fail not given under my hand and seal this the 9th of July
1842.

                 John Welch (Seal)
                 Justice of the peace

Judgement rendered the 29th Jany. 1842 on a note due 25th Decr. 1841 for $10.00 Interest up to the 6th July 1842 31½ cents warrant executed by John L. H. Huddleston - $100 Justice fee for Judgement and two fi fa" Alias Execution by John Welch J. P. Iss. 9th day July 1842 No goods and chattles to be found in my County Levied on one tract of Land sixty acres more or less lying on Fisk's turnpike Road so called in said County. District No. 3 whereon David Philip and Jacob Phillips now lives abounded by Thomas Choate and McComic I think by me J. L. H. Huddleston Const.

July 9, 1842

P-1$ On motion it is considered by the court that said land be condemned and sold to satisfy plaintiff debt and cost aforesaid and also costs of this motion and that a writ of venditioni exponia issue &c.

H. R. & F. Marchbanks)   Motion
    Vs) Plaintiff by attorney dismiss their motion
Alfred Jones) It is therefore considered by the court
) that defendant recover against the plain-
tiff's the cost herein accrued.

Reddin Pippin)   Certo
    Vs) The defendant not appearing to prosecute his writ
Sam Mansel) of certiorari it is condemned by the court that
) the same be dismissed and that the plaintiff re-
cover against defendant the cost in this court accrued.

George Buggs Esqr. took oath of an attorney at law and was admitted to pratice as such in this court.

Elisha Camron)   Warrant
    Vs) Robert Buckhanon Justice of the peace filed here
Har Whitson) in court the following papers to wit -
)
State of Tennessee) To any lawful Officer to Execute and Return
) you are hereby comanded to summons Harrison
Putnam County) Whitson to appear before same acting Justice
) of the peace for said County to answer the
complaint of Elisha Camron in a plea of Debt due by not given tender.

My hand and seal April the 18th A. D. 1842.
                                            Edmond Stamps   (Seal)
                                            Justice of the peace

Executed and set for trial on the 30th April 1842 before Edmond Stamp Esqr.
                                            T. S. Elms   (Seal)

Judgement for the plaintiff for Eight Dollars and twenty three cents Debt and all lawful cost this 30 April 1842.
                                            Ed. Stamps   (Seal)

State of Tennessee) To any lawful Officer in said County to Exe-
Putnam County) cute and return you are   (p-17)   hereby

commanded that of the Goods and Chattles, lands and tenements of Harrison Whitson if to be found in your County you cause the sum of Eight Dollars and twenty four cents and all lawful cost to satisfy a Judgement that Elisha Camron obtained before Edmond Stamps Esqr. on the 30th of April 1842 in this fail not and make due return of this Writ given under my hand and seal this 9th of June 1842.

                Robert Buckhannon
                Justice of peace

  Judgement 30th April 1842 J. P. Justice for Judgement twenty five cents T. S. Elms Serving warrant 50 cents fifa - Allis 25 cents No personal property of any Description to be found in my county, Levied on one tract of land in Putnam County belonging to the defendant where he now lives lying in the Board Valley in district No. 6 Bounded as follows - begining at a sugartree and beach standing near Each other runing thence west 126½ poles to a Hickory and beach and pointers thence south 126½ poles to a beach and white walnut and pointers - Thence East 126½ poles to a large chesnut on a mountain, thence north 126 poles to the beginning containing 100 acres be the same more or less.

June the 13th 1842   Thomas S. Elms Cost.

  On motion it is consider by the court that said land be condemned and sold to satisfied plaintiff debt and costs aforesaid and also the cost of this motion ordered that a writ of venditionecesponias issue &c.

James Snodgrass	)	Warrant
Vs	)	Motion to condemn land George McComick filed
Vinet Henry	)	here in court the following papers to wit -

State of Tennessee	)	To any lawful Officer to Execute and return you
	)	you are hear by commanded to summons Vinet Henry
Putnam County	)	to appear before some acting Justices of the
	)	peace for said County to answer the (p-18)

complaint of James Snodgrass in a plea of debt due by note given under my hand and seal March 26th 1842.

                Edmond Stamps (Seal)
                Justice of the peace

  Executed and set for trial 2nd day of April 1842. Before Edmond Stamps Esqr. - T. S. Elms Const.

  Judgement for the plaintiff for one hundred and two Dollars and forty cents debt and all lawful costs, this given under my hand and seal this 2nd day of April 1842.

                Edmond Stamps
                J. of the peace

State of Tennessee	)	To the sheriff or any lawful officer to
	)	Execute and Return you are hear by com-
Putnam County	)	manded that of Goods and chattles, lands
	)	and tenements of Vinet Henry if to be found

in your county you cause to make the sum of one hundred and one Dollar and thirty one cents Debt, and all lawful costs and Interest that acrees there thereon so much as will satisfy a Judgement that James Snodgrass obtained against the said Vinet Henry before Edmond Stamps Esqr. my predecessor in office on the 2nd day of April 1842 in this writ fail not, and make due Returns of the same, given under my hand and seal this the 4th day of May 1842.

George McCormick (Seal)
Justice of the peace

Came to hand 4th May 1842 Levied on four Feather Beads and furnature one Brown mare and colt one corner cupbord. One cow of the defendants the Beads and furnature were levied on by W. F. Williams before me this the 4th day of May 1842.

T. S. Elems

Warrant served 50 cents one levy made 50 cents two fi fa 25 cents. Sold the property above which is one cow one Bead and furnature and corner cupbord after giving the legal notice, June 10th 1842 for $5.12½.

T. S. Elems Const.

Received on the within Execution Five Dollars twelve and one half cents 10th of June 1842.

T. S. Elems Const.

P-19 No more personal property of any discription to be found in my County, Levied on three tracts of land in Putnam County belonging to the defendant where he now lives lying in Board Valley in district No. 6 . One containing one hundred and thirty acres located and bounded as follows: Beginning on a Beech Marked J. W. Dearing running East 180 poles to Buck eye and to small Dogwoods on the south side of the mountain near a large Cliff of Rocks thence north crossing a spring branch 115½ poles to a sugar tree Beech and Dog wood thence west 180 poles to sugar tree maple and Horn Bean thence south 115½ poles to the beginning - Second tract beginning on the north Boundary line of his 130 acre survey on the side of the mountain 25 poles west of his north East corner of the said 130 acre survey on a Beech Thence north on the mountain 120 poles to a Beech and Elem on the mountain side Thence west 96 poles to a large Rock at a small distance South of a spring Thence south 120 poles to a Black gum and pointers on the line of his 130 acre survey thence East with said line 96 poles to the Beginning containing 72 acres. Third tract Beginning at a Beech on the mountain marked J. G. H. near John W. Deering line at a large Rock running thence south 80 poles to a walnut and Beech thence East 50 poles to a Beech thence south 80 poles to a walnut and Beech Thence East 50 poles to a Beech Thence north 80 poles to the Beginning containing 25 acres.

May 6th 1842   T. S. Elem Const.

On motion it is considered by the court that said land be condemned and sold to satisfy plaintiffs debt and cost aforesaid and also the costs of this motion and that a writ of venditionai Exponias Issue 4 c.

Motion to condemn land.

John Welch
Justice of the peace

Filed herein court the following papers to wit:

Peter Kuykendall) Attachment
Vs) State of Tennessee, Putnam County - To any law-
Gideon Anderson) ful Officer to Execute and return Greetings,
) whereas Peter Kuykendall hath complained on
oath before me John Welch a Justice of the peace in and for said County
that Gideon is Justy Indebted to him to the amount of one hundred Dollars
and oath having also been made that the said Gideon Anderson hath so absconded so that (p-20) the ordinary process of law cannot be served
on him and the said Peter Kuykendall having given bond and security according to law, you are therefore commanded to attach the Estate of the
said Gidion Anderson if to be found in your county as a sufficient quanity
thereof replevable and good and sufficient security that shall be of value
sufficient to satisfy said Debt and costs according to the complaint and
such Estate so attached in your hand to secure or so to provide that the
same may be liable to further proceedings thereupon to have before some
Justice of the peace in and for said county when and where you shall make
known how you have Executed this precept, fail not given under my hand
and seal this 27th day of June 1842.

              John Welch   (Seal)
              Justice of the peace

  Know all men by these presents that we, Peter Kuykendall and John Terry
all of the County of Putnam and State of Tennessee are held and firmly
bound unto Gideon Anderson in the sum of two hundred Dollars to be paid
the said Anderson his certain attorney Executors, administrators or assigns for they which payment well and truly to be made we bind ourselfs
and each of us, one and each, of our heirs, Executors and administrators
Jointly and severally firmly by these presents sealed with our seals and
dated this 27th of June 1842.
  Condition of above obligation is such that whereas the above Boundin
Peter Kuykendall hath the day and date hereof prayed an attachment at
the suit of himself against the Estate of the above named Gideon Anderson
for the sum of one hundred dollars and hath obtained the same Returnable
before some Justice of the peace in and for said County now if the said
Peter Kuykendall shall prosicute his suit with effect or in case he fail
therein shall well and truly satisfy said Gideon Anderson all such costs
as damages as shall be awarded against said Peter Kuykendoll his heirs
Executors administrators in any suit or suits which may be hereafter
brought for wrongfully suing on said attachment (p-21) then the above
obligation to be void otherwise to remain in full force and effect given
under our hands and seal this 27th of June 1842.

Attest   Peter Kuykendall (Seal)
John Welch J. P.   John Terry   (Seal)

State of Tennessee) This day being the 27th day of June 1842 Peter
) Kuykendall appeared before me John Welch a
Putnam County) Justice of the peace in and for said County
) and made oath in due form of law, that he
entered in a note of hand with Gideon Anderson as his security for said
Gideon Anderson for one hundred Dollars made payable to Abraham Buck
there being some small credits made by said Anderson on said note he
said Peter Kuykendall made oath that he has paid on said note one hundred Dollars for principle interest and cost where by he discharged said

note as security and said Anderson stands indebted to him to the same amount and that said Gideon Anderson has absconded that the ordinary process of law cannot be served on him and prays an attachment against the estate of said Anderson made Returnable before some Justice of the peace for said County sworn to and subscribed before me this 27th day of June 1842

Attest
John Welch J. P.   Peter Kuykendall

June 28th 1842 Peter Kuykendall against Gideon Anderson by attachment Daniel W. Hawes D. Sheriff in and for Putnam County returned to me an attachment levied on the property of Gideon Anderson the defendant hath been the security for said Anderson to Abraham Buck for one hundred Dollars which the said Peter Kuykendall hath paid to the same to said Buck which is the amount sworn to in the affidavit upon which this attachment issued, which property remains unreplevied it is therefore   (p-22) considered by me that the plaintiff recover of the defendant the sum of one hundred Dollars for his debt and costs incured for which an order of sale may issue.
    Given under my hand and seal this the date above.
                                                John Welch   (Seal)
                                                Justice of the peace
Justice fee $1.00 Judgment 25 cents No personal property found in my County levied this attachment on two tracts of Land lying on the west side of the Rock Island Road in District No. 3 Putnam County one tract of land Eleven acres the other suppose to be forty five acres adjoining the Lands of John Welch, John Barnes and J. L. H. Huddleston Levied on as the property of Gideon Anderson this 28th June 1842.
                                                D. W. Hawes D. Shff.

    On motion it ordered by the court that said land be condemned and sold to satisfy plaintiff debt and cost aforesaid and also the cost of this motion and that a Writ of venditioni Exsponias issue and &c.

James Snodgrass   )   Warrant
    Vs   )   Motion to condemn land Robert Buchannon Justice
Jeremiah Whitson   )   of the peace filed here in court the following
)   papers to wit:

State of Tennessee   )   To any lawful Officer to execute and return
)   you are hereby commanded to summons Jeremiah
Putnam County   )   Whitson to appear before some acting Justice
)   of the peace for said County to answer the
complaint of James Snodgrass in a plea of Debt due by note given under my hand and seal May 20th 1842.
                                                George McCommac (Seal)

    Judgment for the plaintiff for twenty six Dollars and 25 cents and all lawful cost.
                                                Robert Buchhannon
May 20th 1842   Justice of the peace

    Executed and set for trial on 21st day of May 1842 before Robert Buchhannon.
                                                T. S. Elms Const.

State of Tennessee   )   To any lawful Sheriff or any constable of
)   said County to Execute and return - you are
Putnam County   )   hereby commanded that of Goods and chattles,
)   lands and tenements of Jeremiah Whitson if
to be found in your county you make the sum of   (p-23)   Twenty six
Dollars and Twenty five cents Debt and all lawful Interest and cost of
a judgement that James Snodgrass obtained against said Whitson before me
on 20th day of May 1842 in this fail not and make due return given under
my hand and seal July 6th 1842.

                         Robert Buchhannon (Seal)
                         Justice of the peace

  Judgement 20th May 1842 Debt $26.25 constable Elms serving warrant .50
  J. P. judgement .25 two fi fa's .25.
No personal property to be found of any discription in my County Levied
on one tract of Land in Putnam County belonging to the defendant lying in
the board Valley where he now lives in district No. 6 Butted and Bounded
as follows - Beginning at a white Hickory and sugartree the north west
corner of a tract of land formerly owned of John Lynn and purchased by
him of Joseph B. Dribrell. running thence north 39 poles to a Dogwood on
the hill side thence west to the conditional line thence with the conditional line to the old line thence south East thence with Lynns line to
the beginning corner containing 125 acres be the same more or less.

                         July 6th day 1842
                         Thomas S. Elms Const.

  On motion it is considered by the court that said Land be condemned
and sold to satisfy plaintiff debt and cost aforesaid and also the cost
of this motion and that a writ of venditori Exponi issue &c.

Robert G. Burton   )   Motion to condemn land John Welch a Justice
  Vs   )   of the peace filed here in court the follow-
Gideon Anderson   )   ing papers to wit - "Know all men by these
)   presents that we, Robert G. Burton and Joseph
A. Ray security all of the County of Putnam are held and firmly bound unto Gideon Anderson in the penal sum of Twenty Dollars 23 cents to be paid
to the said Gideon Anderson his certain attorney Executors administrators
as assigns for the which payment well and truly to be made we bind ourselves and Each of us one and Each of us one and Each of our heirs Executors or administrators Jointly and   (p-26)   that the said plaintiff
Recover of said Defendant the sum of Ten Dollars and 23 cents for his
Debt and Interest from the above date and one Dollar and seventy five
cents for cost Incured for which an order of sale may issue, given under
my hand and seal this 20th May 1842.

                         John Welch   (Seal)
                         Justice of the peace

  Justice fee $1.00 for attachment and for Judgment 25 cents constable
fee 50 cents.
  No goods and chattles found in my County levied on a tract of land on
the west side of Rock Island Road of Eleven acres more or less in said
County in Civil District No. 3 adjoining Welches and Barnes lands by me
J. S. H. Huddleston constable. May the 20th 1842.

  On motion it is considered by the court said land be condemned and
sold to satisfy plaintiff Debt and cost aforesaid and also the cost of

this motion and that a writ of venditiori Esponia Issue &c.

Ordered that court adjourn until tomorrow morning at 7 oclock.

Ab. Caruthers

Wednesday 13th July 1842

Court met & there being no more business adjourned till court in course.

P-27   Monday 14 November 1842

State of Tennessee -
Be it remembered that at a Circuit Court begun and held for the County of Putnam in the fourth Judicial Circuit of the State of Tennessee at White Plains in said County on the second Monday being the fourteenth day of November in the year of Our Lord one thousand eight hundred and forty two and of the Independence of the United States the 66th Year - Present the Hon. Abraham Caruthers Judge of the Circuit Court of the State of Tennessee for said Circuit.

Proclamation being made court was opened in due form when James Bartlett Sheriff of Putnam County returned into court the States Writ of vinire facias executed upon the following persons good and lawful men of the County of Putnam to serve as jurors at the present term who had been nominated and designated by the County Court of said County at their August term in the year of ___ Lord one thousand eight and forty two being the next succeeding term of said County Court after the last term of this court to serve as jurors to the present term of court to wit - Reece C. Stewart, John Vaden, John Holliday, Lawson, Clark, Richard F. Cook, John Ditty, Joseph S. Allison, John Barnes, Hugh G. Huddleston, Noah Kuykendall, Burton Marchbanks, Jonathan Fowler, William H. Quarles, James Clark, Jesse Pollard, Hiram K. Hodges, James Jackson, Jesse Rodgers, Dudley Hudgins, Isaac Buck, Zebede P. Dearing, John T. Graham, Joseph Jarred, Samuel T. Vaden, William H. Richardson and Allen Young all good and lawful men of said County of Putnam, out of whom were selected as the Statutes in that case provides a grand inquest and jury to serve at the present term to wit - Isaac Buck, Jesse Rodgers, John T. Graham, John Barnes, Allen Young, Joseph S. Allerson, Reece C. Stewart, John K. Sadler Jonathan Fowler, Joseph Jared, Samuel T. Vaden, James Jackson and Hugh G. Huddleston out of whom the court selected and appointed Isaac Buck foreman of said Grand Jury and said Grand Jury being now here impannelled and sworn to inquire for the state aforesaid and for the body of the County aforesaid received their charge from the court and retired to consider of presentments and indictments attended by Abraham Sims a constable duly chosen and sworn for that purpose and the residue of the jurors who do not compose the grand jury are retained to serve on the traverse jury said Sheriff also returned that he had summoned Abraham Sims & Washington F. Williams to serve as a constable at the present term.

For sufficient reason appearing to the court by affidavit, John Ditty is excused for attending as a Juror at this term.

P-28   Monday Nov. 15, 1842

Lawson Clark who was duly summoned to serve as a juror at this term, failing to appear although solemnly called by the sheriff of this County. It is considered by the court that the State of Tennessee recover against said Lawson Clark for such his default the sum of twenty five dollars unless he show sufficient cause to the contrary and that scire facias issue after the next term of this cause &c.

Jesse Pollard who was duly summoned to serve as juror at this term, failing to appear although solemnly called by the sheriff of this County. It is considered by the court that the State of Tennessee recover against said Jesse Pollard for such his default of the sum of twenty five dollars unless he show sufficient cause to the contrary &c and that scire facias issue after the next term to make known &c.

Hiram K. Hodges who was served to serve as a juror at this term, failing to appear altho solemnly called by the sheriff of this ____. It is therefore considered by the court that the State of Tennessee recover against said Hiram K. Hodges for such his default twenty five dollars unless he show sufficient cause be contrary - and that scire fallias issue after the next term to make known &c.

For sufficient reasons appearing to the court William H. Richards is excused from serving as a juror at this term.

William H. Richard Esqr. took oath of an attorney at law and was admitted as an attorney of this court.

George W. Martin Vs William Vance, William Jared and Mathew R. Jared	In Debt on motion of plaintiff's attorney it is ordered that an an alias Writ of summons issue in this cause.

Abraham Buck Vs John Welch	Certiorari Plff in proper person dismissed this suit It is therefore considered by the court that the debt go hence without day and recover against the plaintiff the cost here in accrued.

Laban Wallis Vs Samuel Mansell	Certiorari On motion of plaintiff a rule is granted him to show cause why defendants certiorari should be dismissed.

P-29 William A. Hall administrator of Samuel Patton Decd. Nancy Patton and Henry Patton	In this cause it appearing the satisfaction of the court that the said Henry Patton and Nancy

Patton are not inhabitants of this State so that the ordinary process of law can not be served upon them. It is therefore ordered by the court that publication be made for three weeks successively in Sparta Gazette a news paper published in the town of Sparta Tennessee commanding the said Henry Patton and Nancy Patton to appear at the next term of Our Circuit Court on the first day of the term to be held for Putnam County at White Plains in said County on the Second Monday of March next then to enter their defence to plaintiff petition or the same will be taken for confessed and set down for hearing Exparte.

Ordered that Court adjourn until tomorrow morning at 9 oclock.

Ab. Caruthers

Tuesday Morning 15 November 1842

Court met pursuant to adjournment.

Carter Whitefield) Cert.
Vs) This day came the parties by their attornies
John Simmons) and the Defendant dismissed his certiorari.
) It is therefore considered by the court that
said certiorari be dismissed and that the plaintiffs recover of the Defendant his cost about his behalf in this cause expended and a procedendo issue to the Justice of the peace.

Moses Grant) Cert.
Vs) In this cause came the parties by their attor-
Joseph Bartlett) nies this day and a motion the plaintiff is
) permitted to amend his petition.

Henry Harpole Admr of) P-30 This day came the parties by their
Jacob Harpole Decd.) attornies and on motion of plain-
Vs) tiff the Defendant and certiorari
Amos Maxwell) dismissed - It is therefore con-
) sidered by the court recover of
the Defendants cost in this cause expended in this court and that procedendo issue directed to the Justice of the peace who tried this cause below that he issue Execution &c.

Alfred Jones) Cert.
Vs) This day came the parties by their attornies and
Hugh W. Carlen) the plaintiff enters his appearance to this suit
) and on motion a rule is granted him for the Defendant to justify his security for the prosecution of this suit on or before the second day of the next term of this court or the same will be dismissed.

Laban Wallace) Certo.
Vs) This day came the parties by their attornies and
Samuel Mansell) on motion of the plaintiff the rule made in this
) cause on yesterday of this term is made final and
the Defendants petition is dismissed. It is therefore considered by the court that the plaintiff and recover of the Defendant his costs by him

about his behalf in this cause expended in this court and that procedendo issue directed to the Justice of the peace who tried this cause below - that he issue execution &c.

Washington H. Irvin)   Case
     Vs   )   This day came the parties by their attorneys,
John Barnes   )   and on affidavit this cause is continued to
)   the next term of this court by the plaintiff
paying the costs of this Term, it is then for _____ by the writ that Defendant Recover against the plaintiff cost of this term.

P-31   Robert G. Burton and Charles F. Burton   )   Debt
                    Vs   )   This day came the
       George Apple   )   parties by their
)   attornies and there
came also a jury of good and lawful men to wit, Burton Marchbanks, William H. Quarles, James C. Clark, Zebibee P. Dering, Richard F. Cooke, Noak Kuykendall, John Hollaway, Dudley Hudgens, John Cates, Elijah Car, Samuel Patton and Mark Harper, who being elected tried and sworn the truth to speak upon the issue joined on their oaths do say that they find the issue in favor of the plaintiff and assess the plaintiff damage by reason of the detention of the debt in the declaration mentioned to Ten Dollars and sixty cents. It is therefore considered by the court that the plaintiff recover against the Defendant two hundred and three dollars and three cents the debt in the declaration mentioned and also the damages aforesaid by the jury assessed and their costs by them about their suit in this behalf expended.

Robert Smith   )   Appeal from Justice of the peace - In this cause it
    Vs   )   appearing to the satisfaction of the court that owing
Clark Harper   )   to the plaintiffs poverty he is not able to procure
)   counsel - It is therefore considered by the court
that Richard Nelson, Esqr. be assigned him as his counsel to attend for him in the prosecution of that suit.

Holden Harget   )   Case - Appl. from Justice of the peace - This
     Vs   )   day came the parties by their attornies, and on
Lewis R. Vance   )   motion and by the consent of the parties this
)   cause is continued till the next Term of this
                                court.

William H. Quarles   )   Debt - Appl - from Justice of the peace.
       Vs   )   This day came the parties by their
James Bartlett   )   attornies and the   (p-32)   plaintiff
)   dismisses his suit - It is therefore considered by the court that the Defendant go hence and recover of the pltff. his court by him about his Defence in this behalf expended.

The grand jury presented Alexander B. McNichol for assault and Battery Harry Hughes and George Hughes for Tipling, George Medley for O. Drunkenness and Snowdown Huddleston and John Jackson for an affray and Daniel

W. Hawes for permitting slaves to sell spiritious liquors and they also brought into court the following indictments to wit: Against Jesse B. Terry for assault and battery and Hugh W. Carlin for assault & Battery and William H. Quarles for assault and Battery Each Endorsed by the foreman a true bill, a fine of Five Dollars and also the cost of this prosecution.

The State)
Vs)
Asa Herald and)
James Haynes)
)

This day came the attorney General for the State and the Defendants in proper person, and the attorney General says he is unwilling further to prosecute this suit. It is therefore considered by the court that the presentment in this case be dismissed and the costs herein certified to the County court for allowance and because it appeared that the offence had been committed - it is ordered by the court that the States Attorney prefer a Bill of indictment against the Defendant exofficio - and that the Defendant enter into recognizance for their appearance here from day to day till the adjournment of this court. Whereupon came the Defendant, James Haynes and Hugh Wallace who acknowledged themselves indebted to the State of Tennessee in the sum of Two hundred and fifty Dollars to be levied of their respective goods and chattels, lands and tenements to be void nevertheless upon condition that said James Haynes make his personal appearance here to tomorrow morning at 9 oclock, and not depart without leave of the court.

The State)
Vs)
Snoden Maddux)
)

Affray

This day came the attorney general for the State and (p-34) the Defendant in proper person and on affidavit of the Defendant this cause is continued till the next term of this court and thereupon came the Defendant.

Benjamin McKee)
Vs)
John L. H. Huddleston)
)

This day came the parties by their Attornies and on motion and affidavit of the plaintiff this cause is continued till the next term of court, on the plaintiff paying the cost of this term it is therefore considered that the defendant recover against the plaintiff the cost aforesaid.

The State)
Vs)
Hardy Chitty)
)

Tipling

This day came the Attorney General for the State and the Defendant in proper person who being charged upon the Bill of indictment saith he is guilty in manner and form as charged and puts himself on the mercy of the court. It is therefore considered by the court that said Defendant pay a fine of one Dollar and also the costs of this prosecution.

The State)
Vs)
Robert G. Hughes)
)

Nuisance

This day came the Attorney General for the State and the Defendant in proper person and the Defendant being charged upon the presentments saith he is not guilty in manner and (p-33) form as charged and for his defence puts himself for the time upon the county and there also came a jury of good and lawful men to wit - James C. Clark, Zebidee P. Dearing, Noah Kuykendall, Richard F. Cooke, John Holladay, Dudley Hudgens Elijah Car, Samuel Patton, Elijah Crowell, Mathew Wallace, John L. Huddleston and Joel Burgin who being elected tried and sworn the truth to speak upon the issue joined on their oaths do say that the defendant is guilty in manner and form as charged. It is therefore considered by the court that the Defendant pay Snoden Maddux and Henry L. McDaniel who acknowledge themselves indebted to the State of Tennessee in the sum of Two Hundred and fifty Dollars to be levied of their respective goods and chattels lands and tenements to be void nevertheless upon condition that the said Snoden Maddux makes his personal appearance at the place of (p-34) holding court for the County of Putnam at the White Plains on Tuesday after the Second Monday of March next to answer the State of Tennessee upon a presentment for an affray and not depart without leave of said court.

For sufficient reason appearing to the court James C. Clark is executed from further attendance as a juror at this Term.

The grand jury returned into open court an indictment in the words and figures following to wit:

State of Tennessee	)	November Term of the Circuit Court in the year of our Lord Eighteen Hundred and forty two.
Putnam County	)	The Grand jurors for the State of Tennessee elected empannelled sworn and charged to en-

quire for the body of the County of Putnam in the State of Tennessee upon their oath present that Mathias Welch yeoman, late of said County on the tenth day of November in the year of Our Lord Eighteen hundred and forty two with force and arms in the County of Putnam in the State of Tennessee with a certain animal commonly called a bitch then and there being feloniously unlawfully wickedly and diabolically and against the order of nature with the said Bitch did commit and perpetuate that detestable and abominable crime of Buggery (not to be named amongest Christians) against the form of the statute in said case made and provided, and against the peace and dignity of the State.

John H. Savage Attorney General of the fourth Solicitorial District in the "State of Tennessee" (p-35) On the Bank of which Bill of Indictment is the following endorsements to-wit: State, Vs Mathias Welch, Buggery, Indictment - Allen Lewis, Prosecutor - Jesse Alvis Lewis, John H. Lewis, Allen Lewis, witness sworn in open court and sent be for the Grand jury to give evidence on behalf of the State upon this Bill of Indictment this 15th of November 1842.

Wm. Carr Clk.

" A True Bill, Isaac Buck foreman of the Grand Jury".

Elizabeth Glover Vs Henry Glover	)))	Petition for Divorse - Came the plaintive by Attorney and on motion this cause it continued till the next Term of court.
John R. James Vs	))	Warrant Motion to condemn Land, James Parson, Justice of Putnam County filed here in court

Robert Lindsey and)	the following papers to wit -
James Allison)	
State of Tennessee)	To any lawful officer of said County, to
)	Execute an Return, you are hereby commanded
Putnam County)	to summon Robert Lindsey and James Allison
)	to appear before some acting Justice of the

peace of said County To answer the complaint of John R. James in a plea of Debt due by note, Herein fail not: given under my hand and seal this the 17th day of August 1842.

                                                 James Jackson
                                                 Justice of the peace

Executed and set for Trial before James Parson Esqr.

On the 1st of September 1842 - James Bartlett Shff. John R. James Vs Robert Lindsey and James Allison I give Judgement in this cause in favor of the plaintiff against the defendants for one hundred and sixty four Dollars 9½ cents and costs of suit. This September 1st 1842.

                                                 James Parsons
                                                 Justice of the peace

P-36 State of Tennessee)	To the Sheriff or any constable of
)	said County Greetings you are hereby
Putnam County)	commanded that of the goods and chattles
)	lands and tenements of Robert Lindsy

and James Allison if to be found in your county, you make the sum of One hundred and sixty four Dollars and 9½ cents and cost of suit it being to satisfy a Judgment that John R. James obtained against the said Lindsey and Allison on the 1st of September 1842 before me fail not, given under my hand and seal this September 5th 1842.

                                                 James Parson   (Seal)
                                                 Justice of the peace

Judgment Sept. the 1st for $164.9¾ cts. Sheriff Jas. Bartlett cost $1.00 Jas. Parson Judgment and fi fa 37½ conit hand the 8th September 1842. James Bartlett Sheriff Recd. on the within fifa one Hundred and two Dollars this 29th Sept. 1842 out of which I retain my cost.

No personal property to be found in my county belonging. To the Defendant Levied on one Tract of Land in district No. 2 of Putnam County Containing by Estimation, Seventy acres, adjoining the Lands of Peter Gouldesby Lying on Cain Creek and Including all the Improvements where Samuel Dunnavin now Lives this 28th day of Sept. 1842.

                                                 James Bartlett Sheriff

On motion of the plaintiff, it is ordered by the court that said Land be condemned and sold to satisfy said Execution and the costs of this motion and that an order of sale issue to the Sheriff Putnam County for that purpose.

Ordered that Court adjourn until tomorrow morning at 9 oclock.

                                                 Ab. Caruthers

P-37   Wednesday Morning No. 16 1842

Court met persuant to ajournment present Hon. Ab. Caruthers Judge.

William Bounds   )   Warrant Motion to Condemn Land
       Vs   )   John Welch, Justice of the peace.
William Kinnard & Wiley Night)

State of Tennessee   )
)   Filed here in court the following papers to
Jackson County   )   wit -

State of Tennessee   )   To any lawful officer of said County to Exe-
)   cute and Return, you are hereby commanded
Jackson County   )   to summons Wm. Kinnaird to appear before
)   some Acting Justice of the peace for said
County to answer the complaint of William C. Bounds in a plea of Debt due
by note herein fail not - given under my hand and seal this 29th day of
May 1842.
                                        John Smith   (Seal)
                                        Justice of the peace

Executed and set for trial 5th day of June 1841 before John Welch Esqr.
June the 5th 1841 - Jacob Harpole June 5th 1841 - William C. Bounds against
William Kinnard by note.
I therefore give Judgment against the Defendant for seven Dollars 87½
cent principle and interest until paid & costs of suit given under my hand
the date above Execution Stayed by Wiley Night.
                                        John Welch   (Seal)

State of Tennessee   )   To any Lawful officer to Execute and Return
)   you are hereby commanded that of the goods and
Putnam County   )   chattels, Lands and tenements of William Kin-
)   naird and Wiley Night his security for stay of
Execution you cause to be made the sum of seven Dollars 12½ cents principle and Lawful interest until paid and costs of suit to satisfy a
Judgment that William C. Bounds, Recovered against said Kinnard before
me on 5 day of June 1841 fail not - given under my hand seal this 5th day
of August 1842.
                                        John Welch   (Seal)
                                        Justice of the peace
Alias Executed
2nd Alias issued 13 Oct. 1842

P-38   Judgment rendered 5 of June 1841 on a note 25 Decr. 1838 for 7.12½
Warrant executed by Jacob Harpole Const. Decr. 50 Interest up to 1st June
1842 - $1.43 3/4 Justices fees for judgment & this fi fa by John Welch
J. P. 37½ alias execution 12½/ .
Levied on 1 horse, 2 mules, 1 yoake of oxen to sell the 17th of August
this 5th of August 1842 J. L. H. Huddleston const. Returned out of Date
by Defendant Runing the above property out of the county J. L. H. Huddleston Const. Created this fi fa by one Judgment that William Kinnard.
Recovered against Mathew Kuykendall for three Dollars 37½ cents this
11th of Jany 1842.

State of Tennessee   )   To any lawful officer to Execute and Return

Putnam County) You are hereby commanded that of the goods
) and chattles Lands and Tenements of William
Kinnard and Wiley Night his security of stay of Execution, you cause to
be made the sum of $3.75 cents principle and all Lawful interest until
paid and costs of suit to satisfy a Judgement that William C. Bounds
Recovered against said Kinnard before me on the 5th of June 1841 for
seven Dollars 12½ cents principle herein fail not, given under my hand
and seal this 15th of Oct. 1842.

               John Welch (Seal)
               Justice of the peace

 Judgment Rendered the 5th June 1842 and a note due the 25th of Decr.
1838 $7.12½ cents Interest up to the 11th of this instant Oct. 1842 $1.50
Warrant and one Levy $1.00 Justice fee for Justice fee for Judgement and
two fi fa 62½ cents credit former fi fa $3.37½ cents due $6.87½.

               John Welch (Seal)

 No goods and chattles to be found in my County Levied on one Tract of
Land belonging to the Defendant four hundred acres more or less, lying in
Putnam County in District No. 3 on the waters of Blackburns fork bounded
as follows by giddeon Terry Land north by Bob Terry East, Carr Terrys
Lands south, Mathew King and Due west where Nathan Vick now lives this
Oct. 15th 1842.

               J. L. H. Huddleston
               Cost.

P-39 On motion of plaintiff it is ordered by the court that said land
be condemned and the sold to satisfy said Execution and the costs of this
motion and that an order of sale issue to the sheriff of Putnam County
for that purpose.

Anna McDaniel   )   Dower
  Vs   ) Be it remembered on this day this cause
the Heirs of her husband) came up for hearing upon the petition
Rily McDaniel Deceased) for Dower of the said Anna McDaniel
) and it appearing to the court that pub-
lication had been made for more than three months in the Sparta Gazett a
news paper printed in this State of the intention of the said petitioner
to make her application to have Dower assigned her in the lands of her
deceased husband it is therefore decreed by the court that a writ of
Dower be awarded to the sheriff of this County commanding him to summon
five free holders therefor unconnected with any of the parties who shall
go upon the premises mentioned in the petition and allot the petitioner
one third in value of the lands therein described to petitioner and certify
the same under their hands and seals to the next term of this court.

 On motion of the Atto. Genl the Clerk of this court produced his re-
ceipt which is ordered to be entered on the minutes to wit - Comptrollers
Office, Nashville, Tennessee 11 Oct. 1842. Received of Wm. H. Carr his
statement of moneys collected as Clerk of Putnam Circuit Court from the
organization thereof to 1 Sept. 1842.
            Amount collected - - - 1.62½
            Commission at 2½ - - - 04

Countersigning and recording 7 horse license   1.75   1.79
Balance due the Clerk on next settlement   17

                                              David Graham Comptroller

   The Grandjury came into court and returned a Bill of Indictment against
Asa Herald and James Haynes for affray - and a Bill of Indictment against
Robert   (p-40)   G. Hughes for nuisance each endorsed by their foreman
a True Bill retired.

William Hughes   )   Petition for certiorari upon petition of Defendant
   Vs   )   verified by affidavit it is ordered that writs of
Land Mansell   )   certiorari and supersedeas be granted him accord-
)   ing to the prayer of petitioner upon his giving
bond and security according to law.

Moses Grant   )   Certiorari - Plaintiff by atto. dismisses his
)   suit - It is therefore considered that the debt
go hence without day and recover against plaintiff the cost of this suit.

William T. Hughes   )   Certiorari
   Vs   )   On motion of plaintiff it is ordered that a
Barnett Lee   )   notice issue to defendant to appear at next
)   term defend his suit &c.

The Bank of Tennessee)   Debt
      Vs   ) Plaintiff by attorney enters a nolle prose-
John Johnson et als   ) qui in this cause as to Alexander C. Robert-
) son and James T. England. It is therefore
considered that the debt go hence without day and recover against the
plaintiff their costs by them about their defence in this behalf expended.

The Bank of Tennessee)   Debt
      Vs   ) On motion of plaintiff it is ordered that
John Potts et al   ) an Alias Writ issue against Debts James
) L. England and John Potts and Alexander
                          C. Robertson.

State   )   Indict. for A. & B. - This day came the
  Vs   )   attorney General for the State, and the
William H. Quarles)   defendant in proper person being charged
)   upon the Bill of Indictment saith he is
guilty in manner and form as charged. It is therefore considered by
the court that the defendant pay a fine of Ten dollars and the costs of
this proceoution - and Stephen D. Burton in court acknowledged himself
security for said defendant for said fine and costs and agrees that execution may issue against him jointly with said defendant for the same.
   And said William H. Quarles and Stephen D. Burton came into court and
acknowledged themselfs indebted to the State of Tennessee in the sum of

five hundred Dollars to be levied of their respective goods and chattels lands and tenements for the use of the State to be void (p-41) on condition that said William H. Quarles keep the peace towards Levi L. Murphree for one year from this time.

John Conger for all &c) Motion Appeal - On motion of plaintiff
Vs) leave is given him to amend his notice,
Mark Harper) and by consent of parties this cause is
) continued until next term.

The State) Presentment for permitting slave to trade in
Vs) spirits - This day came the attorney General
Daniel W. Hawes) for the State and the defendant in proper per-
) son and said defendant being charged upon the
Bill of indictment saith he is not guilty in manner and form as charged and for his trial put himself upon the county and the attorney General for the State doth the like and then came a jury of good and lawful men to wit - Burton Marchbanks, Richard F. Cooke, Noah Kuykendall, Dudley Hudgins, Zebedee P. Dearing, John Holliday, Thomas Welch, Joseph Deering Pleasant Randolph, Robert Peck, Elijah Car, and Peter Anderson, who being elected tried and sworn the truth to speak upon the issue joined upon their oath do say that the defendant is guilty in form and manner and form as charged.
And the defendant moved in arrest of judgment - and deberation being thereon had by the court - It is considered that the judgment in this case be arrested and that the defendant go hence without day and that the cost be certified to the county court for allowance.

The State) First Tipling - By consent this cause is con-
Vs) tinued until next term and Daniel W. Hawes
George Hughes &) came into court and acknowledged himself in-
Harvy Hughes) debted to the State of Tennessee in the sum of
) two hundred and fifty dollars to be levied of
his goods and chattels, lands and tenements for the use of the State, to be void upon condition that said defendants made their personal appearance before the judge of the Circuit Court for the County on the first tuesday after the second Monday of March next to answer the State of Tennessee upon an indictment for retailing spirits and not depart without leave of the court.

The State) Indict for A. & B. - This day came the Attorney
Vs) General for the State and the defendant in proper
Jesse B. Terry) person and said defendant being charged upon the
) Bill (p-42) of Indictment saith he is not
guilty in manner and form as charged in said bill of indictment, and for his trial puts himself upon the County and the attorney General for the state doth the like, and there came a jury of good and lawful men, to wit - William Hudgins, Isaac A. Huddleston, James C. Marchbanks, George Henry, John L. Huddleston, George W. Clinton, Thomas J. McBride, William Whiteacre, Samuel Mansell, John Whiteacre, Jesse Elliott, James J. Brown, who being elected tried and sworn the truth to speak upon the issue joined upon their oaths do say that defendant is guilty in manner and form as charged in said bill of indictment - It is therefore considered by the

court that the defendant pay a fine of five Dollars and the cost of this prosecution and Car Terry and John L. H. Huddleston came into court and as security for said defendant confess judgment jointly with said defendant for said fine and costs. It is therefore considered by the court that the State of Tennessee recover against said defendant and said Car Terry and John L. H. Huddleston the fine and cost aforesaid.

State) Indict. Nuisance - This day came the Attorney
Vs) General for the State and the defendant in
Robert T. Hughes) proper person and the defendant moved in arrest
) of judgment and agreement being thereon had.
It is considered by the court that the judgment in this cause be arrested and that the defendant go hence without day.

The State) Indict Buggery - This day came attorney General
Vs) for the State and says he is unwilling farther
Matthias Welch) to prosecute defendant upon this indictment.
) It is therefore considered by the court that
a Nolle Prosequi fee entered and that the defendant go hence without day and that the State of Tennessee pay the cost of this prosecution.

State) Indict for affray - This day came the attorney General-
Vs) al for the State and the defendant in proper person
James Haynes) and said defendant being charged upon the bill of
) indictment saith he is not guilty in manner and form
as charged and for trial puts himself upon the county and the attorney General like-wise came a jury of good and lawful men to wit - Burton Marchbanks, Richard P. Cooke, Noah Kuykendall, Dudley Hudgins, Zebedee P. Deering, John Holliday, Thomas Welch, Joseph Pearson, Pleasant Randolph, Robert Peek, Elijah Car and Peter Anderson, who being elected tried and sworn the truth to speak upon the issue joined (p-43) the Attorney General with the assent of the court entered a nolle prosequi. It is therefore considered by the court that the defendant go hence without day and the cost be certified by the county court.

The State) Presentment for affray - This day came the Attorney
Vs) General for the State, and the defendant being solemn-
Asa Herald) ly called to come into court and answer the the State
) of Tennessee upon the presentment for affray as he
was bound to do this day came not but made default - It is therefore considered by the court that the State of Tennessee recover against the said defendant the sum of five hundred dollars, the sum mentioned in his bond unless he show sufficient cause to the contrary at the next term of court and that scire facias issue to make known.

State) Indictment for nuisance - This day came the
Vs) defendant and Daniel W. Hawes and Levi L.
Robert G. Hughes) Murphree into open court and acknowledged themselves indebted to the the State of Tennessee
the said Defendant in the sum of two hundred and fifty dollars and the said Daniel Hawes and Levi Murphree in the sum of two hundred and fifty dollars jointly to be levied on their goods and chattels lands and tenements

for the use of the State to be void upon condition that said defendant make his personal appearance before the Judge of the Circuit Court to be held for the County of Putnam at the place of holding court at White Plains in said County on the first Tuesday after the second Monday in March next to answer the State of Tennessee upon a Bill of Indictment for nuisance and not depart without leave of court.

The State)   Forfiture
   Vs   )   This day came the Attorney General who prosecutes
Edward Anderson)   for the State and said Edward Anderson being sol-
)   emnly called to come into court and bring with
him the body of Asa Herald as he was bound to do this day to answer the State upon a presentment for Affray came not, but made default. Neither did said Asa Herald appear - It is therefore considered by the court that the State of Tennessee recover against said Edward Anderson the sum of two hundred and fifty dollars the sum mentioned in his bond unless he show sufficient cause to the contrary at the next term of this court and that scire facias issue &c.

P-44   The State   )   Forfiture
         Vs   )   This day came the Attorney General for
      Samuel T. Vaden)   the State and Asa Herald having been
)   Solemnly called to come into court and
answer the State of Tennessee upon a presentment for affray as he was bound to do this day, came not, but made default - and Samuel T. Vaden being solemnly called to come into court and bring with him the body of Asa Herald to answer the State of Tennessee upon presentment for affray as he was bound to do this day, came not, but made default - neither did said Asa Herald appear. It is therefore considered by their court the State of Tennessee recover against said Samuel T. Vaden the sum of two hundred and fifty dollars the sum mentioned in his bond unless he show good cause to the contrary at the next term and that sci fa issue &c.

Nancy Kirby   )   Case
   Vs   )   This day came Defendant by Attorney and the plain-
Abraham Sims)   tiff being solemnly called into court and prosecute
)   this suit came not, neither is this suit further
prosecuted. It is therefore considered that the plaintiff be non suited and that the defendant recover against the plaintiff his costs by him about his defence in this behalf expended and that he go hence without day.

Henry L. McDanile)   Certiorari
     Vs   )   On motion of plaintiff It is considered that
Elijah C. Crowel)   defendants certorari be dismissed and that the
)   cost in this court accured, and that a proce-
dendo issue to the Justice of the peace who tried this cause.

State   )   It is ordered by the appearing to the court from
  Vs   )   presentments in this case and from the testimony
Robert G. Hughes)   that Robert G. Hughes is guilty of nuisance as
)   owner of a turn pike road in this County, leading
from the foot of Cumberland Mountain by White Plains, to Allens Ferry in

Smith County by permitting said road to be out of repair. It is ordered by the court that the Attorney General prefer a Bill of Indictment against said Robert G. ex officio.

State)
Vs) It appearing to the court that the Defendant having the control of a negro slave Hinny the property of William Marchbanks (p-45) permitted said slave to trade in spiritous liquors in
Daniel W. Hawes)
)
this County, by the presentment in this cause and testimony. It is ordered that the Attorney General at next term prefer a Bill of indictment ex officio, against said defendant for said offence.

Thomas Nicholas Admr. Exparte Time is given petitioner until next term to make report to this court.

Court adjourned until court in course.

A. B. Caruthers

Monday 13th March 1843

State of Tennessee -
    Be it remembered that at a Circuit Court began and held for the County of Putnam in the fourth Judicial Circuit of the State of Tennessee at "White Plains" in said County on Monday being the 13th day of March in the year of Our Lord One Thousand Eight hundred and forty three and of the Independance of the United States the 67th year, present the Honorable Abraham Caruthers Judge of the Circuit Courts of Tennessee and of said Circuit. Proclamation being made court was opened in due form when James Bartlett Sheriff of Putnam County Returned into court the States Writ of Venerafacias Executed upon the following persons to serve as Jurors at the present term of this court - Who had been nominated and designated by the County Court of said County at their December term in the year of Our Lord one Thousand Eight hundred and forty two being the next succeeding term of said County Court after the last term of this court to wit, Wm. Stamps, Jacob Grime, John Brown, Edward Anderson, John West, McClelland Jones, John Officer, William H. Barnes, David Nichols, John Hunter, Joel Burgis, Robert Officer, Lewis Bohannon, Ephraim Elrod, Ridly Apple (p-46) Daniel Campbell, Herald Marchbanks, John W. Carlton John A. Bradford, Edward Elms, Thomas Nicholas, Jacob Hyder and Samuel Mathany, all good and lawful men of said County out whom were selected as the Statutes of that case provides a grand inquest and Jury to serve at the present term of this court to wit -
  William Stamps, Jacob Grime, John Brown, Edward Anderson, John West, McClelland Jones, John Officer, William H. Barnes, David Nicholas, John Hunter, Joel Burgis, Robert Officer, Lewis Bohannon out of whom the court selected and appointed Robert Officer foreman of said grand Jury and said grand jury being here now Empanneled and Sworn to Enquire for the State of Tennessee and for the Body of the County of Putnam Received their charge from the Court and Retired to consider of presentments and indictments attended by Isaac A. Huddleston A constable Duly chosen and sworn for that purpose and the Residue of the Jurors are Retained to serve on the travise Jury Said Sheriff also returned that he had summoned Isaac Huddleston and John L.H. Huddleston to serve as constables at the present term of this court.

Elizabeth Glover)   Pet. for Divorce
   Vs   ) Be it remembered that the above cause came on
Henry Glover)   to be heard before the Honorable Ab. Caruthers
) Judge upon the petition and order for confered
when it appeared that the Defendant and petitioner were married in this
County and she has resided in this County Every sence and it further
appearing that the Defendant maliciously Deserted the petitioner, his
wife about nine years ago and has continued absent every sence it is
therefore decreed by the court that the Bonds of matrimony now existing
between the petitioner and Defendant be dissolved and that (p-47) said
petitioner be restored to all privileges of a single woman and that petitioner pay the cost in the first instance of recovery the same of the
defendant and it is decreed accordingly.

Thomas Nicholas)   Decree
) Be it remembered that on this 13th day of March
   Expartee   ) 1843 the above cause came on to be heard upon
) the Report of Thomas Nicholas Commissioner un-
accepted to the Hon. Ab. Caruthers Judge of the Circuit Court of Putnam
County.
The unassigned administration of the Estate of John Allison Deceased
reports that in obedience to an order of the Circuit Court for Putnam
Made at July Term 1842 be Exposed to public sale at the late residence
of John Allison Decd. in said County the negro woman Ann in his petition
mentioned on a credit of 12 months having first given 20 days notice by
advertisement at White Plains, Kinslows in said County and Millidgeville
and Sparta in White County when David Patton became the purchaser for
the sum of $300.50 cents he being the last and highest Bidder and who
Executed bond for the same with Richard F. Cooke and Samuel M. McCaleb
his securities which securities are good, all of which is Respectfully
submitted.
                                                         Thomas Nicholas

Sworn to and subscribed
in open court 13th March 1843.

Whereupon it is ordered by the court that said report be in all things
confermed and that the Title to the negro slave Ann be divested out of
the administration and distributives of John Allison and that the petitioner pay the cost out of the estate of said Allison in his hand to be
administered.

Bank of Tennessee) John Johnson and Edmond Elms - Debt - This
   Vs   ) day came the parties by their attornies and
Henry B. Johnson) Defendant by leave of the court with-draws
) their pleas in this cause and say they can
not gain say the (p-48) plaintiffs action against them for the sum
of One hundred Dollars Debt and six Dollars sixty cents Damages for the
Detention thereof, it is therefore considered by the court that the
plaintiff recover against Defendants the said sum of one Hundred Dollars
the Debt in the Declaration mentioned and six Dollars and Sixty cents
Damages for the Detention thereof so as aforesaid confesed and also all
costs by her about his suit in this behalf Expended and the Defendant
in mercy.

Bank of Tennessee) Daniel Bartlett, Thomas Welch, Joseph Bart-
Vs) lett and Wm. C. Bounds - This day came the
Joseph L. B. Graham) parties by their attorneys and the Defendants
) by leave of the court, withdraws their pleas
in this cause and say that they can not gainsay the plaintiffs action
against them for the sum of one Hundred Dollars Debt and five Dollars and
42 cents Damages for the Detention thereof it is therefore considered by
the court that the plaintiffs recover against the Defendants the said sum
of One Hundred Dollars the Debt in the Declaration mentioned and five Dollars & 42 cents the Damages for Detention thereof, so as aforesaid confesed and also all cost by her about this suit in this Behalf Expended
and the Defendant in mercy.

Bank of Tennessee) James S. England In Debt - Alexander Robinson
Vs) John Robinson - This day came the parties by
Thomas B. Johnson) their attorneys and the Defendants withdraws
) their pleas in this cause and say that they
cannot gain-say the plaintiffs action against them for the sum of One
Hundred and forty Dollars Debt and Seven Dollars and 25 cents Damages
for Detention thereof so as aforesaid confesed and also all cost by her
about this suit in this Behalf Expended and the Defendant in mercy.

P-49   Bank of Tennessee) Isaac Bumbalough, Wm. Scarborough, Ham-
Vs) son Whitson - This day came the parties
John Bumbalough) by their attorneys and the Defendants
) by leave of the court withdraw their
pleas in this cause and say that they cannot gainsay the plaintiffs action
against them for the sum of One Hundred and forty Dollars Debt and Seven
Dollars and 70 cents Damages for the Detention thereof it is therefore
considered by the court that the plaintiff recover against the Defendant
the said sum of One Hundred and forty Dollars the Debt in the Declaration
mentioned and seven Dollars and 70 cents the damages for the Detention
thereof so as aforesaid confesed and also all cost by her about this suit
in this Behalf Expended and the Defendant in mercy.

Bank of Tennessee) Thomas Welch In Debt - James Jackson, Jas. L.
Vs) B. Graham - This day came the parties by their
Joseph Bartlett) attorneys and Defendants by leave of the Court
) withdraw their pleas in this cause and say
that they cannot gainsay the plaintiff action against them for the sum of
One Hundred and sixty Dollars Debt and Seven Dollars and 50 cents damages
for the Detention thereof it is therefore considered by the court that
the plaintiff recover against the Defendants the said sum of one Hundred
& sixty Dollars the Debt in the Declaration mentioned and seven Dollars
and 50 cents damages for the Detention thereof so as aforesaid confesed
and also all cost by her about this suit in this behalf Expended and the
Defendant in mercy.

Jesse Pollard and Hiram K. Hodges who when fined for non attendance
as jurors this day came into court and upon their affidavit their fines
are released upon the payment of the cost it is therefore considered by
the court that the State of Tennessee recovered against   (p-50)   them

severally the costs in this behalf Expended and fifa issue - Court adjourned till tomorrow morning at 9 oclock.

Ab. Caruthers

Tuesday Morning March 14th 1843

Court met persuant to adjournment present the Hon. Ab. Caruthers Judge presiding &c.

Wm A. Hall administrator of Samuel Patton Decd. Vs Henry Patton and Nancy Patton	Decree Be it remembered that on this 14th day of March 1843 it being the 2rd day of the term the above cause came on to be heard and was heard

before the Hon. Abraham Caruthers Judge presiding upon the petition of complainant was regularly appointed administrator of Samuel Patton Decd. that no assets came into his hand as such administration out of which the Debts of said Estate can be paid thet there is due and unpaid Debts of said Decd to a <u>considerablely</u> amount which there are no assets to satisfy and which there is no way of paying Except by the sale of the Land set forth in complainants petition it is therefore ordered adjudged and Decreed by the court that the Clerk and Master after giving thirty days notice by advertisement in writing upon the door of the court house at White Plains and at three other public places in the County of Putnam and at the courthouse door, in Gainsboro proceed upon the premises to sell at public sale to the highest bidder on a credit of 6 and 12 months all the Lands set forth and Described in complainants petition for the purpose of paying the Debts of the Estate that the purchaser of said land be required to give two and sufficient securities and a lien retained upon said land for the purchase money it is further ordered that the Clerk report his proceedings (p-51) Herein to the next term of court all other things are reserved till the coming of said report.

State of Tennessee Vs Robert G. Hughes	Indictment for nuisance - This day came the attorney General for the State and the Defendant in proper person and said Defendant being charged upon the Bill of Indictment

saith that is guilty in manner and form as charged for his trial puts himself upon the mercy of court, it is therefore considered by the court that the Defendant pay a fine of five Dollars and costs of this prosecution and James I. Hughes came this day in to open court and acknowledged himself security for said Defendant for said fine and costs - and agrees that Execution may issue against him Jointly with the Defendant for the same.

State of Tennessee Vs Hugh H. Carlen	Indictment for Affray - This day came the attorney Genreal for the State and the Defendant in proper person and said Defendant being charged upon the bill of indictment

saitheth that he is not guilty in manner and form as charged and for his trial puts himself upon the county and the attorney general for the Estate doth the like and there came a jury of good and lawful men to wit - Ephraim Elrod, Ridly Apple, Daniel Campbell, H. D. Marchbanks, John W. Carlton, John A. Bradford, Edward Elms, Jacob Kuder, Samuel Matheny, Hugh G. Huddleston, James J. Brown, Elected tried and sworn the Truth to speak upon the issue joined upon their oath say that the Defendant is not guilty in manner and form as charged, it is therefore considered by the court that the Defendant go hence without day and recover against the State of Tennessee the costs of this suit.

P-52   State of Tennessee   )   Indictment for A. & B. - This day came
                  Vs   )   the attorney General for the State and
       Dudley Hunter   )   the Defendant in proper person and the
)   Defendant being charged upon the bill
of Indictment saith that he is guilty in manner as charged and for his trial puts himself on the mercy of the court, it is therefore considered by the court that the Defendant pay a fine of Twenty five Dollars and costs of this prosecution and John L. H. Huddleston came this day into open court and acknowledged himself security for said Defendant for said fine and cost and agrees that Execution may issue against him Jointly with the Defendant for the same.

      State of Tennessee   )   Presentment for Tipling - This
                  Vs   )   day came the attorney General for
    Harvy Hughs and George Hughes   )   the State and the Defendants in
)   proper person and said Defendant
being charged upon the bill of presentment, say that their are not guilty in manner and form as charged and for their trial puts themselfs upon the County and the attorney general for the State doth the like and there came a jury of good and lawful men to wit - Jonathan Buck, Rufus Findly, Robert Rockholt, Jas. L. B. Graham, William Nicholas, James C. Marchbanks, Alfred Jones, Jonathan Fowler, Thomas Nicholas, Thomas F. Watson, Robert Buckhannon and Jesse B. Clark Elected tried and sworn the truth to speak upon the issue joined upon their oath say that they find the Defendant Harvy Hughs guilty in manner and form as charged in the bill of Presentment and they further find the Defendant George Hughes is not guilty it is therefore considered by the court that the Defendant Harvy Hughes make his fine by the payment of one Dollar and all costs in this behalf Expended whereupon came James T. Hughes (p-53) into open court and acknowledged himself security for the fine and costs aforesaid and it is further considered by the court that the Defendant George Hughes go hence without day and recover against the State of Tennessee his costs by him about his suit in this behalf Expended.

    Barnett Lee   )
         Vs   )   Cert.
   William Q. Hughes)   This day came the Defendant and suggested that
)   the plaintiff had departed this life which was
acknowledged to be true by the plaintiffs counsel.

   Bank of Tennessee)   In Debt - This day came the parties by their
          Vs   )   attorneys and the plaintiff Releases the De-
   Henry B. Johnson,)   fendant from the payment of the Debt and
   John Johnson   )   damages in this cause same having been settled.
   Edward Elms   )

George W. Martin)   In Debt by consent of the parties and with
Vs) the assent of the court a rule is Entered
Wm. R. Vance & others) to plead and try at the next term of this
) court, so as not to Delay trial.

James C. Jones Governor for the use) Covenant
of H. D. Marchbank) This day came the parties and
Vs) on affidavit of the Defendant
Alfred Jones & others) this cause is continued till
) next term on payment of cost
of the term, it is therefore considered by the court that the plaintiff
Recover against the Defendant the costs of this term as aforesaid.

P-54   Alfred Jones) Cert.
Vs) This day came the parties by their attor-
Hugh W. Carlen) neys and the plaintiff dismisses this
) suit and the Defendant assumes the payment
of all costs and it is therefore considered by the court that the plaintiff Recover against the Defendant the costs assumed aforesaid.

Washington H. Irwin) Case
Vs) This day came the parties by their attorneys
John Barnes) and thereupon came a Jury of good and lawful
) men to wit - Ephram Elrod, Ridley Apple, Dan-
iel Campbell, H. D. Marchbank, John W. Carlton, Edward Elms, Thomas Nicolas, Jacob Huder, William R. Vance, Samuel M. McCabel, Elected tried and
sworn the truth to speak upon the issue Joined upon their oaths do say
they find the issue in favor of the Defendant it is therefore considered
by the court that the Defendant go hence and recover against the plaintiff his costs about his Defence in this behalf Expended.

Holden Hargett)   This day came the parties by their attorneys and
Vs) the plaintiff dismisses this suit and the Defend-
Lewis R. Vance) ant assumes the payment of all costs it is there
) fore considered by the court that the plaintiff
recover against the Defendant the costs assumed aforesaid.

Green W. Gentry) Case
Vs) This day came the parties by their attorys this
William Willmoth) cause is continued as on affidavit   (p-55)
) of the Defendant till next term of this court
on cost of this term - it is therefore considered by the court that the
plaintiff recover against the Defendant the cost of this term.

The grand Jury returned into court with the following presentments to
wit - the State of Tennessee against Thomas Saylors for Drunkness - signed
by all the Grand Jury - the State against William Morris for Loudness
signed by all the grand jury and Samuel P. Pearin for Drunkness signed by
all the grand Jury and then retired to consider of Further presentments
and Indictments.

36

State of Tennessee   )   Indictment for Affray - This day came the
        Vs   )   Attorney General for the State and the De-
Asa Herald   )   fendant in proper person and being charged upon the Bill of presentment
say that he is not guilty in manner and form as charged and for his trial
puts himself upon the county and the Attorney General for the State doth
the like and there came a jury of good and lawful men to wit - Ephraim
Elrod, Ridly Apple, H. D. Marchbanks, John W. Carlton, John A. Bradford
Edward Elms, Jacob Huder, John L. Huddleston, Thomas T. Nicholas, Mark
Mathews, Daniel Campbell and Bird S. Jones Elected, tried and sworn the
truth to speak upon the issue Joined upon their oath say that the Defendant is guilty in manner and form as charged - it is therefore considered by the court that the Defendant pay a fine of One Dollar and cost
of this prosecution - and Samuel T. Vaden, James Haynes and Hugh W. Carlton came this day into open court and acknowledged themselfs security for
said fine and costs and agree that Execution may issue   (p-56)   against
them Jointly with the Defendant for the same.

State of Tennessee   )   Presentment for affray - This day came the
        Vs   )   attorney General for the State and the de-
Snowden H. Maddux   )   fendant in proper person and said Defendant
)   being charged upon the Bill of Defendant,
being charged upon the Bill of presentment say that he is not guilty in
manner and form as charged and for his trial puts himself upon the County
and the attorney General for the State doth the like and there came a
Jury of good and lawful men, to wit - Ephraim Elrod, Ridly Apple, H. D.
Marchbanks, John W. Carlton, John A. Bradford, Edward Elms, Jacob Huder,
John L. Huddleston, Thomas T. Nicholas, Mark Mathews, Daniel Campbell,
Bird S. Jones Elected tried and sworn the truth to speak upon the issue
Joined do say upon their oath that the Defendant is not guilty in manner
and form as charged in the bill of presentment it is therefore considered
by the court that the Defendant go hence without day and recover against
the State of Tennessee the cost of this suit.

Lawson Clark who fined for none attendance as a Juror at the last term
of court this day came into and upon his affidavit his fine is released
upon the payment of the costs it is therefore considered by the court that
the State of Tennessee recover against him the costs in this behalf Expended and that fi fa issue &c.

The grand Jury returned into court a bill of Indictment against Daniel
W. Hawes for permiting a slave to trade in spirits indorsed by their foreman a true Bill and retired to consider of further presentments and Indictments.

P-57   John Hughes   )   Motion to condemn Land - Lawrence Byrn
             Vs   )   Justice of the peace in putnam County
        Peter McDonald   )   filed in court the following papers to
)   wit -
State of Tennessee:

                        To the sheriff or any constable of Putnam County
Greetings - Whereas John Hughes hath complained on oath to Lawrence

Byrne Justice of peace that Peter McDonald is Justly indebted to him to the amount of seventy four Dollars and forty one and three fourths cents and oath having also been made that the said Peter McDonald absconded or conseals himself that the ordinary process of the Law cannot be served upon him and said John Hughes having given bond and security according to the direction of the act of the General assembly in such case made and proceded, I command you that you attach the Estate of the said Peter McDonald if to be found in your county or so much thereof replevable on security as shall be of value sufficient to satisfy the same Debt and costs according to the complaint and such Estate so attached in your hands to secure or so to provide that the same may be able to further proceedings thereupon to be had before me or some Justice of said County. On the 14th day of Nov. 1842 so as to compell the said Peter McDonald to appear and answer the above complaint of the John Hughes, when and where you shall make known to the said Justice how you shall have Executed this writ.

Given under my hand and seal this 8th day of Nov. 1842.

                L. Byrne   (Seal)
                J. P. for Putnam County.

Executed and returned for trial before Esqr. Byrne on the 14th day of Nov. 1842.

                D. W. Haws
                Dept. Shff.

John Hughes) Peter McDonald - Original Attachment in this case
Vs) the Defendant having been attached by his Lands
Peter McDonald) and not appearing to replevy and the plaintiff
) having (p-58) Established his claim for thirty eight Dollars and seventy Eight and three fourth cents by note and thirty five Dollars and 63 cents in account.

According to Law I do therefore consider that the plaintiff recover of the Defendant seventy four Dollars 41 3/4 cents and cost for which Execution may issue this 14th day of Nov. 1842.

                L. Byrne   (Seal)
                Justice of the Peace.

Know all men by these presents that we John Hughs of Jackson County and Alexander Byrne of Putnam County are held and formerly bound unto Peter McDonald in the sum of one hundred and forty Eight Dollars 83½ cents to be paid to the said Peter McDonald his certain attorney, executors, administrators or assignes for which payment well and truly to be made we bind ourselves and Each of us our and Each of our heirs, Executors or administrators Jointly and severally firmly by these presents sealed with our seals and dated this 8th day of Nov. 1842 the condition of the above obligation is such that whereas the above bounded John Hughes hath the day of the date hereof prayed an attachment at the suit of John Hughes against the estate of the above named Peter McDaniel for the sum of seventy four Dollars and 41 3/4 cents and hath obtained the same returnable to the Circuit Court to be held at White Plains on the 14th day of Nov. Now if the said John Hughes shall prosecute his suit with effect or in case he fail therein shall well and truly pay and satisfy the said Peter McDonald all such costs and damages as shall be awarded and recovered against the said John Hughes his heirs executors or administrators in any suit or suits herein after brought for wrongfully Lying out of said attachment then the above obligation to be void otherwise to remain in full force and effect.

              John Hughes (Seal)
              A. Byrne (Seal)

P-59 State of Tennessee) I do swear that Peter McDonald is Justly
    Putnam County   ) indebted to me after giving all Just
) credits seventy four Dollars forty one and three fourth cents - and that he so absconded or conseals himself that the ordinary process of the Law cannot be served upon him to the best of my knowledge and belief - Sworn to and subscribed before me before me this 8th day of November 1842.

              John Hughes
              L. Byrne J. P.

State of Tennessee) To the sheriff or Lawful constable of said
Putnam County   ) County - I command you that of goods chattles,
) lands and tenements of Peter McDonald if to be found in your County you make the sum of seventy four Dollars & 41 3/4 with interest and costs - to satisfy a judgment that John Hughes obtained against the said McDonald before me the 14th of Nov. 1842 Herein fail not Given under my hand and seal this 14th day of March 1843.

              L. Byrne J. P.(Seal)

Judgment 14th Nov. 1842 $74.41 3/4
Attachment and bond   1.00
Judgment and fifa   .37½

              L. Byrne J. P.

 No personal property found in my County upon which to levy this Execution this 14th of March 1843.

              D. W. Haws D. Sheriff

 Levied on 2 tracts of Land in Putnam County in Dist. No. 1
 1 tract 25 acres adjoining the land of Mathew Rodgers and William Burton Lying on the waters of Indian Creek of Cumberland River, Levied as the property of (p-60) the Defendant this 14th day of March 1843.

              D. W. Haws D. Sheriff of
              Putnam County

 The following endorsement is on the attachment -

              Came to hand on the 14th day of Nov. 1842 and no personal property to be found in my County this 14th of Nov. 1842. Levied on 2 tracts of land in Putnam County Nov. 1842.

              D. W. Haws D. Sheriff

 Executed and returned for trial before Esqr. Byrne on the 14th day of Nov. 1842 D. W. Haws, Shff.

Levied on 2 tracts of land in No. 1st 1 tract containing 25 acres adjoining the Lands of Samuel Young Matthew Rogers and James P. McDaniel the other tract supposed to contain fifty acres adjoining the lands of Mathew Rogers and Wm. Burton both tracts lying on the waters of Indian Creek of Cumberland River - Levied on another property of the Defendant this 14th day of Nov. 1842.

                 D. W. Haw D - Sheriff

On motion of plaintiff it is considered by the court that said Land be condemned and sold to satisfy said Execution and the cost of this motion and that an order of sale of issue to the Sheriff of Putnam County for that purpose.

Court adjourned until tomorrow morning 9 oclock.

                 Ab. Caruthers

Wensday March 15th 1843

Court met persuant to adjournment present the Hon. Ab. Caruthers Judge Presiding &c.

Adam Gardenhire	)	Motion to condemn Land Isaac Buck, Justice of
Vs	)	the peace in Putnam County filed here in court
Hiram K. Hodges	)	the following pappers to wit -

P-61 State of Tennessee) To any Sheriff or any constable for
    Putnam County   ) said County - You are hereby commanded
) to summons Hiram K. Hodges to appear
before me or some other acting Justice of the peace in and on for said County to answer the complaint of Adam Gardenhire assine of Edward Jones in a plea of debt due by note of hand herein fail not but have then and there with your return thereon how you have Executed this precept.

Given under my hand and seal this 1 day of March 1843.

                 Isaac Buck (seal)
                 Justice of the peace

Came to hand 1st day of March 1843 Executed the 3rd of March 1843 and set for trial on the 3rd of March 1843 before Isaac Buck Esqr. at his own house.

                 J. A. Huddleston Cost.

This case I give Judgment for the plaintiff for the sum of one hundred and fifteen dollars & 25 cents interest and all cost in this behalf Expended for which an Execution may issue March the 3rd 1843.

                 Isaac Buck (Seal)
                 Justice of the Peace

State of Tennessee   ) To the Sheriff or any constable for said
Putnam County   ) County I command you that of the goods and

chattles, Lands and tenements of Hiram K. Hodges if to be found in your County you make the sum of one hundred and fifteen dollars and twenty five cents for debt and interest and the further sum of eighty seven and one half cents for cost to satisfy a Judgement that Adam Gardenhire assine of Edward Jones Recovered against him before me on the 3 day of March 1843 herein fail not, but have you then and there the money ready to pay over as the law directs - Given under my hand and seal this 7th day of March 1843.

                Isaac Buck (Seal)
                Justice of the peace

P-62 Debt and Interest $ 115.25
   Cost J. A. Huddleston for
   serving warrant   .50
   Justice fee for Judgment .25
   for fi fa   .12½

                Isaac Buck
                Justice of the peace

  Came to hand the 7th March 1843 there being no goods and chattles to be found in my County belonging to the defendant Levied on three tracts of land of the defendants lying in Putnam County in District No. 5th the first tract bounded as follows, beginning at a double hickory, blackgum and Dogwood running from thence west one hundred and twenty six poles to a chesnut thence north sixty three poles to a chesnut on the side of Cumberland Mountain, thence East one hundred and twenty six poles to a sasafras and shugar tree, thence East south sixty three poles to the beginning containing fifty acres - one other tract beginning at Stake & sugar tree on the south side of a spur of said Mountain and runs west two hundred and forty seven poles to a gopher and white walnut, thence south one hundred and twenty five and one half poles to a hickory, thence east two hundred and forty seven poles to a small hickory and black gum pointers, thence north one hundred and twenty five and a half poles to the beginning, Lying north of the first mentioned tract and containing two hundred acres - also one other tract lying south westardly of the two above mentioned tracts and begins at a stake on the south side of a spur of Cumberland Mountain near a spring and runs south one hundred and eighty poles to a hickory, thence East two hundred and ninty two poles to a Stake and pointers near the old County line, thence south with said Old County line thirty seven poles west thirty two poles south Eight degrees west twenty two poles thence south eight degrees west, thirty two poles, thence north thirty three degrees west thirty three degrees west thirty two poles to a stake and pointers in said old County line, therein (p-63) west one hundred and seventy two poles to the beginning, containing by estimation three hundred acres, said lands including where the said Hiram K. Hodges now lives this 8th of March 1843.
                J. A. Huddleston Const.

  On motion of plaintiff it is considered by the court that said land be condemned & sold to satisfy, said debt and cost of this motion and that order of sale issue to the sheriff of Putnam County for that purpose.

Siman Hogin   )   Attachment
 Vs   ) Motion to condemn land Lawrence Byrne, Justice
Peter McDaniel) of the peace in Putnam County filed herein cost
) the following papers to wit-

State of Tennessee) To the Sheriff to Greetings - Whereas Simon
Putnam County) Hogin hath complained on oath to Lawrence
) Byrne Justice of the peace that Peter McDaniel
is Justly indebted to him to the amount of fifty dollars and fifteen cents
and oath having been also made that the said Peter McDaniel so absconds
as conseals himself that the ordinary process of the law cannot be served
on him and the said Siman Hogin having given bond and security according
to the direction of act of the general assembly in such case made and
provided.

I command you that you attach the estate of the said Peter Mc-
Daniel if to be found in your county as so much thereof repleviable and
security as shall be of value sufficient to satisfy the said debt and
cost according to the complaint and such estate so attacheded in your
hands to secure or so to provide that the Land may be liable to further
proceedings thereupon to be had before me or some other Justice of the
peace on the 17th September 1842 so as to compel the said Peter McDaniel
appear to answer the above complaint (p-64) of the said Siman Hogin
when and where you shall make known to the said Justice how you shall
execute this writ. Given under my hand and seal this 17th Sept. 1842.

L. Byrne (Seal)
J. P. for Putnam County

Came to hand the same day Issue and no personal property to be found
in my county I have levied this attachment on two tracts of land in Putnam County of the defendant this 17th day of Sept. 1842.

Executed returned for trial before Esq. Byrne on the 17th Sept. 1842.

Levied on two tracts of Land in Putnam County in District No. 1st one
tract containing 25 acres ajoining the land of Mathew Rogers and William
Burton both tracts lying on the waters of Indian Creek of Cumberland river,
this 17th day of Sept. 1842.

D. W. Hawes D. Sheriff

Simon Hogin) Original Attachment
Vs) In this case the defendant having being attached
Peter McDaniel) by his lands and not appearing to replevy and the
) plaintiff having established his claim for fifty
dollars & fifteen cents according to law - I do therefore consider that
plaintiff recover of the defendant fifty dollars & 15 cents and the cost
for which execution may Issue this 17th day of Sept 1842.

L. Byrne (Seal)
J. P. for Putnam County

Know all men by these presents that we Simon Hogan and William F. Young
are held and firmly bound into Peter McDaniel in the sum of one hundred
Dollars and thirty cents to be paid to the said McDaniel his administrator
or assigns for the which payment well and truly to be made we bind ourselves
heirs and assigns Jointly and severally firmly by these presents seal with
our seals and dated the 17th day of Sept. 1842 The condition of the above
obligation is such that whereas the above bound Simon Hogan hath this day
prayed an attachment at the suit of Simion Hogan against the Estate of
the above named Peter McDonald for the sum of $50.15 cents and hath ob-
tained the same (p-65) returnable to Lawrence Byrne on the 17th day

of Sept. 1842 - Now if the said Simon Hogan his heirs Executors or administrators in any suit or suits which may be here after brought for wrong fully suing out of said attachment then the above obligation to be void otherwise to remain effect. Given under our hand and seals the day and date above writin.

                                                              Simon Hogan (Seal)
                                                             Wm. F. Young (Seal)

State of Tennessee) I do swear that Peter McDonald is Justly in-
Putnam County) debted to me after giving all Just credits
) fifty Dollars and fifteen cents and he so
absconded or conseals himselves that the ordinary process of the law can not be served on him to the best of my knowledge and belief.

                                            Simon Hogan

Sworn to and subscribed before me on the 17th day of Sept. 1842.

                                            L. Byrne J. P.

One day after date, I promise to pay Simon Hogan forty nine dollars & fifty three cents for virtue recd. witness my hand and seal June 1st 1842.

                                            Peter McDonald (Seal)

On motion of the plaintiff it is considered by the court that the said land be considered and sold to satisfy said Debt and the costs of this motion and that order of sale issue to the sheriff of Putnam County for that purpose.

A. H. Owen to the use of) Motion to condemn Land - James Jackson
John Watson) Justice of the peace in Putnam County
        Vs) filed here in court the following papers
Jesse B. Terry) to wit-

State of Tennessee) To any Lawful Officer to Execute and return
White County) you are here by commanded to summons Jesse B.
) Terry to appear before me or some other Justice
of the peace in said County to answer the complaint of Albert H. Owens.

To the use of John Watson Jr. in a plea Debt due by note herein fail not - Given under my hand and seal - Given under my hand and seal this 10th day of January 1842.

                                          James Bartlett (Seal)
                                          Justice of the peace

Executed and set for trial on the 19th day of January 1842 before James Bartlett Esq.

                                          Wm. K. Bradford Const.

State of Tennessee) Judgment for the plaintiff this 19th day
White County) Jan. 1842 for Debt and Interest $23.10

Const. W. K. Bradford served Warrant   50 cents
Justice James Bartlett for rendering Judgment   25

                                                  James Bartlett   (Seal)
                                                  Justice of the peace

State of Tennessee   )   To the sheriff or any lawful officer of said
Putnam County   )   County Greetings, you are hereby commanded
)   that of the goods and chattles lands and tene-
ments of Jesse B. Terry if to found in your County you cause to be made
the sum of twenty three dollars and ten cents debt and Interest and lawful cost to satisfy a Judgement in favor of Albert H. Owens to the use
of John Watson the he recover against the said Jesse B. Terry on the 19th
of January 1842 before James Bartlett Esqr. an acting Justice of the peace
in and for White County Tennessee at the rendition of said Judgement it
being before the County of Putnam was established or run out that part
of White County which James Bartlett Esqr. lived it being now included
in said County of Putnam and I James Jackson being a lawful acting Justice
of the peace in and for said County of Putnam, and the papers belonging
to the said Bartletts office as Justice of peace being returned to me the
said James Jackson his successors in office as Justice of the peace, herein Fail not - Given under my hand and seal this 24th day of Nov. 1842.

                                                  James Jackson   (Seal)
                                                  Justice of the peace

State of Tennessee   )   I Nicholas Oldham Clerk of White County Court
White County   )   hereby certify that James Bartlett Esq. who
)   rendered the Judgments in this cause was at
the (p-67) date of rendition of said Judgment one of the acting Justice of the peace in and for said County duly commissioned and sworn
and that full credit should be given to all his official acts as such in
testimony whereof - I have hereunto subscribed my name and affixed the
seal of said court at office the 9th Feby 1843.

                                                 Test - N. Oldham Clerk of
                                                 White County Court Clk. 50 cts.

    There being no personal property of the Defendant to be found in my
County on which I can levy this execution levied on 7 tracts of land the
property of Jesse B. Terry two hundred and and sixty acres more or less
including where said Terry now lives and adjoining the land of Benjamin
F. Wroe on the East and Thomas Nicholas on the south and west and North
I. A. Huddleston and Thomas Bullock lying in the County of Putnam on the
waters of the falling waters in district No. 7th Levied on and by me J.
A. Huddleston Constable of putnam County this 24 of Nov. 1842.

    On motion of plaintiff it is considered by the court that said land
be condemned and sold to satisfy said Execution and the costs of this
Execution and that order of sale issue to the sheriff of Putnam County
for this purpose.

Albert H. Owens to the   )   Motion to condemnation of land, James
use of John Watson   )   Jackson Justice of the peace for Putnam

Vs   ) County filed here in court the following
Jesse B. Terry   ) papers to wit -
Joseph L. B. Graham   )

State of Tennessee   ) To any lawful officer to Execute and return
White County   ) you are hereby commanded to summons Jesse B.
) Terry and Joseph L. B. Graham to appear before me or some other Justice (p-68) of peace in said County to answer the complaint of Albert H. Owens to the use of John Watson in a plea of Debt due by note herein, fail not. Given under my hand and seal this 10th day of January 1842.

                 James Bartlett (Seal)
                 Justice of the peace

  Executed and set for trial on the 19th day of January 1842 before William K. Bradford Const.

  I consider Judgment to go against the Defendant for $35.08 considered by me from lawful notice that the said John L. B. Graham is clear of the debt and I for which an Execution maybe issued against Jesse Terry alone this 19th of January 1842.

                 James Bartlett J. P.

State of Tennessee   ) To the sheriff or any lawful officer of said
Putnam County   ) County Greetings, you are hereby commanded
) that of the goods and chattles land & tenements of Jesse Terry if to be found in your county you cause to be in your County you cause to be made the sum of thirty five Dollars and 08 cents to satisfy a Judgment in favor of Albert H. Owen to use of John Watson J. that he recover against the Jesse B. Terry on the 19th of January 1842 before James Bartlett Esq. an Acting Justice of the peace in and for White County Tennessee at the rendition of said Judgment it being before the constable of Putnam was Established or run out that part of White which James Bartlett Esq. lived in being now included in the said County of Putnam - I James Jackson a lawful acting Justice of the peace in and for the County of Putnam and the papers belonging to the said Bartletts office as Justice of the peace being returned to me the said James Jackson his successors in office as a Justice of the peace herein fail not - given under my hand and seal this 24th day of Nov. 1842.

                 James Jackson (Seal)
                 Justice of the peace

P-69 State of Tennessee   ) I Nicholas Oldham Clerk of White County
    White County   ) Court - hereby certify that James Bartlett Esqr. who rendered the Judgment in this cause was at the date of the rendition of said Judgment one of the Acting Justice of the peace in and for said County duly commissioned and sworn and that full faith and credit should be given to all his official acts as such in Testimony whereof I have hereunto subscribed, my hand and affixed the seal of said credit at office this 9th of Feby. 1843.

Test - N. Oldham Clk. of White County Court Clk. fee 50 cts.

There being no personal property of the Defendant to be found in my County on which I can Levy this Execution levied on seven Tracts of land the property of Jesse B. Terry two hundred sixty acres more or less including the place where the said Terry now lives and adjoining the lands of Benjamin F. Wroe on the East and Thomas Nicholas on the South west and I. A. Huddleston and Thomas Bullock on the north lying in Putnam County on the waters of the following waters in district No. 7 Levied on by me I. A. Huddleston a constable of Putnam County this 24th Nov. 1842.

On motion of plaintiff it is considered by the court that the said lands be comdemned and sold to satisfy said Execution and that a order of sale issue to the sheriff of Putnam County for this purpose.

State of Tennessee) Indictment for permitting trade in spirits
Vs) this came the attorney General for the State
Daniel W. Haws) and the Defendant in proper person and said
) Defendant being charged upon the bill of
presentment say that he is guilty in maner and form as charged and for his trial puts himself upon the mercy of the court (p-70) it is therefore considered by the court that the defendant pay a fine of one Dollar and costs of this prosecution and John L. H. Huddleston this day came into court and acknowledged himself security for said Defendant for said fine and costs agrees that Execution may issue against him Jointly with the Defendant for the same.

State of Tennessee) Forfiture
Vs) This day came the attorney General for the State
Samuel T. Vaden) and the defendant in proper person and on motion
) of the Defendant the forfiture is set a side on
the payment of the costs it is therefore considered by court that the State of Tennessee recover against the Defendant all costs in this behalf Expended.

State of Tennessee) Forfiture
Vs) This day came the Attorney General for the
Edward Anderson) State and the Defendant in proper person and
) on motion of Defendant the forfiture is set
aside on the payment of the costs it is therefore considered by the court that the State of Tennessee recover against the Defendant all costs in this behalf expended.

Benjamin McKee) Case app. - this day came the parties by
Vs) there attorneys and thereupon came a jury
J. L. H. Huddleston) of good and lawful men to wit - Ephram Elrod, Ridly Apple, Daniel Campbell, H. I.
Marchbanks, John H. Carlton, John A. Bradford, Edward Elms, Jacob Hyder, Samuel Mathey, Lawrence Byrne, Jabers Watson and Robert Lindsey Elected and sworn well and truly try the matters in dispute upon there oath do say that they find in favor of the plaintiff and assesses his damages to twenty five Dollars, it is considered by the court that the plff recover against (p-71) the Defendant - the sum of twenty five Dollars the damages assessed by the Jury and also all costs by him about his suit in this behalf expended.

Isaac E. Ferrell) Cert.
Vs) On motion of plaintiff it is considered that
Lawson Clark) defendants certiorari be dismissed and that
) the plaintiff Recover against the Defendant
and his security the costs in this court accured and that a procedendo
issue to the Just of the pece who tried this cause.

James T. Hughes) Cert.
Vs) On motion of plaintiff a rule is granted him for
Lewis R. Vance) Defendant to Justify his security for the prose-
) cution of this suit on or before the first day
of the next term of this court or the same will be dismissed.

Robert S. Smith) Case App. - This day came
Vs) the parties by there attorneys and thereupon came
Mark Harper) a Jury of good and lawful men to wit - Ephraim
) Elrod, Ridly Apple, Daniel Campbell, H. D. March-
banks, John W. Carlton, John A. Bradford, Edward Elms, Thomas Nicholos
Jacob Huder, Samuel Matheny, James J. Brown and Ab. Sims, Elected tried
and sworn to well and truly to try the matters in dispute between the
parties upon their oath say that they find in favor of the Defendant is
therefore considered by the court that the Defendant recover against the
plaintiff the costs about his Defence in this behalf Expended.

Robert G. Johnson) App. This day came the party by their attor-
Vs) neys thereupon came a Jury of good and law-
Mark Harper) ful men to wit - William Stamps, John Brown,
) Edward Anderson, John West, McClellan Jones,
William H. Barnes, Robert Officer, Lewis Bohannon, Thomas (p-72)   C.
Choate, William Hudgens, David Nichol, Lawrence Byrne elected, tried and
sworn well and truly to try the matters in disput between the partys upon
their oath say they find in favor of the plaintiff and assess his damages
to sixteen dollars thirteen and one half cents It is there ____ considered
that the plaintiff recover against the defendant the damages assessed a-
foresaid and all costs by him about this suit in this behalf expended.

Hugh Wallace Assignee of) Dept. App.
William Carlin) This day came the partys by their attor-
Vs) neys and thereupon came a Jury of good
Jesse Polard) and lawful men to wit - William Stamps,
) John Brown, Edward Anderson, John West,
McClellan Jones, William H. Barnes, Robert Officer, Lewis Bohannon,
Thomas Choate, David Nichols, William Hudgens and Lawrence Byrnes elected
tried and sworn will and truly to try the matters in dispute between the
partys upon their oaths do say that they find in favor of plaintiff and
assess his damages to ninty nine dollars and it therefore considered that
the plaintiff recover against the defendant the damages assessed aforesaid
and all cost by him about this suit in this behalf expended.

Hugh Wallace Assinee of William Carlin) Debt app. - This day came
Vs) the partys by their attor-
Jesse Pollard) neys and the plaintiffs

releases the Judgement in this case, and assumes half the cost and the defendant the other half it is therefore considered that the partys recover against each other the cost of this suit so by them respectfully assumed aforesaid.

John B. Pointer) Cert.
Vs) On motion it is considered that defendants certi-
Hardy Chitty) orari be dismissed and that the plaintiff recover
) against the defendant the cost herein accured.

Snoden Maddux) Motion App. - Allen Young (p-73) this day
Vs) came in to court an-- acknowledged himself the
Mark Harper) plaintiff security for the prosecution of this
) suit and if he fail therein pay it for him.

Mark Harper) Motion Cert - On motion of plaintiff a rule is
Vs) granted him to show cause why defendants certi-
Amos Maxwell) orari should be dismissed which being understood
) it seems to the court that the law is for the
defendant it is therefore considered by the court that the rule be discharged and this cause set for trial at next term of this court.

William L. Hughes) Cert.
Vs) This day came the partys by their attorneys and
Samuel Mansel) the plaintiff agree to dismiss this suit and the
) defendant assumes the payment of all cost, it is
therefore considered by the court that the plaintiff recover against the defendant the cost assumed aforesaid.

John Conger) Cert.
Vs) This day came the partys and the plaintiff dis-
Snoden H. Maddux) misses his suit and the defendant assumes the
) payment of the cost it is therefore considered
by the court that the plaintiff recover against the Defendant the costs assumed aforesaid.

Henry Robert) Cert.
Vs) On motion of plaintiff a rule is granted to show
Caleb Richardson) cause why certiorari should be dismissed on con-
) sideration it seems to the court that the law is
for the plaintiff it is therefore considered by the court that the rule be made absolute and the plaintiff recover against the defendant the sum of twelve dollars Eighty seven & half cents the amount of a Judgement of the Justice together with the cost in this suit expended.

P-74 James Holaman) Cert.
Vs) This day came the parties and the plain-
John Simmons) tiff dismisses this suit and the Defendant
) assumes the payment of the costs - it is
therefore considered by the court that the plaintiff recover against the

Defendant the costs assumed aforesaid.

Hugh W. Carlen) Case
Vs)
William Jared) This day came the parties by their attorneys and the plaintiff Dismisses his suit it and the Dft. assumes the cost it is therefore considered considered by the court that the plaintiff recover against the Defendant the costs assumed aforesaid.

The grand Jury returned into court a bill of Indictment against Alexander Smith and Samuel Smith for an assault assigned by the foreman not a true Bill - and was thereupon discharged from further attendance at the present turn and the traverse Jury will also Discharged.

Adam Gardenhire administrator of Sarah Rasson Decd. petition to sell Barnett a slave be it remembered that on this day this cause came on for hearing upon petition and the report of the Clerk unexcepted to which is in these words and figures Adam Gardenhire, Administrator of Sarah Rasson Decd., petition to sell a slave the Clerk report that there is no personal Estate except the negro boy Barnett that there are of Judgment against the estate $368 that there is now due of the cost of a suit in which the estate is condemned like $110 the amount not presisely known, that there is also of other debt not now due $456 all of which is reported.

W. E. Car Clk.

It is ordered adjudged and decreed that said report be confirmed and that the petition proceed to sell said slave Barnett for cash in hand at White Plains first advertising the time and place of twenty days of sale at three of the most publick in the County of Putnam and that he report the sale to next court - court adjourned until tomorrow morning.

Ab. Caruthers

P-75 Thursday Morning March 16th 1843

Court met pursuant to adjournment - present the Hon. Abraham Caruthers Judge &c.

James T. Hughes) Certiorari
Vs)
Lewis R. Vance) This day came the parties by their attorneys and on motion of plaintiff a rule is granted him to show cause why the defendants certiorari should be dismissed - and said rule came on to be heard and it is considered by the court that said rule be sustained and the defendants certiorari be dismissed and that the plaintiff recover against said defendant and John Simmons his security in the certiorari bond seventy dollars and thirty five cents the judgment of the Justice below and the further sum of one dollar being interest 12½ per cent per anum from the rendition of the Judgment below and also the costs of suits.

Amy McDaniel) Decree for Dower

Vs	) Be it remembered that the above cause
The heirs at law of	) came on to be heard and was heard on
Riley McDaniel Decd.	) this the 16th day of March 1843 before
	) the Hon. Abraham Caruthers Judge presid-

ing upon the return of the sheriff and the report of E. D. Marchbanks, Samuel T. Vaden, Allen Young, John Rogers and L. Fletcher who were summoned by the sheriff as commissioners to lay off Dower for the complainant in the lands of said Riley McDaniel Decd. which are unexcepted to and from which it appears that the commissioners aforesaid were duly summonsed and qualified that they are free holders and that they are not related either by affinity or consanguinity to this complainant - and it further appearing that they the commissioner aforesaid have laid off and assigned to the complainant her Dower in the lands aforesaid which Dower is discribed in said report as follows - to wit - Beginning on a conditional line between William Burton and said Riley McDaniel Decd running thence East so as to include an old house and half the upper Spring thence down the branch so as to include half the lower (p-76) Spring thence down the branch to the mouth of a lane - thence through the middle of the lane to a south boundary line of the lower 50 acre survey thence west to a sugar tree and two Linns the S - Lower corner of the lower 50 acre tract thence north 96 poles to an Elm - thence East to the S. W. corner of the upper 50 acre tract thence north to the above named conditional line - thence into said conditional line to the beginning so as to include the mansion house and all other out houses the logs and boards that George W. Apple has on the above discribed land - It is thereupon ordered adjudged and decreed by the court that said return of the Sheriff and the report of the commissioners as aforesaid be in all things confirmed and that the said complainant be endowed of the lands as above discribed and that she pay the costs herein &c.

Court adjourned till court in course.

Ab. Caruthers

Monday July 10th 1843

State of Tennessee -

Be it remembered that at a Circuit Court began and held for the County of Putnam in the fourth Judicial Circuit of the State of Tennessee at White Plains in said County on Monday it being the 10th of July in the year of Our Lord One Thousand Eight hundred and forty three and of the Independance of the United States the Sixty Eighth year Present the Honorable Abraham Ab. Caruthers Esqr. one of the Judges of the Circuit Courts of the State of Tennessee and asigned to hold the courts of the fourth Judicial Circuit in said State -

Proclamation being made court was opened in due form when Thomas S. Elms, Sheriff of Putnam County, Returned into open court the State Writ of Venirafacias Executed by James Bartlett former Sheriff of Putnam County Executed upon the following persons, to serve as Jurors at the present term of this court.

Who had been nominated and designated by the County court of said County at their April Term in the year of Our Lord one thousand Eight hundred and forty three being the next succeeding term of said County Court after the last term of this court to wit - Lawrence Byrne, Thomas Watts, John Lee, Elijah Car, William Car, James C. Mitchell, John M. Dowell, James Terry, Isaac Buck, Jonathan Fowler, Burton Marchbanks, William M. Marchbanks, John Madewell, Augustine Lee, George McCormick, Edmond Stamps, Benjamin F. Wroe, James Jackson, Andrew Jackson, Dudley Hunter, William C. Bounds, William K. Bradford, Samuel T. Vaden and James Young all good and lawful men of said County, said former sheriff James Bartlett also returned that he had by virtue of said Writ of venire facias summoned Absolom Sims and Isaac A. Huddleston to serve as Constables to the present term of this court.

Ordered that court adjourn till tomorrow morning at 9 oclock.

Ab. Caruthers

Tuesday morning 9 oclock

Court met pursuant to adjournment - present the Hon. Abraham Caruthers Judge presiding.

Joseph Evans)   Debt Certiorari
Vs)   Came the parties by their attorneys and on motion
Charles Smith)   of the defendant by his attorney leave is granted
)   him to file an amended petition herein.

William Jared)   Debt Certiorari
Vs)   Came the plaintiff by his attorney and dismissed
Hugh H. Carlen)   his writ - It is therefore considered by the court
)   that the defendant go hence and recover of the
plaintiff the costs of suits in this court and (p-78(also the costs that have accured in the same before the Justice of the peace below.

James C. Jones Gov. to the use of)   In Debt
H. T. and R. Marchbanks)   Came the parties by their attor-
Vs)   neys and on motion and affidavit
Alfred Jones and others)   of Harald Marchbanks this suit
)   is continued untill the next
term hereof on the costs of the term. It is therefore considered by the court that the defendant recover against the plaintiff the costs that have accured in this cause at this term.

Barnet Lee)   In Debt
Vs)   Came the defendant by his attorney - and it
William Q. Hughes)   appearing to the court that the plaintiff
)   departed this life more than two terms sence
and that no one has administered upon his estate - that the suit has not been revived but is abated. It is therefore considered by the court that the defendant go hence.

George W. Martin) Came the parties by their attorneys - and
Vs) on motion of the plaintiff by his attorney
William R. Vance and) leave is granted him to amend the writ by
William Jared and) inserting the words George W. Martin assignee
Mathew R. Jared) of Sanders and Martin.
) P-79 This day came the Jurors who were
summoned by the sheriff to appear and serve as such at this term - and out
of whom the following persons all good and lawful men were empanneled as
the statutes in that case provides a Grand inquest and Jury for the State
and for the body of the County of Putnam to wit :

John Lee 1, Dudly Hunter 2, James Jackson 3, George McCormack 4, Augustine Lee 5, John Hadwell 6, Thomas Watts 7, James C. Mitchell 8, William Car 9, John M. Powell 10, Jonathan Fowler 11, Isaac Buck 12, James Young 13, out of whom court selected and appointed Isaac Buck foreman - all of whom were duly sworn and received their charge from the court and retired to consider of presentments and indictments attended by Isaac A. Huddleston a constable duly sworn for that purpose and the residue of the Jury were retained to serve as traverse Jurors.

Benjamin Brown) Trespass
Vs) This day came the parties and on affidavit of
Snodon H. Maddux) the Defendant this cause is contin____ til
) the next term of this court that the plaintiff
recover against the Defendant the costs of this Term as aforesaid.

P-80 John Ray) In Debt
Vs) This day came the parties and
Samuel V. Carick and others) plaintiff by attorney dis-
) miss this suit and the Defend-
ant assumes the payment of the costs it is therefore considered by the
court that the plaintiff Recover against the Defendants the costs Respectfully assumed aforesaid.

Bank of Tennessee) In Debt
Vs) This day came the parties by their
John Potts, Alexander) attorneys and thereupon came a jury
C. Robinson James M.) of good and lawful men to wit -
Johnson and James T. England) William M. Marchbanks, Samuel T.
) Vaden, Burton Marchbanks, Benjamin
F. Wroo, William K. Bradford, William C. Bounds, Elyah Car, Edmond Stamps, Lawrence Byrne, Andrew Jackson, James Terry, and James T. Brown - Elected tried and sworn the Truth to speak upon the issue Joined upon their oaths do say they find the issue in favor of the plaintiff and assess the plaintiff damages accured by the Detention of the Debt in the Declaration mentioned to six Dollars and seven cents, it is therefore considered by the court that the plaintiff Recover against the Defendants the sum of Eighty Dollars and the Damages aforesaid by the Jury assigned and the costs by them about this suit in this behalf Expended.

Nancy Kerby) Trespass
Vs) This day came the partys the plaintiff by attor-
Absolem Sims) ney dismisses this suit it is therefore considered

by the court that the defendant recover against the plaintiff the cost herein accrude.

P-81 Julian Henley) Petition for divorce - Be it remembered that
   Vs) the above cause come on to be heard upon the
  Minah Henley) petition and orders when it appeared from
) the evidence that defendant and complainant
were married about eight years ago in the bounds of this county about five years ago he whiped and drove her from his house and had abandon her maliciously ever sence more than two years before fileing the petition and now lives with another woman in adultry wherefore it ordered and decreed that the bonds of matrimoney now existing between petitioner and defendant be disolved and they be divorced and defendant pay the cost of this suit and execution issue.

 The grand Jury came into court a bill of Indictment against Spencer Phillips for an assault and Battery and Indorsed by their foreman a True Bill.

 The Grand Jury came into court brought with them a bill of Indictment against Joseph Hester and Austin England indorsed by their foreman not a true bill and then retired.

State) Indictment for A. & B. this day came the Atty.
 Vs) General for the State and the Defendant in
Spencer Phillips) proper person and said Defendant being charged
) upon the bill of Indictment saitheth that he
is guilty in manner and form as charged and for his Trial doth put himself upon the mercy of the court, it is therefore considered by the court that for such his offence be fined the sum of Ten Dollars and be Imprisoned in the common Jail of White County there being no Jail in Putnam County for the term of two month from this day and also that all costs in this behalf Expended.

P-82 The grand Jury came into court and brought with them presentments against Nathan Whitaker and Jesse Stanton for an affray also of presentment against Andrew Freeman for Drunkness and also presentments against Allen Lewis and Thomas Welch for an Affray.

State) Presentment for an Affray - This day came the Attor-
 Vs) ney General for the State and the Defendant in proper
Thomas Welch) person and said Defendant being charged upon the bill
) of presentment saitheth that he is guilty in manner
and form as charged and for his trial doth put himself upon the mercy of the court it is therefore considered by the court that the Defendant pay a fine of one Dollar and the costs of this prosecution and John Whitaker Joshua Bohannon and Joseph Bartlett came the day into open court and acknowledged themselfs security for said Defendant for said fine and costs agrees that Execution may issue against them jointly with said Defendant for said fine and costs.

Braxton D. Hunter) In Debt
Vs) Benjamin F. Wroe and acting Justice of
Joseph L. B. Graham and) the peace in and for Putnam County filed
Joseph Bartlett) here in court the following papers to
) wit -

State of Tennessee) To the Sheriff or any constable in said
Putnam County) County, Greetings - I hereby command you
) to summons Joseph L. B. Graham and Jesse
) W. S. Graham and Joseph Bartlett to ap-
pear before me or some other Acting Justice of the peace, in said County
to answer the complaint of Braxton P. Hunter in a plea of debt due by
note here in fail not - given under my hand and seal this the 15th of
April 1843.

                 Benjamin F. Wroe (Seal)
                 Justice of the peace

P-83 Executed and set for trial on the 15th of April 1843 before B. F.
Wroe Esqr. W. F. Williams Constable. Jesse W. S. Graham not in my county
to be found - Judgment in favor of the plaintiff for eighty six dollars
and 11 cents with all costs and interest thereon it being a Judgment that
Braxton D. Hunter obtained against said J. L. B. Graham and Joseph Bartlett before me the 15th day of April 1843 and return as the law directs
herein fail not - given under my hand and seal this May 26, 1843.

                 Benjamin F. Wroe (Seal)
                 Justice of the peace

Judgment rendered the May 15, 1843 for $86.11
Serving warrant on 2 - - - - -   1.00
Judgment 1 fi fa 1 Alias   .50
Williams for an levy   - - -   .50

                 Benjamin F. Wroe (Seal)
                 J. Peace

No other goods and chattles of the defendants in my county to be found
this day levied on three tracts of land of Joseph Bartlett being in the
County of Putnam in district No. 7 on the waters of the dry valley which
three tracts does contain three hundred acres more or less and all joining
each other which said tracts of land Joines the land of Wm. Pryer and
John Watson and John Whiteacre May the 26th 1843.

                 W. F. William Constable

On motion of the plaintiff it is considered by the court that said
lands be condemned and sold to satisfy said Execution and that an order
issue the sheriff of Putnam County for that purpose &c.

Joseph Pearson) In Debt
Vs) Motion to condemn land, John Terry an Acting
James Coale) Justice of the peace in Putnam County filed

here in court the following papers to wit -

P-84 State of Tennessee)   To the sheriff or any constable of
      Putnam County   )   said County - I hereby command you
)   that of the goods and chattles lands
)   and tenements of Samuel Coale Anderson Coale and James Coale if to be found in your county you make the sum of twenty Eight Dollars four and ahalf cents with Interest thereon and all lawful cost to satisfy a Judgment that Joseph Pearson obtained before me on the 11th day of March and pay over the same as the law law directs this 4th day of April 1843.

John Terry (Seal)
Justice of the peace

Judgement for Debt March 11th 1843 $28.04½
Interest - - - - -
Const. Huddleston for serving warrant   1.50
Justice fee for Judgment and fi fa   .37½
Commission - - - -   1.12½

John Terry   (J. P.)

No goods and chattles to be found in my County belonging to the Defendant Levied on 1 tract of Land of the Defendants containing 130 acres more or less   (p-85)   lying in Putnam County in Civil District No. 3rd bounded as follows on the north by John Choate on the East by Lian Bullard on the South John Cates on the West - Isaac Whitaker, where Anderson Coale now lives this 6th April 1843.

J. L. H. Huddleston
Constable.

On motion of plaintiff it is considered by the court that said land be condemned and sold to satisfy said Execution and that on order of sale issue to the Sheriff of Putnam County for that purpose.

A. Gardenhire Administrator Expartee - In this case Adam Gardenhire the administrator, Reports that in pursuance to the Direction of the Interlocutory decree pronounced in this cause at the last term of this court he did proceed to sell the negro mentioned in said decree to the highest and best bidder for cash at White Plains Putnam County Tenn the 10th day of April 1843 having first advertised the time and place of sale for the space of Twenty Days at White Plains Term - and in two other public places in the County of Putnam as discribed by said Decree when Stephen D. Burton became the purchaser of the negro man Barnett for the sum of five hundred and fifty two Dollars and fifty cents he being the highest and best bidder for the same all of which is Respectfully Reported to the Honorable Court July 1843.

A. Gardenhire Administrator

Adam Gardenhier Admistator of Sarah Ranson Deceased Exparte - Be it remembered that on the 2rd day of the Term this cause came on for hearing before the Honorable Abraham Caruthers   (p-86)   Judge presiding upon the interlocutory Decree and the report of the administrator unexcepted to from which it appeared that said administrator on the 12th day of April 1843 after having first advertised the time and place of sale for the space of Twenty Days as Directed in the interlocutory Decree did proceed to sell the slave therein mentioned to the highest bidder at White Plains in Putnam County Tenn and that Stephen D. Benton became the purchaser of said Negro Barnett for the sum of five hundred and fifty two Dollars and fifty and it further appearing from the acknowledgement of Stephen Burton that he said Benton has sold said negro to Adam Gardenhire the administrator in this case and said Burton agreeing that the title to said Slave shall be decreed to said Gardenhier it is therefore ordered adjudged a Decree by the court that the said report be in all things confirmed and that the title to said negro be divested out of the heirs and distributees of Sarah Rawson Deceased and said Benton and vested in said Gardenhier and it is further adjudged and decreed that the _____ be allowed _____ Dollars for his services and that Alvin Collom the solicitor in this cause be allowed the sum of Ten Dollars for his services and that the said allowance and the costs of this proceedings be paid out of the proceeds of said negro.

Bird S. Rhea, Joseph W. Bill and John W. _____ took the oaths of an Atty at law and was permitted as such to practice in this court.

A. Bill C. Nichols) Certiorari
Vs) In this case it is considered by the court that
Lewis R. Vance) an Alias certiorari issue on motion of the Defendant.
)

P-87 Isaac Clendennon) Certiora
Vs) This day came the parties by their attorneys and the plf. suffered a nonsuit it is therefore considered by the court
Henry L. McDaniel)
)
that the Defendant recover against the costs herein accrued.

Green W. Gentry) Case
Vs) This day came the parties by their attorneys
William Willmoth) and thereupon came a Jury of good and lawful
) men to wit - Samiel T. Vaden, Benjamin T. Wroe,
William K. Bradford, William C. Bounds, Elijah Car, Edmond Stamps, Lawrence Byrne, Andrew Jackson, James Terry, Robert Officer, Lewis Bohannon, Allen Young who being Elected Tried, the truth to speak upon the issue Joined upon their oath do say that they find the issue in favor of the plaintiff and assess his damages to seventy five Dollars accasioned by the slanderous words of the Defendant it is therefore considered by the court that the plaintiff Recover against the Defendant the said sum of seventy five Dollars and all costs by him about his suit in this behalf Expended.

Mark Harper) Motion Appeal
Vs) David Patton, Samiel McCabel, Elijah Car, W. H.
Amos Maxwell) Car this day came the partys by their attorneys

and thereupon came a Jury of good and lawful men to wit - William M. Marchbanks, Samuel T. Vaden, Burton Marchbanks, Benjamin F. Wroe, William Y. Bradford (p-88) William C. Bounds, Edmond Stamps, Andrew Jackson, James Terry, Snoden K. Maddux, James J. Brown and Quinton Lowe, who Elected and sworn the truth to speak upon the presentments do say they find for the plaintiff and do confirm the judgment of the Justice of the peace for seventy five Dollars Eighty five cents it is therefore considered by the court that the plaintiff Recover against the Defendants and Samuel Maxwell the security the said sum of seventy five Dollars and Eighty five cents and the further sum of three Dollars damages after the rate of 12½ per cent from the Rendition of the Justice of the peace and all costs in this behalf Expended.

This day the Grand Jury returned into open court a bill of Indictment against Baldwin Rowland for murder Indorsed by the foreman a true bill and retired to consider of further presentments.

State)
Vs) Indictment for murder - This day the Defendant was Brought into court by the sheriff of Putnam County and being Enquired of by the court whether he had procured counsel to Defend him in this cause answered that he had not and owing to his poverty he was unable to procure counsel whereupon the court assigned John A. Minnin William B. Richardson, Joseph W. Bell, William H. Richardson, John W. Bowen attorneys of this court as counsel to aid him in his Defence.
Baldwin Rowland)

State)
Vs) Indictment for murder - This day _____ the Defendant was let to the bar in custody of the Sheriff (p-89) here in open court and arraigned and charged upon the bill of Indictment pleas not guilty thereto and for his Trial puts himself upon the County and the attorney General for the State doth the like.
Baldwin Rowland)

State)
Vs) Indictment for murder - The grand Jury heretofore on this day returned into open court the following Indictment to wit -
Baldwin Rowland)

State of Tennessee)
Putnam County) July Term of Circuit Court in the year of our Lord Eighteen hundred and forty three the grand Jurors for the State of Tennessee Elected Empanneled sworn and charged to Enquire for the body of the County of Putnam in the State of Tennessee upon their oath present that Baldwin Rowland Yoman on the first day of July in the year of Our Lord Eighteen Hundred and forty three with force and aim in the County of Putnam in the State of Tennessee not having the fear of God before his Eyes, but being moved and seduced by the instagation of the Devil in and upon one Delila Raney in the peace of God and of the said State of Tennessee then and there being feloniously willfully maliciously and of his malice afore thought did make and assault and that the said Baldwin Rowland with a certain choping ax of the value of two Dollars which he the said Baldwin Roldwand in both his hands then and there had and held the said Delila Raney in and upon the Right side of the neck of her the

said Delila Raney and upon the Right breast and upon the back of her the said Delila Raney then and there feloniously willfully maliciously and of (p-90) this malice afore thought did strike out and thrust giving to the said Delila Raney then and there with the choping ax aforesaid in and upon the said Right side of the neck of her the said Delila and upon the said Right breast and upon the back of her the said Delila Raney their several mortal wounds of the breadth of three inches and of the depth of six inches Each of said several mortal wounds the said Delila Raney then and there Instantly Died and so the Juror aforesaid upon their oath aforesaid do say that the said Baldwin Rowland the said Delila Raney in manner and form aforesaid feloniously awfully maliciously and of his malice aforethought did kill and murder contrary to the statute in such case made and provided and against the peace and dignity of the State.

John K. Savage Attorney General of the fourth Judicial District in the State of Tennessee upon which bill of indictment is the following Indorsement to wit -

State	)	Murder Indictment - Craven Maddux, George Welch
Vs	)	Prosecutors - William Car, Quinton Lowe, Craven
Baldwin Rowland	)	Maddux and Wilson Stephens witnesses sworn in
	)	open court and sent before the grand Jury to

give evidence in behalf of the State upon this bill of Indictment this the 11th July 1843.

W. H. Car Clk.

A True bill Isaac Buck foreman of the grand Jury.

Ordered that Court adjourn till tomorrow morning.

Ab. Caruthers

P-91 Wednesday July 12st 1843

The court met and persuant to adjournment present the Honorable Abraham Caruthers Judge presiding.

The State of Tennessee	)	Indictment for Murder - This day came the
Vs	)	attorney general who prosecutes for the
Baldwin Rowland	)	State as well as the defendant in proper
	)	person and the said defendant being ar-

raigned and charged upon the bill of indictment says he is not guilty in manner and form as charged upon the bill and for his trial puts himself upon the county and the attorney General doth the Like This entry should have been made on yesterday and being then omitted is made now for them.

James Farris	)	Debt Certiorari
Vs	)	This day came the parties by their attorney and
Amos Maxwell and	)	David Patton and said David Patton acknowledges
Samuel Maxwell	)	himself to owe and stand indebted to the said
	)	James Farris the plaintiff in the sum of one

hundred and fifty dollars to be void on condition that the said defendant shall well and truly prosecute their said writ of certiorari with effect or in case the same shall be dismissed to pay all costs and pay such Judgment as shall be rendered against them for such failure by the court.

Joseph Bartlett) Debt petition certiorari - On the humble
Vs) petition of Joseph Bartlett, Writ of cer-
Zebedee P. Deoring) tiorari and supercedas awarded him direct
) to the Justice of the peace upon his en-
tering into bond and security according to law.

John Eughes) Petition for certiorari
Vs) P-92 On the humble petition writ of defendant writs
James Land) of certiorari and supercedas are awarded him
) directed to the justices of the peace accord-
ing to the prayer of the petitioner. He having taken the oath of a poor person according to law.

Thomas B. Nicholas) Trespass and A. B.
Vs) This day came the parties by their attorneys
Dudley Hunter) and thereupon came a Jury of good and lawful
) men to wit - William M. Marchbanks, Samuel
T. Vaden, Burton Marchbanks, William K. Bradford, Elijah Carr, Edmund Stamps, Lawrence Byrne, Andrew Jackson, James Terry, Henry L. McDaniel H. D. Marchbanks, Mark Masters, who being elected tried and sworn The Truth to speak upon issue Joined upon their oath do say they find the issue in favor of the plaintiff and assess the damages forty four dollars occasioned by the assault and battery in the declaration mentioned, is therefore considered by the court the plaintiff recover against the defendant the said sum of Forty four dollars and all cost by him in this suit in this behalf expended.

George M. Martin assinee of Sanders Martin) This day came
Vs) the attorneys
William R. Vance, William Jared & Matthew Jared) and thereupon
) came a Jury of
good and lawful men to wit, William M. Marchbanks, Samuel Vaden, Burton Marchbanks, William K. Bradford, Elijah Carr, Edmond Stamps, Lawrence Byrne, Andrew Jackson, James Terry, Herald D. Marchbanks, and Mark Mathews who being Elected, Tried and sworn the truth to tell to speak upon the issue Joined upon there oath do say they find the issue in favor of the plaintiff and assess the plaintiff damage occasioned by the detention of the debt in the declaration mentioned to thirty Three Dollars and thirty three cents, it is therefore considered by the court that the plaintiff recover against the defendants the sum of seven Hundred and thirteen dollars (p-93) and ninty one cents and the damages aforesaid - By the Jury assessed and all cost <u>and all cost</u> by him in this suit in This behalf expended.

Snodon H. Maddux) Case appeal
Vs) This day came the parties by there attor-
Mark Cooper and) neys and thereupon came a Jury of good
Jacob Whitfield) and lawful men to wit - Calvin Clark,

Quinton Lowe, William Rawland, William Young, Samuel Mansell, Price M. Draper, Lawson Clark, William H. Barnes, John Whiteacre, Henry Harpole, John L. Hyder who being elected, Tried and sworn to well and truly try the matters in dispute between the parties upon their oath do say they form in favor of the plaintiff and assess his damages to Three dollars and fifty four cents, it is therefore considered by the court that the plaintiff recover against the defendant the said sum of Three dollars and Fifty four cents and all cost by him in this suit in this behalf expended.

Leah Robison) Debt Certiorari
Vs) This day came the parties by their attor-
Robert & James Officer) neys On motion of plaintiff, it is con-
) sidered by court that the defendants
give good and sufficient security for the prosecution of the certiorari of this cause before the rest of this court otherwise to be dismissed.

P-94 Leah Robison) Debt Certiorari
Vs) This day came the parties by their
Robert & James Officer) attorneys and Dudly Hunter came
) into court and acknowledged him-
self to owe and stand in debted to the plaintiff in the sum of Four Hundred dollars to be void on condition that the defendant shall prosecute the certiorari with effect and in case they fail or the same shall be dismissed then to pay all cost and such Judgment as may be rendered against them.

Ordered by court that the grand Jury be discharged from further attendance at the present term of this court.

John Congor to the use) Motion Appeal
of Snoden H. Maddux) This day came the plaintiff and says he
against) intended no further prosecute this suit
Mark Harper) but dismisses the same, it is therefore
) considered by court that (p-95) The
defendant recover against plaintiff all cost in this behalf Expended.

Sampson M. Cassitty) Debt certiorari
Vs) This day came the parties by their consent
Sarah Kinnaird) this cause is set for trial at the next
) term of this court.

State) Motion for murder - This day came the attorney
Vs) General for the State as well as the defendant
Baldwin Rowland) in proper person and appearing to the court
) that Louisa Jane Rowland had been Recognized
to give evidence on behalf of the State in this cause and she failing to attend on motion of the attorney General and attachment in order to issue instanter to compel her attendance instanter to give evidence on behalf of the State.

John Lee)   Debt Certiorari
    Vs) This day came the parties by their attorney, the
Alfred Jones) plaintiff dismisses the suit it is therefore con-
Bird Jones) sidered by the court that the defendants recover
Putnam Jones) against the plaintiff all costs herein Expended.

Joseph Evans) Motion Certiorari - This day came the
    Vs) parties by their attorneys and the
Charles Smith & others) plaintiff motion to dismiss the cer-
) tiorari is over rooled and this cause
is set for trial at next term.

Bank of Tennessee)   Debt
    Vs) This ____ came the plaintiff and dismisses
Samuel H. Williams) this suit as to James Netherton, it is con-
John Henry) sidered by the cause that James Netherton
James Netherton) recover against the plaintiff his cost by
) him in this behalf Expended.

P-96 Bank of Tennessee) On motion of the plain-
    against John Whiteacre & others) tiff by attorney Alias
) summons is awarded
against John Whiteacre one of the defendants.

Bank of Tennessee)   Debt
    Vs) On motion of the plaintiff by attorney
David R. Been and others) Alias Summons is awarded against the
) defendants.

Bank of Tennessee)   Debt
    Vs) This day came the plaintiff by attorney
Thomas Welch and others) and dismisses this suit as to Daniel
) Bartlett, it is therefore considered
by court that said defendant Daniel Bartlet recover against the plaintiff
his cost by him in this behalf Expended.

Bank of Tennessee)   Debt
    Vs) This day came the plaintiff by attorney
John B. Pointer & others) and dismissed this suit as to Anthony
) Dibrell and William P. Ivie it is there-
fore considered by the court that the defendants Anthony Dibrell and
William P. Ive recover against the plaintiff the cost by them in this
behalf expended.

Jesse B. Terry)   Case A. P.
    Vs) This day came the parties and on affidavit of
Joseph L. B. Graham) the defendant this cause is continued till
) the next term on payment of the cost of this
term, it is therefore by the court that the plaintiff recover against the
defendant the cost Expended at the present Term.

Braxton D. Hunter   )   Case A. P.
         Vs   )   P-97   This day came the plaintiff and says
Henry Bohanon   )   he does not Intend to further to prose-
                                 cute this suit and suffers an non-suit
it is therefore considered by the court that the defendant recover against
the plaintiff the cost of this suit in this behalf expended.

Dudley Hunter   )   Case
         Vs   )   This day came the plaintiff and says he intends
Thomas T. Nichols   )   no further to prosecute this suit and dismisses
)   the same, it is therefore considered by court
that Defendant recover against the plaintiff all cost in This suit in this
behalf Expended.

William A. Hall Admr &c.   )   Decree found
         Vs   )   Be it remembered that the above
Henry Patton and Nancy Patton)   cause came on to be heard and was
)   this day, it being the 11th day of
July A. D. 1843 heard before the honorable Abraham Caruthers Judge presiding upon the report of the sale of the lands in complainants petition
set forth and disoribed which report is in the words and figures following:

William A. Hall Admr. & C.   )   report
Henry Patton and Nancy Patton)   In this case the Clerk and Master
)   reports to the Court that on the
20th of May 1843 after giving notice of the time and place as required by
interloctory decree herein pronounced at the last term of this court he
on the premises proceeded to sell all the lands in the petition described
to the highest bidder at public sale when the same were purchased by
Montgomery and Hall they being the highest and best bidders at the price
of seventy five dollars   (p-98) For which he took the notes of said
Montgomery and Hall Due in six and Twelve months with Robert Montgomery
and George W. McWhirter which security is good, lean was also retained
upon the land for purchase money - all of which is respectfully submitted.

                                             W. H. Car Clk. & Master

   And which report being in all things accepted to - it is thereupon
ordered adjudged and decreed by the court that the report of the Clerk
and Master be in all things confirmed and right title and interest to
the following discribed tracts of land lying and being situated in the
County of Putnam State of Tennessee and bounded as Follows - The first
tract beginning on a black oak and bounded on the south by Kings 140
acre and on the west by Benjamin Browns 50 acre tract and on the North
by William Car's Ten acre and Joseph Spears 500 acre tract and on East
by Esther Wilkerson 50 acre and Joseph Ferrell 25 acre tract containing
by estimation one hundred acres an other Tract Granted by the State of
Tennessee by Grant No. 2447 to S. O. Samuel Patton lying on the West
Fork of Mine Lick Creek and bounded as follows to wit - Beginning at a
post oak the N. E. Corner of Samuel Maxwell Old tract running north
Crossing the creek at Forty Eight Poles in all 125 poles to a small maple
and Beech on a branch thence west crossing the Creek at 11 poles in all
11 poles to the beginning 50 acres containing 50 acres more or less be
and the same is hereby divested out of the Henry Patton and Nancy Patton

and their Heirs forever invested in the said Alexander Montgomery and William A. Hall and their Heirs forever it is further ordered by the court that a lien be retained upon said lands for the purchase money George M. McWhirter attorney for the complainant herein be allowed Ten Dollars for procuring the sale of said (p-99) Land which together with the case of suit be paid out of the proceeds of the sale of said land.

Brice M. Draper and others) Petition Certiorari
Vs) On petition of the
Chairman of County Court of Putnam County) plaintiff a writ of
) Certiorari and super-
cedas are awarded them according to the prayer of petition they having entered into bond and security as the law directs _____.

Ordered that Court adjourn till tomorrow morning at 8 oclock.

A. B. Caruthers

Thursday Morning 13th July 1843

Court met according to adjournment, present the same Judge as on Yesterday.

Green W. Gentry) Slander
Vs) Came the parties and the defendant moved in ar-
William Wilmoth) rest of judgment and filed his reasons and the
) same is continued on advisement.

Zebedee P. Dearing) Certiorari
Vs) Came the parties and the plaintiff
William Bartlett, Joseph Bartlett) agrees that the proceedings of
) Justice in rendering the judgment
on motion be quashed and the same appearing to be void for want of jurisdiction - It is considered by the court that they be quashed and that the defendant recover of the plaintiff the costs of suit.

Sims Dearing) On motion of plaintiff ordered
Vs) that defendants give bond and
John Robison and George McComick) security for the prosecution
) of this certiorari on or before
the first day of next Term the present bond being insufficient.

P-100 Ordered by the court that William H. Car, Clerk of this court pay a fine of twenty five dollars for not having an index to this record book, for which an Execution shall issue in behalf of the State of Tennessee Execution is stayed untill the next Term, when the court reserves the power of remitting this fine if a complete index is then made out Here after such an index shall be forthwith made out at the end of every Term.

Zebedee P. Dearing) Motion
Vs) Came the plaintiff and moved the
William Bartlett, Joseph Bullock) court for judgment against the
) defendants and it appearing to
the court that on the 30th day of March 1842 the defendants and plaintiff executed a bill single to William Gentry in the words and figures following -

Twelve months after date we or either of us promise to pay William Gentry one hundred and fifteen dollars for value received as writing.

Our hand and seals this 30th March 1842 - William Bullock (Seal) Daniel Bartlett (Seal) Joseph Bartlett (Seal) Z. B. P. Dearing (Seal) their security " - it also appearing that a suit was duly instituted by warrant and judgment rendered on said bill single by Wm. C. Bounds a justice of peace for Putnam County on the 8th day of April 1843 against the defendants Daniel Bartlett and William Bartlett and the plaintiff Dearing for the sum of one hundred and fifteen dollars on which the plaintiff and the defendant William Bartlett and paid the sum of one hundred and twenty two dollars and 93 cents in equal mouts that is the plaintiff paid sixty one dollars and 43 cents being in full of said judgment interest costs and principal and it appearing from the face of said bill single that the plaintiff was security therein for the defendants. It is therefore considered by the court that the plaintiff recover of the defendants the said sum of sixty one dollars and forty six and $\frac{2}{3}$ cents and the cost of this motion.

P-101 James Farris) Certiorari
Vs) Came the parties and the plaintiff rules
Amos Maxwell) to dismiss the certiorari - it on consideration
) discharged and the cause set down for
trial at the next term on the facts stated in the petition.

State of Tennessee) Indictment Murder
Vs) Came the attorney General and the defendant
Baldwin Rowland) in proper person and on defendants motion
) and affidavit this cause is continued untill
the next Term of this Court The defendant is remanded to the Jail of Jackson County.

Leah Robison) Certiorari
Vs) So for trial on the petition at next Term
Robert and James Officer)

George W. Martin Assignee) Debt
of Samuel Martin) Came the parties and the defendant
Vs) with Lawrence Byrne and Samuel T.
William R. Vance, William Jared) Vaden entered into bond for the
Mathew R. Jardd) appeal prayed and it is granted.

Bank of Tennessee) Debt
Vs) Came the parties by attorney and
Adison A. Maddux, Craven Maddux) the plaintiff dismissed his suit
Robert Lindsy) and the defendants assume the

costs wherefore it is considered by the court that the plaintiff recover of the defendants the costs of suit.

P-102　The President and Directors of　)　　　Motion
　　　　the Bank of Tennessee　　　　　　)　Came the plaintiffs and
　　　　　　　Vs　　　　　　　　　　　　)　on their motion it appear-
　　　　James Bartlett　　　　　　　　　)　ing to the satisfaction of
　　　　　　　　　　　　　　　　　　　　)　the court that on the 30th
March 1843 an execution returnable to this Term of this court issued from the office of and by the Clerk of the Circuit Court of Putnam County in favor of the plaintiffs against Thomas B. Johnson James S. England, Alexander C. Robinson and John Robinson and a judgment obtained against them at the last Term of this court for the sum of one hundred and forty seven dollars and 25 cents debt and damages and ten dollars and forty cents costs directed to the sheriff of Putnam County and it also appears that that the defendant was sheriff of said County and that said Execution came to the hand of Daniel W. Hawes the regularly constituted deputy of the defendant on or about the 8th of April 1843 and said Execution being returned here at this Term with us no other than the following return to wit - "Not Satisfied" the 10th July 1843 -
　　　　　　　　　　　　　　　　　　　　　　Isaac Sollar D. Shff.

And said return being insufficient, It is considered by the court that the plaintiff recover of the defendant the aforesaid sum of one hundred and forty seven dollars & 25 cents and also two dollars and ninety four cents interest on said Judgment at 6 per cents per annum and also Eighteen dollars and seventy seven cents damages of 12½ per cent on said judgment and interest and also ten dollars forty cents the costs aforesaid in all one hundred and seventy nine dollars and 36 cents and also the costs of this motion.

James Bartlett　　　　　)　　　Motion
　　Vs　　　　　　　　　)　Came the parties in proper person and it appear-
Isaac Lollar　　　　　　)　ing on motion of the plaintiff that he was sheriff
　　　　　　　　　　　　)　of Putnam County and the defendant his deputy and
that an execution came to defendants hand sence the last Term of this court in due time in favor of the President and Directors of the Bank of Tennessee against Thomas B. Johnson, James S. England, Alexander C. Robinson and John Robinson for $147.25 and $10.00 cents which defendant failed duly to return and that by reason thereof the said President and Directors have at this Term recovered of the plaintiff $179.36 and also the costs of their motion in that behalf (p-103) and the defendant says he has nothing to say against the plaintiffs recovery against him of said sum of $179.36 and costs - It is therefore considered by the court that the plaintiff recover of the defendant the said sum of one hundred and seventy nine dollars and thirty six cents and the costs that may be taxed in said motion of the Bank Vs plaintiff and also the costs of this motion.

Court adjourned till court in course.
　　　　　　　　　　　　　　　　　Ab: Caruthers

November 13th 1845　　　)　Be it Remembered that at a Circuit Court
State of Tennessee　　　)　began and held for the County of Putnam

in the fourth Judicial Circuit fourth State of Tennessee at White Plains in said County on Monday being 13th day of November in the Year of Our Lord one Thousand Eighteen Hundred and forty three and of the independance of the United States the 68 year.

Present the Honorable Abraham Caruthers Esqr. one of the Judges of the State of Tennessee and assigned to hold the courts of the Fourth Judicial Circuit in said State -

Proclamation being made court was open in due form and Thomas S. Elms Sheriff of Putnam County returned into open court the States Writ of Venira facias to him directed &c. Executed upon the following person to serve as Jurors at the present term of this court who had been nominated and designated.

By the County Court of said County at their August term in the Year of Our Lord one Thousand Eight hundred and Forty three being the next succeeding Term of said County Court after the last term of this court, To Wit - McClelland Jones, John Hollyday, William Carlisle, Thomas Conway, Silas W. Gentry, George Welch, Joseph Peason, John Barnes, Samuel Mansell, Kelly Ward, Austin Webb, Martin Sims, John Officer, Henry Dugger James Officer, Edward Elms, Bethenel Buck, Dudley Hudgins, William Rogers, John T. Graham, David Bradford, James Isbell, Thomas Smith, Joseph Jarred, Alexander Boyd all Good and lawful men of said County out of whom were selected (p-104) as the Statutes in that case provides a grand inquest and Jury to serve at the present term of this court To Wit - William Rogers, John Officer, John T. Graham, Henry Duggar, Thomas Smith, Dudley Hudgens, Joseph Pearson, Samuel Mansell, Alexander Boyd, Edward Elms, Kelly Ward, David Bradford and John Hollyday, out of whom the court selected and appointed William Rogers, Foreman of said grand Jury and said grand Jury Being here now impannelled and sworn to Enquire for the State aforesaid and for the body of the County aforesaid, received their charge from the court and retired to consider presentments and indictments attended by Isaac A. Huddleston a constable duly chosen and sworn for that purpose said Sheriff also returned that he had By virtue of said writ of Vinarie Facias summons Isaac A. Huddleston, Absolam A. Sims to serve as constable at the present term of this court.

For sufficient reason appearing unto the court James Officer is Excused from attending as a Juror at the present term.

Robert G. and C. F. Burton) In Debt
Vs) This day came the parties by
Samuel T. Vaden and James Cantrell) their attorneys and thereupon
) came a Juror of good and lawful men to wit - Bethuel Buck, Joseph Jared, Thomas Conway, Austin Webb, James Isbell, McClelland Jones, George Welch, John Barnes, Martin Sims, William Carlisle, Silas W. Gentry and William M. Marchbanks who being elected, tried and sworn the truth to speak upon the issue joined upon there oath do say they Find the issue in favor of the plaintiffs and assesses their Damages occasioned by the detention of the debt in the Declaration mentioned to Thirty six dollars fifty four cents - it is therefore considered by the court that the plaintiff recover against the defendants the sum of three Hundred and Twenty six dollars and Eighty six cents the Debt in Declaration mentioned, (p-105) and the damages aforesaid by Jury assessed and all cost in this behalf expended.

Bank of Tennessee) In Debt
Vs) This day came the parties by their
Thomas Welch, Joseph Bartlett) attorneys and thereupon came a
and Joseph B. Graham) Jury of good and lawful men to
) wit - Betheul Buck, Joseph Jarred,
Thomas Conway, Austin Webb, James Isbell, McClellan Jones, George Welch, John Barnes, Martin Sims, William Carlisle, Silas W. Gentry, William M. Marchbanks, who being elected tried and sworn the truth to speak upon the issue Joined upon their oath do say they find the issue in favor of the plaintiff and assessed plaintiffs damages occasioned by the detention of the debt - On the declaration mentioned to Eighteen dollars and Twenty cents - It is therefore considered by the court that plaintiff recover against the defendants the sum of Two hundred and forty dollars, the Debt in the Declaration mentioned and the damages aforesaid By the Jury assessed and also cost in this behalf Expended.

Bank of Tennessee) Debt
Vs) This day came the parties by their attornes
John B. Pointer) and thereupon came a Jury of Good and lawful
Mathew E. Wallace) men To Wit - Betheul Buck, Joseph Jared,
) Thomas Conway, Austin Webb, James Isbell,
McClellan Jones, George Welch, John Barnes, Martin Sims, William Carlisle Silas W. Gentry, and William Marchbanks who being elected, tried and sworn the truth to speak upon the issue Joined and upon their oath do say They find the issue in favor of The plaintiff and assess the plaintiff damages to six dollars and Fifty cents occasioned by detention of the declaration mentioned.

It is therefore considered by the court that the plaintiff recover of the defendant the sum of ninty dollars the debt in the declaration mentioned and the damages aforesaid by the Jury assessed and also cost in this behalf Expended.

P-105 November 13th 1843

Bank of Tennessee) This day came the parties by
Vs) their attornies and their upon
John Officer, Robert Officer) came a Jury of good and lawful
William Officer, Alexander Officer) men To wit - Betheuel Buck,
) Joseph Jarred, Thomas Conway,
Austin Webb, James Isbell, McClelland Jones, George Welch, John Barnes, Martin Sims, William Carlisle, Silas W. Gentry, and William M. Marchbanks, who being elected tried and sworn The truth to speak upon the issue Joined upon their oath do say the find the issue In favor of the plaintiff and assess the plaintiff damages to sixteen dollars and forty cents occasioned by the detention of the debt in the declaration mentioned, It is therefore considered by the court that the plaintiff recover of the defendants the sum of Three hundred and sixty dollars the Debt in Declaration mentioned and the damages aforesaid by the Jury assessed and all costs in this behalf expended.

Bank of Tennessee) In Debt
Vs) This day came the parties by
George Henry, Robert Officer) there attornies and thereupon
Andrew Henry) came a Jury of good and lawful

men to wit - Betheul Buck, Joseph Jarred, Thomas Conway, Austin Webb, James Isbell, McClellan Jones, George Welch, John Barnes, Martin Sims, William Carlisle, Silas W. Gentry and William M. Marchbanks, who being elected, tried and sworn the truth to speak upon the Issue Joined upon Their oath do say they find the Issue in favor of the plaintiff and assess the plaintiffs damage to five dollars and sixty cents - occasioned by the detention of the Debt in the declaration mentioned It is therefore considered by the court that the plaintiff recover of the Defendants the sum of ninty dollars the Debt in the Declaration mentioned and the damages aforesaid by the Jury assessed and all costs in this behalf Expended.

P-107 November 13th 1843

Bank of Tennessee)
Vs)
William Scarborough,)
John Bumbalough)
Henry Netherton)
)

In Debt - This day came the parties by their attornies and thereupon came a Jury of good and lawful men To wit - Betheul Buck, Joseph Jarred, Thomas Conway, Austin Webb, James Isbell, McClellan Jones, George Welch, John Barnes, Martin Sims, William Carlisle, Silas W. Gentry and William M. Marchbanks, who being elected tried and sworn the truth to speak upon the issue Joined upon their oath do say they find the issue In favor of the plaintiff and assess the plaintiff damages to Twelve dollars Twelve and one half cents occasioned by the detention of the debt in the declaration mentioned. It is therefore considered by the court that plaintiff recover of the defendant the sum of one hundred and fifty dollars the Debt in the Declaration mentioned and the damages aforesaid by the Jury assessed and all costs in this behalf expended.

Bank of Tennessee)
Vs)
Joseph Bartlet, Joseph B. Graham)
Campbell Bohannon)
)

In Debt
This day came the parties by their attorneys and thereupon came a Jury of good and lawful men To wit - Betheul Buck, Joseph Jarred, Thomas Conway, Austin Webb, James Isbell, McClellan, James, George Welch, John Barnes, Martin Sims, William Carlisle, Silas W. Gentry, and William M. Marchbanks, who the issue Joined upon their oath do say they find the issue Joined upon their oath do say they find the Issue in favor of the plaintiff and assess the plaintiff damages occasioned by the detention of of the debt in the declaration mentioned to Eight dollars and seventy five cents, it is therefore considered by the court that the plaintiff recover of The defendants the sum of one hundred dollars the Debt in the Declaration mentioned and the damages aforesaid by the Jury assessed and all costs in this behalf Expended.

Bank of Tennessee)
Vs)
Snoden H. Maddux and)
Elijah C. Crowell and)
Allen Young)
(p-108))
)

In Debt
This day came the parties by their attornies and thereupon came a Jury of good and lawful men To Wit - Betheul Buck, Joseph Jarred, Thomas Conway, Austin Webb, James Isbell, McClellan Jones, George Welch, John Barnes, Martin Sims, William Carlisle, Silas W. Gentry and William M. Marchbanks, who being Elected tried and sworn the truth to speak upon The upon The issue Joined upon their oath   they find the issue in favor of the

plaintiff and assess the plaintiff damages occasioned by the detention of the declaration mentioned To seven dollars and Eighty cents - It is therefore considered by the court that the plaintiff recover of the defendants the sum of one Hundred and seventy six dollars the Debt in the declaration mentioned and the damages aforesaid by the Jury assessed and all costs in this behalf Expended.

Bank of Tennessee) In Debt
Vs) This day came the parties and plain-
Samuel T. Vaden, Wm. R. Vance) tiff by attorney dismisses this
Russel Marchbanks and) suit and defendants assume the pay-
Herald Marchbanks) ment of all costs, it is therefore
) considered by the court that the
plaintiff recover of the defendants the cost respectfully assumed afforesaid.

Bank of Tennessee) In Debt
Vs) This day came the parties
Herald D. Marchbanks, Russel Marchbanks) and and plaintiff by
John Hollyday, Henry L. McDaniel) attorney dismisses this
Samuel T. Vaden) suit and defendants as-
) sum the payment of all
costs. It is therefore considered by the court that the plaintiff recover of the defendant the costs respectfully assumed afforesaid.

Bank of Tennessee) In Debt
Vs) This day came the parties and plaintiff
Lawson Clark, John Rogers) By attorney dismisses this suit and
) defendants assumes the payment of all
costs. It is therefore considered by the court that the plaintiff Recover of the defendants the costs respectfully assumed afforesaid.

P-109 Joseph Evans) Motion Debt Certiorari - This day came
Vs) the parties by attorneys and the plain-
Charles Smith) tiff dismisses this suit and assumes the
) payment of the balance of the costs and
the defendant assumes the payment of the balance of the costs. It is therefore considered by the court that the parties recover against each other the costs Respectfully assumed aforesaid.

Simon Hogan Administator) Debt Certiorari - Upon petition of de-
of Anthony Hogan Decd.) fendant It is ordered by the court that
Vs) Writ of certiorari and super cedas issue
Thomas Hollyday) according to the prayer of petitioners
) suit defendant Having given bond and
security as the law directs for the prosecution of the same.

William B. Campbell Esquire Took the oath of an attorney and was permitted to practice as an attorney at this Bar.

Ordered that court adjourn till to morrow a __9 oclock.

Ab. Caruthers

Tuesday November 14th 1843

Court met persuant to adjournment present the Honorable Abraham Caruthers, Judge presiding.

State   )   O Drunkness
Vs   ) This day came the attorney General for the State
George Medley) and said defendant in proper person and said de-
) fendant being charged upon the bill of presentment
says he is guilty in manner and form as charged and for his trial doth put himself upon the mercy of the court and the attorney general for the State doth the like. It is therefore considered by the court that said defendant pay a fine of one Dollar and the costs of this prosecution.

P-110 And Snoden H. Maddux and Joseph Y. McKee came this day into open court and acknowledged themselfs security for said defendant for said fine and costs, and agrees that Execution may issue against them Jointly with said defendant for the same.

State   )   Drunkness
Vs   ) This day came the Attorney General for the State
Thomas Saylors) and said defendant in proper person and said de-
) fendant being charged upon the bill of presentment
and saith he is guilty in form and manner as charged and for trial doth put himself upon the mercy of the court and the attorney General for the State doth the like it is therefore considered by the court that said defendant pay a fine of Five Dollars and the cost of this prosecution and Zebedee P. Hearing came this day into open court and acknowledged himself security for said defendant for said fine and cost and agrees that Execution may issue jointly against him with said defendant for the same.

State   )   Affray
Vs   ) This day the attorney General for the State and the de-
Hugh Owen) fendant in proper person and said defendant being charged
) upon the bill of presentment saith he is not guilty in
manor and form as charged and for his trial doth put himself upon the County and the Attorney General for the State doth the like and thereupon came a jury of good and lawfull men to wit - Bethuel Buck, Joseph Jarred, James Isbell, McClellan Jones, George Welch, John Barnes, Martin Sims, William Carlisle, Silas W. Gentry, Jackson Maxwell and Hugh G. Huddleston who being Elected tried and sworn the truth to speak upon the issue joined upon their oath doth say that the defendant is not guilty in manner and form as charged, it is therefore considered by the court that said defendant go hence without day and recover of the State of Tennessee the costs of this prosecution and that the same be certified to the County court for allowance.

State   )   This day came the attorney General for the
Vs   )   State (p-111) and said defendant in pro-
Nathan Whiteaker)   per person and said defendant being charged
)   upon the bill of presentment saith he is not
guilty in manner and form as charged and for his trial doth put himself
upon the county and the Attorney General for the State doth the like and
thereupon came a Jury of good and lawful men to wit - Jonathan Fowler,
Thomas Anderson, Ranson Mahany, George Apple, Snoden H. Maddux, Joseph
L. B. Graham, Jesse W. S. Graham, Waddy Carlisle, David H. Nicholes,
Moses N. Scarlett, Joshua Bartlett and William Norris, who being Elected
tried and sworn the truth to speak upon the issue joined upon their oath
do say that said defendant is not guilty in manner and form as charged.
It is therefore considered by the court that said defendant go hence
without day and recover against the State of Tennessee the cost of this
prosecution and that the same be certified to the County Court for allowance.

State   )   Forfeiture
Vs   )   This day came the Attorney General for the State
Spencer Phillips)   and said Spencer Phillips being solemnly called
)   to come into court as he was bound to do this
day to take the benefit of the Insolvent Debtors oath came not but made
default, it is therefore considered by the court that the State of Tennessee recover against the said Spencer Phillips the sum of Five Hundred
Dollars the sum mentioned in his Bond unless good cause shown to the contrary at the next term of this court and that scifa Issue to make known &c.

State   )   Forfeiture
Vs   )   This day came the Attorney General for the State
James Jackson   )   and said James Jackson being solemnly called to
)   come into court and bring with him the body of
Spencer Phillips to take the benefit of Insolvent Debtors oath as he was
bound to do this day came not but made default neither did said Spencer
Phillips appear, it is therefore considered by the court That the State
of Tennessee recover against the said James Jackson the sum of Five Hundred Dollars the sum mentioned in his Bond unless good cause shown to the
contrary at the next term and scifa issue to make known &c.

P-112   November 14th 1843

State   )   Forfeiture
Vs   )   This day came the Attorney General for the State
Joseph D. Hider)   and said Joseph D. Hider being solemnly called
)   to come into court and bring with him the body
of Spencer Phillips to take benefit of the Insolvent Debtors oath as he
is bound to do this day came not but made <u>defalt</u>, it is therefore considered by the court that the State of Tennessee recover against the said
Joseph D. Hider the sum of Five Hundred Dollars the amount mentioned in
his bond unless good cause be shown to the contrary and that sci fa Issue to make known &c.

State   )   Forfeiture
Vs   )   This day came the Attorney General for the
Nathaniel Whiteaker)   State and said Nathaniel Whiteaker being

solemnly called to come into court as he is bound to do this day to answer the State of Tennessee upon a presentment for an affray came not but made default, it is therefore considered by the court that the State of Tennessee recover against the said Nathaniel Whiteaker the sum of Two Hundred and Fifty Dollars the sum mentioned in his bond unless good cause shown to the <u>contrarty</u> at next term and that scifa Issue to make known &c.

State   )   Forfeiture
  Vs   )   This day came the Attorney General for the State
Joseph S. Henry)   and said Joseph S. Henry being solemnly called
)   to come into court and bring with him his <u>boddy</u>
of Nathaniel Whiteaker to answer the State of Tennessee upon a presentment for an affray as he is bound to do this day came not, but made default, it is therefore considered by the court that the State of Tennessee recover against the said Joseph S. Henry the sum of Two Hundred and fifty Dollars the sum mentioned in his unless good cause be shown to the contrary and that scifa Issue to make known &c.

State   )   Forfeiture
  Vs   )   This day came the Attorney General for the State
James Brooks   )   and James Brooks being solemnly called to come into
)   (p-113) November 14th 1843, court and bring with
him the <u>boddy</u> of Nathaniel Whiteaker to answer the State of Tennessee upon presentment for an affray as he is bound to do, this day came not but made default, it is therefore considered by the court that the State of Tennessee recover against the said James Brooks The sum of Two Hundred and fifty Dollars the sum mentioned in his bond unless good cause can be shown to the contrary at next term and that scifa issue to make known &c.

State   )   Forfeiture
  Vs   )   This day came the Attorney General for the State
Henry W. Sadler)   and the said Henry W. Sadler being solemnly called
)   to come into court as he was bound to do this
day to give evidence in behalf of the State of Tennessee upon a presentment against Hugh Owen and Nicholas McDonald for an affray came not but made default, it is therefore considered by the court that the State of Tennessee recover against the said Henry W. Sadler the sum of one Hundred and twenty five Dollars - being the penalty of his summons unless sufficient cause be shown to the contrary at the next term and that scifa Issue to make known &c.

State   )   Forfeiture
  Vs   )   This day came the Attorney General for the State
Nathaniel Whiteacre)   and the defendant in proper person   (p-114)
)   November 14th 1843, and a motion of the defendant the forfeiture in this case is set aside on the payment of the cost, it is therefore considered by the court that the State of Tennessee recover against said defendant all costs in this behalf Expended.

State   )   Forfeiture
Vs   )   This day came the Attorney General for the State and
Asa Herrald   )   the defendant in proper person and on motion of the
)   defendant the forfeiture in this case is set aside
on the payment of the cost, it is therefore considered by the court that
the State of Tennessee recover against said defendant all costs in this
behalf Expended.

State   )   A. & B.
Vs   )   Simeon Bramlet Jailor for White County on a
Spencer Phillips)   charge for biting off the ears of Bohannon and
)   sentenced to be imprisoned by the Circuit Court
of Putnam County at the July term thereof A. D. 1843 from the 12th 1843
day of July up to the 30th of the same month and making in all 18 days
at 2/3 per day and two lawful turnkeys 3/ - Each making in all the sum
of $7.75.
   Being sworn to by said Jailor and certified by the Attorney General
it was ordered by the court the same should be allowed and taxed in the
bill of cost.

   The grand Jury came into open court and brought with them the following
presentments to wit - One against Samuel P. Perrin for drunkness, one a-
gainst Thomas Cates and Thomas Pointer for an affray, one against Zechariah
Sullens and Henry Ayres for an affray, one against Jesse A. Bounds for
drunkness and also a bill of Indictment against Thomas Wattson and John
Sutton for an affray Endorsed by the foreman a true bill and then retired
to consider of further presentments and inditements.

P-115   November 14th 1843

Simon Hogin Administrator of   )   In debt Certiorari - Plaintiff by
Anthony Hogin Dec.   )   attorney Enters his appearance and
         Vs   )   this cause is set for trial at the
Thomas Holiday   )   next term.

A. B. Nichols   )   Debt Certiorari - On motion of defendant it is
Vs   )   ordered that plaintiff give security for the
Lewis R. Vance   )   maintainance of this suit before the causes
)   reach the Docket or the same will be dismissed.

A. B. McNichols   )   On motion of defendants it is or-
Vs   )   dered that the plaintiff give
R. G. Benson & Lewis R. Vance) security for the maintainance of
)   this suit before the causes reached
the Docket or the same will be dismissed.

A. B. McNichols)   Certiorari
Vs   )   On motion of defendants it is ordered that the
Thomas Smith &   )   planntiff give security for the maintainance
Lewis R. Vance   )   of this suit before the cause reached the
                      Docket or the same will be dismissed.

Thomas T. Watson)   App
  Vs   ) This day came the partys by there attorneys
Zechariah Gass) and on affidavit of the defendant this cause
) is continued untill next term on the payment
of the cost of this term, it is therefore considered by the court that
the plaintiff recover of the defendant the cost afforesaid.

Thomas T. Watson)   App
  Vs   ) This day came the parties and on affidavit of
Zechariah Gass) defendant this cause is (p-116) November
) 14th 1843, continued till next term on the
payment of the costs of this term it is therefore considered by the ____
that the plaintiff recover the costs of the defendant afforesaid.

Sims Dearing Administrator of Joshua Fox Deceased)   In Debt
       Vs   )   Came the plain-
John Robison & George McCormack   )   tiff by his at-
)   torney and the
time having expired for the defendants to give security for the prosecution
of the certiorari and c - whereupon it is considered by the court that the
defendants petition be dismissed and that the plaintiff recover against
defendants the costs that have accrued in this cause and that a procendendo issue to the Justice below &c.

John Lee   ) This day came the parties in proper
  Vs   ) person and they here in court agree-
Alfred Jones, Bird S. Jones) ing that there is a mistake in render-
and Vurdarn Jones   ) ing the Judgment in this cause at
) the last term of this court by render-
ing the Judgment against the plaintiff for the costs &c when the Judgment
should have been against the defendants - It is therefore considered by
the court that the Judg____ment be corrected according to the understanding
and agreement of the parties - and that the plaintiff accordingly recover
against the defendants said costs - & that plaintiff have execution.

P-117 James Pharris)   Debt Certiorari
     Vs   ) Came the parties by their attorney and agree
   Amos Maxwell) to dispence with with a Jury and submit it
) to the court to decide the matters in con-
troversy and it appearing to the satisfaction the court that the defendant
was not denied the benefit of stay as alledged in the petition, it is
therefore considered by the court that pltff recover against the defendants
Samuel Maxwell and David Patton fifty eight dollars the sum adjudged by
the Justice of the peace together with two dollars thirty two cents damages
sence the rendering of Judgment before the Justice amounting together the
sum of $60.32 and that execution issue for the same together with costs
before the Justice of the peace & the costs of suit in this court.

Ordered that court adjourn till tomorrow morning 9 oclock.

                            Ab. Caruthers

Wednesday November 15 1843

Court met persuance to adjournment present the Honorable Abraham Caruthers Judge presiding.

John Hughes) In Debt
Vs) Motion to condemn Land Lawrence Byrns an acting
Needham Apple) Justice of the peace in and for Putnam County Filed
) herein open court the following papers to wit -

State of Tennessee) To any lawfull Officer to Execute and return
Putnam County) you are hereby commanded to summons Needham
) Apple and Elizabeth Eoleford his wife to
appear before me or some other Justice of peace for said County to answer the complaint of John Hughes of a plea of Debt under Fifty Dollars due by note made and delivered by the said Elizabeth Holeford to John Hughs while a single woman and which note is herewith filed herein fail not.
Given under my hand and seal this 23th day August 1843.

McClellan Jones
J. P. of Putnam
County

Executed and set for trial on the 25th of August 1843 before L. Burns Esqr. at his house.

J. L. H. Huddles-
ton Const.

P-118 Judgement in favor of Plaintiff against Needham Apple and Elizabeth Holdford his wife for Thirty one Dollars and Thirty cents and cost for which Execution may issue this 25th day of August 1843.

L. Byrne (Seal) J.P.

State of Tennessee) To the sheriff or any constable of said County
Putnam County) I command you that of the goods and chattles
) Lands and tenements of Neadham Apple and Elizabeth Holford his wife if to be found in your county you make the sum of Thirty one Dollars and thirty cents with interest and Lawful cost to satisfy a Judgement that John Hughes obtained against the said Apple and Elizabeth Holford his wife before me on the 25th of August 1843 and pay over the same as the law directs this the 7th day of September 1843.

L. Byrne (Seal)
J.P. of Putnam County

Judgement 25th August 1843 $31.30
J. H. Huddleston serving warrant   1.00
Judgment & fi fa   .37½

L. Byrne J.P.

No personal property found in my County Levied this fi fa on two tracts of Land of the defendants September 13th 1843.

Allen Young D.S.

Levied on a tract of Land in Putnam County District No. 1 Tennessee on Indian Creek of Cumberland River Deeded by Elizabeth McDaniel to Elizabeth Holeford the wife of Needham Apple lying on the north side of said Creek adjoining the lands of Washington Sadler on the north west of Indian Creek on the East containing five acres also on the tract belonging to the defendant being one third of the tract of land laid off by commissioners as said Elizabeth dowers adjoining the land Heirs of Jonathan Holford Decd on the North of William Sadlers on the East Garrett Sadlers on the west including the mansion house where said Jonathan Holford Decd. formly lived.

Sept. 13th 1843
Allen Young D. Shff.

On motion of plaintiff it is considered by the court that Land be condemned and sold to satisfy said execution and the cost of this motion and that order of sale issue to the shff of Putnam County for that purpose.

P-119   November 15th 1843

John Hughes   )   In Debt - Motion to condemn land L. Byrne an
   Vs   )   acting Justice of the peace in and for Putnam
Needham Apple   )   County Filed herein open court the following
)   paper To wit -

State of Tennessee   )   To the Sheriff or any lawful Officer of
Putnam County   )   said County - I command you to summons
)   Needham Apple to appear before me or some
Justice of said County to answer the complaint of John Hughes in a plea of debt due by note under one hundred Dollars herein fail not - Given under my hand and seal This 24th day of August 1843.

McClellan Jones (Seal)
J. P. of Putnam County

Executed and set for trial on 25th of August 1843 before L. Byrne Esqr. at his house J. S. H. Huddleston const. fee 50 cents Judgment in favor of the plaintiff against defendant for sixty three dollars and Twenty two cents and the costs for which execution may issue this 25th day of August 1843.

L. Byrne J. P. (Seal)

$59.$\frac{79}{100}$ One day after date I promise to pay John Hughs on order fifty nine dollars and sixty nine cents with Interest from the 1st day of Jany. last for William Dec. witness my hand and seal this 11th October 1842.
         His
Needham X Apple (Seal)   Atest   R. Judgment $63.22
         Mark

State of Tennessee)
                    To any sheriff or constable for said county - I command you that of the goods and chattles and lands and Tenements of Needham Apple if to be found in your County - You make the sum of sixty three dollars and twenty Two cents, and costs of suit to satisfy a Judgment that John Hughes obtained the said Apple before or on 25th August 1843 and pay

over the sum as the law directs this 7th day of September 1843.

                L. Byrne (Seal)
                J. P. for Putnam
                County.

Judgement 25 August 1843 $63.22 J. L. Huddleston Warrant 50 cts. Judgment & fi fa 37½ cents - L. Byrne J. P.

No Personal property found in my County Levied the fi fa on Two tracts of Land of the defendants Sept. 13th 1843.

                Allen Young Shff.

P-120   Nov. 15th 1843

Levied on a tract of Land in Putnam County Tennessee district No. 1 on Indian Creek of Cumberland river Deeded by Elizabeth McDaniel to Elizabeth Holford the wife of Needham Apple lying on the North side of said Creek adjoining the lands of Washington Sadler on the North West of Indian Creek on the East containing five acres also on the tract belonging to the defendant being one third of her tract of land laid off by commissioners as said Elizabeths dower adjoining the land of the Heirs of Jonathan Holford Decd, on the North William Sadlers on the East Garrett Sadlers on the west including the mansion house where said Jonathan Holford Decd. formerly lived September 13th 1843.

               Allen Young D. Sheriff

On motion of plaintiff it is considered by the court That said land be condemned to satisfy said Execution and the costs of this motion and that an order of sale issue to the sheriff of Putnam County for that purpose.

James C. Jones Gov. to the use of   ) In Debt on constable
E. R. and T. Marchbanks   ) land - This day came
     Vs   ) the parties by their
Alfred Jones, Bird S. Jones, Robert   ) attorneys and there-
Alcorn, Galant Anderson and Edward Anderson) upon came a Jury of
) good and lawful men

To wit - Betheul Buck, Joseph Jarred, George Welch, John Barnes, Martin Sims, William Carlisle, Silas W. Gentry, William H. Quarles, Jackson Maxwell, Hugh G. Huddleston, John H. Young and Jonathan Nicholas who being elected tried and sworn the truth to speak upon the issue joined upon their oath do say that they find the issue in favor of the plaintiff and assess this damages (p-121) To Eighty dollars and Sixty cents besides costs of suit it is therefore considered by the court that the plaintiff recover from the defendants the sum of Four Thousand dollars the amount of the penalty of the bond in the declaration mentioned which sum may be discharged by the payment of said sum of Eighty dollars and sixty cents the damages aforesaid, By the Jury assessed and the costs of this suit.

Simon Hogan administrator of Anthony Hogan Decd.) Debt Certiorari
       Vs   ) This day came
Thomas Hollyday   ) the parties by

their attorneys and thereupon came a jury of good and lawful men to wit, Betheul Buck, Joseph Jarred, Thomas Conway, Austin Webb, James Isbell, McClellan Jones, George Welch, John Barnes, Martin Sims, William Carlisle, Silas W. Gentry, and William K. Bradford, who being elected tried and sworn and truly to try the maters in this dispute between The parties upon their oath do say they find in favor of the plaintiff and assess his damages to Twelve dollars - It is therefore considered by the court that the plaintiff recover of the defendant the damages aforesaid by the Jury assessed and all costs In this behalf Expended.

Bank of Tennessee) In Debt - This day came the
  Vs) parties and on motion the
Snodon E. Maddux, Elijah C. Crowel) Judgment in this cause as to
Allen Young) the debt and damages and re-
) leased the same having been
settled.

P-122 A. B. McNichols) Certiorari
  Vs) This day came the defendant by attorney
 Lewis R. Vance) and the time having Expired for plain-
) tiff to give security for maintainance
of this suit according to a rule made heretofore for the purposes - Wherefore it considered by the court that plaintiff Be nonsuited and the defendant recover of the plaintiff His costs about his defence in this behalf expended.

A. B. McNichols) App.
  Vs) This day came the defendant by at-
Lewis R. Vance & R. G. Benson) torney and the Time having Expired
) for the plaintiff to give security
for the maintainance of this suit according to a rule made heretofore for that purpose wherefore it is considered by the court that said plaintiff be non suited and that the defendant recover of the plaintiff his costs by him about his defence in this behalf expended.

John Watson) Debt Certiorari
  Vs) This day came the defendant by attorney and
Jesse W. S. Graham) motion he is permitted to amend his petition.
) The Grand Jury came this into open court and returned a presentment against Hampton Pittito and Bethel Boman for an affray one Bill of indictment against Peter McDonald for Larceny endorsed by their foreman a true bill also a bill of indictment against James Mc-Broom for forgery Endorsed by their foreman not a true Bill and retired to consider of further presentments and indictments.

State) Drunkness
 Vs) November 15th 1843
Samuel P. Perrin) P-123 This day came the attorney General
) for the state and the defendant in
proper person and said defendant being charged upon the presentment sayeth that He is not guilty in manner and form as charged and for his trial doth

78

put himself upon the country and attorney doth likewise and upon came a Jury of good and Lawful men, to wit - James Jackson, Lawson Lee, Samuel Simpkins, William McDaniel, Bird I. Jones, Daniel W. Haws, William Stephens, George Medly, Godfrey Austin, James H. Sutton, Brice M. Draper, John Dyer, who being elected tried and sworn the truth to speak upon the issue Joined upon their - do say that said defendant is not guilty in manner and form as charged, It is therefore considered by the court that said Defendant go hence without day and recover against the State of Tennessee the cost of this prosecution, and that the same <u>sertified</u> to the County court for allowance.

State) Affray
Vs) This day came the Attorney General for the State
Bethel Bowman) and defendant in proper person and said defendant
) being charged upon the presentment sayeth He is
guilty in manner and form as charged and for his Trial puts himself upon the mercy of the court, it is therefore considered by the court The said defendant pay a fine of one dollar and the costs of this prosecution and David Bradford came into open court and acknowledged himself security for said defendant for said fine and costs and agrees that execution may issue against him jointly with defendant for the same.

State) This day came the attorney General for the
Vs) State and says that he is unwilling further
James Brewington and) to prosecute this suit but dismisses the
Alexander Brewington) same and it appearing to (p-124) To
) (November 15th 1843) the satisfaction of
the court that the same is a frivolous and malicious prosecution it is therefore considered by the court that said defendants go hence without day and recover against John Welch pay the prosecution in this case all costs in this behalf Expended.

State) Murder
Vs) This day came the attorney for the State and the
Baldwin Rowland) Defendant in proper person when the sheriff of
) Putnam County returned into court pannels of
one Hundred and six Jurors of which Jurors one was peremptorialy challenged by the State Fire perentorialy By defendant and one Hundred Challenged by defendant for cause and it appearing to the court that defendant can not have a fair and impartial trial in the County of Putnam By consent of the Attorney General of the defendant in proper person it is ordered By the court the vinire in this cause be changed To the County of Smith in the fourth Judicial District of the State of Tennessee.

State) Murder
Vs) This day came the Attorney General and Craven
Baldwin Rowland) Maddux and George Welch and each Acknowledged
) themselves to owe and stand indebted to the
State of Tennessee in the sum of two hundred and fifty dollars each to be levied of their respective goods and chattles lands and tenements to the use of the State nevertheless to be void on condition that the said Craven Maddux and George Welch made their personal appearance before the Judge of Circuit Court of Smith County at the Courthouse in the town of

Carthage on the first thursday after 3rd Monday of Decr. next then and there to prosecute in behalf of the State of Tennessee on a charge against Baldwin Rowland for murder and thereon not depart without leave first had and obtained of the court   (p-125)   November 15th 1843, .

This day came William Car, Quinton Lowe, Hezekiah Dun, George Sells, Washington Williams, Mark Harper, William Elrod, Mathew Cowen, John Lee, Pleasent Hooten, Absolom Sims, Champ Stanton, William W. Stephens and each acknowledged themselves to owe and stand Indebted to the State of Tennessee in the sum of Two Hundred and fifty dollars each to be Levied of their respective goods and chattles, lands and Tenements for the use of the State - never the less to be void on condition that they make their personal appearance before the Judge of the Circuit court of Smith County at the court in the town of Carthage on the first Thursday after the 3rd Monday in December next - Then and there to give evidence in behalf of the State of Tennessee on a charge against Baldwin Rowland and not depart without leave first had and obtained by the court.

State   )   Indictment for Murder - This day came Felix A.
Vs   )   Badger, William Elrod, James Carter, Albert A.
Baldwin Roland)   Anderson, Batey Mansell and William R. Vance
)   and each in open court acknowledged themselves
to owe and stand indebted to Baldwin Rowland the defendant in the sum of Two hundred and fifty dollars each to be Levied of their Respective goods and chattles lands and Tenements to the use of the said Baldwin Rowland to be void never the less upon condition that they make their personal appearance before the Judge of the Circuit Court of Smith County at the Courthouse in the town of Carthage on 1st thursday after 3rd Monday in Decr. next Then and there to give evidence in behalf of Baldwin Rowland on a charge of murder and not depart leave first had and obtained of said Baldwin Rowland.

P-126 State   )   Indict for Murder - Akilias Hare Jailor
       Vs   )   for Jackson County filed this day in
       Baldwin Rowland)   open court the following account for
)   keeping Baldwin Roland on a charge of
Murder committed in putnam County in the State of Tennessee from the 19th March 1843 to the 11th July 1843 and from 13th July 1843 to the 14th Nov. 1843 making in all 240 days at 37½ cts. per day $90. Four Turn keyes 3/0 each $2.00 making In all the sum of $92. being sworn to by S. C. Hare and certified by the attorney General the same was ordered by court allowed and Taxes in a bill of costs.

Ordered that Court adjourn till tomorrow 9 oclock.

                                                      Ab. Caruthers

            Thursday Morning nine oclock November 16th 1843

Court met pursuant to adjournment present Abraham Caruthers Judge presiding.

80

Leah Roberts) Debt Certiorari - Came the parties by their at-
Vs) torneys who agree to dispence with a Jury in
Robert Officer) this cause and submit the matter in controversy
James Officer) to the court and it appearing to the satisfaction
) of the court that the plaintiff did not agree
that the issuance of the Executions should be suspended as is alledged in
the defendants petition. It is therefore considered by the court that the
defendants petition be dismissed and that the plaintiff Leah Roberts recover against the defendant and Dudly Hunter the security in the bond for
prosecution of the certiorari in the costs in this cause and that a procedendo issue directed to the Justice below that he proceed to issue
Execution (p-127) upon the Judgments mentioned in the petition and
that the original papers be by the clerk of this court delivered over to
said Justice.

Hugh W. Carlin) Case
Vs) This day came the parties by their attorneys and
William Jared) it appearing to the court by admission of the
) parties that the judgment rendered at the March
term 1843 against defendant in this cause for the costs of suit was entered by mistake by consent of the parties by attorneys said Judgment is
set aside and annuled and it is considered by the court that the defendant recover against the plaintiff the costs in this suit accrued.

Hugh W. Carlen) Debt
Vs) This day came plaintiff and dismisses his suit -
William Jared) It is therefore considered by the court that the
) defendant go hence without day and recover against
the plaintiff his costs by him about his defence in this behalf expended.

John Hughes) Certiorari
Vs) On motion of plaintiff a rule is granted him to
James Land) show cause why defendants certiorari should be dis-
) missed and said rule coming on for agreement, it
is considered by the court that defendants certiorari be dismissed and that
a procedendo be issued to the Justice who tried the cause below - and that
plaintiff recover against defendant the costs herein accrued.

Jesse W. S. Graham) Certiorari
Vs) Ordered by the court that this cause be placed
John Watson Senr.) on the trial docket at next term, and defend-
) ant Graham by Atto. agrees that plff may take
any exception to his petition at next term that he could have taken at this
term.

Jesse B. Terry) Appeal from J. P. - This day came the parties
Vs) by attorneys and (p-128) plaintiff enters
Joseph L. B. Graham) a non suit in this cause - It is therefore
) considered that defendant go hence without
day and recover against plaintiff his cost by him in this behalf expended
&c.

Snoden H. Maddux   )   Appeal
      Vs   )   This day came the parties by attorneys and on
Mark Harper   )   affidavit plaintiff this cause is continued
)   until next term and it is considered that de-
fendant recover against plff the costs of this term.

William K. Bradford)   Appeal
      Vs   ) This day came the parties by their attor-
Samuel Mansel   ) neys and on motion this cause is ordered
) to be strucken from the docket and it is
considered by the court that the plaintiff recover against the defendant
the costs that have accrued in this cause in this court whereupon the defendant presented here in court his petition praying that a cortiorari
& supercedes issue which is granted him whereupon the plaintiff by his
attorney appeared and it is agreed by both sides that the cause be placed
on the trial docket at next term.

Lawson Clark   )   Appeal
      Vs   )   This day came the parties by their attorneys and the
Wesly Harvy   )   plaintiff dismisses his suit - It is therefore con-
)   sidered by the court that the defendant go hence and
recover against the plaintiff the costs of suit.

Lawson Clark   )   Appeal
      Vs   )   Came the parties by their attorneys and the plaintiff
Mathew Cowen   )   dismisses his (p-129) suit. It is therefore con-
)   sidered by the court that the defendant go hence
and recover against the plaintiff the costs of suit.

Lawson Clark   )   Appeal
      Vs   )   Came the parties by their attorneys and the plaintiff
Mathew Cowen   )   dismisses his suit It is therefore considered by the
)   Court that the defendant go hence and recover against
the plaintiff the costs of suit.

The State   )   Forfeiture
      Vs   )   This day came the attorney General and the defendant
James Jackson   )   Whereupon motion of said defendant the forfeiture of
) $500 heretofore entered against him at this term is
set aside upon the payment of costs which defendant agrees to pay and
confesses Judgment for said costs. It is therefore considered by the
court That the State of Tennessee recover against said James Jackson the
costs that have accrued herein.

The State   )   Forfeiture
      Vs   )   This day came the attorney General and the defend-
Joseph D. Hyder   )   ant - when upon motion of said defendant the for-
)   feiture of $500. heretore at this term entered him
is set aside upon payment of the costs which defendant agrees to pay and
confesses Judgment said costs - It is therefore considered by the court
that the State of Tennessee recover against the said defendant the costs
aforesaid.

State) Forfeiture
Vs) Came the attorney General and the defendant and
Spencer Phillips) on motion of said defendant the forfeiture here-
) tofore at this term entered against him at this
term (p-130) is set aside on the payment of costs.
It is therefore considered by the court that the State of Tennessee
recover against said defendant the costs that have accrued herein.

The State) Indictment Assault & Battery - Came the Attor-
Vs) ney and thereupon came James Jackson into open
Spencer Phillips) court and acknowledged himself the defendants
) security for the costs of this prosecution and
confesses Judgment for the same. It is therefore considered by the court
that the State of Tennessee recover against the said James Jackson jointly
with said defendant the costs aforesaid and the attorney General agrees
to stay execution eight months.

The State) Peace Warrant
Vs) Came the attorney General and the defendant and up-
Quinton Lowe) on the examination of the evidence it is considered
) by the court that the defendant go hence and be discharged from his recognizance and it appearing to the court the prosecution
is frivolous - It is considered by the court that Craven Maddux the prosecutor in this cause pay the costs of this prosecution and that execution
issue &c.

John A. Humble) Motion
Vs) This day came the plaintiff by his attor-
Moses Scarlet, John Lee) ney and moved the court for Judgment
Thomas Scarlet Joseph) against said defendants - and after argu-
Lacock his securities) ment had and heard - It is considered by
) the court that the said plaintiff take
nothing by his motion and that the defendants go hence without day and
recover against the said John Humble the costs of motion &c and that Execution issue.

P-131 The State) Horse Stealing
Vs) This day came the attorney General and
William McDonald,) says he is unwilling further to prose-
Wilson McDonald) cute in this behalf and on his motion
Lawson Lee) a nole prosequi is entered herein. It
) is therefore considered by the court
that the defendants go hence and be discharged from their recognizance
and that the defendants recover against the State of Tennessee the costs
of this prosecution.

The State) Indictment for horse stealing - This day came
Vs) the Attorney General and the defendant and on
Peter McDonald) motion and affidavit of said defendant this
) cause is continued till next term whereupon came
the defendant Peter McDonald together with James McDonald, William Mc-
Donald, Middleton McDonald and Henry Sadler his securities who acknowledged

themselves to owe & stand indebted to the State of Tennessee that is to say the said Peter McDonald in the sum of one thousand dollars and the said James McDonald, William McDonald, Middleton McDonald & Henry Sadler Jointly in the sum of one thousand dollars to be levied of their respective goods and chattles, lands and tenements to the use of the State but to be void on condition that the said Peter McDonald shall well and truly make his personal appearance before the Judge of the Circuit Court of Putnam County at White Plains the place of holding the Courts in said County on the first Tuesday after the second Monday of March next and then and there answer the State of Tennessee upon an Indictment for horse stealing and not depart without leave of the court.

Isaac Buck Chairman of the County Court of Putnam County) This day
Vs) came the
Brice M. Draper, Obadiah Evans, Edward Draper) parties
) by their
attorney (p-132) and the court being satisfied from the evidence adduced on the trial herein that the order made by the County Court establishing the road mentioned in the petition should be quashed – Whereupon it is considered that said order be quashed and that the defendants recover against the said Isaac Buck the costs that have accrued herein.

The State) Indictment Malicious Mischief – This day came the
Vs) attorney General and the defendant this cause is
Bennet Watts) continued till next term of court whereupon Lawson
) Clark and Mason Watts came into court and acknowledged themselves to owe and stand indebted to the State of Tennessee Jointly in the sum of two hundred and fifty dollars to be levied of their proper goods and chattles land and tennements, to the use of the State but to be void on condition that the defendant Bennet Watts shall make his personal appearance before the judge of the Circuit Court of Putnam County at White Plains the place of holding the courts in said County on the first Tuesday after the second Monday of March next and then and there answer the State of Tennessee on an Indictment for mischief and not depart without leave of the court.

The Bank of Tennessee) This day came the parties by at-
Vs) torney and thereupon came a Jury
Robert Alcorn, Alfred Jones) of good and lawful men to wit –
Bird S. Jones, Prettyman Jones) Betheul Buck, Joseph Jared, Thomas
Gallant Anderson) Conway, Austin Webb, James Isbell,
) George Welch, John Barnes, Martin
Sims, Silas W. Gentry, William Car, Thomas Nicholas, and Jackson Maxwell, who being elected, tried and sworn the truth to speak upon the issue Joined upon their oath say they find the issue for the plaintiff and they assess their damages (p-133) to twenty two dollars and forty two and a half cents besides costs – It is therefore considered by the court that the plaintiff recover against the defendant the sum of two hundred and fifteen dollars the debt in the declaration mentioned together with the damages aforesaid in form aforesaid assessed by the jury and costs of suit.

Lawson Clark) Appeal
Vs) This day came the parties by their attorneys and

Edward Anderson) thereupon came a Jury of good and lawful men
Thomas Anderson) to wit - Bethuel Buck, Joseph Jared, Thomas
) Conway, Austin Webb, James Isbell, McClellan,
Jones, George Welch, John Barnes, Martin Sims, William Carlisle, Silas
W. Gentry, and Jackson Maxwell who being elected tryed and sworn the
truth to speak upon the matters in controversy upon their do say they
cannot agree by consent of the parties, George Welch one of said Jurors
withdraws the rest of the Jury from rendering their verdict are discharged
& the cause continued.

Sampson W. Cassitty) Certiorari
Vs) This day came the plaintiff by attorney and
Sarah Kinnaird) the defendant failing to appear and prosecute
) her certiorari - It is considered by the court
that defendants certiorari be dismissed and that the plaintiff recover a-
gainst the defendant three dollars the amount of the Judgment of the justice below and the costs of this suit.

The Grand Jury came into court and returned a Bill of indictment against
Bennett Watts for Malicious mischief indorsed by William Rogers their foreman a true Bill and also a Bill of indictment against Jesse B. Terry &
David Graham for affray endorsed by their foreman a true bill and there
being no further business before said grand jury they are discharged.

State) William Duvall jailor of Smith County presented
Vs) his account sworn to for keeping William Mc-
Wm. McDaniel) Daniel in jail one day 37½ (p-134) 2 turn
Wilson McDaniel) keys $1.00 - $1.37½ For keeping Wilson McDaniel
) in jail one day 37½ two turnkeys a 50¢ - $1.37½
both on a charge of feeding securiting A.B.M. Nichols knowing that he had
stolen a horse - It is ordered by the court that said account be allowed
and taxed in the Bill of costs in said cause.

On motion of attorney, William H. Carr Clerk of this court the following receipts comptrollers Office Nashville Tennessee 11 Oct. 1843 received
from Wm. H. Car his statement of revenue, collected as Clerk of Putnam
Circuit Court from 1st Sept. 1842 to 1st Sept. 1843.

Amount Collected	44.93
Commission	1.11
Countersigning and recording 12 Licence	3.
Ray Bennet and Bound	9.11
Warrant No. 2047 this day for	35.92

Daniel Graham Comptroller Nashville 11th Oct. 1843

Received of Wm. H. Car Esq. thirty five dollars 82 cents audited to
him by No. 2047 and due on account of revenue by him collected as clerk
of Putnam Circuit Court from 1st Sept. 1842 to 1st Sept. 1843.

Signed duplicate M. Francis Trustee Pro. T.

Trustee's Office - White Plains 30th Oct. 1843

Received from Wm. H. Car his statement of monies collected as Clerk of Putnam Circuit Court from 1st Sept. 1842 to 1st Sept. 1843.

Amount collected		53.00
Commission at 2½ per cent	1.32½	
Making settlement with Trustee	1.00	2.32½
Amount Recd.		$50.67

J. M. Goodbar Trustee

Richard Johnson, Washington G. Hargis, Margaret Hargis, Sally Michel, Joseph Johnson, Samuel Johnson, John Bradly, Nancy Bradly, William C. Johnson, John Johnson, Thomas B. Johnson, Henry Johnson, (p-135) Albert V. Horn, Jane Horn Heirs at law of Samuel Johnson Decd.

Expartee) Petition to sell land and Slaves

Be it remembered that the above cause came on to be heard and was heard this 15th Nov. 1843 before the Honorable Ab. Caruthers Judge presiding to upon said petition from which it appears that Samuel Johnson, lately departed this life intestate in the County of Putnam State of Tennessee leaving petitioners his only heirs at law that petitioner, John Johnson and John Bradly - have sence took out letters of administrator on his Estate and give bond and security to the County Court of said County for the faithful performance of the same and also appearing that when said Samuel Johnson departed this life he was the owner of the land and the negros in the petition mentioned and that the same cannot be divided amoung said heirs without being sold and the proceeds thereof divided among them and it also appears that Winie Johnson the widow of said Deceased has taken a portion of said land for her dower in the same and that it would be for the interest of said heirs that said land and negros be sold it is therefore ordered adjudged and decreded by the court that said administrators John Johnson and John Bradly be appointed Special commissions to sell said land and negros that they expose the same to public sale on a credit of twelve months at the late residence of said land Decd. after advertizing the same at least thirty days before said sale at the White Plains (p-136) at Sparta Tennessee and at least five other public places in the County of Putnam and White and that they divide said land into such portions as would be likely to make it bring the most that they take bond with approved security for the purchase money for said land and negros and also retain a lien on the land for the purchase money and that they report to the next term of this court all other matters being reserved for the comming in of said report.

David H. Nichols) Appeal
Vs) Came the parties by their attornies and a Jury
Joseph McKee) of good and lawful men to wit - Bethuel Buck,
) 2 Joseph Jared, 3 Thomas Conway, 4 Austin Webb,
5 George Welch, 6 James Isbel, 7 John W. Lindsy, 8 John Brown, 9 Martin Sims, 10 Silas W. Gentry, 11 Jackson Maxwell, 12 William Carlisle, who being elected tried and sworn the truth to speak on the matters in controversy do say they find for the plaintiff three dollars and seventy

five cents, subject to the opinion of the court on the defendants liability to work as a hand under plaintiff as overseer under the following state of fact: Plaintiff was appointed overseer of the road which he sues defendant in this case for not working on and defendant assigned as a hand to work under him at April Term 1843 of Putnam County Court and again at September Term 1843, at July Term 1843 of said Court the defendant was appointed overseer of another road, all other facts are for the plaintiff - If defendant was not liable under the above orders of the County Court to work as a hand under plaintiff they find for defendant.

David H. Nicholls)
  Vs   )
John Webb)
)

Came the parties and agree that the facts of the foregoing case of Nichols Vs McKee are the facts of this case except that by order of the County Court of Putnam appointing McKee overseer defendant was assigned as one of his hand being also one of plaintiff hand assigned in the order appointing him overseer and agree that this case abide the Judge.

P-137 David H. Nicholls)
    Vs   )
   John Webb   )
)

Overseer Appeal - Came the parties and a jury of good and lawful men to wit - 1 Betheul Buck, 2 Joseph Jared, 3 Thomas Conway, 4 Austin Webb, 5 George Welch, 6 James Isbel, 7 John W. Lindsy, 8 John Barnes, 9 Martin Sims, 10 Silas W. Gentry, 11 Jackson Maxwell and William Carlisle who being elected tried and sworn the truth to speak on the on the matters in controversy do find for the plaintiff seventy five cents subject to the opinion of the court on the facts, to wit - At April (and also) at September Term of Putnam Court 1843, plaintiff was appointed overseer of the road which defendant is sued for not working on defendant assigned him as a hand - At July Term of said Court Joseph McKee was appointed overseer of another road and defendant assigned him as a hand.

David H. Nicholls Overseer)
    Vs   )
Hiram Hallums   )
)

The parties agree that this cause shall abide the judgment of the court in the above case of plaintiff Vs John Webb the amount of judgment to be two dollars and twenty five cents if deft. is liable.

David H. Nicholls Overseer)
    Vs   )
Samuel Simpkins   )
)

The parties agree to abide the judgment in the above case of plaintiff Vs John Webb, for three dollars and 75 cents.

David H. Nicholls Overseer)
    Vs   )
Archibald Hallum   )

Appeal, Same agreement $3.25

David H. Nicholls Overseer)
    Vs   )
James Sutton   )

Same agreement for $2.25

David H. Nicholls Overseer)
           Vs   )   Appeal - Same agreement for $3.75
Almarine Sutton   )

David H. Nicholls Overseer   )
           Vs   )   Appeal - Same agreement for $3.75
Joseph Evans   )

P-138   David H. Nicholls Overseer   )
                   Vs   )   Same agreement for $1.50
        Joseph Evans   )

David H. Nicholls Overseer   )
           Vs   )   Same agreement for $3.75
Paschal Hunt   )

State of Tennessee   )   Assault and Battery Recog-
           Vs   )   nizance &c.
Spencer Phillips, James Jackson   )   Came the attorney General
Joseph D. Euder   )   and the defendants when by
)   agreement all the orders and
forfeitures made and taken in this case at the present Term of the Court
an set aside and the defendants jointly assume all the costs accrued in
the prosecution of defendant Phillips for an assault and battery in which
judgment for fine and costs and imprisonment was rendered against him at
the last Term of this court - It is therefore considered by the court that
the plaintiff recover of the defendants the costs accrued in this prosecution from the beginning and execution shall issue against the defendants
jointly the fine and costs to be levied of the property of Phillips and
the costs of the property of all the defendants - The attorney General
stays Execution Eight months.

   Court adjourned until court in course.

                                            Ab: Caruthers

                           March 11 1844

   Court met pursuant to adjournment and no judge attending court was by
the Clerk of this Court adjourned until tomorrow morning 9 oclock.

                                            W. H. Carr Clerk

                           March 12th 1844

P-139   Court met pesuant to adjournment and no Judge attending court was
by the Clerk of this court adjourned untill tomorrow morning 9 oclock.

                                            W. H. Car, Clerk

March 13th 1844

Court met pursuant to adjournment and no Judge attending court was by the Clerk of this Court adjourned until tomorrow morning 10 oclock.

W. H. Car Clerk

Court met pursuant adjournment and no Judge attending.

The State)
Vs)
Peter McDonald)
) The Defendant being solemnly called to come into court and answer the State of Tennessee upon an indictment for horse stealing as he was bound to do this day came not But made default - It is therefore considered that the State of Tennessee recover against the said Peter McDaniel the sum of one Thousand dollars the sum mentioned in his recognizance unless good cause shown to the contrary at next Term and that Sci fee issue to make known &c.

The State)
Vs)
James McDonald, William McDonald)
Middleton McDonald, Henry Sadler)
) Forfeiture
Defendant being solemnly called to come into court and Bring with them the Body of Peter McDonald as they were Bound to do this day to answer the State of Tennessee upon a bill of indictment for horse stealing, came not But made Default neither did said Peter McDonald appear it is therefore considered that the State of Tennessee recover against the said James (p-140) March 14th 1844. McDonald, William McDonald, Middleton McDonald and Henry McDonald the sum of one Thousand dollars unless good cause shown to the contrary at next Term &c and that Sci fee issue to make known &c.

The State)
Vs)
Thomas Watts)
) Indictment affray - This day the Defendant being solemnly called to come into court as he was Bound to do this day to answer the State of Tennessee upon a Bill of Indictment for an affray came not But made Defalt it is therefore considered that the State of Tennessee recover against the said Thomas Watts the sum of five hundred dollars the sum mentioned in his Bond without sufficient cause shown to the contrary at next term and that scifee issue to make known &c.

The State)
Vs)
Bennett Watts)
) Indictment Malicious Mischief - This day came the Defendant being solemnly called to come into court as he was bound to do this day came not but made Default it is therefore considered that the State of Tennessee recover against the said Bennett Watts the sum of two hundred and fifty dollars the sum mentioned in his Recognizance unless sufficient cause be shown to the contrary at next Term and that scifee issue to make known &c.

The State)
Vs)
Lawson Clark)
) Forfeiture &c - This day the Defendants being Solemnly called to come into court and Bring with them the Body of Bennet Watts as they were bound

to do this day to answer the State of Tennessee upon a bill of indictment for malicious mischief, came not but made Default - neither did said Bennett Watts appear it is therefore considered that the State of Tennessee recover against   (p-141)   March 14th 1844 the said Lawson Clark and Mason Watts the sum of two hundred and fifty dollars the sum mentioned in the recognizance unless good cause shown to the contrary at the next Term and that sci fee issue to make known &c.

The State) Present Affray - This day came the defendant to-
Vs) gether with Joseph Pearson into open court and
Thomas Cates) acknowledged themselves to owe and stand indebted
) to the State of Tennessee Jointly in the sum of
five hundred dollars to be levied of their respective goods and chattles Lands and tenements to the use of the State to be void nevertheless upon condition that the said Thomas Cates make his personal appearance Before the Judge of the Circuit Court of Putnam County of White Plains in said County the place of holding said Courts on the first Tuesday after the second Monday in July next and then and there to answer the State of Tennessee upon a charge for an affray and not depart without leave first had and obtained of the court.

Court adjourned till court in course.

W. H. Car Clerk

P-142   Arrived in the United States at the Port of Neworleans on the Sixteenth day of January 1847.

E. Edward Andrea age 38 years born Sachen Meningre (?)
Agnes Andrea his wife age 39 years born Sarceboling
Eliese Weiring age 18 years born Scarceboling
Emma Weiring   "   16 years born   "
Fanny Andrea   "   12 "   "   "   Newhoure
Maximillian Andrea 10 "   "   "
Clara Andrew   "   8 "   "   "
Caroline Andrea   "   6 "   "   "
Anna Andrea   "   4 "   "   "
Ada Andrea   "   18 Mo.   "   "   Germany   Europe

State of Tennessee) This 31st day of March 1847 personally appeared
Jackson County) before me B. B. Washburn Clerk of Circuit Court
) of said County Ernest E. Andrew and made oath
in due form that the above statements as to the age place of birth and time of arrival in the United State of the above named persons is true to the best of his knowledge and belief and subscribed the same in my persence the date above.

B. B. Washburn Clk.

Attest - W. B. Eaffa   Ernest Edward Andrea

Circuit Court Dec. Term 1854

State of Tennessee) Be it remembered on this 11th day of December
Putnam County) 1854 the same being the second Monday in

December 1854 present H. L. Davidson Judge of the Fifth Judicial Circuit of the Circuit Courts of said State by interchange with Hon. John L. Goodall, Judge of the Fourth Judicial Circuit of the Circuit Courts aforesaid Proclaimation being made &c who then proceeded to oranganize the first Circuit Court for said County under the re-organization of said County in pursuance of the Act of the General Assembly passed on the 14th day of February 1845 at New Salem Meeting House the same being a house on the premises of Lewis Huddleston in said County: Therefore Curtis Mills presented to the court the following certificate of his election to the office of Clerk of the Circuit Court of said County and moved the court be inducted into said office and tenderred the following official bonds as required by the several statutes of the State aforesaid all of which was executed and acknowledged by the several obligors in open court and the solvency of the obligors and their ability to pay the aggregate penalty of the same being made to appear to the satisfaction of the court by the oaths of Pleasant Bohanan and Russel Moore and all of said bond being examined by the court and approved it was ordered that they be spread upon the minutes and which are severally as follows, preceded by said certificate of election:

State of Tennessee - I, I. H. Moore sheriff pro tempor of Putnam County appointed but the County court of said County pursuant to the provision of the Act of Assembly passed February fourteenth 1854 establishing said County of Putnam Certify that on the 3 day of June 1854 at the precincts in the (p-143) several districts for the purpose of electing Clerk of the Circuit Court for said County as provided in same Act when Curtis Mills was duly and constitutionally Elected Clerk of said Circuit Court.

Given under my hand & seal this 5th June 1854.

            I. H. Moore Shrff
            Pro tem of Putnam Co.

Bond No. 1 - Know all men by these presents that we Curtis Mills and William E. Barnes, John Barnes, William C. Bounds, David Nicholas, Lewis Huddleston, I. H. Moore, James McKinney and Robison Dyer all of the County of Putnam and State of Tennessee are held and firmly Bound unto the State of Tennessee in the sum of ten thousand Dollars current money which payment and truly to be made and adm. we bind ourselves our heirs, Executors and administrators Jointly and severaly firmly by these presents sealed with our seal and dated this the 11th day December A. D. 1854.

The condition of the above obligation is such at wherein the above Bound, Curtis Mills was on the last Saturday in June last day & constitutionaly Elected Clerk of Circuit Court in and for the County Putnam for the next ensuing four years now if the same Curtis Mills shall well and truly and safely keep all the Records of the Circuit Court of Putnam County and shall faithfully discharge all the duties appertaining to said office of Clerk according to law then above obligation to be null and void are else to be and remain in full force and effect.

Joseph Brown	Curtis Mills (Seal)
Executed and acknowledged	H. C. Bounds (Seal)
by the several obligarn	J. L. M. Huddleston
before me in open court	James M. McKinney (Seal)
and examed and approved	David Nicholas (Seal)
by me Decr. 11th 1854.	

H. L. Davidson, Judge
                                              His
                                       H. G. X Huddleston
                                         Mark   (Seal)
                                     John Barnes   (Seal)
                                     J. H. Moore   (Seal)
                                   Robison Dyer (Seal)
                                   James Bartlett (Seal)

P-144   Cirt. Term 1854 Bond No. 2

   Know all men by these presents that we Curtis Mills and William H. Barns, Lewis Huddleston, J. H. Moore, James Bartlett, Hugh G. Huddleston James M. McKinney, John Barns and Robinson Dyer all the County of Putnam and State of Tennessee are held and firmly bound unto the State of Tennessee in the sum of one thousand Dollars current money which payment will truly to be made and done we bind ourselves and heirs Executors and administrators Jointly and severally firmly by these presents sealed with our seals and dated this the 11th day of December A.D. 1854 - The condition of the above bound Curtis Mills was on the Last Saturday in June last duly and constitutionally elected Clerk of the Circuit Court in and for the County of Putnam for the next ensuing for years. Now if the said Curtis Mills shall well and truly account for and pay over all fines and forfitures, which may be paid unto his office to the proper officer of said State authorized by Law to recover the same then the above obligation to be null and void else be and remain in full force and effect.

Test: Joseph Brown
Executed and acknowledged by the several obligers
before me in open court and
Examined and approved Dec. 11th 1854.

H. L. Davidson, Judge &c.

                                     Curtis Mills   (Seal)
                                       Wm. C. Bounds   (Seal)
                                       James M. McKinney (Seal)
                                       David Nicholas (Seal)
                                       W. H. Barns   (Seal)
                                       His
                                     H. G. X Huddleston (Seal)
                                     Mark
                                     John Barns   (Seal)
                                     J. H. Moore   (Seal)
                                     Robison Dyer   (Seal)
                                     James Bartlett (Seal)

                                No. 3

   Know all men by these presents that we Curtis Mills, William H. Barnes, Lewis Huddleston, J. H. Moore, James Bartlett, Hugh G. Huddleston, James M. McKinney and John Barnes and Robison (p-145) Dyer all of the County of Putnam and State of Tennessee in the sum of three thousand dollars current money which payment well and truly to be made and we bind ourselfs our heirs executors and administrators Jointly and severally firmly by these presents sealed with our seals and dated this the 11 day of December A.D. 1854 the condition of the above obligation is such that whereas the above bound Curtis Mills was the first Saturday in June last duly and constitutionly Elected Clerk of the Circuit Court for Putnam County Tennessee the next ensuing four years.

   Now if the said Curtis shall well and truly account for and pay over all State and County Tax which may be paid into his office upon suits in

92

said court to the proper office authorized by Law to receive the same then this obligation to ___ null and void else be and remain in full force and effect.

Test - Joseph Brown	Curtis Mills (Seal)
Executed and acknow-	Wm. C. Bounds (Seal)
ledged the several	J. L. H. Huddleston (Seal)
obligators before me	James M. McKinney (Seal)
in open court and	David Nicholas (Seal)
examined and approved.	W. H. Barnes (Seal)
Dec. 11th 1854.	His
	H. G. X Huddleston (Seal)
H. L. Davidson Judge &c.	Mark
	John Barnes (Seal)
	J. H. Moore (Seal)
	Robison Dyer (Seal)
	James Bartlett (Seal)

No. 4

Know all men by these presents that we Curtis Mills and William H. Barns, John Barns, William C. Bounds, David Nicholas, Lewis Huddleston, J. H. Moore, James McKiney and Robison Dyer all of the County of Putnam and State of Tennessee in the sum of ten thousand dollars current money which payment well and truly to be made and done to Bind ourselves and heirs and Executors and administrators   (p-146)   Jointly in severly formly but this presents sealed with our seals and dated this the 11th day of December A.D. 1854 the condition of the above obligation is same, whereas the above bound Curtis Mills on the first Saturday in June last duly and constitutionly elected of the Clerk Circuit Court of Putnam County for the four years next ensuing.

Now if the said Curtis Mills shall well and truly collect and pay over all monies which may come into his hands as commishoner appointed by said court or which may come to hand as arising from the sale of any propperty unless a decree or order of said court to the person or persons entitled by law to Recover the same or to their legally acknowledged agents or Attorneys then this obligation to be null and void else be and remain in full force and effect.

Test - Joseph Brown	)	Curtis Mills (Seal)
Executed and acknowledged	)	Wm. C. Bounds (Seal)
by several obligators before	)	J. L. H. Huddleston (Seal)
me in open court	)	James M. McKinney (Seal)
and examined and approved	)	David Nicholas (Seal)
Dec. 11th 1854.	)	W. H. Barry (Seal)
	)	His
H. Davidson	)	H. G. X Huddleston (Seal)
	)	Mark
	)	John Barns (Seal)
	)	J. H. Moore (Seal)
	)	Robison Dyer (Seal)
	)	James Bartlett (Seal)

No. 5

Know all men by these presents that we Curtis Mills and William H. Barnes

John Barns, William C. Bounds, David Nicholas, Lewis Huddleston, J. H. Moore, James Bartlett, H. G. Huddleston, James McKinney and Robison Dyer all of the County of Putnam and State of Tennessee and held and firmly bound unto the State of Tennessee in the sum of five thousand dollars current money which payment well and truly to be made and done we bind ourselves and (p-147) each of our heirs Executors administrators Jointly and severally firmly by these presents sealed with our seals and dated this 11th December A.D. 1854 the condition of the above obligation is such that whereas the above bond Curtis Mills was on the first Saturday in June Last duly and constitutionally Elected Clerk of Circuit Court of Putnam County for the next four years ensuing.

Now if the said Curtis Mills shall well and truly pay over all monies which shall come into his hands from any delinquent Revanue officer the proper officers authorized by law to Recover the same according to the provision of an act of the General Assembly of said State passed 15 January 1844 the the above obligation to be null and void else to and Remain in full force and effect.

Test Joseph Brown)	Curtis Mills	(Seal)
Executed and acknowledged)	Wm. C. Bounds	(Seal)
by the several obligators before)	J. L. H. Huddleston	(Seal)
me in open court and examined)	James McKinney	(Seal)
and approved.)	David Nicholas	(Seal)
Dec. 11th 1854)	W. H. Barnes	(Seal)
)	His	
E. L. Davidson Judge)	H. G. X Huddleston	(Seal)
)	Mark	
)	John Barns	(Seal)
)	J. H. Moore	(Seal)
)	Roberson Dyer	(Seal)
)	James Bartlett	(Seal)

Whereupon the said Curtis Mills Clerk elect took an oath to support the Constitution of the United States and the State of Tennessee and an oath against _____ and the oath of Office as Clerk of Putnam County Circuit Court and thereupon entered upon his duties as such.

This day Pleasant Bohannon Sheriff of Putnam County entered here into open court the States Writ of Venirafacias to him directed from the County Court of Putnam County Commanding him to summons the following named persons to attend this Term of the Court (p-148) as Jurors to wit - J. W. Cotton, John West, Lewis Barnes Sr., William Peek, David Mansel, Charlie Hunter, James Robison, James J. Bohannon, John Johnson, Spencer Phillips, James M. Brooks, Richard Ray, William Webb, Samuel McCaleb, R. C. Allison, Amos Mott, John B. Campbell, G. W. Apple, Bird S. Jones, Garland Stanton, Howard A. Ensor, John K. Saddler as Jurors and Samuel Hughes and John W. Carr as constables to attend thereon as court officers came to hand the same day issued Executed and all the Jurors and Court officers this the 11th day of December 1854.

P. Bohannon Shff.
R. Dyer D. Shff.

Out of which venirafacias and Jurors aforesaid the Court proceeded to elect and empanell a Grand Jury as the Act of the General Assembly in such case provides when the following named persons were drawn and elected to wit,

Lewis Barons Sr., Garland Stanton, R. G. Maddux, Samuel McCaleb, Spencer Phillips, M. D. Apple, John E. Campbell, John K. Saddler, Bird S. Jones Charles Hunter, Howell H. Briant, R. D. Allison, William A. Ensor of whom the court appointed R. D. Allison foreman of the Grand Jury all of whom are good and lawful men, house holders and free holders of Putnam County, who being elected, Empannelled and sworn.

Ordered that Court be adjourned until tomorrow morning 8 oclock.

H. L. Davidson

Tuesday Morning December 12th A. D. 1854

Court met persuant to ajournment Present the Honorable H. L. Davidson Judge Presiding.
Thomas B. Murry Attorny Gen'l of the fourth Judicial District having failed to attend the Term of Court therefore the court appoints Wilburn Goodpasture Attorny Genl Protem during the present Term of court who appeared in open (p-149) court and took an oath to support the constitution of United States and the constitution of the State of Tennessee and the oath of Attorney General Protem and thereupon entered upon his duties as such.

William Austin) Damage appeal came the parties by attornies and
Vs) on motion and affidavit of the plaintiff this
Isam Smith) cause is continued untill the next Term of this
) court and on motion of the Deft. by attorney it
is ordered that he give security for procecution of this suit on or before the first day of the next Term of this court or the same shall stand Dismissed.

State) Peace Warrant - Came the attorney General for
Vs) the State and the _____ Whereupon the
Elias Whitacre) same is ordered to be continued until the next
) term of this court.

Isaac Clark) Debt Appeal
Vs) On afft. of the plaintiff this cause is continued
Dudley Hunter) until the next Term of this court.

Ordered by court that Wednesday the third day of this court here after be set for States day.

This day came the Honorable Court charged the Grand Jury as a Grand inquest for the State of Tennessee to enquire for the Boday of the County of Putnam who retired to their room to consider of presentments, Indictments &c attended by Samuel Hughs a constable sworn in due form of Law to attend thereon.

P-150 Grand Jury returned into court a Bill of Indictment of the State against Isam Smith Endorsed by the foreman a true Bill and again retired to consider of Presentments Indictments &c.

State	)	Indictment for A. & B. William Austin Prosr. Came
Vs	)	the attorney General for the State and the Deft in
Isam Smith	)	proper person, who being arraigned and charged upon
	)	said Indictment says he is not guilty as therein

charged against him and for his trial puts himself upon the County and attorney General for the State doth the like whereupon came a Jury of good and Lawful men to wit: James J. Bohanon, James Robison, John West, John Johnson, William Peek, Amos Mott, William Webb, J. W. Cotton, G. W. Apple, David Mansell, Reubin Whitson and Thomas T. Watson, who being elected tried and sworn the truth to speak upon the issue of traverse joined upon there oaths do say the defendant is not guilty in manner and form as is charged in said Indictment.

It is therefore considered by the court that the defendant go hence without day and that the County of Putnam pay all such costs herein as she is by law bound to pay and that the same be certified to the County Court for allowance.

The State of Tennessee	)	Indictment for Larceny - In this case
Vs	)	the Grand Jury returned and filed in
Joseph Floyd	)	open court a Bill of Indictment endorsed
Elizabeth Floyd	)	by their foreman, not a True Bill, or-
	)	dered by the court that said defendants

be discharged and that the State of Tennessee pay the costs of prosecution in the cause and that the same be certified to the Treasurer of the State of Tennessee for payment.

P-151   April Term 1855 Monday

The Grand Jury this day returned and filed in open court a bill of Indictment against William Austin for an Assault & Battery Endorsed by their foreman A true Bill ordered that a capias issue.

Court then adjourned until court in course.

                                                                               H. L. Davidson

State of Tennessee -

                     Be it remembered that at a Circuit Court Began and held for the County of Putnam in the State of Tennessee in the Court house in the Town of Cookeville on the Second Monday it Being the ninth day of April in the Year of our Lord One thousand Eight hundred and fifty five and in the seventy ninth year of American Independance. Present the honorable John Goodpasture Judge of fourth Judical Circuit of the State of Tennessee - This day Pleasant Bohannon Sheriff of Putnam County Returned herein to open court the States Writ of Venirafacias to him directed from the County Court of Putnam County commanding him to summons the following named persons to attend this Term of Court as Juror to wit: Abasalom Sims, Elijah Carr, Sr., John Whitson, Thomas Nicholass, John G. Graham,

George Henry, Thomas L. Watson, John Madwell, Drury Sims, George Mc-Cully, Reubin H. Dowell, Amos Maxwell, James B. Lowery, John A. Roberts Robert Smith, Joseph Mitchell, William Gipson, John Lee, Isaac A. Huddleston, John Jarred, Henry Sadler, Allen Maneer, Edward Anderson, John Officer, John S. Watson as Jurors to attend this Term of court and Hampton Ramsey and Alexander Boyd as constables to attend thereon as Court officers (p-152) came to hand 20th January 1855. Executed on all the within Jurors Except John Whitson this the 9th day of April 1855.

            P. Bohannon Shrff.
            R. Dyer D. Shrff.

 Out of which venirafacias and Jurors aforesaid the court proceeded to elect and impannell a Grand Jury as the Act of General assembly in such case provides when the following persons were drawn and elected to wit: Elijah Carr Sr., Reubin H. Dowell, Dury W. Sims, Robert Smith, John A. Roberts, Isaac A. Huddleston, John Lee, John S. Graham, Allen Maneer, Henry W. Sadler, James B. Lowery, Amos Maxwell and John Officer of whom the court appointed Henry W. Sadler foreman of the Grand Jury all of whom are good and Lawful men, house holders and free holders of the County of Putnam who being elected, empanelled, sworn and charged a Jury of Grand Inquest for the State of Tennessee to inquire for the Body of the County of Putnam who retired to their room to consider of presentments, Indictments &c attended by Hampton Ramsey a constable, sworn in due form of Law to attend thereon.

John S. Bartlett	Trespass Eject - Came
James Bartlett	the plaintiff by attor-
Daniel Bartlett	ney and dismissed their
Jesse Bartlett	suit - It is therefore
Nathan Bartlett, Jane Bartlett his wife	considered by the court
Vs	that the Defendant go
Benjamin H. Watson and Lucy Watson	hence and Recover against
	the plaintiffs and James

Bartlett and Henry Whitacre their securitys in this cause all costs here in and that Executed on issue &c.

P-153 Nancy Norriss) Pt. for Divorce - On motion of the Plff.
    Vs   ) by attorney and for reason appearing to
   William R. Norris) the court from the petition in this
) cause which is sworn to by said plain-
tiff it is ordered that publication be made for three successive weeks in the Hearald of the Times in the Town of Sparta Ten requiring said Deft. to appear at the next Term of this court and defend the same or the same will be taken for confessed and set down for hearing Expartee.

State of Tennessee) Indictment for A. & B. Isam Smith Prosr.
   Vs   ) Came the attorney General for the State and
William Austin   ) the Defendant by attorney moved the court to
) Quash the Indictment in cause which motion
was overruled by the court.

97

On affidavit of William Mitchell and for reason to the Court shown it is ordered that Joseph Mitchell, A Juror be released and discharged from further attendance as such at this term of the court on account of sickness.

Ordered by the court that Monday the first day of this court be set for States day in place of Wednesday the third day.

Isaac Clark)
Vs)
Dudley Hunter)
)

Damage Appeal - Came the parties by attornies and on motion of the Deft by attorny it is ordered by the court that the plaintiff Give security for the prosecution of this suit on or before calling of the same for trial or the same shall stand, dismissed (p-154) where upon came herein to open court William Clark and acknowledged himself to stand and be indebted to Dudly Hunter the Deft in the Sum of Two hundred and fifty Dollars void on condition should the same be adjudged against him upon a final hearing of the same.

Elijah W. Brown)
And)
Alvira Brown)
Vs)
Thomas Pullian)

Ejectment - Came the Defendant and came along with him James G. Terry and as security acknowledged themselves to owe and stand Indebted to the plaintiffs in the sum of Five hundred Dollars void on condition should the same be adjudged against them upon a final hearing of the same.

Thomas Bounds)
Vs)
Jesse B. Terry)
)

Debt Cert. - On motion of the Defendant by attorny it is ordered by the court that the plaintiff give security for the prosecution of this suit on or before the first day of the next term of this court or the same shall stand dismissed &c.

Andrew J. Grogan)
Vs)
H. H. Bryan & Milton Stanton)
)

Debt Appeal - On motion of Defendant by attorny it is ordered that the plaintiff Give Security for the prosecution of this suit on or by tomorrow morning or the same shall stand dismissed and the plaintiff by attorney moved the court to amend the warrant by inserting the name of William Grogan as a Deft which was over ruled by the court.

P-155 Isaac Clark)
Vs)
Dudley Hunter)
)

Damage Appeal - Came the parties by their attorney and there came a Jury of good and lawful men to wit: James M. McDaniel George McCully, John S. Watson, William Gipson, John Jarred, William Gentry, Thomas J. Watson, Absalem Sims, Thomas Nicholass, John Madewell, John Grider and Spencer Phillips, who being elected tried and sworn well and truly to try the matters in controversy between the parties upon their oaths do say they find the same in favor of the Defendant. It is therefore considered by the court that the Defendant Recover off the plaintiff and William Clark his security in this suit and that Execution issue for the same &c.

State of Tennessee)	The Grand Jury returned into court a Bill of
Vs)	Indictment against said Defendant for Pettie
William J. Taylor)	Larceny Endorsed thereon on a true Bill by
)	their foreman, which bill of Indictment is

in the wards and figures following to wit, State of Tennessee Putnam County April Term of said court in the year of ____ Lord one thousand Eight hundred and fifty five.

    The Grand Jurors for the State of Tennessee elected empannelled sworn and charged to enquire for the Body of the County of Putnam in the State of Tennessee upon their oath presents that William J. Taylor yeoman on the nineteenth day of December, one thousand eight hundred and fifty four with force and arms in the County of Putnam and State aforesaid did unlawfully steal take and carry away one bag of the value of one Dollar two Bushels (p-156) and one Peck of corn of the value of two Dollars and twenty five cents the property of James B. Lowery there and then being in the possession of James B. Lowery against his will contrary to the form of the State in such cases made and provided and against the peace and dignity of the State the Grand Jurors aforesaid upon their oaths aforesaid to further present that William J. Taylor yeoman on the nineteenth day of December one thousand Eight hundred and fifty four with force and arms in the county of Putnam and State aforesaid and unlawfully steal take and carry away one Bag of the value of one Dollar two Bushels and one Peck of corn of the value of Two Dollars and twenty five cents the property one Elijah Hicky then and there Being in the possession of James B. Lowery, Bailer of Elijah Hickey against his will contrary to the form of the States in such cases made and provided and against the peace and dignity of the State.

                                                                  Tim H. Williams
                                                                  Atty. General 4th Circuit.

    Upon the Back of which Bill of Indictment are the following Endorsements to wit:

    State Vs William T. Taylor Larceny James B. Lowery sworn in open court and sent before the Grand Jury to give Evidence on the within Indictment this 9th April 1855.

                                                                                  Curtis Mills Clerk

    A True bill Henry M. Saddler foreman of the Grand Jury.

State of Tennessee)	Indictment for murder R. Brown
Vs)	Pros. – In this cause the
William Crabtree & Isaac Crabtree)	following (p-137) Record
)	from the Circuit Court of

Fentress County by the Clerk of said court was filed in this court in the above cause and was ordered to be spred upon the record of this court to wit: State of Tennessee – Be it remembered that at a Circuit Court Begun and held for the County of Fentress in the Court house in Jamestown on the second Monday the same being the twelfth day of February A.D. one thousand Eight hundred and fifty five and of the Independance of the United States the 78th Year, Present the Honorable John L. Goodall Judge of the fourth Judicial Circuit presiding.

Proclamation being made court was opened in due form when Wilson L. Wright Shrff. of Fentress County returned into the States Writ of venira facias to him Directed by the County Court of Fentress County which is in words and figures following to wit - State of Tennessee Fentress County November Term of the County Court 1854 Nov. 6th this day the court proceeded to appoint a venira of Jurors to serve at the February Term of the Circuit Court 1855 when they appointed the following persons good and lawful men to wit: District No. 1 William R. Beaty and Robert Whited 2nd District Jesse Cobb and Jesse Wood 3rd James Crocket, James Rains and Thomas Livingston, 4th District Robert King and E. M. Roberson 5th District Aris Alexander 6th District Elijah Noland and Benjamin Beech 7th District Berdine Young John Duncan Thomas Riley 8th Jesse Rich Theopolis Williams 9 Isaac A. Dawson Soloman Morris 10th John Stepp, Jesse Davis 11th Leonard Huddleston, and George Smith 12th William Anderson as constables to wit on the Grand Jury and it is ordered by the court that the sheriff of Fentress County summons them accordingly (p-158) witness D. C. Travis Clk: at office the first Monday in Nov. 1854.

            Davis C. Travis Clerk
            By R. T. Hildreth D. C.

 Executed upon all except Jesse David and George Smith to serve as Jurors at the present term of this court and who had been nominated and appointed by the County Court of Fentress County at the November Term thereof it being the first sessian of said court after the last Term of this court whereupon the court proceeded to select out of the Jurors aforesaid as the statutes provides a Grand inquest and Jury for the body of the County of Fentress in the State aforesaid to wit Jesse Wood Burdine Young, Emanuel M. Roberson, Thomas Riley, Theopolis William, James Crocket, Thomas Livingston, Leonard C. Huddleston, William Anderson, Whited Arys Alexander, Jesse Cobb, and Robert King all good and lawful men of said County out of whom the court appointed Thomas Riley foreman of said Grand Jury and said grand Jury now being here empanneled and sworn to inquire for the body of the County of Fentress received their charge from the Honorable Court and Retired to their room to consider of indictments and presentments attended by John Williams A. constable duly appoined summoned and sworn for the purpose and the balance of the Jurors who do not compose the Grand Jury are retained to serve as Traverse Jurors at the present term of this court Tuesday Morning February the 13th 1855 Court met pursuant to adjournment Present the Honorable John L. Goodall Judge presiding State of Tennessee Vs William Crabtree & Isaac Crabtree indictment for murder Robert Brown Prosecutor _____ In this case the Grand Jury Returned and filed in open court a bill of Indictment against William Crabtree and Isaac Crabtree for murder and Endorsed by the foreman a true Bill which Bill of Indictment is in (p-159) words and Figures following to wit:

State of Tennessee) February Term of Circuit Court for said
Fentress County   ) County in the year of Our Lord one thous-
) and eight hundred and fifty five the Grand
Jurors for the State of Tennessee Elected Empannelled Sworn and charged to Enquire for the Body of the County of Fentress in the State of Tennessee upon their oath present that William Crabtree Laborer and Isaac Crabtree Laborer Late of said County on the 18th day of February in the year of our Lord One thousand and eight hundred and fifty four without the fear of God before their Eyes and being moved and seduced by the instigation of the Devil with force and arms in the County of Fentress and the State of Tennessee in and upon one Ephraim Brown in the peace of God and our said State

then and there being Feloniously, wilfully wickedly, Deliberately, Maliciously and premediately and their malice afore though did make and assault and that they the said William Crabtree and said Isaac Crabtree with a certain knife of the value of one Dollar which they the said William Crabtree and Isaac Crabtree in their Right hands then and there held the said Ephraim Brown in and upon the Right side of the Belly Just above the Nable of him the said Ephraim Brown then and there feloneously wilfully wickedly deliberately maliciously premoditatedly and of their malice afore thought did strike and thrust giving to him to said Ephraim Brown then and there with the knife aforesaid in and upon the said right side of the belly just above the navel of him the said Ephraim Brown one mortal wound of the Breadth of six inches and of the Depth of six inches of which said mortal wound the said Ephraim Brown from the said 18th day of February in the year aforesaid untill the 21st of February (p-160) in the year of our Lord one thousand Eight hundred and fifty four in County and State aforesaid did languish and languish, did live on which said 21st day of February in year aforesaid the said Ephraim Brown in County and State aforesaid of said mortal wound Died and the Juror aforesaid and upon their oath aforesaid do say that the said William Crabtree and said Isaac Crabtree him the said Ephraim Brown in the manner and by the means aforesaid felonously wickedly wilfully deliberately maliciously premeditatively and of their malice afore thought did kill and murder in the first Degree contrary to the form of the Statute in such case made and provided and against the peace and dignity of the State.

               Erasmus L. Gardenhire

P-161 Endorsed on the back Atty. General 4th Civ. Dist. Murder State Vs William Crabtree and Isaac Crabtree Indictment Robert Brown Prosecutor William Brown, P. F. Lossdon, Perry Hatfield, Robert Brown sworn in open court and sent before the Grand Jury to give Evidence on this Bill of Indictment February 13th 1855 R. T. Hildreth A. true Bill Thomas Rily former Clerk on the Grand Jury.

Wednesday morning February the 14th 1855 court met persuant to adjournment Present the Honorable John L. Goodall Judge Presiding.

State of Tennessee	Indictment for murder R. Brown
Vs	Prosecutor - Come the attorney
William Crabtree & Isaac Crabtree	General for the State and the
	Defendant in proper person who

Being arraigned and charged upon the Bill of Indictment in this cause pleads not Guilty to the same and for their trial put themselves upon the County and the Attorney General for the State doth the Like and the Court Proceeded to empanell a Jury and Exausted a panell of ninety two and Elected out of said panell George A. Harris and Evander Walker as Jurors and said Jurors sworn are put under the care of John Williams a Constable who is sworn to keep them together in some convenient apartment Separate and apart from all other citizens and not to allow any person to have any (p-162) communication with them until the meeting of the Court tomorrow morning to resume the consideration of this cause ordered that the Defendant be remanded to Jail this order should have been on the minutes of Yesterday, But is now for then February 14th 1855.

State of Tennessee) Indictment for murder Robert
        Vs) Brown Prosecutor - Came the
William Crabtree & Isaac Crabtree) Attorney General for the
) State and the defendants in
proper person and the Jurors elected in this cause on a former day of this term and the court again preceeded to the empanelling of a jury in this cause when another panell of Seventy four Jurors was exausted out of which Eli Stars and Alexander Evans were elected and retained as jurors and placed upon the panell in this cause and said Jurors having Received their charge from the court were put in charge of Jeremiah Right an officer duly sworn for that purpose by him to be conveyed to some suitable apartment to be kept together separate and apart from all other persons and all manner of communication between them and other persons to be Prohibited until the meeting of the Court on Friday Morning next.

Friday February 16th 1855 Court met pursuant to adjournment Present the Honorable John L. Goodall Judge Presiding.

State of Tennessee) Indictment Murder R. Brown Pros.
        Vs) Came again the attorney General
William Crabtree & Isaac Crabtree) for the State and the defendants
) is brought to this bar in custody of the Sheriff of Fentriss County and came again the Jurors elected in this cause on a former day at this term to wit George A. Harris, Alexander Evans, Evander Walker and Eli Stars in care of the Officer Jeremiah Right and the court proceeded again to the empanelling of a jury in the cause when three panells were Exausted out of which William King and James Frogg were elected and retained as jurors and placed upon the panell and the court being of opinion that a <u>fore</u> and impartial trail can not be had in the County of Fentress in this cause on motion of the defendants it-is ordered by the court that the venire of this cause be changed from the County of Fentress to some other County in the fourth Judicial Circuit or to Some County out of the fourth Judicial Circuit adjoining the County of Fentress and thereupon the defendants by themselves and attornies elects the County of Putnam in the fourth Judicial Circuit as the County to which the venire shall in this cause be changed the same adjoining the County of Fentress It is further considered by the court that the venire in this cause be changed from the County of Fentress to the County Putnam aforesaid and that the Clerk of this Court make out and transmit a full true and perfect copy of the Record and Proceedings in this cause and file the same together (p-163) with the original papers in this cause and file the same with the clerk of the Circuit Court of Putnam County on or before the 2nd Monday of April next and it appearing to the Court that the common Jail of Fentress County is unsafe and insufficient to keep the defendants it is ordered by the court that the sheriff of Fentress County fourthwith after the adjournment of the Court take the defendants and deliver them to the Sheriff or Jailor of Overton County and there to be kept in the Jail of Overton County until the Circuit Court of Putnam County to be holden in the town of Cookeville on the 2nd Monday of April next and that the Sheriff of Overton County deliver them to the sheriff or Jailor of Putnam County on or before the Second Monday of April next unless they give the proper Security whereupon came here into open court the said Isaac Crabtree together with Samuel Crabtree and Hiram Crabtree Hiram Crabtree Sr., Hiram Crabtree Jr., Joel T. McGhu, John Williams, M. B. Bledsoe, Barthoelot Lee, Mitchell Wright, and John R. McGhu who acknowledged themselves to owe and be indebted to the State of Tennessee in

the sum of two thousand dollars that is to say the said Isaace Crabtree in the sum of one thousand and the said Samuel Crabtree, Hiram Crabtree Sr., Hiram Crabtree Jr., Joel T. McGhu, John Williams, M. B. Bledsoe, Barthaelet Lee, Mitchel Wright, & John R. McChu jointly and severally in the Sum of one thousand Dollars to be levied on their proper goods and chattles, Lands and tenements to the use of the State to be rendered But to be void on condition that the said Isaac Crabtree make his personal appearance before the Honorable Circuit Court of Putnam County to be holden in the Court House in the Town of Cookeville on the 2nd Monday in April next then and there to answer the State of Tennessee on (p-164) a charge of murder in the first degree and not to depart until legally discharged by said court also came here in open court Caleb Stephenson, Samuel Crabtree, James Crabtree, Alfred Holm, Washington Upchurch, Martin Cruch, James M. Brite, Phillip Lossdon, Henry Hatfield, Robert Brown, John N. Simpson, Sidney Mason, Asa Johnson, Manuel Hatfield, Sherell Dilk, Robert Young, Sames C. Latham, Goldman Craig, Willburn Williams & James Crabtree for his wife Nancy Crabtree who severally acknowledges themselves to owe and be indebted to the State of Tennessee in the sum of two hundred and fifty Dollars each to be levied on their proper goods and chattles, Lands and tenements to the use of the State to be rendered, but to be void on condition that they make their personal appearance before the Honorable the Circuit Court of Putnam County in the Court House in the town of Cookeville on the 2nd Monday in April next then and there the said Robert Brown to prosecute on behalf of State and the other named witnesses to give Evidence in favor of the State of Tennessee in the cause of the State of Tennessee against William Crabtree and Isaac Crabtree for murder in the first degree and not depart untill Legally discharged also came here in open court Hiram Crabtree, James Crabtree, Goldwon Craige, Sherell Dilk, James V. Latham, Ephram Crabtree, Fidelry Mason, James M. Wright, James Kniss, Pernila Craig, Minny Dilk, Jeffry N. Richardson, Robert Young, John Williams, Amy Morgan acknowledge themselves severally to owe and be indebted to the State of Tennessee in the sum of two hundred Each to be levied upon their Respective goods and chattles, lands, and tenaments to the use of the State to be rendered void on condition that they make their personal appearance before Honorable Circuit Court to be holden for the County of Putnam in the court house in the town of Cookeville on the second Monday in April next then and there to give evidence in favor of the Defendants in cause of the State of (p-165) Tennessee against William Crabtree and Isaac Crabtree for murder in the first degree and not depart until legally discharged.

Saturday February 12th 1855   State of Tennessee Vs William Crabtree and Isaac Crabtree. The State in accounts with John Culaer inn keeper for keeping two of the jurors in the above cause at the rate of nine dollars
per day the whole day the whole jury $ 6.00
To keeping two others three days   4.50
To two others   1.50

                                                            $12.00

This includes boarding & lodging sworn to in open court John Culaer Beb. 17th 1855.

R. L. Heildrelh Clerk

And the Attorney General having reported the sum correct ordered by the court that the sum be allowed and taxed in the bill of costs.

Bill of Costs - Clerk R. T. Heildreth entering Indictment on the minutes
25 cents charging plea 50½ ¢ order putting jury under charge of officer
25¢ order remaining Debts to Jail 25¢ order putting Jury under care of
Jury Officer 25¢ order to change venire 25¢ order to change venire to
Putnam County 25¢ order for Clerk to make transcript file it 25¢ order
take Debts to Overton County Jail 25¢ order for sheriff of Overton
County to Deliver Debts to Sheriff of Putnam County 25¢ 30 recognizance
for the State $7.50 order to tax inn keeper acct. 25 Bill of costs 25¢
Transcript of the cause for Putnam County $1.62 preparing 2 supeonas
for State 25¢, 21 witnesses probates $1.31¼ half Jury 6½ $14.00 .
(P-166)   Sheriff Wilson L. Wright for carrying Debt William Crabtree
from James Town to Livingston Jail and returning from 56 miles $15.60
summons 2 witnesses for State 50¢ half of Jury 6½¢ calling cause $7.10½
Guard R. Murphy 56 miles 6¢ per mile   3.36
Andrew Murphy 56 "   "   "   "   3.36
Innkeeper John Cullaer for keeping 2 of the jurors in the above case at
the rate of nine dollars per day for the whole Jury $6.00 to keeping two
others three days at $4.50 to two others 1 day $1.50 $12.00 .

Witnesses for the State

Parks Hatfield 3 days at 75¢ & 24 miles at 4¢	3.21
Phillip F. Lossden 3 days at $1.00 & 50 miles at 4¢	5.00
Martin Cronch 3 days at 75 & 26 miles at 4¢	3.29
Isaach Wright 3 " " Each	2.25
William Brown 3 " " "	2.25
Goldmon Craig 3 days & 21 miles	3.09
Alfred Helm - 3 days at 75¢ & 21 miles	3.09
Perry Hatfield - 3 days at 75¢ & 28 miles	3.31
Sherell Dilk - 3 days at $1.00 & 160 miles at 4¢	9.40
Manuel Hatfield - 3 days at $1.00 & 160 miles at 4¢	9.40
Fidley Mason - 3 days at $.75 & 24 miles at 4¢	3.21
Wilburn Williams - 3 days at $.75 & 24 miles at 4¢	3.21
Asa Johnson - 3 days at $.75	2.25
James M. Wright - 3 days at $.75	2.25
Caleb Stevens 3 " " "	2.25
Henry Dilk 3 " " " & 20 miles	3.05
Samuel Crabtree 3 days at $.75 34 "	3.61
S. M. Upchurch 3 " " " 24 " 4¢	3.21
Robert Brown 3 days at 75½ each	2.25
James Crabtree 3 " " " "	2.25
John M. Simpson 3 " " " "	2.25

State Vs Crabtree Bill of cost continued	$ 114.96½
Clerk R. T. Helidreth Taking 15 Recognizances for Deft.	3.75
Witnesses for Deft Minny Delk 2 days at 75¢	1.50
Amy Morgan 3 days 75¢ each	2.25
Perandy Delk 3 days & 22 miles	3.13
Hiram Crabtree 3 days & 22 miles	3.13

P-167

Jeffry M. Richardson 1 day at 75¢	.75
Robert Hatfield 3 days and 28 miles	3.75
James Kaip 3 days at 75½	2.25
Ephram Crabtree 3 days & 24 miles	3.21

104

Robert Brown claim transferred to R. L. Heildreth and Samuel Crabtree, Fridley Mason, Derry Hatfield, Manuel Hatfield, claim transferred to Henry Gatewood, Alfred Helm claim transferred to John M. Simpson $4.62 of Sherell Dilks claim transferred to E. Lee and $5.00 to Hiram Millsap.

State of Tennessee) I Reece T. Heildreth of the Circuit Court and
Fentress County   ) for the County and State aforesaid do hereby
) certify that the foregoing is a full true and
perfect copy of the transcript of the record and proceedings in the cause here-tofore prosecuted in the Circuit Court of said County wherein the State of Tennessee is plaintiff and William Crabtree and Isaac Crabtree is defendants as fully and entirely as the same remains of Record in my office in testimony whereof I have hereunto set my hand and private Seal having no public offical seal provided for this office at office in Jamestown this 29th day of March 1855.

(L.S.)   Reece T. Heildrith Clerk

Ephraim Dunavin Exparte Petitioner to be Restored to citizenship.

Be it remembered that on this 9th day of April 1855 the above cause came on to be here and was heard before the Honorable John L. Goodall Judge presiding and upon the petition of the complainant and proof when it appeared to the court that petitioner had hertofore been convicted upon a charge of counterfeiting (p-168) in the County of Anderson Tennessee and sentenced to confinement in the penitentiary of said State for the term of three years and also rendered infamous. That he has served out said term of imprisonment and has since been a citizen of Jackson County (now Putnam) since July 1851 and as such has deported himself as an industrious, honest, and orderly citizen. It is therefore ordered adjudged and decreed by the court that the petitioner be restored to all rights privileges enjoyed by good honest citizens of the State of Tennessee and that he pay the costs of this proceedings for which execution may incur.

Ordered that court be adjourned until tomorrow morning after 8 oclock.

John L. Goodall

Tuesday Morning April the 10th 1855 court met pursuant to agreement. Present the Honorable John L. Goodall Judge Presiding.

James Brooks   )   Trespass
    Vs   ) Parties by attorneys agree to plead and try at
James Bartlett) the next term of this court so as not to delay
) the trial of the same.

Jesse Hale   )   Debt Appeal
   Vs   ) Came the plaintiff by attorney and dismissed his
M. N. Presley) suit. It is therefore considered (p-169)
) by the court that the Defendant go hence and recover against the plantiff and Willis Juggins his securitor in the appeal

Bond in this case all cost here in and that Execution issue for the same.

State of Tennessee) Indictment for A & B Isam Smith Pros. Came
Vs) the attorney General for the State and on
William Austin and) affidavits of Defts. this cause is ordered
Ira Carr) to be continued untill the next Term of this
) court whereupon came here into open court
the Defts. together with R. S. Allcorn, Robert Allcorn, and James Allcorn and acknowledged themselves to owe and stand indebted to the State in the sum of one thousand dollars that is to say, the said William Austin and Ira Carr Defts in the sum of five hundred dollars jointly and the said R. S. Allcorn, Robert Allcorn, and James Allcorn in the sum of five hundred dollars jointly to be levied on their proper goods and chattels lands and tenaments to the use of the State to be rendered, But to be void on condition that the defendants make their personal appearance before the Judge of the Circuit Court of Putnam County to be holden in the Court house in the Town of Cookeville on the 2nd Monday of August next then and their to answer the State on a charge of assault and battery and not depart untill legally discharged.

Jeremiah Hugin) Scifa
Vs) Came the parties and on motion of plantiff
William C. Mitchell) by attorney moved and obtained leave of the
) court to amend the Scirfacias in this cause
by inserting after the words "to give Evidence according to supeno" the following words to wit - (p-170) Rugularly issued by S. P. Maxwell a justice of the peace fore said County on the 16th day of February 1855" and also after the words" had been summoned" the following words to wit, "By M. G. Stephens a constable for said County on the same day issued thereupon the defendant moved the court to quash the Scirafacias in the cause which was overruled by the court and on motion and affidavit of plaintiff this cause ordered to be continued untill the next Term of this court upon the payment of all cost Expended at this term of the court by said plaintiff. It is therefore considered by the court that Deft - recover against the plaintiff the costs of this Term and that Execution for the same.

Expartee - Petition to the restoration to citizenship upon the petition of James Allcorn it appearing from the proof that he had been convicted in the County of Jackson for counterfieting and it appearing that he had served in the penitentiary and had been discharged more than three years and had demeaned himself as a good industrious, honest citizen and his character is such it is ordered that he be restored to all the privileges of other good citizens of this state and it is further ordered that he pay the cost of this proceedings and Execution issued.

Robert G. Burton) Debt motion - In the matter of this motion
Vs) of the following paper was duly returned and
Stephen Ward) filed in this County to wit Warrant, State
) of Tennessee Putnam County To the sheriff
or any constable of said County I command you to summons Stephen Ward to appear before me or some other Justice of said County to answer the complaint of Robert G. Burton in a plea of Debt in sum under ten Dollars he

in fail not   (p-171)   Given under my hand and seal this 20th Febr. 1855.

Thompsons for 10 cts - J. P.   E. L. Thompson   (Seal)

   Endorsed thereon to wit, Executed and set for trial the 22nd day of February 1855 before E. L. Thompson Esqr. H. Ramsey Const. for 50¢ R. G. Burton Vs Stephen Ward I give judgement in this case for the plantiff and against the Defendant for $8.87 and cost of suit for which Execution may issue this 22nd Febr. 1855.

                                                E. L. Thompson J. P.

   Execution State of Tennessee Putnam County To the Sheriff or any constable of said County I command you that on the Goods and chattels Lands and tenaments of Stephen Ward if to be found in your County you make the sum of Eight Dollars and Eighty seven cents and the costs of suit to satisfy a judgement that Robert G. Burton obtained against him before me on the 22nd Febr. 1855 and pay over the same as the Law directs this 27th Febr. 1855.

E. L. Thompson   (Seal)   J. P. for P. Cty.

   Endorsed to wit, amount of Debt up time of Rendering Judgement $8.87 Justice fee for Wt. & Jd. issue .50 H. Ramsey for serving & levying issue 1.00 came to hand the same day issued returned no personal property to be found in my county Levied on a certain tract of Land as the Land of Stephen Wards whereon he now lives joining the lands of Stephen Wards whereon he now lives joining the lands of John Pharris and Jonathan Moore supposed to be one hundred acres more or less in District No. 1 Putnam County Tennessee this 27th Febr. 1855.
                                                Hampton Ramsey
                                                Constable

   Thereupon on motion it is considered by the court that the Land so levied upon aforesaid and the same is hereby condensed and ordered to be sold to be sold to Satisfy the plantiff debt and costs and the cost of the motion and that an order of sale issue &c.

P-172   Curtis Terry   )   Debt Cost
            Vs   )   Came the plaintiff here into open court
        Thomas Pullin   )   and dismissed his suit it is therefore con-
)   sidered by the court that the Deft go hence
and recover against the plaintiff all costs in this suit and that execution issue.

   Grand Jury returned into court following Presentments to wit, State of Tennessee Vs James Lowe Tipling, State against George Dillard for Tipling State Vs Jasper Lowe for Tipling and State Vs George Dillard for Tipling all of which presentments is signed by the foreman of the Grand Jury and all the balance of the Grand Jurors in due form of Law &c ordered that execution issue.

Martin Whitton   )   Debt Appeal

107

Vs) On motion and affidavit of the plaintiff It is
Jackson Maxwell) ordered by court that this cause be continued
) untill the next Term of this court upon paying
the costs of this term. It is therefore considered by the court that
the defendant recover against the plaintiff the cost of this term and
that execution issue &c.

Andrew J. Grogan) Debt Appeal - Came the parties
Vs) by attornies and there came a
E. H. Bryant and Milton Stanton) Jury of good and lawful men to
) wit, Moses A. Jarred, Samuel
Hughes, James M. McKinny, John R. Carr, William N. Baron, Moses Canard,
Thomas Pullim, Hugh Green, Huddleston, James Rector (p-173) Andrew
Masson, James Bennett, and Martain Dowell who being elected tried and
sworn well and truly to try the matters in controversy between the parties
upon their oaths do say they find the same in favor of the Defendant It
is therefore considered by the court that the defendant Recover against
the plaintiff all costs herein and that execution issue.

William Austin) Damage Appeal - Came the parties by their attor-
Vs) nies and then came a Jury of good and lawful
Isam Smith) men to wit, George Henry, Thomas T. Watson,
) John C. Watson, James McDaniel, George W. Mc-
_____, John Jarred, William Gentry, Thomas Nicholas, Absalom Simms, John
Drain, William Grisson, and John Madewell, who being elected, tried and
sworn to try the matters in controversy Between the parties, who after
having received their charge from the Honorable court returned to consider of their verdict and again returned into court and upon their
oaths do say they can not agree upon a verdict in this cause and by
consent of the parties by attorneys and with the assent of the court a
mistrial is Entered in this cause and the Jurors were permitted to disperse.

State of Tennessee) Indictment in the first de-
Vs) gree. Robert Brown Pros.
William Crabtree, & Isaac Crabtree) Came the attorney General
) for the State and the de-
fendants in proper persons and on motion and affidavit of Robert Brown
the prosecutor in the case it is ordered by the court (p-174) that
this case be continued until the next term of this court, Whereupon came
here into open court Isaac Crabtree one of the above named defendants together with G. M. Crabtree, Hiram Crabtree Sr., Hiram Crabtree Jr., Ephram
Crabtree, Samuel Crabtree, Asa Johnson and Robert Young and acknowledged
themselves to owe and stand indebted to the State of Tennessee in the sum
of Two thousand dollars that is to say the said Defendant Isaac Crabtree
in the sum of one thousand dollars and said Hiram Crabtree Sr., Hiram
Crabtree Jr., Ephram Crabtree, Samuel Crabtree, Asa Johnson, and Robert
Young jointly and severally his the sum of one thousand dollars to be
levied on their respective goods and chattles Lands and tenaments to be
use of the State to be rendered, nevertheless to be void on condition
that the said Isaac Crabtree make his personal appearance before the
Judge of the Circuit Court for Putnam County ten in the court house in
the Town of Cookeville on the Second Monday in August next then and
there to answer the State upon a charge of murder in the first Degree
now pending in said Court against him and not depart untill Legally

Discharged. Whereupon the said William Crabtree one of the above named Defendants having failed to enter into Bond and Security as required by Law and it appearing to the court that there is no public Jail in Putnam County It is ordered by the court that the Sheriff of Putnam County It is ordered by the court that the sheriff of Putnam County convey said Deft, William Crabtree to the sheriff and Jailor of Overton County there to be kept in the Jail of said County of Overton untill the next Term of the Circuit Court for Putnam County to be held at the Courthouse in the Town of Cookeville on the second Monday of August next and at that term the Sheriff of Overton County redeliver the said Defendant William Crabtree (p-175) to the sheriff of Putnam County on or before the Second Monday in August next unless he give the proper security to appear and answer said charge of murder.

Gallant Anderson) Debt Cert. In This cause came the plain-
Vs) tiff by attorney came here into open
William McDaniel Admr.) court and dismissed his suit It is there
) fore considered by court that said Anderson
pay the cost of this suit and that Execution issue. It is further ordered by the court that a procedendo be awarded to the Justice of the peace Rendering the Judgement in this cause.

State of Tennessee) Indictment first Degree R. Brown Prosr.
Vs) This day came here into open court Will-
William Crabtree and) iam Brown, Galeman Craig, Alfred Helm,
Isaac Crabtree) Shered Delk, Mancell Hatfield, Wilburn
) Williams, James M. Wright, Caleb Stephens,
Samuel Crabtree, S. M. Upchurch, Robert Brown, James Crabtree, J. W. Simpson, Robert Young, James C. Lathan, Henry Delk, Asa Johnson, who severally acknowledged themselves to owe and be indebted to the State of Tennessee in sum of Two hundred and fifty Dollars each to be Levied of their proper goods and chattels Lands and Tennements to the use of the State to be rendered But to be void on condition that they make their personal appearance before the Honorable Circuit Court of Putnam County in the courthouse in the Town of Cookeville on the Second Monday in August next (p-176) then and there the said Robert Brown to prosecute on behalf of the State and the other named witnesses to give Evidence in favor of the State of Tennessee in the case of State against William Crabtree and Isaac Crabtree for murder of first degree and not depart until Legally discharged.

State of Tennessee) Indictment for murder in the first degree
Vs) Robert Brown Prosr. - Came here into open
William Crabtree and) Court James C. Lathan, James W. Wright,
Isaac Crabtree) James Kimp, Hiram Crabtree Sr., Hiram
) Crabtree Jr., James Crabtree, Galemon
Craig, Ephraim Crabtree, Shered Delk, Robert Young, G. W. Crabtree, Minnie Delk and Permelia Craig and acknowledged themselves severally to owe and stand indebted to the State of Tennessee in the sum of two hundred and fifty Dollars each to be levied of their Respective goods and chattles Lands, and tenements to the use of the State of Tennessee to be rendered But to be void on condition that their personal appearance before the Honorable Circuit court of Putnam County to be holden in the court house in the Town of Cookeville on the second Monday in August next then and

there to give Evidence in favor of the Defts in the case of the State of Tennessee against William Crabtree and Isaac Crabtree for murder in the first Degree and then and there attend untill Legally Discharged.

Benton Hawes) Debt Motion - In the matter of this motion
Vs) the following papers was duly returned and
Benjamin H. Watson) filed to wit: Warrant, State of Tennessee
) Putnam (p-177) County to the sheriff
or any constable of said County - I command you to summons B. H. Watson to appear before me or some other Justice of peace for said County to answer the complaint of Burton and House in a plea of Debt due by note herein fail not.

Given under my hand and seal this 9th day of February 1855.

Joseph D. Hyder (Seal)
Justice of the peace

Endorsed thereon to wit: Executed and Returned before J. D. Hyder Esqr. at his house and set for trial on the 17th day of February 1855 T. Bohannon Sheriff Burton and House Vs B. H. Watson I give Judgement in this case for plaintiff and against the Defendant for sixty seven dollars & eighty two cents for which an Execution may Issue this 17th day of February 1855 Joseph D. Hyder (Seal) Justice of the Peace.

Execution State of Tennessee Putnam County -

To the Sheriff or any constable of said County I command you that of the Goods and chattles Lands and Tenements of B. H. Watson if to be found in your county you make and collect the sum of sixty seven dollars and eighty two cents with Interest thereon and all Lawful cost that Burton and House obtained against him before me on the 17th day of this Instant Herein fail not.
Given under my hand and seal this 21st day of February 1855 Joseph D. Hyder (Seal) Justice of the Peace Endorsed thereon to wit, Judgement 17th February 1855.

$67.82 Bill of cost Justice Hyder for Wt. 50 Joseph D. Hyder Justice of the peace.
Came to hand the 22nd day of February 1855 No. Perishable property to be found in my County Levied upon a tract of land of the Defendant Lying in Putnam County in District No. third adjoining the Lands of Joshua Brown and said to contain Eighty four acres This Levy was made about nine oclock in the morning the 23rd day of February 1855.

P. Bohannon Shff.

Therefore on motion it is considered by the court that the Land so levied upon as aforesaid be and the same is hereby condemned and ordered to be sold to satisfy (p-178) the plaintiff Debt and cost and also the cost of this motion and that an order of sale Issue.

Burton & Hawes) Debt Motion In the matter of this motion the
Vs) following papers was filed to wit:
B. H. Watson)

State of Tennessee)   To the sheriff or any constable of said
Putnam County   )   County I command you to summons B. H. Watson
)   son to appear before me or some other Justice
of the peace for said County to the complaint of Burton & Hawes in a plea
of Debt by Note Herein fail not. Given under my hand and seal this the
9th day of February 1855.

    Joseph D. Hyder Justice of the Peace Endorsed thereon, Executed and
returned before Joseph D. Hyder Esqr. at his house and set for trial on
the 17th day of February 1855.

                                                                     P. Bohannon Shff.

Burton and Hawes Vs B. H. Watson I give Judgement in this case for the
plaintiff and against the Defendants for nine dollars and three and a
half cents and cost for which on Execution may Issue this 17th day February 1855, Joseph D. Hyder Justice of the peace Execution State of
Tennessee Putnam County to the sheriff or any constable of said County
I command you that of goods and chattles Lands and Tenements of B. H.
Watson if to be found in your county you make and collect the sum of nine
dollars and three cents with Interest thereon and all lawful costs to
satisfy a judgement and cost that Burton and House obtained against him
before me on the 17th day of this Instant herein fail not.

    Given under my hand and seal this 21st day of February 1855.

Joseph D. Hyder (Seal)   Justice of the Peace

    Endorsed therein to wit: Judgement 17th of February 1855 (p-179)
Judgement 17th February 1855 $9.03 Bill of cost Justice Hyder Fee for
warrant and Judgement & fifa 50 Shff Bohannon Returning warrant 50 Joseph D. Hyder Justice of the Peace came to hand the 22nd day February
1855 No goods and chattles to be found in my County.

    Levied on a tract of Land of the Defendants lying in Putnam County
Des. No. 3 and adjoining the Lands of Joshua Brown and said to contain
Eighty four acres this the 23rd day February 1855.
                                                            P. Bohannon Shff.

    Whereupon it is considered by the court that the Land Levied upon as
aforesaid be and the same is hereby condemned and ordered to be sold to
satisfy the plaintiffs Debt and cost and also the cost of this motion
and that an order of sale issue.

Burton & Hawes   )   Debt Motion - In the matter of this motion the
    Vs   )   following papers was duly Returned and filed to
B. H. Watson   )   wit - Warrant State of Tennessee Putnam County
)   to the Sheriff or any constable of said County,
I command you to summons B. H. Watson to appear before me or some other
Justice of the peace for said County to answer the complaint of Burton
and Hawes in a plea of Debt due By note herein fail not. Given under
my hand and seal this 9th day of February 1855 Joseph D. Hyder Justice
of the Peace Endorsed thereon to wit: Executed and Returned before Joseph D. Hyder Esqr. at his house and set for trial on the 17th day of
February 1855 P. Bohannon Sheriff Burton and Hawse Vs B. H. Watson I

give Judgement in this case in favor of the plaintiff and against the Defendant for forty one dollars and thirty one cents and cost for which Execution may Issue this the 17th day of February 1855.

Joseph D. Hyder
Justice of the Peace

Execution - State of Tennessee Putnam County - To the sheriff or any constable or any constable of said County I command that of the Goods and chattles   (p-180)   Lands and Tenements of B. H. Watson if to be found in your county you make and collect the sum of forty one dollars and thirty one cents with Interest there and all Lawful cost to satisfy a judgement and cost that Burton & Hawse obtained against him before me on the 17th day of this Instants Herein fail not. Given under my hand and seal this 21st day of February 1855.

Joseph D. Hyder
Justice of the Peace

Endorsed thereon to wit Judgement 17th Feb. 1855 $41.31 Bill of cost Justice Hyder fee for Wt. 10 for Judgement and fifa 40 Shff Bohannon Returning warrant 50 Joseph D. Hyder Justice of Peace Executed by levying on yoke of oxen and Yoke this 22nd day of February 1855 after giving Legal notice sold the property mentioned in the above Levy at John Bohannon's Mill to the Highest bidder for $28.00 this the 5th day of March 1855 no more Goods and chattels to be found Levied upon a tract of Land of the Defendants Lying in Putnam County Dis. No. adjoining the lands of Joshua Brown and said to contain Eighty four acres this the 21st day of March 1855 P. Bohannon Sheriff of Putnam County it is considered by the court that the land Levied upon as aforesaid being the same is hereby condemed and ordered to be sold to satisfy the plaintiff Debt and cost and also the cost of this motion and that an order of sale issue.

Burton and Hawes)   Debt Motion - In the matter of this motion the
      Vs   )   following papers was duly returned and filed
B. N. Watson   )   in this court to wit, Warrant State of Tennessee
)   Putnam To the Sheriff or any constable of said
County I command you to summons B. N. Watson to appear before or some other Justice of the peace for said County to answer the complaint of Burton and Haws in a plea of Debt and by note here in fail not. Given under my hand and seal this   (p-181)   9th day of February 1855.

Joseph D. Hyder (Seal)

Endorsed thereon to wit, Executed and returned before J. D. Hyder Esqr. and set for trial on the 17th day of February 1855.

P. Bohannon Sheriff

Burton & Haws Vs B. N. Watson I give judgment in this case for the plaintiff and against the defendant for Eighty two dollars and 12½ cents and the cost for which an Execution may issue this 17th day of February 1855.

Joseph D. Hyder (Seal)

Execution State of Tennessee Putnam County to the Sheriff or any constable of said County I command you that on this Goods and chattels, lands

112

and tenaments of B. H. Watson if to be found in your county you make and collect the sum of Eighty two Dollars and twelve and a half cents with interest thereon and all lawful cost to Satisfy a judgement and cost that Burton and Hawes obtained against him before me on the 17th day of this instant herein fail not. Given under my hand seal this 21st day of February 1855.

                                        Joseph D. Hyder (Seal)
                                        Justice of the Peace

Endorsed thereon to wit, Judgement 17th February 1855 - $82.12½ Bill of cost Justice Hyder fee for judgement and fifa and Wt. 50¢. Sheriff Bohannon returning warrant 50¢.

                                        Joseph D. Hyder J. P.

No goods and Chattels to be found in my County Levied on a tract of Land of the defendant Lying in Putnam County in Dist. No. 3rd adjoining the lands of Joshua Brown said to contain Eighty four acres this the 23rd day of February 1855.

                                        P. Bohannon Sheriff
                                        of Putnam County

(p-182) Whereupon it is considered by the court that the Land so Levied upon as aforesaid be and the same is hereby comdemned and ordered to be sold to satisfy the plaintiffs Debt and cost and the costs of this motion and that an order of sale issue &c.

R. G. Burton   )   Debt Motion - In the matter of this motion the
   Vs   )   following paper was duly returned and filed to
Anderson Cole   )   wit, Warrant State of Tennessee Putnam County To
)   the Sheriff or any constable of said County I
Command you to summons Anderson Cole to appear before me or some other Justice of said County to answer the complaint of Robert G. Burton in a plea of Debt due by note in a Sum under one hundred Dollars this 17th January 1855.

                                        John Terry   (Seal)
                                          J. P. for Putnam Cty.

Endorsed thereon to wit, Executed and returned before John Terry Esqr. and set for trial on the 19th day of January 1855 James B. Terry Const. brought Jan. 19th 1855 for $77.35½ Robert G. Burton Vs Anderson Cole, I give judgement in this cause for the plaintiff against the defendant for seventy seven Dollars and thirty five ½ cents all cost for which Execution may issue this January 19th 1855.

                                        John Terry   (Seal)
                                        Justice of the Peace
                                        Putnam County

Execution State of Tennessee Putnam County - To the Sheriff or any constable of said County I command you that of the Goods and chattels Lands and Tenements of Anderson Cole if to be found in your county you make the sum of Seventy Seven Dollars and thirty nine cents with interest thereon with all Lawful cost to satisfy a Judgment that Robert G. Burton obtained against him before me on the   (p-183) 19th day of January 1855 & pay over the same as the Law Directs this the 23rd of January.

                                        John Terry   (Seal)
                                        Justice of Peace Putnam Cty.

Endorsed thereon to wit, Debts with interest up to January 25th 1855 $77.39 Justice fee for Wt. Judgment and fifa 50¢ const. J. B. Terry for Serving warrant 50¢ $78.39 John Terry Justice of the peace.

No personal property to be found in my county Levied upon a tract of Land Lying in Putnam County the property of the Defendant and whereon he now lives containing by Estimation fifty acres adjoining the Lands of Columbus Kirby on the north and Edward Shoat on the South and Jefferson Cole on the west Lying in Civil District Number first this 22nd January 1855.

James B. Terry Const.

Whereupon a motion is ordered by the court that the Land so Levied as aforesaid being the same is hereby condemned and ordered to be sold to satisfy the plaintiff's debt and cost and also the cost of this motion and that an order of sale issue.

Hiram Hellem)   Debt Motion
Vs)   In this cause the following paper was only returned
R. G. Dukes)   and filed to wit, Warrant.
)

State of Tennessee)   To the Sheriff of said County I command you to
Jackson County   )   summon R. G. Duke & Pretyman Jones to appear
)   before me or some other Justice of the peace
for said County to answer Hiram Hellum assignee of Prityman Jones in a plea of Debt Due by note for a sum under one hundred dollars fail not Given under my hand and seal this 21st day of May 1855. (p-184)

E. G. Growell J. P.
for Jackson County

Endorsed thereon to wit, I acknowledged the serving of the within warrant R. G. Duke, Hiram Hellum Vs R. G. Duke by confession judgement in favor of the plaintiff and against the defendant for thirty nine dollars and fourteen and cost of suit for which Execution may issue this 21st May 1855.

E. C. Growell J. P.

Stand by Wm. Duke

Execution State of Tennessee Putnam County - To the Sheriff or any constable of said County I command you that of the Goods and Chattels, Lands and tenements of R. G. Duke and William Duke his Security for stay of Execution if to be found in your county you make the sum of twenty dollars and 90 cents with interest from the 13th of February 1854 and cost of suit to satisfy a Judgement to that Hiram Hellem obtained against the said R. G. Duke 1854 here in fail not and pay over as the law directs this October the 4th 1854 M. A. Jared J. P. for Putnam County Endorsed therson to wit no goods and chattels to be found in my county Levied upon a tract of land of the defendant lying in Putnam County in district No. 13th the adjoining the lands of E. Anderson, Lilly McApper, P. Jones, and Hugh Wallace, and said to contain 65 acres this 27th day of October 1854.

M. Boyd Const.

Whereupon a motion it is considered by the court that the Lands so Levied upon as aforesaid being the same is hereby condemned and ordered to be sold to Satisfy the plaintiff Debt and cost and the cost of the motion and that an order of sale issue.

Ordered that court be adjourned until after 8 oclock.

Jno. L. Goodall

P-185   Wednesday morning April 11th A. D. 1855 - Court met pursuant to agreement, Present the Honorable John L. Goodall Judge Presiding.

Benjamin N. Watson)   Ejectment
          Vs   ) By agreement of the parties by attorneys they
Samuel Madewell   ) agree to plead and try at the next Term of
) this court so as not to delay the trial of
                       the same.

Daniel W. Haws assignee of) Debt Motion - In the matter of this
Samuel Madewell   ) motion the following papers was duly
          Vs   ) returned and filed to wit, Warrant
B. N. Watson   ) State of Tennessee Putnam County To
) the sheriff or any constable of said
County I comman_ you to summon B. N. Watson to appear before me or some other Justice of the peace for said County to answer the complaint of D. W. Haws assignee of Samuel Madewell in a plea of Debt due by note herein fail not.

Given under my hand and seal this 16th day of February 1855.

Joseph D. Hyder   (Seal)
Justice of the peace

Endorsed thereon to wit, Executed and set for trial before J. B. Clark Esqr. at his home on the 20th day of February 1855.

J. Henry Const.

D. N. Haws Vs B. N. Watson I give judgement on the within for twenty five Dollars principle & Sixty Eight cents Interest and all lawful costs for Which Execution may issue this Watson principle and Roberson Dyer and William H. Barons (p-186)   Securities this 15th day of February 1855.

James McKinny   (Seal)

Endorsed thereon to wit, Justice McKinny Judgment 25¢ Execution 25 warrant 10¢ Shff. Bohannon for serving Warrant $1.50.

No Goods and chattles to be found in my County Levied on a tract of Land of the Defendant Lying in Putnam County District No. 3rd adjoining the lands of Mary A. and Hiram Brown and said to contain one hundred and eleven acres this the 19th day of February 1855.

P. Bohannon Shff.

Thereupon on motion it is considered by the court that the Land so Levied upon as aforesaid be and the same is hereby condemned and ordered to be sold to satisfy the plaintiffs Debt & cost and the cost of this motion and that an order of sale issue.

D. W. Hawes)   Debt Motion
  Vs)   In the matter of this motion the following papers
B. E. Watson)   was duly returned and filed to wit, warrant State
)   of Tennessee Putnam County - To the Sheriff or any constable for said County - I command you to summons said B. E. Watson and Samuel Madewell to appear before me or some other Justice of the peace for said County to answer the complaint of D. M. Haws assinee of Samuel Madewell in a plea of Debt due by note herein fail not - Given under my had & seal this 1st day of April 1855.

                                           Lee R. Taylor   (Seal)
                                           Justice of the peace

20th day of February 1855 Staid by)   I. B. Clark   (Seal)
)   J. P. for P. C.

F-187   Execution State of Tennessee Putnam County - To the Sheriff or any constable of said County I Command you that of the Goods and chattels Lands and Tenaments of B. M. Watson if to _found in your County you make the sum of twenty five Dollars and sixty Eight cents with Interest thereon and all lawful cost to satisfy a Judgement that D. W. Haws assignee of Samuel Madewell obtain against him before me on the 20th day of February 1855 and pay over the same as the law Directs this February 23rd 1855.

                                           I. B. Clark   (Seal)
                                           Justice of the peace

Endorsed thereon to wit, Judgment rendered February 20th 1855 $25.68 Justice fee for Judgement & fila & 10¢ Justice Hyder issuing Wt. 10¢ const. Henry serving Wt. 50¢ February 23rd 1855.

                                           I. B. Clark   (Seal) J.P.

Paid on the within fifa one dollar and ten cents and all the cost Except the Levy this March 9th 1855.
                                           J. Henry Const.

Came to hand February 23rd 1855 No goods and chattles Lands to be found in my County Levied upon a tract of Land of the Defendant lying in Putnam County in Dist. No. 3rd adjoining the Lands of Joshua Brown and said to contain 84 acres this February 26th 1855.
                                           I. Henry Const.

Whereupon on motion it is considered by the court that the Land so Levied upon as aforesaid be and the same is hereby condemned and ordered to be sold to satisfy the plaintiffs Debt and cost and the cost of this motion and that an order of sale issue.

Levi L. Murphy and)   Debt Motion
Thomas T. Watson)

Administrators of Jno. Watson Dec.) P-163 In the matter of this
        Vs) motion the following
Benjamin H. Watson & others) papers were filed to
) wit, State of Tennessee Putnam County, To the sheriff or any constable of said County -
I command you to summons B. H. Watson, Roberson Dyer and William H. Barons
to appear before me or some other Justice of the peace for said County to
answer the complaint of Levi Murphy and Thomas T. Watson administrators
of the Estate of John Watson Decd. in a plea of Debt due by note herein
fail not. Given under my hand and seal this 30th day of October 1854.

                                                      Joseph D. Hyder (Seal)
                                                      Justice of the peace

    Endorsed thereon to wit, Executed and returned before James McKinney
Esqr. and set for trial on the 11th day Novr.
                                                P. Bohannon Shff.

    In this case I Give Judgment against Defendant $306.27 cents this the
10th day of February 1855 - James McKinny J. P. (Seal) Execution State
of Tennessee Putnam County - To the sheriff or any constable of said
County - I command you thereof the Goods and chattles Lands and tenements
of Benjamin H. Watson, Roberson Dyer and William H. Baron if to be found
in your County you make the sum of three hundred and six Dollars and
twenty seven cents principle and Interest & cost a Judgment obtained before me on the 10th day of February 1855 in favor of Thomas T. Watson
and Levi L. Murphy Executors of John Watson Deceased against the said
Benjamin H. Endorsed there are to wit:

    Executed and (p-189) set for trial before J. D. Hyder Esqr. at
his own house on the 7th day of April 1855.
                                                J. Henry Constable

    D. M. Haws assinee of Samuel Madewell I give Judgment in this case by
the plaintiff and against the Defendant for seventy five Dollars and twelve
and ahalf cents for which an Execution may issue this April the 7th 1855.

                                                        Joseph D. Hyder
                                                        Justice of the peace

Execution State of Tennessee Putnam County - To the Sheriff or any constable of said County _____ I command you that of the Goods and Chattles
Lands and Tennements of B. H. Watson and Samuel Madewell if to be found
in your County make and collect the sum of twenty five Dollars twelve
and a half cents with interest herein fail not.

    Given under my hand and seal this the 11th day of April 1855.

                                                      Joseph D. Hyder (Seal)
                                                     Justice of the peace

    Endorsed thereon to wit: Judgment 7th April 1855 for $25.12½ Constable
Henry returning warrant 50 ¢ Esqr. Taylor for wt. 10¢ Justice Hyder for
Judgment and fifa 40¢.
                                                     Joseph D. Hyder J. P.

Issue 11th April 1855 came to hand same day issue No goods and Chattles to be found in my County Levied upon the tract of Land of the Deft Lying in Putnam County in District No. 3rd adjoining the Lands of Joshua Brown Mary Allen and Henry Whitaker and said to contain 220 acres (p-190) this 11th April 1855.

                      J. Henry Constable

Whereupon on motion it is considered by the court that the Land so Levied upon as aforesaid be and the same is hereby condemned and ordered to be sold to satisfy the plaintiff Debt and cost and that an order of sale issue.

Samuel Stone and)   Debt Motion
Leroy Suttle)   In the matter of this motion the
  Vs)   following papers was filed to wit,
John Boyd, Joseph Johnson et al)   Warrant, State of Tennessee Jack-
)   son County to any Lawful Officer
of said to summons John C. Boid, Joseph Johnson, and Thomas Hall a day to appear before me or some acting Justice of the Peace for said County to answer the complaint of Sam Stone and Leroy B. Suttle assign of Bransford Boid in a pleas of Debt Due by note under five hundred fail not.
Given under my hand and seal 6th day of April 1854.

                      Peter G. Cox J. P.
                      (seal)

Endorsed thereon to wit, for P. C. Executed and set for trial before Moses Jarred on the 9th day of April 1854.

                      William Davidson D.
                      Sheriff

Cost $1.00 Judgement in favor of the plaintiff and against the Defendants for seventy one Dollars and seventy two cents with all lawful interest for which Execution may issue this the 8th April 1854. M. A. Jarred J. P. Execution State of Tennessee Putnam County to the Sheriff or any constable of some County I command that (p-191) of the goods and chattels, lands and tennaments of John C. Boyd, Joseph Johnson, A. L. Boyd, if to be found in you County their security for the stay of Execution if to be found in your County you make the sum of Seventy one Dollars and seventy two cents with Interest & cost to satisfy a Judgement that S. E. Stone and Leroy B. Smith obtained against them before me on the 8th day of April 1854 for seventy one dollars & seventy two cents and costs and pay even the same as the Law Directs this January the S. P. 1855.

                      M. A. Jarred J.P.
                      for Putnam County

Endorsed thereon to wit, Judgement $71.72 Davidson $1.00 Jarred 40¢ No Goods and chattels to be found in my County levied upon a tract of land of Joseph D. Johnson Lying in Putnam County in Districts No. 11 and 12 adjoining the Lands of R. E. Farris, B. Boyd, John Whitefield and William Ensor and said to contain fifty acres this 10th January 1855.

                      A. Boyd Constable

Whereupon on motion it is considered by the court that the Lands so

Levied upon as aforesaid being the same is hereby condemned and ordered to be sold to satisfy the plaintiff's Debt and cost and the cost of this motion and that an order of sale issue.

Absalom Johnson)   Debt
   Vs   ) In the matter of this motion the following papers
Ingram Bustle   ) was duly returned and filed to wit, Warrant State
) of Tennessee Putnam (p-192) County to the
Sheriff or any constable of said County I command you to summons Ingram Bustle to appear before me or some other Justice of the Peace for said County to answer the complaint of Absalom Johnson in a plea of Debt due by account under fifty Dollars this 12th day of August 1854.

               R. N. Dowell (Seal)
               J. P. for Putnam Co.

  Endorsed to wit, Returned and set for trial on the 14th day of October 1854 before Isaac Laller Esqr. J. H. Carr const. I give Judgement in favor of the plaintiff against the Defendant for $33.50 Debt with 85 cents cost for which Execution may issue this 14th October 1854.

               Isaac Loller (Seal)
               Justice of the peace

State of Tennessee Putnam County – To the Sheriff as any constable of said County you are hereby commanded that of the goods and chattels, lands and tenaments of Ingram Bustle if to be found in your County you make the sum of thirty three Dollars and fifty cents Debt with interest and all lawful costs of suit to satisfy a judgment that Absalom Johnson obtained before hand on the 14th October 1854 herein fail not. Given under my hand and Seal this 30th of October 1854.

               Isaac Lollar (Seal)
               Justice of the peace

Judgement $33.50 R. N. Dowell for Wt. 10¢ J. N. Carr for serving warrant 50¢ for Judgement 10¢ fifa 40¢ No goods and chattels to be found in my County levied upon a tract of land of the Defendant lying in Putnam County in (P-193) District No. 8 injoining the Lands of James Crowder on the East and Amos Mott on the West and Amos Mott on the north and said to contain one hundred acres this the 1st day of Nov. 1854.

               J. N. Carr Const.

  Whereupon on motion it is ordered by the court that the Land so levied upon as aforesaid being the same is hereby condemned and ordered to be sold to satisfy the plaintiff's Debt and cost and the cost of this motion and that an order of sale issue.

Rhea & Burton   )   Debt Motion
to use of T. A. Rhea   ) In the matter of this motion the following
   Vs   ) papers was duly returned and filed to wit,
Ingram Bustle &   ) Warrant State of Tennessee Putnam County:
Jacob Bar   ) To the Sheriff or any constable of said

County, I command you to summon Ingram Bustle and Jacob Bar to appear before me or some other Justice of said County to answer Rhea & Burton to the use of J. A. Rhea in a plea of Debt under a sum of twenty Dollars this the 9th of October 1854.

            Howell H. Bryant (Seal)
            J. P. for said County

  Executed and set for trial on the 14th day of October 1854 before Isaac Loller Esqr. J. N. Carr Const.
  I give Judgement in favor of the plaintiff against the Defendant for ten dollars and sixty seven cents Debt with $1.35 cost this 14th of October 1854 Isaac Loller (p-194) State of Tennessee Putnam County To the sheriff or any constable of said County you are hereby commanded that of the Goods, and chattels Lands and tenaments of Ingram Bustle and Jacob Bar if to be found in your County you make a cause to be made the sum of ten Dollars and sixty seven cents debt and Interest with lawful cost of suit to Satisfy a judgement that Rhea & Burton to the use of T. A. Rhea obtained before me on the 14th of October 1854 here in fail not.
  Given under my hand and seal this 30th of October 1854.

            Isaac Loller (Seal)
            Justice of the peace

Judgement $10.67 H. H. Bryant for Wt. 10¢ T. N. Carr for serving warrant $1.00 for judgement & fifa 40¢.
  No goods and chattels to be found in my County levied upon a tract of Land of the Defendants Lying in Putnam County in District No. 8 adjoining the lands of James Crowder on the East and Amos Mott on the West & north said to contain one hundred acres this 1st day of Nov. 1854.

            J. N. Carr Const.

  Whereupon on motion it is considered by the court that the Land so levied upon as aforesaid being the same is hereby condemned and ordered to be sold to Satisfy the plaintiff's debt & cost and that an order of sale issue.

Douglass & Ford)   Debt Motion
  Vs   ) In the matter of this motion the following papers
A. N. Hargret) was duly (p-195) returned and **filied** to wit:
) State of Tennessee Jackson County to the Sheriff
or any constable of said County I command you to summon H. N. Harget to appear before me or some other Justice of Peace for said County to the complaint of Douglass and Ford on a plea of Debt due by note in a sum under fifty dollars. Given under my hand and seal 28th day of February 1854.

            E. C. Crowell (Seal)
            J. P. for said County

  Executed the within an A. N. Hargret and set for trial before Esqr. Crowell on the 3rd day of March February the 28th 1854.

            J. Carr D. Sheriff

  Judgement for the plaintiff for $41.45 with all lawful Interest & cost for which Execution may issue this 3rd of March 1854.

E. C. Crowell J.P.

Execution State of Tennessee Putnam County to the Sheriff or any constable of said County I command you that of the Goods and chattels lands and tenaments of A. N. Harget and R. G. Duke and John Duke his security for the stay of Execution if to be found in your County you make the sum of forty one dollars and forty five cents with interest thereon and all cost to satisfy a Judgement that E. F. Douglass and Charles R. Ford partners in trade who done business under the name Style of Douglass and Ford obtained against the said Harget before E. C. Crowell on the 3rd day of March 1854 for forty one Dollars and forty five cents and costs and pay over the same as the law Directs this January 3rd 1855 N. A. Jarred (Seal) J. P. for Putnam (p-196) Co. Judgement for $41.45 Interest & Leving for & Cam Crowell 35¢ Jarred 30¢ No. Goods and chattels to be found in my County Levied on a tract of land of the debt lying in Putnam County District No. 13 adjoining the Land of William McGinnis, John Jainer and Charles Smith and said to contain thirty acres this January 30th 1855.

A. Boyd Const.

Whereupon on motion it is ordered by the court that the Land so Levied upon as aforesaid be and the same is hereby condemn and ordered to be Sold to satisfy to satisfy the Plaintiff Debt and cost and the cost of this motion and that an order of Sale issue &c.

Love & Null)   Debt Motion
Vs   )   In the matter of this motion of the following papers
R. G. Duke   )   was filed in this cause to wit, Warrant State of
)   Tennessee Jackson To the Sheriff or any constable
of Said County I command you to summon R. G. Duke to appear before me or some other Justice of Said County to answer the complaint N. Love and John W. Null partners in trade trading under the form of Love & Null in a plea of Debt Due by account under fifty Dollars herein fail not. Given under my hand and Seal this 21st day of April 1853.

E. C. Crowell (Seal)
J. P. for said County

Executed and set for trial before Esqr. Crowell at his house on the 7th of May 1853 J. Maxwell Const. fee 50¢ (p-197) Love & Neull Vs R. G. Duke in this case I give Judgement in favor of the plaintiff against the Defendant for $18.25 principle with all lawful Interest & cost which Execution may issue this 18th April 1853.

E. C. Crowell (Seal)
J. P.

State of Tennessee Putnam County To the Sheriff or any constable of said County I command you that of the Goods and chattels Lands and Tenements of R. G. Duke and C. Anderson his Security for Stay of Execution if to be found in your County you make the Sum of Eighteen Dollars & 25 cents and cost of Suit to Satisfy a Judgement as that Null and Love obtained against the Said R. F. Duke before E. C. Crowell on the 7th May 1853 for Eighteen Dollars and twenty five cents and cost and pay over the Same as the Law directs this October the 4th 1854.

M. A. Jarred (Seal)

J. P. for Putnam County

Amt. of Debt $18.25 Interest Maxwell $1.00 Crowell 50¢ & Wt. B. A. Lee 50¢ Jarred 15¢.

No goods and chattels to be found in my County Levied upon a tract of Land of the Defendant Lying in Putnam County in District No. 13 adjoining the Land of E. R. Anderson, Lilly McGuffin, P. Jones Hugh Wallis said to contain 65 acres this 27th October 1854.

A. Boyd Const.

Whereupon on motion it is ordered by the court that the Land So Levied upon as aforesaid be and the same is hereby condemned and ordered to be sold to satisfy the plaintiff (p-198) Debt and cost of this motion and that an order of Sale issue.

James T. High)   Debt Motion
Vs   )   In the matter of this motion the following papers
Joseph Johnson)   was duly returned and filed to wit - Warrant State
)   of Tennessee Jackson County To the Sheriff or any
constable of said County I command you to summon Joseph Johnson to appear before me or some other Justice of said County to answer the complaint of James H. High in a plea of Debt due by note under Fifty Dollars herein fail not.

Given under my hand and seal this 1st of May 1854.

J. E. Ferrell   (Seal)
J. P. for said County

Executed and set for trial before J. E. Ferrell Esqr on the 13th of May 1854 William McDonald const. In this cause I Give Judgment against Joseph Johnson for $8.11 for which Execution may issue in favor of J. J. High this 13th May 1854.

J. E. Ferrell J.P.

State of Tennessee - Putnam County: To the Sheriff or any constable of said County I command you that of the Goods and chattls Lands and tenements of Joseph Johnson if to be found in your county you make the sum of Eleven Dollars & Eight cents with Interest and all cost to satisfy a Judgment that James T. High obtained against the said Johnston before me on the 13th day of May 1854 and pay over the same as the Law directs this 14th August 1854.

J. E. Ferrell J.P.
for said County

(p-199) Debt $8.11 Wt. 50¢ Justice 50¢ No personal property found. Levied this fifa upon a tract of Land Lying in Putnam County on the Walton Road Supposed to be two hundred acres Bounded as follows on the cost by the Lands of Hughs on the North by Whitefield on the west by William Ensor on the South by Bransford Boyd this 14th August 1854.

William McDonald Const.

Whereupon it is considered by the court that the Land Levied upon is as aforesaid be and the same is hereby condemned and ordered to be sold to satisfy the plaintiffs Debt and cost and that an order of sale issue.

State) Peace Warrant - Came the attorney General and
Vs) Deft. in proper person and the prosecutrix fail-
Elias Whitaker) ing to attend and prosecute and it appearing to
) the court that prosecution is frivolous. It is
ordered that the Deft be discharged and that the prosecutrix Zilly Whitaker pay the cost of this prosecution It is therefore considered by the court that State Recover against said Zilly Whitaker all cost here in and that Execution issue.

State) Indictment for P. Larceny came the attorny Gen-
Vs) eral and the Defendant in proper person and an
W. T. Taylor) affidavit of the Defendant (p-200) this cause
) is continued untill the next term of this court
be cause there is no Jail provided by the County of Putnam and the Defendant failing to give security he is ordered to the Jail of the County of Overton there to be kept by the Jailer of said County untill the first day of the next term of court.

The Grand Jurors this day returned into open court an Indictment against Andrew Grogan and Jane Bruce for Ludness Endorsed by their foreman a true Bill ordered that a capias issue.

Ordered that court adjourn untill court in course.

Jno. L. Goodall

State of Tennessee -

Pleas at a Circuit Court Began and held for the County of Putnam in the State aforesaid in the courthouse in the Town of Cookeville on the second Monday being the thirteenth day of August in the year of our Lord One Thousand Eight hundred and fifty five in the seventy ninth year of American Independance Present the Honorable John L. Goodall Judge of the fourth Judicial Circuit in the state of Tennessee presiding.

P-201 State of Tennessee) Indictment Intent to com-
Vs) mit Rape - This cause
Major - Alias - Negro a slave) being brought to this
) court by change of Venue
This day the following papers was filed in this cause by the Clerk of the Circuit Court of Fentress County which was ordered to be spread on the minutes of this court to wit: June Term 1855. State of Tennessee - Be it remembered that at a Circuit Court began and held for the County of Fentress in the court house in Jamestown on the second Monday the same being 11th day of June in the year of our Lord One thousand Eight hundred and fifty five Present the Honorable John L. Goodall Judge presiding.

Proclamation being made court opened in Due form when Wilson L. Wright Sheriff of said County returned into court the States Writ veniree facias to him directed by the county court of Fentress County Executed upon the following persons good and lawful men of said County to wit: Granville

Gwinn, George Beaty, Samuel Albertson, John Price, Phillip Conatser Sr.
George Upchurch, John Richards, George Coples, Parker Young, John D.
Hale, Robert Young, John F. Riley, William Pile, William B. Williamson
Robert Ramsey, William Young, William Smith, Charles Reagan, David Greer,
John Hovver, Edward Downs, Alfred Williams and Jesse Brewster and Levi
Shepherd and James A. Huddleston as constables. To serve as Jurors at the
present Term of this court and who had been nominated and appointed by
the County Court of Fentress County at the March Term thereof it being
the first session of said court after the last term of this court.

Whereupon the court proceeded to select out of the Jurors aforesaid
as the statutes (p-202) provide a grand Inquest and Jury for the Body
of the County of Fentress in the State aforesaid to wit: William Pile,
Edward Downs, Charles Regan, John Cobb, Samuel Albertson, Phillip Conatser, Jesse Brewster, John F. Riley, Alfred Williams, Granville Gwinn,
George Coply, Parker Young and William Smith all good and lawful men
of said County out of which the court appointed Charles Reagan foreman
of said Grand Jury and said Grand Jury now being here empaneled and sworn
to Enquire for the body of the county received their charge from the Honorable Court and Retired to their Room to consider of Indictments and
presentments attended by James A. Huddleston a constable duly summoned
and sworn for that purpose and the balance of the Jurors who do not compose the Grand Jury are retained as Traverse Jurors at the present Term
of this court.

State of Tennessee) Bill of Exceptions Circuit Court for Fen-
Vs) tress County October Term 1854, Be it Rem-
Major Alias Neg.) embered that the above cause came and at
) the present Term of this court before his
Honorable H. L. Davidson and a Jury of said County the Attorney General
offered to read the following Record which was objected to by the Deft.
and the objections overruled and the Record Read that is the Indictment
only was read to the Jury the Balance considered as read.

Tuesday morning October 10th 1854 Court met pursuant to adjournment
present the Honorable H. L. Davidson Judges Presiding (p-203) The
Clerk of the Circuit Court of Morgan County filed with the Clerk of the
Circuit Court of Fentress County on the 9th day of October 1854 the following proceedings which is ordered by the court to be spread on the minutes
of this court which is in the words and figures following to wit:

The Clerk of the Circuit Court of Scott County filed with the Clerk of
Circuit Court of Morgan County the 23rd day of June 1854 The following
proceedings to wit:

The State) Indictment for Rape - The venire of this cause
Vs) having been changed from the County of Scott
Major Alias, Nig) by an order of the Circuit Court of said County
) to the County of Morgan the Clerk of the Cir-
cuit of Scott County this day filed in the office of the Clerk of the
Circuit Court of said Morgan County a Transcript of this cause which is
in words and figures following to wit:

The State of Tennessee Be it Remembered that heretofore to wit: Upon
the 18th of August 1853 upon the affidavit of Mirah Looper a warrant was

Issued from office Henderson Pemberton an Acting Justice of the peace for Scott County in said State which said warrant is in the words and figures following to wit -

State of Tennessee, Scott County - to the Sherriff or any constable of said County Mirah Looper having given information to me on oath that Nig otherwise called Magor, a slave the propperty of Riley Long did on the 17th day of August 1853 with force and violence by laying violent hands on the said Mirah Looper did assault her (p-204) touching her person with violence with intent to Ravish the said Mirah Looper contrary to her will and against the peace and Dignity of the State: These are therefore to command you to take the Body of said Nig otherwise called Magor a slave the property of Riley Long and Bring him before me or some other Justice for said County to answer the charge and be delt with according to law Given under my hand and seal this 18th day of August 1853.

Nelly Looper
Prosecutor

H. Pemberton (Seal)
Justice of the Peace
Scott Co.

Which said warrant is tendered in the words and figures following to wit: Warrant the State Vs Nig a slave Executed on the 18 of August 1853 and Returned to the Pemberton Esqr. this 18th day of August 1853.

R. Newport Const.

The State
Vs
Nig otherwise called Magor the propperty of Riley Long

In this case the Defendant was brought forward and after hering the Evidence it is considered by me that the Defendant is guilty of the charge alledged and that he be commited to Jail of Scott County and there safely kept so that he shall appear at the next Term of Circuit Court to be held for said County on the fourth Monday and succeeding days of November for to answer the charge an be further Delt with according to law this 18th day of August 1855.

H. Pemberton, J. P.
for Scott Co.

Endorsed State Vs Nig otherwise called Magor
the propperty of Riley Long

H. Pemberton for writing warrant and Judgment	1.00
R. Newport for serving warrant	.90
for taking prisoner to Jail	.50
H. Pemberton C.	.50

H. Pemberton J.P.
(Seal)

P-205 After words to wit: At the Court November Term of the Circuit Court for said County of Scott held at the Court house in Huntsville Honorable E. Alexander Judge presiding the following proceedings were had and following Entries were made of Record to wit, State of Tennessee Scott County - Be it remembered that at a Circuit Court began held for the County of Scott and State of Tennessee on the fourth Monday of November one thousand Eight hundred and fifty three it being the twentyth day of said month Present and presiding the Honorable E. Alexander one of the Circuit Judges of the State of Tennessee assigned to hold the courts for the Second Judicial Circuit in said State the following proceedings were had to wit, John Lewellon High Sheriff of Scott County by virtue of the States writ venirafacias to him Directed returned that he has summoned the following named persons to wit, 1 Evan Roberts 2 Joseph Watters, 3 C. C. Reed 4 Rewbin West, 5 Rayburn Thompson 6 William Burtram 7 Lenard C. Cain, 8 James Burtram, 9 B. S. Newport, 10 Joel Hamby 11 Jacob Lawson, 12 John Phillips, 13 Emanuel Lewellon, 14 Whitley Rich, 15 John Sharpman, 16 Phillip Low, 17 A. Wm Cross, 18 James Acres, 19 C. Duncan 20, Caswell Cross 21 Joel Ryan, 22 William Chitwood, 23 James L. Chitwood, 24 Josiah Ivy, 25 Abner Thomas he also returned by virtue of writ he had summoned Andrew Bolin and Stewart Pemberton constables to attend upon the court at the present term and out of the Jurors summoned aforesaid the const. proceeded as the Statute in such case made and provided and directs to Elect and empanell a Grand Jury when were Elected 1 A. W. Cross, 2 Champlin Duncan, 3 Emanuel Duncan, 4 William Burtram, 5 John Phillips, 6 Lenard C. Kain, 9 Abner Thomas, 10 Joel Hamby, 11 Wily Rich, 12 Phillip Low, 13 Rewbin West all Good and Lawful men of said County of Scott of whom the court appointed A. M. Cross foreman who together with the Rest of the said Jurors having been Elected Empannelled sworn and charged according to Law to Enquire for the Body of the County of Scott retired to consider of their presentments attended by Andrew Bolinn a constable who was summoned Qualified accordingly.

State Vs Major Alias Nig a slave Rape Tuesday November the 29th 1853 - Came into court the Grand Jury in a body headed by their foreman with a Bill of Indictment against Major Alias Nig a slave Which Bill of Indictment is in the words an figures following to wit -

State of Tennessee Scott County - Second Judicial Circuit November Term of the Circuit Eighteen hundred and fifty three The Grand Jurors for the State of Tennessee being duly summoned Elected Empanneled sworn and charged to Enquire for the body of the County of Scott in the State aforesaid upon their oaths aforesaid present that Major otherwise called Nig a negro slave Late of said County Laborer on the seventeeth day of August in the year of our Lord one thousand Eight hundred and fifty three with force and (p-207) armes in the County of Scott aforesaid unlawfully feloniously and violently in assault did make upon the Body of one Mirah Looper a free white woman in the peace of the State then and there being with the Intent of him the said Major otherwise called Nig a slave her the said Mira Looper violently forceably and against her will unlawfully and feloniously to Ravish and carnally know contrary to the form of the Statute in such case made and provided and against the peace and Dignity of the State and the Jurors aforesaid upon their oaths aforesaid do further present that Major otherwise called Nig a negro slave Labourer on the seventeenth day of August in the year of Our Lord one thousand Eight hundred and fifty three with force and arms in the County of Scott aforesaid unlawfully forciably and feloniously an assault did make on the Boddy of one Mira Looper a free white woman in the peace of the State then and there bring her the said Mira Looper unlawfully forceably and against the will of her the said Mira Looper violently and feloniously did Ravish and carnally know contrary to the form of the statute in such case made as provided and against the peace and dignity of the State.

> Wm. S. McAdoo
> Attorney General

Which Bill of Indictment is Endorsed as follows Indictment the State Vs Major Alias Nig a slave Rape Nelly Looper prosecutor Mira Looper witness for the state sworn in open court and sent before the Grand Jury November 29th 1853.

> J. L. Smith Clerk

A True Bill Absalom M. Cross foreman of the grand Jury Wendesday Novr. 30th 1853 State Vs Major Alias Nig Rape came the State by attorny General and the Defendant being (p-208) at the bar in custody of the Sheriff and Defendant having no counsel and no person being willing to employ counsel for him the court orders that David H. Cumings William C. Kain and N. A. Patterson Esqr. be assigned as counsel for said Defendant & thereupon this cause was continued as on affidavit of the Defendant untill the next Term of this court and because the court is satisfied that the said Defendant can not be safely kept in the Jail of this county. It is ordered by the court that the Sheriff and Jailor of Scott County Deliver that Body of the said Defendant to the Jailer or sheriff of Campbell County to be kept in the common Jail of said County untill the fourth Monday of March next when the Jailer of said Campbell County shall deliver the Body of said Defendant to the Sheriff of Scott County Tuesday 28th March 1854.

The State of Tennessee) Indictment assault with intent to com-
Vs) mit a Rape on a free white woman came
Major Alias Nig a slave) the attorney General for the State and
) Defendant having been placed at the Bar
in custody of the sheriff and having heard the Indictment Read in this case for plea there to say he is not guilty in manner and form as therein charged and for his trial puts himself upon the county and the attorney General doth the like and thereupon the court having proceeded to empannell a Jury in this cause according to Law and having Examined several pannells of Jurors without being able to select and empannell a Jury there from who were good and Lawfull men free from Like Exceptions and the court being satisfied from said unsuccessful attemps to select and empanell a Jury that a fair and impartial trial can not be had (p-209) in this cause in the county of Scott. It is therefore ordered by the court that the venure in this cause be changed to some other County in this the second Judicial Circuit of Tennessee or some adjoining County out of this Judicial Circuit free from the same or like Exception and the court there upon called upon the Defendant to Elect to what County the venue in cause shall be changed and therefore the Defendant by himself and attorneys chosen and Elects the County of Morgan in the State of Tennessee as the County to which the venue in this cause shall be changed it is thefefore considered by the court and that the venue in this cause be changed from the County of Scott to the County of Morgan aforesaid this the second Judicial Circuit of Tennessee there to be tried in due form of Law and it is further ordered by the court that the Clerk of this court make out a full true and perfect Transcript of all the Record and proceedings

in this cause together with all the original all papers in this cause and transmit the same to the Clerk of said Morgan on or before the third Monday of July next and thereupon came into open court Nelly Looper, Mirah Looper, Joel Looper, Granville Looper, and Fountain Sexton, who acknowledged themselves to owe and be indebted to the State of Tennessee in the penal sum of Two hundred and fifty Dollars Each to be Levied of their Respective goods & chattles Lands and Tennements yet to be void if they and Each of them shall well and truly make their personal appearance before the Judge at the Circuit Court at a Court to be held for the County of (p-210) Morgan at the court house in the Town of Montgomery on the first Tuesday after the third Monday of July next then and there the said Nelly Looper to prosecute and the said Joel Looper, Mirah Looper, Granville Looper and F. Fountain Sexton to give Evidence on the part of the State of Tennessee against Major Alias Nig a slave for assault with intent to commit a Rape upon a free white woman and not depart the court without Leave the Defendant produced no witness to be Recognized and thereupon the Defendant was remanded to Jail. It is further ordered by the court that the Sheriff of Scott County as soon as practible Delivered the Defendant again to the Jailer of Campbell County there to be kept until the sitting of the Circuit Court for the said County of Morgan and that the Sheriff of Campbell County then and there at said Court deliver him to the sheriff and Jailer of Morgan County to further answer the charge of the State Exhibited against him in said cause.

Costs State Tax - - -	$ 2.00
Justice H. Pemberton warrant 50, Judgment 50	1.00
Cost R. Newport S. warrant - - -	.50
Berry Guard 1 day Guard - -	.50
H. Pemberton 1 day " - - -	.50
Clerk entering Indictment	.25
2 Continuance 37½ - - - -	.75
1 affidavit - - -	.06¼
7 Spas - - 12½	.87½
Recognizance - - - -	.25
Rranscrip - - -	1.62½
2 orders 25 - - - -	.50
Shff. Chambers 1 spa. S. W.	.25
Shff. Burtram 6 " " " - - - 25	1.25
George McDonald for keeping prisoner 113 days 37½	42.37½
10 Turnkeys - - 50	5.00
keeping Jury 6 25	1.50

State of Tennessee) I, T. F. Smith Clerk of the said County Cer-
Scott County   ) tify the foregoing to be a full true perfect
) Transcript of the (p-211) proceedings
in the case of the State against Major Alias Nig a slave for Rape as the Same remains of Record in my said office June 19th 1854.

T. F. Smith Clerk

The State   ) Indictment for Rape the venue of this cause having
   Vs   ) been changed from the County of Morgan to the County
Major Alias) of Fentress by an order of the Circuit Court of the
) said County of Morgan thereupon the clerk of the
Circuit Court of the County Court of the County of Morgan filed in the

office of the Clerk of the Circuit Court of Fentress a full and perfect Transcript of this cause which is as follows at the July Term of the Circuit Court for the County of Morgan held at the Court house in the Town of Montgomery the Honorable E. Alexander presiding as Judge the following proceedings were had in the cause of the State against Major Alias, Nig a slave and the following Entrys were made of Record to wit- Monday July 17th 1854 State of Tennessee second Judicial Circuit - Be it Remembered that at a Circuit court open and held for the County of Morgan at the courthouse in the town of Montgomery in the State and Circuit afore said and on the Third Monday of July being the 17th day of said month in the year of our Lord one thousand and Eight hundred and fifty four present and presiding the Honorable Ebenezer Alexander one of the Judges of the State of Tennessee and assigned to hold the court in the second Judicial Circuit in said State Hansley Human Esqr. Sheriff of Morgan County Returned into court the States Writ of Veniraficious issued from the April Term of Morgan County which court is at court of Record Executed upon the following persons Good and Lawful men Citizens of Morgan County as Jurors to the present Term of Court to wit; William M. Williams, William Williams, Thomas E. Davis, William L. Schooler, James B. Schooler, William A. Field, Levi Summer, Henry Brown, Larkin B. Liew, Daniel Honeycutt, (p-212) John McCoy, Pleasant McCart, John Young, Jr., Mathew McCowen, John Cook, Pemberton Satwood, M. J. Davidson, Wesley Ballwin, Duro Adams, Thomas A. Elmore, I. R. Henry, Enoch Farmer and said sheriff also Returns that he has by virtue of said Writ summoned Henry Chiles and Ethbert Caulk to attend at this present Term of the Court as constables and thereupon from the Jurors summoned as aforesaid the court proceeds as the Statute in such case made and provided Directs to select and Empannel a grand Jury for said County of Morgan at the term of the court when are Elected 1 Nathaniel Horn, 2 David Honeycutt, 3 Larkin B. Liew, 4 John Cook, 5 Duro Admas, 6 William M. Williams, 7 William A. Fields, 8 Enoch Farmer, 9 Pleasant McCurt, 10 Mathew McCowen, 11 M. J. Davidson, 12 Henry Brown, 13 William Williams of whom the court appointes Mathew McCowen foreman who together with the rest of said Grand Jurors having been duly Elected Empanneled sworn and charged according to Law to Enquire for the Body of the County of Morgan Retire to consider of their presentments Henry Chiles constable summoned as aforesaid was sworn to attend upon the Grand Jury Ethbert Caulk who was summoned as a constable was assigned to wait upon the court Tuesday July 18th 1854.

The State of Tennessee) Assault with intent to commit a rape
Vs) upon a free white woman and this cause
Major Alias Nig a slave) being so regularly in the Circuit Court
) of this Morgan County By change of venue
as aforesaid came the attorney General for the State and the Defendant being at the Bar in custody of the sheriff and having heretofore been arraigned on the Bill of Indictment in this cause and pleaded not Guilty, where to the court proceeded to select and Empannel a jury to try their issue joined and having Exhausted several pannels of Jurors Returned here into court By the Sheriff without being able to select therefrom a Jury of (p-213) good and Lawful men free from Like Exceptions and being satisfied from said unsuccessful Efforts that a fair and impartial trial in this cause cannot be had in the County of Morgan and being of the opinion that the contingence contemn stated by the Act of Assembly authorizing change of venire in crimal cases has arisen in this case it is ordered by the court that the venue in this case be changed from the County of Morgan to some other County in this Judicial Circuit of Tennessee or to some other County adjoining the County of Morgan out of said

Judicial Circuit and thereupon the defendant by himself and Attorney's Elects the County of Fentress in the fourth Judicial Circuit of Tennessee as the County to which the venue in this case shall be changed. It is further considered by the court that the venue of this cause be changed from this the County of Morgan to the said County of Fentress it adjoining the County of Morgan and that the Clerk of this Court make out and transmit a full true and perfect Transcript of all the Records and proceedings in this cause and file the same together with all the original papers in this cause with the Clerk of the Circuit Court of said County of Fentress on or before the Second Monday of October next and thereupon came into open court Nelly Looper, Joel Looper, Granville Looper, Fountain Sexton, who Each acknowledge themselves to owe and be indebted to the State of Tennessee in penal sum of two hundred and fifty Dollars to be Levied of their Respective goods and chattles Lands and tenements yet to be void if they Each shall well and truly make their personal appearance before the Judge of Circuit Court of the County (p-214) of Fentress at a Court to be held for said County at the Town of Jamestown on the Second Monday of October next and on Tuesday of that Term the said Nelly Looper to prosecute and try the said Joel Looper, Mirah Looper Fountain Sexton and Granville Looper to testify and Give Evidence in behalf of the State in the case of the State Tennessee against Major Alias Nig a slave for Rape upon a free white woman and do not depart the court without leave and came also Fountain Sexton who acknowledged himself to be indebted to the State of Tennessee in the penal sum of two hundred and fifty Dollars to be Levied of goods and chattles Lands and tenements yet to be void if Amanda Sexton his wife and Daughter shall well and truly make her personal appearance before the Judge of Circuit Court at a Court to be held for the County of Fentress at the Court house in the town of James Town testify and Give Evidence on behalf of the State in the case of the State of Tennessee against Major Alias Nig a slave for Rape on a free white woman and not to depart the court without Leave and it appearing to the satisfaction of the court that the Jail of Morgan and and Fentress County are insecure. It is ordered by the court that the Defendant be delivered by the sheriff of County immediately to the Sheriff and Jailer of Rone County to be there confined in the common Jail of said County untill the setting of the court for the County of Fentress and that he be then delivered by said Sheriff of Rone County to the sheriff of Fentress County and thereupon the said Defendant was remanded to jail.

```
Bill of cost Clerk Bryant for Recording 6000 words   10¢          $6.00
Six Recognizance 25 1 afft. 6½                                    1.56¼
Enrolling the cause brought up from Scott      (p-215)            1.62½
1 order                                                             .25
John H. Brient Clerk                                              11.06
```

State of Tennessee)   I John H. Brient Clerk of the Circuit Court
Morgan County   )   in and for the County of Morgan aforesaid do
)   hereby certify that the foregoing contains
a full true and perfect transcript of the Record & proceedings had in said Court in the case of the State of Tennessee against Major Alias Nig a slave for Rape as the same remains of Record in said Court in testimony whereof I have hereunto Subscribed my hand and affixed my seal at office in Montgomery the 21st day of September A. D. 1854.

(O.R.) Tenn.   John H. Brient Clerk
(L.S.)

Some of the objections to the Record were 1st the name of a valued certificate from the Circuit Court of Scott County 2nd the Record from the Morgan Circuit Court does not embrace the Record and Indictment from Scott County 3rd that there are Divers recitals and statements of the Clerk of Each Court and the manner in which said got to this court and there were no Evidence in the Records showes that the Record and proceedings from Scott County had Evan been Recorded in Morgan County and divers other objection all of which were overuled and the Record read as above the atto. Genl then Introduced Mirah Looper she said she was about 16 years old that some time August about a year ago she went to Sextons to stay all all night with his children as himself and wife had gone to set up with a sick woman about Dark she had got the children a sleep and Laid Down directly she heard some one knock at the door. She got up and made up a light and opened the door and seen the Defendant Jump up and run the Loom Bench was near the Door down through the corn field (p-216) she then waked up the children and started home with them she was toating one of the Little children when she got out side of the fence about forty yards he jumped from behind a tree with his head all Bundled up with Rags caught the child and slung it away off from her and caught hold of her and threw her down on her back and got on her and choked her with one hand & tried to pull up her clothes with the other she said he chocked her so she could not hollow, But when she could she said Quit Nig she strugled with him she supposed about 3 minutes and Jumped up and rum off in the woods and squatted behind a tree she never seen him any more that night he scratched her neck and hurt her side when he knew her - this all occured in Scott County that she was Daughter of Nelly Looper there were 3 children with her when it happened she then went home and told her mother what had happened the attorney General acked her what she told her mother and others this was objected to by the Defendant and sustained. The Defendant is a Black man and belonged to her uncle Rily Long her dress was torn, most torn off at the rise and 5 Buttons Broke off the Back of her Dress the children were screaming and crying & Examioned she said when he first knocked at the Door it was about Dark that she was then Badly frightened and just as she opened the Door he jumped off the Loom Bench and run off and said never was so bad scared in all her life she then fixed and started as soon as she could and when he jumped at her he Looked Like a Ghoste with his head all Bundled up she thought it was a bed Quilt over him she never was so much alarmed in her life and did not speak a word at the (p-217) house or that place that he did not touch her private parts. She had been intimately acquainted with the Defendant for several years, he never made any attempt before never said Evan a smutty word in her presence she had Lived on the same plantation and in a half mile of him for 3 or 4 years before this dificulty had seen him frequently in passing about and he never said or offered any thing wrong to her in his life she said she never lived in the same house with Defendant that she never had any familiarity with him in any way she went to Sextons that evening she had not seen him - Nig that day nor for several days previous could not remember the Last time she did see him, she thought as he run he Droped off the cloths off his head Reexamined said she thought he Droped off the rags or bed quilt as Jumped off her and he carried them off with him run down where he had slung the child said the moon was shining very Bright.

Nelly Looper the prosecutor proved Mirah Looper was her Daughter that she came home crying from Sextons with the children Early in the night her dress torn at the waist 4 or 5 Buttons off of the Back her next scratched

131

with the Defendants fingers nails this was in August 1853. She went the next day and took out the warrant Deft is Black and belongs to Rily Long the Attorney General asked her to state what her Daughter said to her when she came home this was objected to and overruled and she said her Daughter told her in substance and about as did and said the Deft. Major or Nig had done it and she also detailed all the particulars about as Mirah detailed them all of which was objected but admitted an authority of case of State Vs Phillips (p-218) Humephys Mirah was a Daughter and a free white woman X Examioned said she knew Deft had lived on the same plantation several years and had Lived one year in the same house her other Daughter and family had one other daughter next to Mirah Nig slept in the house on the floor never knew him to use a Smuter word or attempt anything indecent in her life she has great feeling against Defendant.

Granville Looper for the State next Examinoned said he was a brother of Mirah Looper went the next day and seen the place about 100 yards from the fence seen where he had stood besides the tree seen his track at the tree found some Buttons seen her Dress torn and the scratches on the neck, he was asked what she told him about it and who done it and where it was, all of it in substance as did Mirah in her Evidence she told him the Defendant done it where it was she nor no one else showed him where it was but he found the place from what she told him the tracks were made with broad toed shoes When she came home it was just after dark and she was crying X Examinoned said he did not know it was Defendant tract he had not seen him have a pair of shoes for a good while as he remembered he used to have a pair of Broad towed shoes but he had not seen them for several months as he knew of he saw the Defendant between sun Down and Dark the same Evening and he was Bar footed at his masters house, which was about three fourths of a mile from Sextons he left him there near the peach orchard said he had greate feeling against Defendant This was all the proof - The change of the court being satisfactory in all respects (p-219) be copied to the several opinions of the court Deft. Excepts and tenders this Bill of Exceptions which is signed and sealed and made a part of the Record in this case.

H. L. Davidson (Seal)

Friday Morning October the 13th 1854

Court met persuant to adjournment - Present to adjournment Present the Honorable H. L. Davidson Judge Presiding.

State of Tennessee	)	Assault with intent to commit a Rape
Vs	)	Nelly Looper Prosecutor - Came the
Major Alias Nig a slave	)	Attorney General Thomas b. Murry for
	)	the State and the Defendant in proper

person is brought to the bar in custody of the Sheriff of Fentress County who being arraigned and charged upon the bill of Indictment in the cause pleads not guilty to the same and for his trial puts himself upon County and the Attorney General for the State doeth the Like and thereupon the Court proceeded to empannell a Jury to try the issue in this cause as the Law Directs wherson elected Hansel Prichard, Pearson H. Davison, Samuel Scroggins, Joseph Griffin, John Calvin, Michael Marian, William A. Gilreath, Jonathan Wilson, Pleasant Miller, James Read, Armestead Miller all good and Lawful men and citizens of Fentress County and all free holders of Fentress County who being Elected tried and sworn the truth to speak upon the issue found in the cause wherein the State of Tennessee is plaintiff and Major alias Nig, a slave is Defendant and true deliverance made after hearing all of the Evidence in the case and a part of the argument of the Counsil are put under the charge of Enoch Brown and William A. Edwards constable who are sworn by the court to keep the Jury together in some convenient apartment (p-220) separate and a part from other citizens and not to allow any other person to have any conversation with them on any subject nor not to speak to them themselfs in relation to the trial until the meeting of this court to morrow to resum the consideration of this cause ordered by the court that the Deft be Remanded to Jail.

Saturday Morning October 14 1854 - Court met pursuant to adjournment, present the Honorable M. L. Davidson Judge presiding.

State of Tennessee)
Vs)
Major Alias Nig)
)

Rone County Presented in open court his account for conveying Deft from Rone County to the Jail of Fentress County which acct. is ordered to be spread upon the minutes of Court to be taxed in the Bill of cost in said cause and which is as follows for conveying Major Alias Nig by Deputy Sheriff James R. Roberson of Roan County from Montgomery Morgan County to Kingston Roan County a distance of 33 miles by himself at 8 cents per mile at two cents Each and 8 Ferriages at 10 cents Each To Sterling T. Turner Shrf for conveying said Prisoner, Major Alias Nig from Kingston Roan County to James Town Fentress County a distance of fifty seven miles and back home making 114 miles at 8 cents per mile one Guard fifty seven miles and back 114 miles at six cents per mile one other Guard part of the way saving Eight miles back home say 16 miles at six cents per prisoner 57 miles at 4 cents 3 Ferriages at 5 cents and 3 ds. at 10 cents.

              Sterling T. Turner

Sworn and subscribed before me in open court.

October the 12th 1855   R. T. Hildreth Clerk

State of Tennessee)
Vs)
Major Alias Nig a slave)
)

Rape
Came again into open court (p-221) the jury heretofore sworn and charged in this cause also the Defendant being brought to the bar of the court in the custody of the sheriff and the Jury aforesaid upon their oaths aforesaid do say they find the Deft. Guilty of an assault with intent to commit a Rape on Mirah Looper as charged in the Indictment the Defendant then by his counsel moved the court to set aside the verdict of the Jury and Grant the Defendant a new trial also in arrest of Judgment a new trial both of which motions the court overruled. It is therefore considered by the court that the Defendant for such his offence as found by the Jury in their verdict be hung by the nect until he is Dead on the first Monday in November 1854 within one mile of the town of James town in Fentress County between the hours of 6 oclock A.M. and two oclock P.M. and that the sheriff of said County be ordered to carry this sentence and Judgment into Execution ordered that Defendant be remanded to Jail untill the day of Execution of said Judgment it is further considered by

the court that the State of Tennessee pay the costs of this prosecution which by law she is bound to pay and that the same be certified to the Treasurer and thereupon the Defendant by his attorney prayed an appeal from said several opinions and Judgment of the court in the manner of a Writ of Error to the next term of the surpreme court of Errors and appeals to be held in the Citty of Nashville on the first Monday in December next which to him is Granted and it being suggested and satisfactorialy appearing to the court that the Jail of Fentress County is insecure it is therefore ordered by the court that the Sheriff of said County forth-with convoy the Deft to the Jailor of Davidson County Tennessee to be secured by him and safely kept in the Jail of said County of Davidson (p-222) untill his cause is Reached for trial and disposed by said supreme court.

State of Tennessee) Defendant convicted and sentenced
) to Hang and Appealed to Surpreme
No. 322 - Vs) Court (See Minute Page) Clerk
Major Alias Nig a slave Rape) R. T. Hildreth Copying the Record
) from Morgan County on the Minutes
3500 words at 10¢ $3.50 charge Plea 50 Jury 12½ct. order remanding Dft. to Jail 25 motion to set aside the verdict 25 order overuling motion 250 motion in arrest of Judgment 25 order overuling motion 25 Judgment final 75 order for sheriff Executed 25 order remanding Deft. to Jail 25 order to take Deft to Nashville Jail 25 Bill of cost 25 Transcript of cause for Supreme Court $1.62½ Bill of Exceptions and other papers there annexed 4200 words at 10 cts per hundred $4.20 6 witness probates 37½ .

$ 13.32½
Witness for State Granville Looper 4 days & 35 mi   4.44
Nelly Looper 4 days at 75 ct. Each   3.00
Mirah   "   "   "   "   "   "   .300
Manda Sexton 5   "   " $1.00   each & 60 mi   7.40
Fountain "   5   "   1.00   "   60 mi   7.40
Jailor of Roan County Sterlin T. Turner keeping Deft in Jail 32 days at
37½¢ Each $30.75 2 Turnkeys   50¢ each   31.75
D. S. James R. Roberts Conveying Deft from Morgan County Jail to Roan
County Jail 33 miles at 8 cents per mile   2.64
2 Guards 33 miles Each at 6 cents Each   3.96
Prisoner at 4 cts per mile 33 miles   1.32
and 8 Ferrigage at 10 cents Each 8 packages 10 cts Each 80¢   7.52

Sheriff Sterling T. Turner taking Nig from Kingston to Jamestown and back home 114 miles at 8 cents per mile $9.12 one Guard at 114 miles at 6 cents per mile $6.12 another Guard part of way say 16 miles at 6 cents per mile (p-223) 96 cts for prisoner 57 miles at 4 cents $2.28 3 packages at 5 cents Each 15 cents and 3 packages at 10¢ Each 30 cents $19.65.
Shff W. L. Wright calling cause 4 cts Jury 12½ cents   16½

Friday Feb. 16th 1855

Court met persuant to adjournment present the Honorable John L. Goodall Judge presiding.

State of Tennessee   )   Indictment for Rape came the attorney
         Vs   )   General for the State and the Defendant
Major Alias Nig a Slave   )   is brought to the Bar in custody of the
)   Sheriff of Fentress County and for want
of time to try this cause and the opinion of the supreme Court not being
here the cause is continued until the next Term of court and on motion
it appearing to the court that the common Jail of Fentress County is insufficient and unsafe to keep the Deft in it is ordered by the court
that the Sheriff of Fentress County forthwith after this court convoy
the Deft to the Sheriff and Jailor of Overton County and that he be Received and kept there untill the next term of this court - December Term
A.D. 1854 of the Surpreme Court of Tennessee Nashville - Present the
Honorable Robert McKinny Robert L. Caruthers and A. W. O. Talton Judges
Major Alias Nig Vs State of Tennessee assault with intent to committ
Rape this day came the attorney General of the State and the said prisoner was Lead to the Bar by Sheriff of Davidson County whereupon as well
the Record and proceedings aforesaid as the matters for Error assigned
by the said major Alias Nig being seen and heard by the court how fully
understood for that it appears to the court   (p-224)   that in the Record and proceeding aforsaid as well as in rendering the Judgment afore
said there is Error.   It is therefore considered by the court that the
Judgment rendered in this cause in the courts below be reversed annulled
and for nothing held and that the State of Tennessee pay the costs of
this court and that the same be certified to the Treasurer of the State
for payment and it is further considered by the court that said cause
be remanded back to the Circuit Court of Fentress County for a New trial
to be therein had and it is now ordered by the court that said prisoner
be now remanded back to the Jail of Davidson County from whence the
Sheriff of said County will at his Earliest convenience return take and
safely convoy and deliver over to the sheriff and Jailor of Fentress
County who will him Receive and safely keep until tried again or be
otherwise Legally discharged.

Opinion of Court.

The prisoner a negro Slave was Indicted in the Circuit Court of Scott for
an assault with intent to committ a rape on Marah Looper a free white woman the venire was changed to the County of Morgan and then it was changed
to the County of Fentress at the October Term of Circuit Court of Fentress
the prisoner was tried and convicted of said offence he moved for a new
trial and in arrest which motions were severaly overuled and judgment
of death pronounced against him whereupon he appealed in Error to this
court several Errors and assigned in argument by the prisoners counsel
First that the Record sent from the Circuit Court of Scott to the Circuit
Court of Morgan is not duly authorenticated there being no seal to the
Clerks Certificate it is true that Records of Courts in the same State
are proved by Exemptifications   (p-225)   under the seal of the of the
Court and attestation of the clerk and it is said a record so proved is
Denied of Higher Credit than a sworn copy as having passed under a more
Exact critical Examination.
                                            Vail Vs Smith

Lesson Vs Jenkins 2 John Ca - 113
1 green Ev 502

   The attorney General insisted unto the County that the seal of court was not necessary because the court to which the record was sent could notice Judicially that the person who verified and attested the Record was the Clerk of said court and cases in Civil Suits are referred to in support of this position Stinson Lesse Vs Russell 2 term R. 42 Britton Vs Patterson 5 pages R.444 Bennett Vs State M. & Z. 133 1 Green Ev. Sec. 6 It is certainly true that the courts will Judicially Recognize the public officers of the State under whose Laws and organization they act, as the chief Executive the heads of Departments - Judges of Courts of general Jurisdiction attornys for the State Sheriffs and we see no reason why the Clerks of the Courts should not also be included - 1 Green Ev. S-6 Rex Vs James 2 Champ 14 - Burrett Vs State M. 133 - Be this However as it may we observe that when the case came to the Circuit Court of Morgan the prisoner was put on his trial and attempt which proved inaffective was made to procure a Jury and thereon the Vinire was changed to the County of Fentress now in this proceeding Counsel for the prisoner made no objection to the validity of the Records as to the manner of its authentication and this we consider a waver of the objection if indeed it could be made at all.

Second the Error next assigned was not Entered in full upon the minutes of the Circuit Court of Morgan (p-226) as required by the Act of 1839 Ch. 9-S-2 on change of Vinire In Adams Vs State 1 Swan R. 466 the transcription was Entered of Record in the progress of procuring a Jury and the directions of the Statutes ordering the transcript to be entered upon the Records of the Circuit Court of the County to which the vinire may be changed was sufficiently complied with. It was not therefore a thing necessary to be done to confer upon the court Justification of the cause see State Vs Cahann 8 Humphrys R. We consider this statute to be merely directorially and that the omission of the court to comply with it will not vitiate its Judgment - The intention was to preserve the Records from Causalty and Loss and it is the duty of the Court to comply with its provisions - But whether the Records be copied on the minutes or not is a matter of no interest pregnant to the prisoner - We observe further that this construction conforms to the policy of the Recent Legislation on practice in Criminal Cases Viz Act 1852 C. 25-6 Third objection is made as to the correction on the merits of the case - We have carefully considered the case as set fourth in the Bill of Exceptions and certainly it contains much cogent proof tending to Estabish the Guilty of the prisoner but seems to us from what is stated in the Record that partious of the case perhaps material have been omitted the Record of the proof is imperfect and in some Respects obscure the Jointity of the prisoner with the person who committed the assault is a point in which it seems to us more full and satisfactory proof may be advanced we are not content to affirm the conviction in the present State of the case and remand it with the prisoner for another trial Judgment reversed and case Remanded Follows Judge McKinny I concured in the Judgment ordering a new trial upon the facts (p-227) But dissented upon the 2rd point being of opinion that the Act of 1839 requiring the transcript to be Entered in full upon the minutes of the Court to which the vinire is changed is imperative upon the court and that the omission to do so constitutes Error.

State of Tennessee

I James P. Clark Clerk of the Surpreme Court of the State aforesaid at Nashville do hereby certify that the foregoing is a full true and perfect copy of the Judgment and opinion of said Court in the case of Major, Alias, Nig Vs the State Indictment for assault with intent to committ Rape is as the same remains on Record and of file in my office In Testimony whereof I have hereunto set my hand and affixed the seal of said court at office in Nashville this 28th day of December A.D. 1854 and 79th year of American Independance.

J. J. Rich)
   Seal   )   J. P. Clark Clerk
   1855   )

Tuesday Morning June 12 1855

Court met pursuant to adjournment present Honorable John L. Goodpasture.

State of Tennessee   )   Indictment for Rape - Nelly Looper
      Vs   )   Prosecutor came the attorney General
Major, Alias Nig, a slave   )   for the State and the Defendant &
                                          Brought to the Bar in custody of the
Sheriff and the court proceeded to Empanell a Jury and two pannells are Exhausted and David Green is Elected as a Juror in the cause and said Green is put under the care of James A. Huddleston a constable who is sworn to keep him separate and apart from other citizens in some convenient apartment and not to allow any person to have any communication with him untill (p-228) Wednesday Morning at this Term to resum the consideration of this cause ordered that the Defendant be remanded to Jail Wednesday Morning June the 13th 1855.

Court met pursuant to adjournment present the Honorable John L. Goodpasture Judge presiding.

State of Tennessee   )   Indictment for assault with intent to com-
      Vs   )   mit a Rape in this cause the following
Major Alias Nig Slave   )   account now filed the State of Dr. to C.
)   M. Maxwell for keeping Eight of the Jury
in the cause of the State Vs Major Alias Nig, from Friday Dinner to Saturday night of the Last Term of Court one day and two thirds $10.00 to keeping the other four Jury man from friday supper to Saturday Charles Maxwell $4.00 Sworn to in open court February 17th 1855.

                                                                             R. T. Hildreth Clerk

And the Attorny General for State having reported the same correct. It is therefore ordered by the court that the same be Taxed in the Bill of cost in this cause and certified for payment State of Tennessee Vs Major Alias Nig Rape in this cause following account now filed to wit:

The State Dr. to John Hamilton Shff. or Jailer of Overton County for keeping Deft. Nig in the Jail of Overton County from the 18 day of February 1855 to Term 9th 1855 making in all 111 day at 37½ per day $41.62½
Two Lawful Turnkeys   50   1.00

                                                                                     42.62½

John Hamilton Shff and Jailer of Overton County.

Subscribed to and sworn to before me June 12th 1855.

                                                                             R. T. Hildreth
                                                                              Clerk

And the Attorny General for the State having Reported the same correct It is therefore held by the court that the same be Taxed in the Bill of cost in the cause and certified for payment.

Thursday Morning June 14th 1855

Court met pursuant to adjournment Present the Honorable John L. Goodall Judge Presiding State of Tennessee Vs Major Alias Nig a slave Indictment (p-229) for Rape Nelly Looper Prosecutor came again the attorney General for the State and the Defendant is brought to the bar in the custody of the Sheriff of Fentress County and came into court David Green the Juror Elected on a former day at this term in the care of the constable James A. Huddleston and the Court proceeded to the Empannelling of a Jury in this cause and after Exhausting several pannells George Scott, Elijah York, Ephraim P. Lewis and William S. Hill were Elected and placed upon the pannell and the court being of opinion that a fair and impartial trial could not be had in the County of Fentress in this cause on motion of the Defendant It is ordered by the court that the venire of this cause be changed from the County of Fentress to some other county in the fourth Judicial Circuit or to some County out of the fourth Judicial Circuit adjoining the County of Fentress and thereupon the Defendant by himself and his attornys Elects the County of Putnam in the 4th Judicial Circuit as the County to which the venire in this cause shall be changed the same adjoining the County of Fentress It is therefore considered by the court that the venire in this cause be changed from the County Fentress to the County of Putnam aforesaid and that the Clerk of the Court make out and transmit a full true and perfect coppy of the Record and proceedings in this cause and filed the same together with the original papers in this cause and file the same with the Clerk of the Circuit Court of Putnam County on or before the second Monday of August next and it appearing that the common Jail of Fentress County is unsafe and insufficient to keep the Deft in ___ It is ordered by the court that the Sheriff of Fentress County fourthwith after the adjournment of this court take the Defendant (p-230) and deliver him to the Sheriff and Jailer of Overton County and there to be kept in the Jail of Overton County untill the Circuit Court of Putnam County to be holden in the town of Cookeville on the Second Monday of August Next and came here in open court Nelly Looper, Mirah Looper, Armstead Miller, Marian B. Bledsaw, Wilson L. Wright, Granville Looper and Fountain Sexton and acknowledged themselves to owe and be indebted to the State of Tennessee in the sum of Two hundred and fifty Dollars to be Levied of their proper Goods and chatls Lands and tenements to the use of the State to be rendered but to be void on condition they make their personal appearance before the Honorable Circuit Court of Putnam County to be holden in the courthouse in the Town of Cookeville on the 2rd Monday of August next then and there the said Nelly Looper to prosecute and Give Evidence in said cause on behalf of the State and the said others to give Evidence on behalf of the State in said cause and not depart untill Legally Discharged.

Friday June 15th 1855

Court met persuant to adjournment present the Honorable John L. Goodall Judge presiding.

State of Tennessee Vs Major Alias Nig, Slave

Prosecutor Indictment for Rape Nelly Looper – In this cause the following

Bill of cost if filed to wit, State of Tennessee Dr. to Mitchell Wright, Jailer of Fentress County for keeping Deft in Jail from 9th day of October 1854 to the 16th of Same at 37½ per day making 8 days $3.00
Six Lawful Turnkeys 50¢ 3.00
Also from the 3rd day of Feb. 1855 to the 18th of the Same at 37½ per day making 16 days 6.00
from Lawful Turnkeys $2.00 Also from 10th June 1855 to the 15th of the same making 5 days at 37½ per day $1.87½ (p-231) nine Lawful Turnkeys at 50¢ $4.50 Keeping Jury in the above cause at the June Term 1855 1 Jury man 2 day at 75¢ per day 1.50
4 at 75¢ 3.00

Total $ 24.87½

Subscribed and sworn to before me the 15th June 1855.
R. T. Hildreth Clerk Maxwell Wright Jailer of Fentress County.

And the same having been Examined by the attorny General and reported correct it is ordered by the court that the same be Taxed in the Bill of cost in this cause and that the same be certified for payment according to Law.

Bill of Cost

Clerk R. T. Hildreth Continuance 37½ order to take Deft to Jail 25 order remanding to Jail 25 order for officer to take Juror 25. Order to tax turnkey account Dr. Jailer account 25 affidavit 6¼ motion to change venire 25. order to change venire Transcript 25 order to take Deft to Overton County Jail 25 Taking 7 Recognizances $1.75 9 Spas. $1.12½ witness probats 13 Transcripts of counsel $1.62½ others papers there to annex 5350 word $5.35 order to tax Inn Keepers account 25 order to Tax Jailer account 25 two other Spas. $13.82½
S. B. Lee sumaning 5 witnesses 1.25
Innkeeper C. H. Maxwell keeping Eight of the Jurymen from Friday Dinner to Saturday night one day and two thirds $10.00 keeping the other four Jurymen from Friday supper to Saturday night supr. $4.00 Jailer John H. Hamelton keeping the Deft in Jail from 18th Feby 1855 to June 1855 making 111 days a 37½ per day $41.62½ and 2 Lawful Turnkeys 50 $1.00 Shff. John L. Kenny carring Deft 52 $10.00 two Guards Each 100 miles and returning 6¢ $6.00 Each (p-232) paid by said Keny $12.00 witness for state Nelly Looper 7 days at 75¢ E- $5.25 Mirah Looper 3 days at $1.00 and 3 days 75¢ and 60 miles at 4 cents $6.90 John Looper 3 days 75¢ $2.25 M. B. Bledsaw 3 days and 22 miles $3.57 Pleasant Miller 3 days $2.25 Granville Looper $1.00 and Coroners $4.65 Fountain Sexton 3 days and 60 miles $4.65 Shff. Baily Burtram sumoning 2 witness 50 Innkeeper Mitchell Wright keeping 1 Juror 1 day 75¢ $3.00 Jailer Mitchell Wright keep Deft in Jail from the 9th day of Oct. 1854 to 16 of Oct. making 8 days $3.00 Six Lawful Turnkeys at 50¢ Each $3.00 also from the 3rd day of Feby 1855 to the 18th of the same at 37½ making 16 days 6.00 four Lawful Turnkeys at 50¢ Each $2.00 also from the 10th June 1855 to the 15th of the Same and making 5 days $1.87½ 9 Lawful Turnkeys at 50 cts Each $4.50

$ 20.37½

Shff. John Lewellon Carrying Deft from Burksville to Jacksboro 3 trips 24 miles Each making 144 miles at 10¢ $4.40 2 Guard at each trip at 6 cents Each 17.28
Total cost 110.28

Robert H. Balaim is Entitled to Nelly Looper and Mariah Looper witness Claims and C. C. Maxwell to Granville Looper Oct. 1854.

R. T. Hildrith Clerk

State of Tennessee)
Fentress County) I Reece T. Hildrith Clerk of the Circuit Court
) of said County do certify that the within and
) foregoing is a full true and perfect coppy of
the Record and proceedings had in the case State of Tennessee against Major Alias Nig a slave for a Rape Nelly Looper prosecutor heretofore prosecuted in the Circuit Court of Fentress County as fully and entirely as the same remains of Record and on file in my office and in testimony whereof I have here unto set   (p-233)   my hand and private seal having no Public Seal prepaired for this office this 31st day of July 1855.

( )
(Seal)   R. T. Hildrith Clerk
))   of the Circuit Court of
                                Fentress County Tennessee

This day Pleasant Bohannon Sheriff of Putnam County returned here in to open court the States venirefacia to him directed from the County Court of Putnam County commanding him to summons the following named persons to attend the Term of the court as Jurors to wit, Noah Kerkendoll, Washington Burgess, William M. Marchbanks, John Pennington, Theophalus Malone, William Hudgins, Campbell Bohannon Sr., W. H. Miller, John Johnson, Jackson Lee, Anderson West, Isaac Whitaker, William H. Gentry, John Grime, Luther Clark, George H. Harper, John Montgomery, Josiah Whitefield, Joseph Fletcher, Wilson M. McDaniel, William G. Young, Joshua Bartlett, Thomas Anderson, Julian Edwards, Jackson Wallis, and John Meritt as Jurors and William M. McDonald and Jacob Henry as constables to attend thereon as court officers came to hand 20th May 1855.

Executed by sumoning all the Jurors and court officers this the 13th of August 1855.
R. Bohannon Shff.
R. Dyer D. Shff.

Out of which venirefacias and Jurors aforesaid the court proceeded to Elect and Empannell a Grand Jury as the Act of the General Assembly in such case provides when the following named persons were drawn and Elected to wit - William M. Marchbanks, Noah Kerkendall, Luther Clark, John Montgomery, John Grime,   (p-234)   Julian Edward, Thomas Anderson, Joshua Bartlett, Jackson Wallis, Wilson M. McDonald, William H. Gentry, Ward H. Miller and John Pennington of whom the court appointed William M. Marchbanks foreman of the Grand Jury all of whom are good and Lawful men house holders and free holders of the county of Putnam who being Elected Empanelled sworn and charged a Jury of Grand inquest for the State of Tennessee to Enquire for the Body of the County of Putnam who retired to their room to consider of presentments Indictments and attend by Jacob Hany a constable sworn in due form of Law to attend thereon on affidavit of Joseph Fletcher and for reasons to court shown it is ordered by the court that Joseph Fletcher, William G. Young, and Josiah Whitefield that they be released from further attendance at this Term court as Jurors.

This day T. H. Williams attorny for the fourth solicitorial Dist.

appeared in open court and refused to prosecute in behalf of the State on account of sickness whereupon the court appointed William H. Botts attorney General protem who being present in open court took an oath to support the constitution of the United States and the State of Tennessee and the oath of Office and thereupon Entered his Duties as such.

Thomas Bounds)   Debt Appeal
Vs) This day came here into open Charles Isam and as
Jesse B. Terry) security for the plaintiff and acknowledged him
) self to owe and stand indebted to Jesse B. Terry
the Deft in the sum of Two hundred and fifty Dollars to be void on condition should the same be adjudged against (p-235) the said plaintiff upon a final hearing of the same that he will pay all such costs as shall be adjudged against him.

State of Tennessee) Presentment for Tipling - Came the attorny
Vs) General for the State and the Defendant in
James Lowe) proper person and he being arraigned and
) charged on the presentment says he is Guilty
as therein against him charged It is therefore ordered that for such his offence he pay a fine of one Dollar and all costs whereupon came here in to open court J. A. Lowe and Jackson Maxwell and as security for said Deft. confesses Judgment Jointly with said Deft for said fine and cost this day adjudged against him. It is therefore considered by the court that the court Recover against said Deft and J. A. Lowe and Jackson Maxwell the sum (p-236) of one Dollar the fine aforesaid and also all cost herein and that Execution issue.

State of Tennessee) Indictment for an assault and Battery
Vs)
William Austin) Isam Smith Prosecutor came the Attorney
) General for the State and the Defendant in
proper person who being arraigned and charged upon the Indictment says he is not guilty as therein against him is charged and for his trial puts himself upon the County and the attorny General for the State doth the like whereupon came a Jury of good and Lawful men to wit - William Webb, Isaac Whitaker, John Johnson, Campbell Bohannon, John Meritt, William Budgins, Washington Burgess, Theophalus Malone, Anderson West, Jackson Lee, John Grider and Moses A. Jared who being Elected tried and the truth to speak upon the issue Joined upon their oaths do say that said Defendant is Guilty in manner and form as herein charged against him. It is therefore ordered that he pay a fine of two Dollars and fifty cents and all costs whereupon came here into open court Robert Allcorn, Prettiman Jones, W. M. Allcorn, R. S. Allcorn and James Allcorn and as security for said Deft confessed Judgment Jointly with said Deft for said fine and costs this day adjudged against - It is therefore considered by the court that the State of Tennessee Recover against said Deft the sum of two Dollars and fifty cents and also against his security for said fine and costs and that Executed Issue.

State of Tennessee)   Indictment for A. & B.
Vs) Isam Smith Prosecutor came the attorny Gen-
Ira Carr) eral for the State and the defendant in

proper person and the Deft being arraigned and charged upon the Indictment says (p-237) he is not guilty as therein against him charged and for his trial puts himself upon the County and the attorny General for the State doth the Like whereupon came a Jury of good and Lawful men to wit, William Webb, Isaac Whitaker, John Johnson, Campbell Bohannon Sr., John Meritt, William Hudgins, Washington Burgess, Theopholus Malone, Anderson West, Jackson Lee, John Grider and Moses Jared who being Elected tried and sworn the truth to speak upon the issue Joined upon their oaths do say they find the same in favor of the Deft that he is not Guilty in manner or form as therein charged and that the State of Tennessee pay all costs and part of the prosecution in this cause and that the same be certified for allowance.

State of Tennessee) Indictment for murder in the first Degree
Vs) Robert Brown Prosr. came the Attorney Gen-
William Crabtree and) eral for the State and the Defendants in
Isaac Crabtree) proper person and there came a Jury of good
) and Lawful men to wit: L. J. Jones, Amon Jones
John Lee, William Buck, William Peak, John Hunter, Samuel K. Wilson, Dudly Hunter, Joseph Holloway, Robert Macky, Bird S. Jones, and John S. Watson who being Elected true and sworn well and truly to try and true deliverance to make between the State of Tennessee and the Defendants at the bar who after having heard part of the Evidence in this cause and there not being time this Evening to finish the trial of this cause the Jurors were placed in charge of Robinson Dyer D. Sheriff of Putnam County who was sworn according to Law to take them (p-238) to some comfortable convenient Room to keep them separate and apart from all other person to suffer no person to have any conversation with them and return again at the meeting of this court.

The Defendant is ordered in custody of the Sheriff ordered that court be adjourned untill tomorrow morning 7 oclock.

Jno. L. Goodall

Tuesday morning August 14th A.D. 1855 Court met persuance to adjournment present the Honorable John L. Goodall Judge presiding.

State of Tennessee) Indictment for murder in the first Degree
Vs) Robert Brown Prosecutor - Came again the at-
William Crabtree) torney General for the State and the Defendant
Isaac Crabtree) Lead to the bar of the court in the custody
) of the Sheriff of Putnam County and came also
the same Jury Elected true and sworn in this cause on yesterday in charge of Robison Dyer D. Shff who after having heard the Ballance of the Evidence in this cause and heard all of the arguments of counsel in this cause and received their charge from the Honorable Court and there not being time this day to finish the trial of this cause this day and the Jurors were placed in charge of Robinson Dyer D. Sheriff sworn to take charge of the Jurors to meet again tomorrow morning at the meeting of this court.

Ordered that court be adjourned untill tomorrow morning 7 oclock.

Jno. L. Goodall

P-239 Wednesday Morning August 15th A.D. 1855 - Court met persuant to adjournment Present the Honorable John L. Goodall Judge Presiding.

State of Tennessee) Indictment for Murder in the 1st Degree
Vs) Robert Brown Prosecutor - Came the attorny
William Crabtree and) General for the State and the Defendant
Isaac Crabtree) in proper person and said Defendant being
) arraigned and charged upon the Bill of
Indictment in this cause say they are not Guilty in manner and form as there ___ charged against them and for their trial put themselfs County and the attorny General for the State doth the Like, whereupon came a Jury of good and Lawful men to wit, L. J. Jones, Amon Jones, John Lee, William Buck, William Peek, John Hunter, Samuel K. Wilkerson, Dudly Hunter, Joseph Holloway, Robert Macky, Bird S. Jones and John S. Watson who being Elected tried and sworn well and truly to try and true Deliverance to make between the State of Tennessee and the Defendant at this Bar - who after having heard part of the Evidence in this cause and there not being time this day to finish the trial of this cause the Juror were placed in charge of Robison Dyer D. Shff of Putnam County, who was shown according to Law to take them to some comfortable convenient Room to keep them separate and apart from all other persons to suffer no person to have any conversation with and return again at the meeting of this court and the Defts is ordered in custody of the sheriff the entry should have appeared upon the minuts of Monday Last at this Term of the Court but is made now for them.

P-240 Joseph Mitchell) Debt Appeal - Came the parties by their
Vs) attornies and the Deft having filed at
A. T. Wallis) this Term of court a Bill of Discovers
) against said plaintiff whereupon the
same is ordered to be continued untill the next term of this court upon the payment of the costs of this Term by said Deft. It is therefore considered by the court that the plaintiff Recover against said Defendant the costs of this Term and that Execution issue for the same This Entry should appeared upon the Minutes of Yesterday but is made now for then.

State of Tennessee) Indictment for Pettit Larceny James B. Lowry
Vs) Prosecutor - Came the attorny General for the
William J. Taylor) State and the Defendant Led to the Bar in
) custody of the sheriff of Putnam County who
being arraigned and charged upon this Bill of Indictment in this cause says he is not Guilty in manner & form as therein against him is charged and for his trial puts himself upon the County and the attorney General for the state doth the Like Whereupon came a Jury of good and Lawful men to wit: William Gipson, Jesse Elliott, Henry T. Hughes, Joseph Bray, William Bennett, Elmore Carrington, James Lack, James Mahan, John Grider, William Webb, Campbell Bohannon and John Jackson, who being Elected tried and sworn well and truly to try and true Deliverance to make Between the State of Tennessee and the Deft at the Bar, who after having heard all of the Evidence in this cause and the argument of counsel and Received their charge from the Honorable court Retired in charge of Robison Dyer A D. Shff. of Putnam County sworn for that purpose and again return into court and upon their oaths do say that said Defendant is not guilty in manner and form (p-241) as in the Bill of Indictment in this cause is charged

against him It is therefore considered by the court that said Deft be discharged and Recover against the State of Tennessee all cost in this cause on part of the prosecution in this cause and that the same be certified for allowance.

William Richardson and) Ejectment came the plaintiffs by their
John Richardson) attorney and Entered a nola prosequi in
Vs) this cause as to Edward Vaughn one of
John Robards and) the above named Defendants it is there-
Edward Vaughn) fore considered by the court that the
) Deft go hence and recover against the
plaintiffs the costs in this suit incident to making him a Deft in the same and that Execution issue this Entry should have appeared upon the minutes of yesterday But is made now for then.

John Richardson and) Eject
William Richardson) Came the Defendant and came a Long with
Vs) him Felix N. Patterson and Holland Denton
John Robards) and as security for said Deft acknowledge
) themselves indebted to the said plaintiff
in the sum of Two hundred and fifty Dollars for the payment of all cost in this suit should the same be adjudged against the Deft upon a final hearing of the same.

Hezekiah Love) Trespass
Vs) By the consent of the parties by attornies this
Riley R. Leigue) cause is set for Friday next for trial etc.
) This entry should have appeared upon the Minutes of Monday Last But is made now for then.

Robert Allcorn) Debt Quiditimit Cert. - Came the plaintiff
Vs) by Attorny and Entered a nola prosequi as
Edward Anderson and) to Edward Anderson one of the Defts above
V. W. Anderson) named causes. It is therefore considered
) by the court that the Deft go hence and
Recover against the plaintiff all costs in this cause incident to making him a Deft in this cause and that Execution issue and it appearing to the court on motion and affidavit of the Deft that the plaintiff security heretofore Given in this cause is insufficient it is ordered by the court that the plaintiff Justify his present or Give other and additional security on or before the first day of the next Term of this court and in case of failure this cause be dismissed whereupon came here into open court R. S. Allcorn and acknowledged himself held and firmly bound unto the Deft in the sum of one hundred Dollars as such additional security as aforesaid conditioned that the said plaintiff shall prosecute his said suit with Effect or in case of failure shall well and truly pay and satisfy all such costs as may be adjudged against said plaintiff.

State) The said Defendants having been Brought into
Vs) court for contempt commitment in the face of
John Kirby and) the court proceeded to hear the proof and is
Henry Bohannon) of opinion that the said John Kirby is not

Guilty of any offence and that the said Henry Bohannon is Guilty and for such his offence he pay a fine of five Dollars and costs It is therefore considered by the court that the said Deft John Kirby be discharged and that the State of (p-243) Tennessee Recover against the said Henry Bohannon the sum of five Dollars the fine aforesaid and cost and that Execution issue for the same & etc.

Isaac Burton) Debt Appeal – Came the parties and plaintiff
Vs) having filed at the present Term of this court
Thomas Lancaster) his Bill of Discoveris against said Deft and
) this being the Trial Term of this cause and
the same opperating as a continuance untill the next term of this court upon the payment of the cost of the present term of this court by said plaintiff It is therefore considered by the court that the Deft Recover against said plaintiff the costs of this Term and that Execution issue.

State of Tennessee) Indictment for an assault with intent
Vs) to commit a Rape – Nelly Looper Prose-
Major, Alias Nig a slave) cutor came the attorney General for
) the State and the Defendant being Led
to the Bar in custody of the Sheriff of Putnam County who being arraigned and charged upon the Bill of Indictment in this cause says he is not guilty in manner and form as therein against him is charged and for his trial puts himself upon the county and the attorny General for the State doth the like whereupon came a Jury of good and lawful men to wit– Albert G. Davis, R. H. Lowell, Jackson Maxwell, Barnett Richerson, K. D. Exum, Elijah Carr, James B. Lowery, Joseph Mitchell, John Merett, John Johnson William Hudgins, and Campbell Bohannon (p-244) who being Elected, tried and sworn well and truly to try and true Deliverance to make Between the State of Tennessee and the Defendant at the Bar who after having heard all of the Evidence in this cause and apart of the argument of consel thereon and there not being time this day to finish the trial of this cause the Jurors were placed in charge of Robison Dyer D. Shff of Putnam County sworn in due form of Law to take them to same comfortable convent Room and keep them separate and apart from all other persons and suffer no person have any conversation with them himself in relation to the trial of this cause and return again with them at the meeting of this court.

S. D. Burton assine of) Debt Motion to condem Land In the matter
T. T. Pointer) of this motion the following papers were
Vs) duly returned and filed in this cause to
John B. Pointer) wit –
Warrant

State of Tennessee Jackson County – To the sheriff or any constable of said county I command you to summons John B. Pointer and Thomas Pointer to appear before me or some other Justice of said County to answer the complaint of Stephen D. Burton assine the said Thomas Pointer in a plea of debt Due by note under one hundred dollars herein given under my hand and seal this 27th day of February 1854.

John Terry
J.P. for Jackson Co.

Endorsed to wit - Executed and set for trial on the 4th of March 1854 before John Terry Esq. at his house - J. H. Moore Constable S. D. Burton asine of Thomas T. Pointer Vs John B. Pointer and the said Thomas T. Pointer I give judgment in this case for the plaintiff for seventy five dollars and forty nine for cost (p-245) for which Execution may issue this March 4th 1854. John Terry J. P. for Putnam County - State of Tennessee Putnam County to the sheriff or any constable of same county I Command you that of the goods and chattles land and tenements of John B. Pointer and Thomas B. Pointer if to be found in your county you make the sum of Eighty one dollars and sixty three cents with interest there on to satisfy a Judgment that S. D. Burton assinee of said Thomas T. Pointer obtained against them before me on the fourth of March 1854 and pay over the same as the law Directs this 15th July 1855.

           John Terry
           J. P. for Putnam County

Endorsed thereon to wit - Debt with Interest up to July 13th 1855 $81.63½ const. J. H. Moore for serving Wt. $1.00 J. Terry for Wt. Judgment 2 fifa 65 cents - $83.28½ John Terry J. P. No personal proppertty of the Deft. to be found in my County I levy this fifi on one tract of land containing one hundred acres more or less in Dist. No. first in Putnam County Bound by Jacob Jud on the west and Moses Charles on the North and Choate Ayres the east levied on as the property of John J. Pointer this the 15 day of July 1855 Robison Dyer D. Sheriff all of which being seen and hereby the court on motion it is ordered by the court that Land so Levied on as aforesaid be and the same is hereby commanded and ordered to be sold to sattisfy by plaintiff Debt and cost and also the cost of this motion and that an order of sale issue.

State of Tennessee	)	Indictment for Murder in the 1st Degree
Vs	)	Robert Brown Prosecutor - (p-246) Came
William Crabtree	)	again the attorny General for the State and
Isaac Crabtree	)	the Defendants Lead to the Bar in custody of
	)	the Sheriff of Putnam County and came also

the same Jury Elected tried and sworn in this cause and received their charge from Honorable court on yesterday in charge of Robison Dyer D. Sheriff of Putnam County, who retired to considered of their verdict in charge of Robison Dyer D. Shff. and again returned into court and upon their oaths do say that Defendant Isaac Crabtree one of the above named Defendants is not Guilty in manner and form as in the Bill of Indictment in this cause is charged against him and the Juror aforesaid upon their oths aforesaid do say that said Defendant William Crabtree is guilty of man slaughter and that he be imprisoned in the common Jail and penitentiary house of the State of Tennessee for the Term of six years.

William Austin	)	Damage Appeal - Came the parties and on motion
Vs	)	and affidavit of the Defendant it is ordered by
Isam Smith	)	the court that the plaintiff Give security for
	)	the prosecution of this suit on or before the

calling of the same for trial or the same shall stand dismissed whereupon came them into open court the plaintiff and took the oath prescribed by Law permitting poor persons to prosecute without giving security and the rule was discharged.

146

Jo. O. Haws) Debt - Motion to condem Land in the matter of this
Vs) motion the following papers were duly returned and
D. W. Sims) filed to wit-

Warrant

State of Tennessee, Putnam County - to the sheriff or any constable of said County I command summon on D. W. Sims to appear before me on some other (p-247) Justice of same County to answer the complaint To Hawes in a plea of Debt due by note herein fail not. Given under my hand and seal this the 18 day of April 1854.

J. B. Clark
J.P. for Putnam County

Endorsed thereon to wit - Executed and set for trial before J. M. Brooks Esq. on Saturday the 29th April 1854. S. Hughs. Costs D. W. Sims - I give Judgment against Deft in favor of the plaintiff for twenty dollars and 65 cents and all lawful cost for which execution may issue this the 27th April 1854 James W. Brooks Justice of Peace for Putnam County - Execution State of Tennessee Putnam County to the sheriff or any constable of same County I command you to summons you that of the goods and chattles lands and tenements of Drury W. Sims and Charles V. Robertson and Pleasant Randolph securities if to be found in your county you make the twenty one dollars and 47½ cents and all cost to sattisfy a Judgment that I J. O. Hawes and to obtain against them before me J. W. Brooks Esq. on the 29 of April 1854. This given under my hand and seal this the 10th day of Jan. 1855 James W. Brooks Justice for Putnam County Endorsed there to wit; No goods and chattels to be found in my County I this day levi upon a tract of land of the Deft lying in Putnam County in District No. 5 adjoining the lands of Martin Stephens and said to contain 75 acres this the 1st day of Feb. 1855 S. Hughs const. Debt twenty one dollars and 47½ cents I have for serving Wt. 50 J. Clark for warrant 10 J. W. Brooks for fife 15 cents (p-248) all of which being seen and heard by the court on motion it ordered by the court the Land so Levied upon as aforesaid be and the said is hereby condemed and ordered to be sold to satisfy the plaintiffs Debts and the cost of this motion for which an order sale to Issue.

Thersay Winchester) Debt Motion to condem Land in the matter of
Vs) this motion the following paper was Returned
R. G. Duke) and filed to wit - Warrant State of Tennessee
) Putnam County to the sheriff or any constable
for said County I command you to summon R. G. Duke to appear before or some other justice of said County to answer the complaint of Thersay Winchester in a plea of debt due by note under forty dollars herein fail not given under my hand and seal this 22 of April 1853.

E. C. Crowel (Seal)
J.P. for Putnam County

Endorse thereon to wit - Executed and set for trial before Esq. Crowell at his house on the 7 of May 1853 J. Maxwell Const. Thersay Winchester Vs R. G. Duke In this case I give Judgment in favor of the plaintiff and against the Deft for ten dollars and thirty five cents and cost of said for which Execution may Issue this 7th May 1853.

E. C. Crowell J. P.
Executive

State of Tennessee - Putnam County, to the Sheriff or any constable of said ____ I command you as you have been commanded before that of the goods and chattles lands and (p-249) Tennements of R. G. Duke if to be found in your county you make the sum of ten dollars and 35 cents with interest and cost.)

) Ten dollars paid on the Execution Oct. 6th 1854 to satisfy Judgment that Thersay Winchester obtained before M. C. Crowell etc. on the 7th day of May 1853 against the said Duke for $10.35 and cost and pay over the same as the law directs this Nov. 9th 1854.

M. A. Jarred J. P.
for Putnam County.

Oct. 6th 1854 Credit $.3.00 Judgment $10.35 interest Maxwell 50 Crowell 35 Jarred 60 Endorsed thereon to wit: No goods and chattels to be found in my county Levied upon a tract of Land of the Defendant lying in Putnam County in District No. 13th adjoining the Lands of E. Anderson Lilly ...Duffy P. Jones and Hugh Wallace and said to contain 65 acres this the 15 Nov. 1854 A. Boyd cost all of which being seen and hereby the court on motion it is ordered by the court that the Land so Levied on as aforesaid be and the same is hereby condemed and ordered to be sold to satisfy the Plaintiffs Debt in cost and cost of this motion for which an order of sale may Issue.

Ordered that Court be adjourned untill tomorrow morning 7 oclock.

Jno. L. Goodall

Thursday Morning August 16th A.D. 1855

Court met persuant to adjournment present the Honorable John L. Goodall Judge Presiding.

State of Tennessee	)	On a charge of Eastaray - Came the attorney
Vs	)	General and the Defendant by attorny moved
A. J. Grogan	)	to Quash the proceedings in this cause.

P-250)
State of Tennessee	)	Indictment for Ludness - Harvil H.
Vs	)	Briant Prosecutor Came the attorney
A. J. Grogan	)	General for the State and the Defendant in proper person and said Defendant

being arraigned and charged upon the Bill of Indictment says he is not Guilty as therein against him is charged and for his trial puts himself upon the Country and the attorny General for the State doth the like; Whereupon came a Jury of good and Lawful men to wit: William Webb, Isaac Whitaker, M. A. Jarred, John Grain, Washington Burgess, Theophalis Malone, Anderson West, Jackson Lee, William Peek, S. P. W. Maxwell, Joseph Hester, and James K. Peek who being Elected tried and sworn the truth to speak upon the issue of Traverse Joined upon their oaths do say that said Defendant is Guilty in manner and form as therein against him is charged and it is ordered by the court that for such his offence he pay a fine of one Dollar and the cost of this prosecution.

148

James Brooks)   Trespass on the case - Came the parties by their
Vs) attorneys and the plaintiffs Demur to the Defend-
George Henry) ants plea is sustained and the Deft have Leave
) to plead soon.

William Austin) Damage Appeal-Came the parties by their attorneys
Vs) and there came a Jury of good and Lawful men to
Isam Smith) Wit: Campbell Bohannon, M. A. Jarred, William Webb,
) Jackson Lee, (p-251) S. H. Maxwell, Preston
Stewart, William Hudgins, Theopholis Malone, Anderson West, Joseph Hester
John Johnson, Isaac Whitaker, who being Elected tried and sworn well to
try the matters in constroversy Between the parties upon their oaths do
say they find the same in favor of the plaintiff and assess his Damage
to the sum of five Dollars - It is therefore considered by the court that
the plaintiff Recover against the Defendant the sum of five Dollars the
Damages aforesaid by the Jury aforesaid assessed and also the sum of five
Dollars in cost and that Execution issue for the collection of the Same.

State)   This day the Grand Jury returned into court
Vs) the following Bills of Indictment to wit -
John Bohannon) State against James Bullington for an assault
James Bullington) and Battery, State against James Lowery and
James Lowery) G. W. Collier for an assault and Battery and
G. W. Collier) the State against H. I. Brock and John Watson
) for an assault and Battery all of which Bills
are signed by their foreman A. true Bill William M. Marchbanks foreman
of the Grand Jury, and also returned in court at presentment of the State
against John Bohannon for an assault and Battery which was signed by the
foreman of the Grand Jury and all the Ballance of the Grand Jurors in due
form of Law and again retired to consider of present Indictments & etc.

On affidavit of Julious Elmore one of the Grand Jurors on account of
sickness he is discharged and released as such.

State) Indictment for Ludness - E. H. Briant Prosecutor
Vs) P-252   State of Tennessee   )   Indictment
Janie Bruce) Vs) for an as-
) Major Alias Nig a slave) sault with
) intent to
commit a Rape - Nelly Looper Prosecutor Came again the attorny general
for the state and the Defendant Lead to the bar in custody of the Sheriff
of Putnam County and came also the same Jury Elected tried and sworn in
this cause on yesterday in charge of Robison Dyer D. Sheriff of Putnam
County sworn to take charge of them who after having heard the Ballance
of the argument of counsel thereon and received their charge from the
Honorable Court retired in charge of Robison Dyer to consider of this
verdict and again returns into court and upon their oaths do say that
said Defendant is Guilty on the first count in manner and form as in the
Bill of Indictment in this cause as charged against him and not guilty
on the second count as charged in said Bill of Indictment.

149

State of Tennessee) Presentment for Tipling - Came the attorney
    Vs) General for the State and the Defendant in
George Dillard) proper person who being arraign and charged
) upon the presentment in cause says he is not
guilty in manner and form as therein against him is charged and for his
trial puts himself upon the county and the Attorny General for the State
doth the Like whereupon came a Jury of good and Lawful men to wit:
Campbell Bohannon, John Johnson, William Hudgins, John Meritt, J. M. Mc-
Daniel, Samuel McCaleb, John West, William H. Barons Jr., Ridly Draper,
Thomas A. Matheny, G. W. Apple, and William Gipson who being Elected
tried and sworn the truth to speak upon the issue joined upon their other
oaths do say that said Defendant is not guilty in manner and form as in
the presentment is (p-253) charged against him. It is therefore ordered
that the defendant be discharged and that the State of Tennessee pay all
cost in this cause and part of the prosecution and that the same be certified to the County Court of Putnam County for allowance as the Law directs.

State of Tennessee) Peace Warrant Came the attorny General for
    Vs) the State and the Defts and the prosecutor
Francis Bright) Hannah Elrod failing to attend and prose-
Louisa Bright) cute. It is therefore ordered that Defts
Mary Bright) be discharged and recover against the State
Francis Bright Jr.) of Tennessee all costs on part of the prose-
) cution in this cause and that the same be
certified for allowance as the Law directs.

State) Indictment for Murder in 1st Degree Robert
  Vs) Brown Prosr. This day came Mitchell Wright
William Crabtree and) Jailer of Fentress County produced and read
Isaac Crabtree) here in open court account for keeping Isaac
) Crabtree one of the above named Deft in the
common Jail of Fentress County on the above charge from 13th Feby 1855 to
16th day of same month making 3 days at 37½ c E. $1.12½
12 Lawful turnkeys at Feby court at 50   6.00

Making in all the sum of $ 7.12½

Which account having been Examined by the Att. General and certified to
be correct the same is allowed by the court and ordered to be Taxed in
the Bill of cost in this cause.

State of Tennessee) Indictment for Petit Larceny - James B.
    Vs) Lowery Prosecutor - This day came John H.
William J. Taylor) Hamilton (p-254) Sheriff of Overton
) County produced and read herein open court
his account for keeping said Deft in the common Jail of said County on a
charge of Pettit Larceny from the 11th day of April 1855 to the 13th day
of August 1855 one hundred and twenty four days at 37½ cents per day $46.50
Two lawful Turnkeys putting him in Jail on the 11th April 1855 and
taking him out on the 13th of August 1855 as aforesaid at 50 cts, Each 1.00

                                  Total $ 47.50

Which account having been Examined and certified by the attorny General to be correct the same is allowed by the court and ordered to be Taxed in the Bill of cost in this cause.

State of Tennessee) Indict. for assault with intent to com-
Vs) mit Rape - Nelly Looper Prosecutor.
Major Alias Nig a slave) This day John H. Hamilton Shrff. and
) Jailer of Overton County produced and
read herein open court his account for keeping said Defendant in the common Jail of Overton on a charge of assault with intend to commit a rape from the 18th day of June 1855 to the 13th day of August 1855 when he was taken to the Circuit Court of Putnam County for trial fifty five days at 37½ cents. $20.62½
For two lawful Turnkeys putting him in 18th June 1855 and taking him out on 13th August 1855 as aforesaid at 50 ct.   1.00

                    Making in all the sum of $ 21.62½

which account having been Examined and certified by the Attorny General to be correct the same is allowed by the court and ordered to be Taxed in the Bill of cost in this cause.

State of Tennessee) Indictment for murder 1st degree - Robert
Vs) Brown, Prosecutor, This day John H. Hamilton
William Crabtree) Sheriff and Jailer of Overton County Produce
) (p-255) and read here in open court his
account for keeping said Deft in the common Jail of Overton County on a charge of murder now pending in the Circuit Court of Putnam County from the 11th day of April 1855 to the 13 day of Augst 1855 one hundred and twenty four days at 37½ cents per day $ 46.50
For two Lawful Turnkeys putting him in and taking him out of Jail on the days aforesaid at 50 cents each   1.00

                    Making in all the sum of $ 47.50

Which account having been Examined and certified by the Attorny Genl. to be correct the same is allowed by the court and ordered to be Taxed in the Bill of cost in this cause.

State of Tennessee) Indictment for murder in the 1st De-
issued - Vs) gree Robert Brown Prosecutor.
William & Isaac Crabtree) This day F. H. Daugherty special
) Deputy Sheriff of Overton County Pro-
duced and read here in open court his account for conveying Deft. William Crabtree from Livingston Overton County to Cookeville Putnam County to be tried upon a charge of murder in all in going and returning 48 miles
for sheriff $ 4.85
Two Guards each $1.50 for each 25 miles   5.75
for defendant 1.00 for Each 25 miles   1.92

                    Making in all the sum $ 12.52

Which account having been Examined and certified by the Attorny General to be correct the same is allowed by the court and ordered to be Taxed in the Bill of costs in this cause.

State of Tennessee)	Indictment for Pettit Larceny James B. Lowrey
Vs)	prosecutor – This day Russell Moore produced
William T. Taylor)	and read here in open court his account for
)	feeding Deft. six meals at 25¢ each $1.50

(p-256) To feeding two Guards B. H. Watson and J. H. Moon 1st
August Term 1855 seven meals. 1.75

Making in all the sum of 3.25

Which account having been Examined and certified by the Attorney General to be correct and it appearing to the court that there was no public Jail in the county of Putnam therefore the same is allowed by the court and ordered to be Taxed in the Bill of costs in this cause.

State of Tennessee)	Indictment for murder in the first Degree
issued – Vs)	Robert Brown prosecutor – This day Russell
William Crabtree)	Moore produced and Read here in open court
)	his account for feeding William Crabtree at

April Term 1855 six meals at 25 cents each. $1.50
Fed Guard B. H. Watson and Robison Dyer six meals each 2.25
At the August Term 1855 feeding William Crabtree nine meals at
25 cents Each. 3.00
Fed Eight meals by Mill & co. 2.00
Guard Claburn Brown fed nine meals 2.25
To feeding Isaac Crabtree and Guard seven meals at 25 ct. Each 3.50

Making in all sum of $12.50

Which account having been Examined and certified by the attorney to be correct and it appearing to the court that there was no public Jail in the County of Putnam therefore the same is allowed by the court and ordered to be taxed in the Bill of cost in this cause.

State of Tennessee)	Indictment for Murder in the 1st Degree.
Vs)	Robert Brown Prosecutor Came again the at-
William Crabtree)	torney General for the State and the Defend-
)	ant Led to the Bar of the Court in custody

of the Sheriff of Putnam County and on motion and affidavit the defendant by (p-257) attorney moved the court for a new trial in this cause which was over ruled by the court and the Defendant moved the court in arrest of Judgment which was overruled by the court, and it being demanded of the Defendant if he has anything further to say why the Judgment of the Law should not be passed upon him nothing further being urged – Therefore It is considered by the court that the Defendant be imprisoned in the common Jail and penitentiary house of the State of Tennessee for six years at hard Labor and that the Sheriff of Putnam County convey and deliver said Deft. to the keeper of said penitentiary as soon as practible after the adjournment of this court and it is further considered by the court that the State of Tennessee Recover against said deft all cost in this Suit and that Execution issue and etc.
Whereupon the Defendant by attorny prays an appeal in nature of a writ of Error to the next Term of the supreme Court of Errors and appeals to be held in the courthouse in the citty of Nashville which to him is Granted whereupon came here into open court the Defendant William Crabtree together with Samuel Crabtree, Hiram Crabtree, Isaac Crabtree and W. E. D. Jones

and acknowledged themselfs to owe and stand indebted to the State of Tennessee in the sum of Four thousand Dollars to wit: The defendant William Crabtree in the sum of Two thousand Dollars and the said Samuel Crabtree, Hiram Crabtree, Isaac Crabtree, and W. E. B. Jones in the sum of two thousand Dollars Jointly to be Levied of their proper Goods and chattles, Lands and Tennements to the use of the State of Tennessee to be remanded nevertheless to be void if the said William Crabtree the Defendant make his personal appearance before the surpreme Court in the Citty of Nashville on the first Monday of December next then and there to answer the State of Tennessee upon a charge of man slaughter and then and there attend   (p-258)   untill Legally discharged.

J. A. Ray) Debt Motion to condem Land In the matter of this
Vs) motion the following papers were duly returned
G. W. Crabtree) and filed by the Justice of the peace who re-
) manded the Judgments wit -

Warrant State of Tennessee Putnam County Greetings -, You are hereby commanded to summons George W. Crabtree to appear before some Acting Justice of peace for said County to answer the complaint of J. A. Ray in a plea of Debt and by account under warrant herein fail not.
Given under my hand and Seal this 26th of March 1855.

                Isaac Lollar (Seal)
                Justice of the peace

Endorsed thereon to wit - Executed and set for trial on the 3rd of April before R. D. Allison Esqr. fee 50 cents.
                J. W. Carr Const.

I, Loller fee S. warrant 10 cents In the above case I Give Judgment for plaintiff for fourteen Dollars 98 cents with all Lawful cost April the 3 1855.

                R. D. Allison (Seal)
                J. P. for sd. County

Execution State of Tennessee - Putnam County to the sheriff or any Lawful officer of said County I command you that of the Goods and chattles Lands and tenements of George W. Crabtree if to be found in your County you make the sum of fourteen Dollars and ninty Eight cents and costs of suit to satisfy a Judgment that J. A. Ray obtained against him before me on the third of April 1855 and pay over the same as the Law directs this the 10th day of May 1855.
                R. D. Allison (Seal)
                J.P. for said County

Endorsed Debt $14.98 Justice fee 50¢ constable J. W. Carr 50 cents No goods and chattles   (p-259)   to be found in my county Levied on a tract of land of Land of the Defendant Lying in Putnam County in District No. 13 adjoining the tract of Joseph Roberts heirs on the East and on the north and Benjamin Prickets on the south and said to contain one hundred and twenty five acres this the 24th of May 1855 my fee 50 cents.
                J. W. Carr Const.

All of which being seen and heard by the court on motion it is ordered by the court that the Land so Levied upon as aforesaid be and the same is hereby condemed and ordered to be sold to satisfy the plaintiff Debt and cost and also the costs of this motion and that an order of sale issue.

Ordered that Court be adjourned until tomorrow morning 7 oclock.

Jno. L. Goodall

Friday Morning August the 17th A.D. 1855

Court met persuant to adjournment present the Honorable John L. Goodall Judge Presiding.

James Brooks) Trespass on the Case - Came the parties by at-
Vs) torney and on motion and affidavit of the plain-
James Bartlett) tiff this cause is ordered to be continued untill
) the next Term of court upon the payment of all the costs in this suit by said plaintiff It is therefore considered by the court that the Defendant Recover against the plaintiff all costs in this suit and that fifa issue and by agreemnt of the parties by attorney this cause is not to be tried untill the next April Term of this court.

Elijah Brown) Ejectment - Came the parties by their (p-260)
Vs) attorny and on motion and affidavit of the plain-
Thomas Pullin) tiff it is ordered by the court that this cause
) be continued untill the next Term of this court upon the payments of the costs of this Term of the court by said plaintiff It is therefore considered by the court that the Defendant Recover against the plaintiff the cost of this Term and that Execution issue for the collection of the same and on motion of the plaintiff by attorny and for reasons to the court shown it is ordered by the court that attendance of Mathew Smith be stricken from the Bill of cost in this cause at the present term of this court and etc and by agreement of the parties by attornies this cause is not to be tried untill the next April Term of this court.

Nancy Norris) Pettition for Divorce - In this cause the
Vs) Petitioner moved the court to take the pe-
William R. Norris) tition for confessed and have the cause set
) down for hearing Expartee and it appearing to the court that the subpoena had been in the hands of the Sheriff of Putnam County three months next before this Term of this court It is therefore ordered that the petitioned be Taken for confessed and set down for hearing Expartee.

Benjamin H. Watson) Ejectment - Came the parties by their attor-
Vs) neys and the plaintiffs Demer to the second
Samuel Maxwell) place of the Declaration Defendants is sus-
) tained and is over ruled as to the fourth place and the plaintiff is allowed to amend his Declaration.

State of Tennessee) Indictment for assault with intent to
Vs) commit a Rape.
Major Alias Nig a slave)

This day J. Perkins In keeper proceeded and read in open court his account (p-261) for boarding and Lodging the Jury while on the Trial of the above cause at the August Term 1855 two days at nine Dollars per day making in all the sum of $18.00.

Which account having been Examined and certified by the attorny General to be correct the same is allowed by the court and ordered to be taxed in the Bill of cost in this cause.

State of Tennessee) Indictment for murder in 1st Degree - Robert
Vs) Brown Prosr.
William Crabtree) This day Jourdon Perkins Innkeeper produced
Isaac Crabtree) and read herein open court his account for
) Boarding and Lodging the Jury while on the
trial of the above cause at this Term of the court two days at nine Dollars per day making in all the sum of $18.00.

Which account having been Examined and certified by the attorny General to be correct the same is allowed by the court and ordered to be Taxed in the Bill of cost in this cause.

Campbell Bohannon) Debt motion to condem Land - In the matter
Vs) of this motion the following papers were duly
Levi Phillips) returned and filed to wit: Warrant State of
John Jackson) Tennessee Putnam County to any Lawful officer
) of said County Greetings - You are hereby to commanded to summons Levi Phillips to appear before me or some other Justice of the peace in and for said County to answer to the complaint of Campbell I Bohannon in a plea of Debt due by note herein fail not.

Given under my hand and seal the 9th of October 1854.

                 Lee R. Taylor (Seal)
                 Justice of the Peace

P-262 Endorsed to wit: Executed and set for trial before Lee R. Taylor Esqr. at his home on the 10th day of October 1854.

                 J. Henry Const.

Judgment In this case I give Judgment in favor of the plaintiff against the Defendant for seventy Dollars Debt and 81 cents Interest all cost of suit which Execution may issue this 10th October 1854.

                 Lee R. Taylor (Seal)
                 Justice of Peace

Execution - State of Tennessee Putnam County - To the sheriff or any constable of said County, I command you that of the Goods and chattles Lands and tenements of Levi Phillips - Spencer Phillips and John Jackson his securitys for the stay of Execution if to be found in your County you make the sum of seventy Dollars 87½ cents with Interest thereon and all cost to satisfy a Judgment that Campbell I Bohannon obtained before me on the 10th day of October 1854 for seventy Dollars 87½ cents and cost and pay

over the same as the Law Direct the 13th day of June 1855 Lee Taylor (Seal) Justice of the peace of Putnam Co. Endorsed Judgment on the 10th day of October 1854.
Amount of Debt $70.87½
Justice Taylor for Writ Judgment and fifa   .50
Constable Henry for serving warrant   .50

              Lee Taylor   (Seal)
              Justice of the peace

No Goods and chattles to be found in my County Levied upon a tract of Land of Defendant Lying in Putnam County in District No. 5 adjoining the Lands of D. W. Sims and said to contain 75 acres the 14th day of June 1855.

              Jacob Henry Const.

All of which being seen and heard by the court on motion it is ordered by the court that the Land so Levied upon as aforesaid be and the same is hereby condemned and ordered to be sold to satisfy the plaintiffs Debt and   (p-263)   cost also the cost of the motion and that an order of sale issue.

R. G. Burton) Confession of Judgment In the matter this motion
  Vs   ) the following papers were duly returned and filed
Walker Brown) to wit, R. J. Burton Vs Walker Brown Debt this
) day Walker Brown appeared before me and confessed
Judgment in favor of Robert G. Burton for one hundred and fifty Dollars and thirty cents due by two notes one dated the 2rd day of January 1854 for $85.14 the other the 31st Dec. 1855 for $72.87½ it is therefore considered by the court that the said Robert G. Burton recover of the said Walker Brown the sum of one hundred and fifty Dollars and thirty cents and all costs this the 21 Feby. 1855.

              James M. McKiny (Seal)
              J. P.

Execution State of Tennessee - Putnam County,

To the Sheriff or any constable of said County I command you that of the Goods and chattles Lands and tenements of Walker Brown if to be found in your County you make the sum of one hundred and fifty Dollars and thirty cents on a Judgment obtained Before me in favor of R. G. Burton against the said Walker Brown by confession this the 22 day of March 1855.

              James M. McKinny (Seal)
              J.P. for Putnam County

Endorsed, Bill of cost Justice McKinys issuing Execution Judgment 65 cents no more personal property found in my County - Levied on undivided shears of a tract of Land where the widow Harpoole now lives as the property of Walker Brown Lying in Civil District number in Putnam County ten - known as the Harpoole Stand another tract adjoining the widow   (p-264)   Harpool containing acres Joining James Carr and Elias Green, where Walker Brown Lives these Lands Lying in Putnam County Tennessee Levied on as the property of Walker Brown this 22rd day of February 1855.

              J. B. Terry Const.

All of which being seen and heard by the court on motion it is considered by the court that the Land so Levied upon as aforesaid be and the same is hereby condemned and ordered to be sold to satisfied the plaintiffs Debt and cost and also the cost of this motion and that an order of sale issue.

James Brook)
Vs)
George Henry)
)

Trespass on the case - Came the parties by attornys and there came a Jury of good and Lawful men to wit: John Terry, William Webb, Isaac Whitaker, John Grider, S. H. Matticks, Joshua White, Theopholus Malone, Anderson West, Jackson Lee, Washington Burgess, M. A. Jarred, and William Z. Buck, who being Elected tried and sworn the truth to speak upon the issue joind upon their oath do say they find the same in favor of the plaintiff and assess his Damages to the Sum of one Dollar - It is therefore considered by the court that the plaintiff Recover against the Defendant the sum of one Dollar the Damages aforesaid by the Jury aforesaid by the Jury aforesaid assessed and also the sum of one Dollar of the cost and that an Execution issue for the collection of the sum and c.

State of Tennessee)
Vs)
William J. Taylor)
)

Indictment for Pettit Larceny James B. Lowery This day Pleasant Bohannon and Robinson Dyer Sheriff and D. Sheriff of Putnam County Produced and read herein open court their account (p-205) for conveying and bring the Deft William J. Taylor from the Jail in White County to Cookeville in Putnam County at the April Term 1855 38 miles at 10 cents per mile . $ 3.80
B. H. Watson Guard at 6 cts per mile.   2.28
Also Dr. as above for conveying said Taylor from Cookeville to the Jail in Overton County for safe keeping at the April Term 1852 42 miles at 10 cents per mile.   4.20
E. D. Watson Guard at the same Time 42 miles at 6 cts per mile.   2.52
For Guarding said Taylor 3 days and 2 nights at the August Term 1855 B. H. Watson.   3.00
Also P. Bohannon for Guarding said Deft Taylor 3 days and 2 nights   3.00

Making in all a sum of $18.80

Which account having been Examined and certified by the Attorny General to be correct and there being no public Jail in Putnam County the same is allowed by the court and ordered to be Taxed in the Bill of cost in this case.

State of Tennessee)
Vs)
William Crabtree)
)

Indictment for murder in first degree. Robert Brown Prosecutor - This day Pleasant Bohannon Shff. and Robison Dyer D. Shff of Putnam County produced and read herein open court their account against said Deft. To conveying said William Crabtree from Cookeville to the Jail in Overton County at the April Term 1855 for safe keeping 42 miles at 10 cents per mile. $4.20
2 guards J. H. Moon - and Samuel Hughes Each 42 miles at 6 cents E Per mile.   5.04
To Guarding said Crabtree at same Term of the Putnam Court 2 days and 2 nights.   2.00

B. H. Watson and Roberson Dyer Each day and night as Guard	$2.00
P-266 Lewis Huddleston and H. Ramsey Each one day as Guard 50 cts. Each.	1.00
Also for Guarding said Crabtree and William Crabtree 4 days and 3 nights at the August term 1855.	7.00
J. H. Moon and M. C. Brown 4 days and 3 nights Each for Each of the Defts Crabtree.	14.00
Deduct ½ half day and 1 night over charged for Isaac Crabtree at August Term 1855 for the 3 persons above named at $1. per day 75 cents Each.	2.25
Making in all the sum of	$ 32.99

Which account having been Examined and certified by the attorney General to be correct and it appearing to the satisfaction of the court that there was no public Jail in Putnam County. The same is allowed by the court and ordered to be Taxed in the Bill of costs in this cause.

Jeremiah Coggin) Case agreed upon scirefacia appeal from J.P.
Vs) Came the parties by their attornys when the
William C. Mitchell) above cause came on to be heard before the
) Honorable John L. Goodall Judge and etc.
upon the proceedings had in said cause and the facts agreed to by the parties before the Justice below who tried said cause who after having seen and heard the same was of the opinion that in said proceedings heard there was no error in the proceedings aforesaid and therefore affirms the Judgments of the Justice aforesaid - It is therefore considered by the court that the plaintiff recover of the defendant and Hezikiah Love his security for appeal the sum of twenty five dollars the amount of the Judgment of the Justice aforesaid together with all costs herein and that execution issue etc.

Whereupon the Defendant by attorny moved the court for a new trial in this cause which was over ruled by the court whereupon the Defendant prays an appeal to the next Term of the surpreme of Tennessee and he   (p-267) having given Bond with Isaac Burton and John Meritt as his security said appeal is granted and the Defendant tendered herein open court his Bill of Exception which was signed and sealed by the court and ordered to be made a part of the Record in this cause.

Hezekiah Love) Trespass
Vs) Came the parties by their attorny and there came
Riley R. Liegue) a Jury of good and Lawful men to wit: William
) Webb, Isaac Whitaker, John Johnson, Campbell
Bohannon, William Hudgins, Washington Burgess, Theopholis Malone, John Grider, M. A. Jarred, Jackson Lee, Anderson West, and Benjamin H. Watson who being Elected tried and sworn the truth to speak upon the issue Joined who after having heard all of the Evidence in this cause and the argument of counsel thereon and received their charge from the Honorable Court retired to consider of this verdict and again return into court and upon their oaths do say they could not agree upon a verdict in this cause and there not being time this day to finish the trial of this cause the Jurors were permitted to Disperse untill tomorrow morning the meeting of this Court to resum the further consideration of this cause.

State of Tennessee) Indictment for Ludness M. H. Brient Prosr.
Vs   ) Come the attorny General for the State and
A. J. Grogan   ) the Defendant in proper person whereupon came
) herein to open court Allin Young and as se-
curity for said Deft confessed Judgment Jointly with said Defendant for
said fine and cost adjudged against said Defendant on a former day at
the   (p-268)   present term of this court. It is therefore considered
by the court that the State of Tennessee Recover against said Deft. Allen
Young the sum of one Dollar the fine aforesaid and also all costs herein
and that Execution issue & etc..

State of Tennessee) On the charge of Bastardy appeal from the
Vs   ) County Court of Putnam County - Came the at-
A. J. Grogan   ) torny General for the State and the deft in
) proper person the above cause came on to be
tried before his honor John L. Goodall whereupon and because to the Court
it seems that the proceeding of the County Court is in error it is ordered
that the Judgment of the County Court of Putnam be reversed and this cause
remanded back to said court and it is further considered by the court that
the County of Putnam pay all cost herein and that the same be certified
for allowance and it is further ordered by the court that said Defendant
enter into bond and security for his appearance at the next term of the
County Court of Putnam County Whereupon came the Deft together with Allin
Young hereinto open court and acknowledged themselves to owe and stand
indebted to the State of Tennessee in the sum of five hundred Dollars to
wit, the said Deft A. J. Grogan in the sum of two hundred and fifty Dollars and the said Allin Young in the sum of two hundred and fifty Dollars
to be Levied of their proper Goods and chattles Lands and tenements to
the use of the State to be rendered nevertheless to be void if the said
A. J. Grogan shall make his personal appearance before the County court
of Putnam County Term to be holden in the court house in the Town of
Cookeville on the first Monday in September next then and there to answer the State of Tennessee upon a upon a charge of Bastardy (p-269)
and then attend untill Legally Discharged.

State of Tennessee) Presentment for Tipling came the attorney
Vs   ) General for State and the Defendant in proper
George Dillard   ) person and said Deft being arraigned and
) charged upon the presentment in this cause
says he is not guilty in manner and form as therein charged against him
and for his trial puts himself upon the county and the Attorny General
for the State doth the Like whereupon came a Jury of good and Lawful men
to wit, Campbell Bohannon, John Johnson, William Hudgins, John Merrits,
J. W. McDaniel, Samuel McCabel, John West, William H. Barons Jr., Ridly
Draper, Thomas R. Matheny, G. W. Apple and William Gipson who being
Elected tried and sworn the truth to speak upon the issue joined upon
their oath do say that said Deft is not guilty in manner and form in the
presentment as charged against him. It is therefore ordered that the Deft.
be discharged and the state of Tennessee pay all cost on part of the prosecution in this cause Expended and that the same be certified for allowance
as the Law Directs.

J. James C. Officer Adm.   )   Debt Appeal

of W. G. Sims - Decd) There not being time at this term of court
Vs) to try this cause and by consent of the
William Courton) parties by attornys this cause is ordered
) to be continued until the next April Term
of this court.

P-270 Martin Whitton   )   Debt Appeal
            Vs   ) Came the parties by attornies and the mat-
       Jackson Maxwell   ) ters of Law arrising on the motion being
) seen and heard by the court and fully
understood - It is therefore ordered that the motion be Dismissed and that
the Defendant go hense without day and recover against the plaintiff all
cost in this suit and that Execution issue for the collection of the same
& etc.

James Brown   )   Trespass
    Vs   ) By consent of the parties by their attornies
Elizabeth Franklin   ) and there not being time to try this cause
) at this Term of the court the same is con-
tinued untill the next April Term of this court.

State of Tennessee   ) Indictment for an assault with intent
        Vs   ) to commit a Rape Nelly Looper Prosr.
Major, Alias Nig a slave   ) This day W. D. Wright Sheriff of Fen-
) tress County produced and read here
in open court his account for conveying Defendant from Jamestown to
Livingston Jail 28 miles and Back making 56 miles at 10 cents at Feb.
Term. $ 5.65
For Guards Andrew Murphy 56 miles at 6 c pr. mile   3.36
For John G. Simpson 56 mi. at c. per   3.36
For carring Deft from Livingston to Jamestown and back at June
Term making 4 trips at 28 miles each at 10c pr. mile.   11.25
Guard Robt. Murphy the same at 6 c pr. mile.   6.72
Guard Robt. Boles 1 trip 56 miles at 6 cents per mile.   3.36

                    Making in all the sum of $36.90

Which account having been Examined and certified by the attorney General to be correct the same is allowed by the court and ordered to be
Taxed in the Bill of cost in this cause.

State of Tennessee   ) P-271 Indictment for an assault with
       Vs   ) intent to commit a Rape. Nelly Looper
Major Alias Nig a slave   ) Prosr. Came again the attorny General
) for the State and the Defendant Lead
to the bar in custody of the sheriff of Putnam County and on motion and
affidavit the Defendant moved the court for new trial in this cause and
which was overruled by the court whereupon the Defendant by attorney
moved the court in arrest of Judgment which was overruled by the court
and it being demanded of the defendant if he had any thing further to
say why the judgment and sentence of the Law should not be passed upon
him and nothing further being urged. It is therefore considered by the
court that the Defendant for such his offence as found by the Jury in

their verdict be hung by the neck untill he is Dead on the first Monday in October next within one mile of the Town of Cookeville in Putnam County and that the sheriff of Putnam County carry this sentence and Judgment into Execution.

And it is further considered by the court the State of Tennessee pay all cost and part of the prosecution in this cause and that the same be certified to the Treasurer of Tennessee for payment as the Law Directs, and thereupon said Defendant prays an appeal to be held in the city of Nashville on the first Monday of which to him is granted December next and there being no public Jail in the County of Putnam. It is ordered by the court that the sheriff of Putnam County forthwith convey the Defendant and deliver him over to the Jailer of Davidson after the adjournment of this court secured by him in said Jail of said County of Davidson untill his cause is reached for trial and disposed of by said supreme court.

P-272 Ordered that court be adjourned untill tomorrow morning 7 oclock.

Jno. L. Goodall

Saturday Morning August 18th A.D. 1855

Court met pursuant to adjournment - Present the Honorable John L. Goodall Judge presiding.

Nancy Norris) Pet. for Divorce Decree - Be it Remembered
Vs) that this cause came on to be heard before
William R. Norris) the Honorable John L. Goodall Judge and etc.
) on this 18th of August 1855 upon petition
order proconfesso and proof when it appeared to the court that the Defendant had Deserted the petitioner willfully and maliciously and without Just cause for the space and term of more than two years before the filing of the petition of the petitioner and that he failed to provide her with the necessarys of Life - It is therefore ordered adjudged and Decreed by the court that the bonds of matrimony now existing and subsisting between the petitioner and William R. Norris be forever dessolved and that she be restored to all rights and priviledges of a single woman and that the Defendant pay all cost of this suit and that an Execution will issue for the same.

State of Tennessee) Indictment for an assault with intent
Epd. Vs) to commit Rape - Nelly Looper Prosr.
Major Alias Nig a slave) This day James B. Terry produced and
) read here in open court his account
for feeding said Deft at the Term of the Court 5 meals at 25 c.E. $1.25
To feeding shff and 3 men as Guards 5 meals Each at 25 c.E.   4.00
To feeding 1 man as Guard 2 meals 25 c E.   .50

                  Making in all the sum $5.50

P-273 Which account having been Examined and certified by the attorney General to be correct and it appearing to the court that there is no public Jail in Putnam in Putnam County the same is allowed by the court and ordered to be Taxed in the Bill of cost in this cause.

Hezekiah Love   )   Trespass
    Vs   )   Came again the parties by attorneys and came al-
Rily R. Leigue   )   so the same Jury Elected tried and sworn and re-
)   ceived their charge from the Honorable court on
yesterday and upon their oaths do say they find the issue in favor of the
plaintiff and assess his Damage to the sum of two hundred Dollars. It is
therefore considered by the court that the plaintiff Recover against the
Defendant the sum of two hundred Dollars the Damages aforesaid by the jury
aforesaid assessed and also all cost herein and that Execution issue for
the collection of the same.

P-274   State of Tennessee   )   Indictment for A. & B. Randall
            Vs   )   Bright Prosr. - Came the attorney
        James B. Lowrey and   )   General for the State and the Defts.
        G. W. Collier   )   in proper person and there not being
)   time to try this cause at this Term
of this court the same is ordered to be continued until the next term of
court Whereupon came the Defendants together with Joseph Collier herein
to open court and acknowledged themselves to owe and stand indebted to
the State of Tennessee in the sum of seven hundred and fifty Dollars to
wit* The Defendants in the sum of five hundred dollars and the said
Joseph Collier in the sum of two hundred and fifty Dollars to be levied
on their proper Goods and chattles Lands and Tennements to the use of
the State of Tennessee to be remanded nevertheless to be void if the said
James B. Lowery, G. W. Collier make their personal appearance before the
Honorable Judge of the Circuit Court for Putnam County to be holden in
the court house in the Town of Cookeville on the second Monday of December
next then and there to answer the State upon a Bill of Indictment now pending in this court against them and not depart untill Legally Discharged.

William H. Barons Jr.   )   Came the parties by attorneys and
Admr. of Thos. Saylor Decd.   )   there not being time at this Term
    Vs   )   of court to try this case by consent
William H. Baron Sr.   )   of the attornys this cause is ordered
)   to be continued untill the next April
Term of this court.

   This day the Grand Jury returned into court the bill of Indictment to
wit - State against Macky for an assault and Battery Endorsed thereon a
true Bill - William M. Marchbanks foreman of the Grand Jury - State against
Randall Bright for Pettit Larceny (p-275) and State against James
Brooks for keeping a Rowdy house both of which Bills are Endorsed by this
foreman of the Grand Jury also returned into court at the same time the
following presentments to wit - State against D. W. Sims for Tipling and
State against D. W. Sims for Tipling both of which presentments are signed
by the foreman of the Grand Jury and Eleven of the Rest of the Grand Jurors
in our form of Law.

Thomas Bounds and   )   Debt Appeal
Charles Isam   )   Came the parties by their attornys and
    Vs   )   there came a Jury of good and Lawful men
Jesse B. Terry   )   to wit, J. W. McDaniel, John Merit, John

All corn, E. I. Buck, K. D. Ervin, Snowden Matticks, Hezikiah Love, Bird Sexton, Robert Allcorn, Joshua White, Isaac Burton, William Mitchell, who being Elected tried and sworn well and truly to try the matters in controversy Between the parties upon their oaths do say that they find that the Execution in this cause has been paid off - It is therefore considered by the court that the Execution in this cause be quashed and that the Defendant Recover against the plaintiff and Charles Isam his security for the prosecution in this suit all cost here in and that Execution issue &c.

Hezekiah Love) Trespass
Vs) Came the parties by their attornys and a motion
Rily R. Leigue) of Defendant by attorny and for reasons to the
) court shown it is ordered by the court that no
witness on part of the plaintiff in this cause Except S. P. W. Maxwell H. L. Smith (p-276) H. H. McDaniel, J. J. Maxwell, Bird Sexton, R. Helm, J. M. Butler and the Depositions in the cause to be Taxed against the Defendant in the Bill of cost.

State of Tennessee) Indictment for an assault to commit
Vs) a Rape - Nelly Looper Prosr. This
Major, Alias Nig a slave) day Russell Moon produced and read
) here in open court his acct. for feeding said Deft. at this Term of court nine meals at 25¢ Each. $2.25
Two Guards, J. D. Hyder and Henry Whitaker nine meals Each at 25¢ Each meal. 4.50

Making in all the sum of $ 6.75

Which acct. having been Examined and certified by the attorney General to be correct and it appearing to the court that there was no public Jail in Putnam County the same is allowed by the court and ordered to be Taxed in the Bill of cost in this cause.

Benjamin H. Watson) Covenant
Vs) Came the parties by attornies and the Demur
Samuel Madewell) of the plaintiff to the second and fourth plea
) of Defendant came on and after argument it
seems to the court that said second plea is not sufficient in same but Because said Demur reaches the first Error in pleading and it appearing to the court that the covenant in this Deed profered in plaintiffs Declaration is not correctly set fourth in said Declaration and that said Declaration is defective - It is therefore considered by the court that said Demur be sustained to said Declaration and that plaintiff have Leave to amend his Declaration and said demur to defendants fourth plea is over ruled.

The Grand and Traverse Jurors having no further Business to perform at this Term, They are discharged as such.

P-277 State of Tennessee) Indict. for an assault with
Vs) intent to commit a rape.
Major Alias Nig, a slave) Nelly Looper Prosr.

The Defendant by attorney tendered here in open court his Bill of Exceptions which was signed and sealed by the court and ordered to be made a part of the Record in this cause.

State) Indict for Murder 1st Degree - Robt Brown Prose-
Vs) cutor - The Deft by attorny tendered here in open
William Crabtree) court his Bill of Exceptions - which was signed
) and sealed by the court and ordered to be made
a part of the Record in this cause.

Ordered that court be adjourned untill court in course.

Jno. L. Goodall

State of Tennessee -

Pleas at a Circuit Court Began and held for the County of Putnam and State aforesaid in the courthouse in the Town of Cookeville on the second Monday it being the tenth day of December in the year of Our Lord one thousand Eight hundred and fifty five and in Eightith Year of American Independence Present the Honorable John L. Goodall Judge of the fourth Judicial Circuit in the State of Tennessee Presiding etc.

This day Pleasant Bohannon Sheriff of Putnam County Returned here in to open court the States Writ of (p-278) Monday 10th December 1855 venirafacias to him directed from the County Court of Putnam County commanding him to summons the following named person to attend this term of the court as Jurors to wit - J. H. Moon, Mathew S. Smith, Joel Burgess, Dabner Pennington, David Whitaker, Robert Whitaker, George McComick, A. V. Horn, Zachariah Lee, Owen B. Rector, Lewis T. Barons, Carrell Dyer, S. M. McCabel, William Courton, Henderson Tilly, Floyd M. Banks, Carter B. Whitefield, Jefferson Rolin, Jerremiah Coggins, John H. Young, James Carlin, W. W. Cowen, John Collins, Hugh Wallis, Patrick Brady as Jurors and John Jackson and John Carr as constables to attend thereon as court officers came to hand the 6th Sept. 1855 Executed by summoning all the within Jurors Except George McCormick, this the 10th day of December.

P. Bohannon Shff.
R. Dyer D. Shff.

Out of which venirafacias and Jurors aforesaid the court proceeded to Elect, empannell a Grand Jury as the Act of the General Assembly in such case provides when the following named person were drawn and elected to wit - Samiel M. McCaleb, J. H. Moore, John Collins, Dabner Penington, Jefferson Rolin, Carter B. Whitefield, John H. Young, William Courton, Owen B. Rector, W. W. Cowen, Lewis T. Barons, Carrall Dyer, and Joel Burgess whom the court appointed Samiel M. McCaleb foreman of the Grand Jury all of whom are good and lawful men householders or free holders of the County of Putnam who being Elected Empannalled sworn and charged a Jury of Grand Inquest for the State of Tennessee to enquire for the Body of the County of Putnam who retired to their Room to consider of presentments Indictments etc. attended by John Carr a constable sworn to attend thereon.

P-279 Left Out

P-280   Monday 10th December 1855

On affidavit and for reasons to the court shown Henderson Tilly, Robert Whitaker, Jeremiah Coggin, F. M. Banks, George McCormick, James Carlin, and Patrick Brady ordered that they all be released and Discharged from further attendance as Jurors at this court.

Isaac Burton) Appeal
Vs) By consent of parties the cause is ordered to
Thomas Lankister) be continued untill the next Term of this court.

State of Tennessee) Indict for Drunkness on motion of Attorney Gen-
Vs) eral ordered that an Alias Capias issue against
John Watson) said Deft. Directed to the sheriff of White and
) Dekabb Countys returnable.

State of Tennessee) Indictment for A. & B. - John Grider Prosr. Came
Vs) the attorny General for the State and the De-
James Bullington) fendant in proper person and on affidavit of
) Deft. this cause is ordered to be continued un-
till the next Term of this court Whereupon came the Deft together with Henry Bullington herein open court and acknowledged themselves to owe and stand Indebted to the State of Tennessee in the (p-281) sum of Five hundred Dollars to wit the Deft in the sum of two hundred and fifty Dollars and the said Henry Bullington in the sum of two hundred and fifty Dollars to be Levied of their Respective proper goods and chattles Lands and tenements to the use of the State of Tennessee to be rendered nevertheless to be void on condition that said Deft make his personal appearance before the Judge of the Circuit Court of Putnam County to be held in the Court house in the Town of Cookeville on the second Monday in April next then and there answer the State upon the above charge and then and there attend untill Legally discharged.

State of Tennessee) Indictment for A. & B. W. H. Baron Prosecutor.
Vs) Came the attorny General for the State and
Robert Macky) the Defendant in proper person and said Deft.
) being arraigned and charged upon said Indict-
ment says he is guilty as therein charged against Him. It is therefore ordered by the court that for such his offince he pay a fine of ten Dollars and the cost of this prosecution. Whereupon came here into open court William W. Peek and as security for said Deft confessed judgment jointly with said Defendant for said fine & cost this arraigned against said Defendant It is therefore considered by the court that the State of Tennessee Recover against said Deft. and William R. Peek the sum of ten dollars this fine aforesaid and all costs herein and that Execution issue for the collection of the same, etc.

State of Tennessee) Presentment for Tipling - Came the Attorney
Vs) General for the State and the Defendant in
Drury W. Sims) proper person (p-282) and he being ar-
) raigned and charged upon the presentment in

the cause says he is guilty as therein charged against him. It is therefore considered by the court that said defendant for such his offence pay a fine of two Dollars and the cost of his prosecution, whereupon came here into open court James A. Malon and as security for said defendant confessed judgement jointly with said Defendant for said fine and cost this day adjudged against said Deft. It is therefore considered by the court that the State of Tennessee Recover against said Deft and James A. Mahan the sum of Two Dollars the fine aforesaid and all costs herein and that Execution issue for the collection of the same.

State of Tennessee)
Vs)
Drury W. Sims)
)

Presentations for Tipling came the attorney General for the State and the Defendant in proper person and he being arraigned and charged upon the presentiments in the cause and says he is guilty as charged against him. It is therefore considered by the court that said defendant for such his offence pay a fine of Two Dollars and the cost of this prosecution whereupon came here into open court James A. Mahan and as Circuit for said Defendant confessed judgement jointly with said defendant for said fine and cost this day adjudged against him said defendant It is thereupon considerable the court that the State of Tennessee recovered against Deft. and James A. Mahon This sum of Two Dollars the fine aforesaid and all costs herein and that execution issue for collection of the same.

P-283   State of Tennessee)
Vs)
N. J. Prock)
)

Indictment for Drunkenness – Came the attorney General for the State and the said defendant in proper person and he being arraigned and charged upon the said indictments says he is not guilty in manner and form as therein against him is charged and for this trial puts himself upon the County and the attorney puts himself upon the County and the Attorney General for the State doth the like whereupon came a jury of good and Lawful men to wit, Hugh Wallace, David Whitacre, Zachariah Lee, William M. Peek, John Jarred, Elijah Crowell, James Carlin, James Baker, Ruebin Whitson, M. J. Centry, John Grimes and Mathis Smith who being elected tried and sworn the truth to speak upon the issue found upon their oaths do say that the said Deft is guilty as therein charged against him It is therefore considered by the court that said Deft for such his offence pay a fine of Five Dollars and the cost of this prosecution. It is therefore considered by the court that the State of Tennessee recover of the said deft the fine and cost aforesaid and that he be and remain in the custody of the sheriff until the fine and cost is paid or security given for the same.

State of Tennessee)
Vs)
John Bohannon)
)

Presentment for Assault and Battery – Came the attorny Gen. for the State and the defendant in proper person and he being arraigned and charged aforesaid presentments says he is not guilty as therein charged against him and for his trial puts himself upon the mercy of the county and the attorny General for the State doth the Like whereupon came a Jury (p-284) of Good and Lawful men to wit, Bird S. Jones, Absolom Sims, Pleasant M. Hider, William Insor, John M. Amonett, Joseph D. Hyder, John Jackson, James R. Jarr, Ammon Jones, Wilson Wilmoth, John Terry, and Spenser Phillips who being Elected tried and sworn the truth to speak upon the issue of travis Joined upon their oath do say that said defendant is guilty in manner and form as therein charged against him.

Joseph Mitchell) Debt Appeal - On affidavit of plaintiff this
Vs) cause is ordered to be continued until the
A. J. Wallace) next Term of this court upon the payment of
) the cost of this Term by said plaintiff - It
is therefore considered by the court that the Defendant recover against
the plaintiff the cost of this term of the court and that execution issue
for the collection of the same.

Robert Alcorn) Debt Certiorari - Came the parties by their
Vs) attorneys and there came a Jury of Good and
V. W. Anderson) Lawful men to wit: David Whitacre, Zachariah
) Lee, William M. Peek, John Jarred, John Grim
James Baker, Reubin Whitson, M. J. Gentry, Mathew Smith, Charles Crook,
John Earns and William Buckner who having heard all the evidence in
this cause therein and the Honorable charge of the court retired to
considered of their verdict and again returned into court and upon their
oath declare that they could not agree upon a verdict in this cause and
there not being a true this day (p-285) to finish the trial of this
cause - The Jurors were permitted to disperse until the meeting of this
court tomorrow morning.

John and William Richardson) Ejection
Vs) Came the parties by attorney and by
John, Robert and Eward Vaughn) consent this cause is continued
) until next Term of this court.

John Farly) Came the defendants and came along with
Vs) them James Farly and Thomas C. Martin
Jessy and Jefferson Farly) and as security for said defendant
) acknowledged themselves to owe and stand
indebted to the pltff in the sum of Two hundred and fifty Dollars for the
payment of all cost in this suit should the same be adjudged against said
defendant upon a final hearing of the same.

Wiley Knight) Ejectment
Vs) Came the defendant and came along with him Rily
William Bean) Draper, Kirchin Pippin, Vencent M. Terry and Frazier
) Anderson and as security for said defendant acknowledged themselves to owe and stand indebted to said plaintiff in the sum
of Two hundred and fifty Dollars for the payment of all the costs in this
suit should the same be adjudged against said deft upon the final hearing
of the same.

R. D. Allison) Debt motion to condem Land. In the matter of
Vs) this motion the following papers was duly Re-
Drury M. Sims) turned and filed to wit (p-286) Warrant,
John Cadewell) State of Tennessee Putnam County - To the
R. M. Dowell) Sheriff or any constable of said County, I
) hereby command you to summons Drury W. Sims,

John Madewell, and R. H. Dowell to appear before me or some Justice for said County to answer the complaint of R. D. Allison, T. M. McKinny, J. W. McDaniel, J. D. Hyder, and W. H. Barons in a plea of Debt Due by note herein fail not. Given under my hand and seal this 13th day of August 1855.

              Wm. C. Bounds (Seal)

Bounds fee for Wt. 10   J. P. for Putnam County

Endorsed Executed and set for trial before Wm. C. Bounds Esqr. on Saturday the 15th day of August 1855.

              S. Hughes Const.

R. D. Allison and other Vs D. W. Sims and others - I give Judgt. in this case for the plfft against the Defendant for $40.75 on note due the 15th July 1855.

            Wm. C. Bounds J.P.

Execution - State of Tennessee Putnam County - To the sheriff or any constable of said County I hereby command you that of the Goods and chattles Land and Tennements of Drury W. Sims, John Madewell, and Reubin H. Powell, you cause to be made the sum of forty Dollars and seventy five cents Debt with Interest and costs to satisfy a Judgment that R. D. Allison and others Recommend against them before me on the 15th day of August 1855 and pay over as the Law directs this the 29th day of September 1855.

             Wm. C. Bounds (Seal)
             J.P. for Putnam Cty.

Endorsed Judgt the 15th August 1855 for $40.75 on note due the 15th July 1855 (p-287) Const. Hughes for S. Wt. $1.50 - J. P. Bounds for Wt. 10 - Judgt. 25¢ fifa 15 fifa 15¢ W. C. Bounds J.P.

No personal property of the Defendant to be found in my County I levy this fifa on a Tract of Land containing Eight hundred and five acres Bounded by Levi Phillips on the west and Abraham Ford on the East and others Lying in Putnam County in Dist. No. 5 on the head waters of Falling Water Levied on as the property of D. W. Sims this the 29th of Sept. 1855.

             Robison Dyer
             Dept. Sheriff

 All of which being seen and heard by the court on motion is considered by the court that the Land so Levied upon as aforesaid be and the same is hereby condemned and ordered to be sold to satisfy the plaintiffs Debt. and cost and also the cost of this motion and that an order of sale issue.

Thomas T. Pointer)	Debt Motion to condemn Land in the matter
Vs)	of this motion the following papers was
John, C. Boyd, B. Boyd)	duly returned and filed to wit: Warrant
and Josiah Jarred)	State of Tennessee, Putnam County - To
)	the sheriff or any Lawful officer to

Executed and return - I command you to summons John C. Boyd and B. Boyd and Josiah Jarred to be and appear before some other acting Justice of the peace in and for said County to answer the complaint of Thomas Pointer. in a plea of Debt Due by note herein fail not.

Given under my hand and seal this the 6th day of Feby 1855.

Wm. C. Bounds (Seal)
J.P. for Putnam County

Endorsed Executed in full and (p-288) set for trial before M. A. Jarred on the 24th day of Feby. 1855.

R. Dyer D. Shff.

T. T. Pointer Vs J. C. Boyd and B. Boyd and Josiah Jarred - In this case I give Judgment for the plaintiff and against the Defendants for two hundred and twenty four Dollars and fifteen cents and cost for which Execution may issue this 24th of Feby 1855.

M. A. Jarred J.P.

R. Dyer fee $1.50

Execution State of Tennessee Putnam County - To the sheriff or any constable of said County I command you that of the goods and chattles, Lands and Tenements of John C. Boyd, B. Boyd, Josiah Jarred and J. W. Boyd their security for the stay of Execution if to be found in your county you make the sum of Two hundred and twenty four Dollars and fifteen cents with Interest thereon and all cost to satisfy a Judgment that T. T. Pointer Obtained against them before me on the 24th day of Feby. 1855 and pay over the same as the Law directs - this the 30th day of October 1855.

M. A. Jarred (Seal)
J.P. for said County

Endorsed - Judgment $226.15 Interest R. Dyer $1.50 Jarred 40¢ Bounds 10¢ No property of the Defendant to be found in my County I Levy this fifa on a Tract of Land containing one hundred and Eighty acres more or Less Bounded by B. Boyd on the North Josiah Jarred on the South R. Fain, on the west Lying in Putnam County in Dist. No. 11 in Rock Spring Valley Levied on the property of John C. Boyd this the 3rd day of November 1855.

Robison Dyer D. Shff.

(p-289) All of which being seen and heard by the court on motion it is considered by the court that the Land so Levied on as aforesaid be and ordered to be sold to satisfy the plaintiffs Debt and cost and also the costs of this motion that an order of sale issue.

William M. Huddleston) Debt Motion - In the matter of this
to the use of T. T. Pointer) motion the following papers was duly
Vs) returned and filed to wit:
John C. Boyd and others) Warrant, State of Tennessee Putnam
) County - To the sheriff or any lawful officer to Execute and return I command you to summons John C. Boyd Bradford Boyd, Josiah Jarred to be and appear before me or some other Acting Justice of Peace in and for said County to answer the complaint of W. M.

Huddleston to the use of Thomas T. Pointer in a plea of Debt due by note herein fail not.

Given under my hand and seal this 6th day of Feby 1855.

Wm. C. Bounds (Seal)
J.P. for Putnam County

Endorsed Executed in full and returned set for trial before M. A. Jarred on the 24th day of Feby 1855.

R. Dyer D. Shrff.

W. M. Huddleston to use of T. T. Pointer Vs J. C. Boyd, B. Boyd, Josiah Jarred. In this case I give Judgment for the plaintiff and against the Defendant for one hundred and six Dollars and ninety cents and costs for which Execution may issue this Feby the 24th 1855.

M. A. Jarred J.P.

Execution - State of Tennessee Putnam County - To the Sheriff or any constable of said County - I command you that of the (p-290) Goods and Chattles Lands and tenements of John C. Boyd, B. Boyd, and Josiah Jarred J. W. Boyd their security for the stay of Execution if to be found in your county you make the sum of one hundred and six Dollars and ninety cents with Interest thereon and all cost to satisfy a Judgment that W. M. Huddleston obtained against them before in the use of T. T. Pointer on the 24th day of Feby 1855 and pay over the same as the Law directs.

This the 30th of October.

M. A. Jarred (Seal)
J.P. for Putnam County

Endorsed Judgment $106.90 Interest and cost R. Dyer $1.50 Jarred 40 Bounds 10¢.

No personal property of the Defendant to be found in my County - I Levy on a tract of Land containing one hundred and Eighty acres more or Less Bounded by B. Boyd on the north Josiah Jared on the South R. Fain on the West lying in Putnam County in Dist. No. 11 in the Rock Spring Valley Levied on as the property of John C. Boyd this the 3rd day of November 1855.

Roberson Dyer
D. Shff.

All of which being seen and heard by the court on motion it is considered by the court that the Land so Levied on as aforesaid be and the same is hereby condemned and ordered to be sold to satisfy the plaintiffs Debt and cost and also the cost of this motion and that an order of sale issue.

A. J. Grogan)   Debt Motion - In the matter of this motion the
    Vs   )   following papers were duly Returned and filed
G. W. Harper)   to wit:

P-291   Monday December 10th 1855

Warrant State of Tennessee Putnam County – To the sheriff or any constable of said county I command you to summons George Harper to appear before me or some other Justice of Peace of said County to answer the complaint of Andrew J. Grogan of a plea of Trespass on the case for unlawfully Taking and selling two milch cows and a crop of Tobacco Belonging to complainant to his damage fifty Dollars this January the 27th 1855.

                  I. E. Ferrell J. P.
                  for Putnam County (Seal)

Endorsed Executed and set for trial before I. E. Ferrell Esqr. the 1st day Feby 1855 this 29th day of January 1855 – William McDaniel Constable George W. Harper In this case we Give Judgment against Defendant for nineteen Dollars and all Lawful cost.

Feby. the 1st 1855.   I. E. Ferrell J.P.
                  J. W. McDaniel J.P.

Execution State of Tennessee Putnam County – To the sheriff or any constable of said County – I command you that of the Goods and chattles Lands and tenements of George W. Harper if to be found in your County you make the sum of nineteen Dollars with Interest and all cost to satisfy a Judgment that Andrew J. Grogan obtained against him before me on the 1st day of February 1855 for the use of John Hughs and pay over the same as the Law directs this the 18th day of Sept. 1855.

                  I. E. Ferrell J.P.
                  for Putnam Co.

Endorsed Debt $19. Writing Warrant 50¢ Summoning 3 Witnesses 75¢ Wt. issue 10¢ Judgment 25¢. 3 spas. 20¢ Overton Pate 1 day 50¢ Milton D. Stanton 50¢ (p-292) A. M. Boland 50¢ fifa 15¢ Alias 15¢ .

                  I. E. Ferrell J.P.

No personal property found the 20th September 1855 Levied upon for this fifa G. W. Harpers <u>Intrust</u> in a certain Tract of Land where Ellmore Carrington now lives Lying on Martins Creek in Putnam County Bounded by S. Gillum Joseph Shaw and Montgomery this the 20th day of September 1855.

                  William McDaniel Cost.

All of which being seen and heard by the court on motion it is considered by the court that the Land so Levied upon as aforesaid be and the same is hereby condemned and ordered to be sold to satisfy the plaintiffs Debt and cost and also the cost of this motion and that an order of sale issue.

James High	) Debt Motion Condemned Land – In the matter of
Vs	) this motion the following papers were returned
Joseph Johnson	) and filed to wit: Execution, State of Tennessee
	) Jackson County – To the sheriff or any constable

of said County I command you to summons Joseph Johnson to appear before me or some other Justice of said County to answer the complaint of James J. High in a plea of Debt due by note under fifty dollars herein fail not this the 1st day of May 1855.

J. E. Ferrell J. P. for
Putnam County

Endorsed Executed and set for trial before I. E. Ferrell Esqr on the 13th day of May 1854 William McDaniel Const. In this case I Give Judgment against (p-293) Joseph Johnson for Eight Dollars and Eleven cents in favor of J. J. High for which Execution may issue this the 13 day of May 1854.

I. E. Ferrill J.P.

Execution State of Tennessee Putnam County - To the Sheriff or any constable of said County I command you that of the goods and chattles Lands and Tenements of Joseph Johnson if it be found in your county you make the sum of Eight Dollars and Eleven cents with Interest and all cost to satisfy a Judgment that James J. High obtained a against him the said Joseph Johnson on the 13th day of May 1854 and pay over the same as the Law directs this 14th day of August 1854.

I. E. Ferrell Justice of
the peace said County.

Endorsed Debt $8.10 warrant 50¢ Justice for 50 cents.

No personal property to be found Levied upon for fifa a Tract of Land Lying in Putnam County Tennessee on the walton Road as the property of Joseph Johnson supposed to be two hundred acres on the East by the Land of Hughs on the North Whitefield on the West by Wm. Ensor on the South by Bransford Boyd this the 14th day of August 1854.

William McDaniel Const.

All of which being seen and heard by the court on motion it is considered by the court that the Land so Levied on as aforesaid be and the same is hereby condemned and ordered to be sold to satisfy to the plaintiff Debt and cost and also the costs of this motion and that an order of sale issue.

P-294   John Shoat to the use of   )   Debt Motion condemn Land.
        S. D. Burton and D. W. Haws   )   In the matter of this motion
                    Vs   )   the following papers were
        Daniel Kirby   )   duly returned and filed to
)   Wit:

State of Tennessee Putnam County - To the sheriff or any constable of said County - I command you to summons Daniel Kirby to appear before me or some other Justice of said County to answer the complaint of John Shoat to the use of S. D. Burton and D. W. Haws in a plea of Debt Due by note in a sum under one hundred Dollars herein fail not under the penalty prescribed by Law.

Given under my hand and seal this the 13th day of Feby 1855.

E. L. Thompson (Seal)
J.P. for P. County

Endorsed Judgment by confession before E. L. Thompson on the 24th of Feby 1855 for $90.30 Staid by J. B. Terry.

John Shoat against Kirby I give Judgment in this case for the plaintiff and against the Defendant $90 Dollars and 30 cents and cost of suit to the use S. D. Burton and D. W. Haws for which Execution may issue this 24th day of Feby 1855.

E. L. Thompson J.P.

Execution State of Tennessee Putnam County – To the Sheriff or any constable of said County – I command you that of the Goods and chattles Lands and tenements of Daniel Kirly and J. B. Terry his security if it to be found in your county you make the sum of ninety Dollars and thirty cents which Interest and all Lawful cost to satisfy a Judgment that S. D. Burton and D. W. Haws obtained against him before me on the 24th of February 1855 (p-295) and pay over the same as the Law Directs this the 30th day of October 1855.

E. L. Thompson J.P.
for Putnam County

Endorsed amount of Debt up to time of rendering Judgment $90.30 Thompson for warrant Judgment fifa 50¢.

E. L. Thompson J.P.

Came to hand the same day issued Returned no property to be found in my County Levied on a certain Tract of Land of Daniel Kirby where Benjamin Gabbard now lives adjoining the Land of Esqr. Thompson and Hampton Ramsey supposed to be one hundred acres more or Less in Dist. No. 1st Putnam County Tennessee this the 30th of October.

James B. Terry Const.

All of which being seen and heard by the court on motion it is considered by the court that the Land so Levied on as aforesaid be and the same is hereby condemned and ordered to be sold to satisfy the plaintiff Debt and costs and the costs of this motion and that an order of sale issue.

This day the Grand Jury Returned into courts Bill of Indictment of the State against John Cates and Hickman Whitaker for an affray – Endorsed thereon by the foreman a True Bill also a presentment against Joseph Brown for an assault and Battery Endorsed thereon by the foreman of the Grand Jury and all the Rest of the Grand Jurors in due form and again retired to consider of presentments Indictments etc.

Samuel Maxwell)   Debt Appeal
Vs   )   Came the parties by their (p-296) and on motion
Alexander Boyd)   and affidavit of the Defendant and it is ordered by
)   the court that the plaintiff give security for the
prosecution of this suit on or before the calling of the same for trial or the same shall stand dismissed.

Patty Medly by his) Debt Cert. — Came the Defendant
next friend George Medly) by his attorney and the plaintiff
by his next friend Patty Medly) being solemnly called to come into
) court and prosecute her suit came
not It is therefore considered by the court that the Defendant go hence
and Recover against the plaintiff all costs herein and that Executor issue for collection of the same.

Ordered that court adjourn untill tomorrow morning, 8 oclock.

                  Jno. L. Goodall

Tuesday Morning December 11th A. D. 1855

Court met persuant to adjournment Prest. the the Honorable John L. Goodall Judge Presiding and etc.

Samuel Maxwell) Debt Appeal
 Vs) Came the Defendant by his attorney and the plain-
Alexander Boyd) tiff being solemnly called to come in to court
) and prosecute his suit, came not It is therefore
considered by the court that the Defendant go hence and Recover against the plaintiff all cost herein and that Execution issue.

P-297 Margret Irwin) Debt Cert.
   Vs) Plaintiff by attorney moved the court to
  John B. Pointer) Dismiss the petition in this cause.

G. W. Puckett) Debt Motion to condemn Land in the matter of
 Vs) this motion the following papers were duly re-
G. W. Crabtree) turned and filed to wit,

Warrant State of Tennessee Putnam County — To the sheriff or any constable of said County I command you to summons G. W. Crabtree to appear before me or some other Justice of said County to answer the complaint of G. W. Pucket in a plea of Debt in a sum under three hundred Dollars.

Given under my hand and seal this Sept. 19th 1855.

                 M. A. Jarred (Seal)
                 J.P. for said County

Endorsed Executed and set for trial before E. C. Crowell Esqr. on the 6th day of October 1855.
                 A. Boyd Const.

Judgment in favor of the plaintiff and against the Defendant for four Dollars and 62 cents with all lawful Interest and cost for which Execution may issue this 6th Oct. 1855.
                 E. C. Crowell J.P.

174

Execution State of Tennessee Putnam County - To the Sheriff or any constable of said County I command you that of the Goods and chattles Lands and Tenements of G. W. Crabtree if to be found in your County you make the sum of four Dollars and fifty two cents principle with all Lawful Interest and cost to satisfy a Judgment that G. W. Pucket obtained against him before me on the 6th day (p-298) of October 1855 collect and pay over as the Law directs.

Given under my hand and seal this 23rd of October 1855.

            E. C. Crowell (Seal)
            J. P. for Putnam County

Endorsed Debt $4.52 J. P. Crowel 40 Jarred 10.

No Goods and chattles to be found in my County Levied upon a tract of Land of the Defendants Lying in Putnam Count in Dist. No. 13 adjoining the lands of Joseph Roberts Decd. and others and said to contain one hundred and twenty five acres this 16th of November 1855.

            A. Boyd Const.

All of which being seen and heard by to court on motion it is considered by the court that the Land so Levied upon as aforesaid be and the same is hereby condemned and ordered to be sold to satisfy the plaintiffs Debt and cost and also the cost of this motion and that an order of sale issue.

Abraham Sutton   )   Appeal
 Vs   ) Came the Deft by his attorny and the plain-
William Whitefield) tiff being solemnly called to come into court
) and prosecute his suit came not - It is there-
fore considered by the court that the Defendant go hence and recover of the plaintiff all cost herein and that Execution issue.

Josiah Brown   )   Debt Appeal
 Vs   ) Came the plaintiff by attorny and Entered a
William Rodgers) note (p-279) prosequi in this cause a-
James Julin   ) gainst James Julin one of the above named
) Defendants - It is therefore considered by
the court that the Deft go hence and Recover against the plaintiff all cost in this suit incident to making him a Deft in this cause and that Execution issue.

Josiah Brown   )   Debt Appeal
 Vs   ) Came the parties by their attornys and the plain-
William Rodgers) tiff by attorny agrees to take a non suit in
) this cause . It is therefore considered by the
court that the Deft go hence and Recover against the plaintiff all costs herein and the Execution issue.

State   ) Prest for A & B - Came the attorney General for the
Vs   ) State and the Deft - Whereupon it is considered by
John Bohannon) the court that the Deft who was tried upon the
) above charge and yesterday pay a fine of one Dollar
and the cost of this prosecution. It is therefore considered by the court
that the State Recover against said Deft the fine and costs aforesaid and
the Execution issue etc.

State   ) Indictment for Drunkness John Grider Prosecutor.
Vs   ) Came the attorney General for the State and the De-
N. I. Brook) fendant in proper person - Whereupon came herein
) to open court Thomas Anderson, Edward Anderson,
Jefferson Roland, and Edward McGuffy (p-300) and as security for said
Defendant confessed Judgment Jointly with said Deft for the sum of five
Dollars the fine and the cost adjudged against said Deft on yesterday. It
is therefore considered by the court that the State Recover against said
Deft and the above named securitys the sum of five Dollars the five afore-
said and also all cost herein and that Execution issue.

James H. Smith and   ) Ejectment - Came the parties
E. L. Smith and M. E. J. Smith) and the plaintiff security hav-
J. R. Smith and A. S. Smith) ing filed his notice that he
N. I. A. Smith and J. K. Smith) would not stand as plaintiffs
the last five minors by   ) security and the plaintiff fail-
their Guardian I. H. Smith   ) ing to give other security It
Vs   ) Is ordered by the court that
James McDaniel and C. F. Burton) the same be Dismissed for want
) of security. It is therefore
considered by the court that the Defendant go hence and Recover against
the plaintiff and Gideon Smith, E. Lewis, S. P. Maxwell, their securities
all cost herein and that Execution issue.

State   ) Indict. for A. & B. Randal Bright Prosr.
Vs   ) Came Attorny General for the State and the Deft
J. B. Lowery &) by attorny moved the court to Quash the Indict-
G. W. Collier) ment in this cause which was overruled by the
) court.

State of Tennessee   ) Indictment for A. & B. Randal
Vs   ) Bright Prosecutor - (p-301)
James B. Lowery & G. W. Collier) Came the attorny General for
) the State and the Defendant in
) proper person and said Defendant
being arraigned and charged upon the Indictment says they are not guilty
as therein charged against them and for their trial puts themselves upon
the County and the attorny General for the State doth the Like. Whereupon came a Jury of Good and Lawful men to wit, Hugh Wallis, Hampton Ramsey, W. H. Barons, Austin Shoat, D. W. Sims, Joshua White, James Mahan,
Jesse Farly, John Haws, James W. McDaniel, J. C. Clinton, and Jefferson
Cole who being Elected tried and sworn the truth to speak upon the issue
of Traverse Joined upon their oaths do say that said Defendants is Guilty
in manner and form as therein charged against them. It is therefore considered by the court that said Defendants for such their offence pay a
fine of Ten Dollars and cost of this prosecution. It is therefore considered by the court that the State of Tennessee Recover against said

Defendants the sum of Ten Dollars the fine aforesaid and all costs here in and that Execution issue whereupon the Defendants moved the court for a new trial in this cause which was overruled by the court whereupon the Defendants moved the court in arrest of Judgment which was overruled by the court from which opinion of the court the Deft prays an appeal in the nature of a writ of Error to the next Term of the supreme Court of the State of Tennessee to be held in Nashville Tennessee to be held on the first Monday in December 1856, which to them is Granted Whereupon the Defendants tendered herein open (p-302) court their Bill of Exceptions which was signed and sealed by the court and ordered to be made a part of the Record in this cause.

Whereupon came the Defendants together with Thomas B. Murry and Isaac Lollar here in open court and acknowledged themselves to owe and stand Indebted to the State of Tennessee in the sum of five hundred Dollars to wit, the Defendant in the sum of Two hundred and fifty Dollars and the said Thomas B. Murry and Isaac Lollar in the sum of two hundred and fifty Dollars to be Levied of their Respective Goods and chattles Lands and Tenements to the use of the State of Ten. to be rendered nevertheless to be void on condition that said Defendants make their personal appearance before the Judge of the Circuit Court for Putnam County to be held in the Court house in the Town of Cookeville Tennessee on the Second Monday of April 1857 then and there to abide by and perform the Judgment of Supreme Court of the of the State of Tennessee in the above cause and then and there attend untill Legally discharged.

Robert Allcorn)   Debt Cert. Came again the parties by their at-
Vs   )   torneys and came also the same Jury Elected tried
V. W. Anderson)   and sworn in this cause on yesterday and upon
)   their oaths do say that said Defendant is guilty
of swearing three profane oaths. It is therefore considered by the court that (p-303) the plaintiff recover against the Defendant the sum of ninety three and three Quarters cents the amount of the amount of penalty made and approved and also all costs herein and that Execution issue.

Hezekiah Love)   Motion to correct Taxation of cost. On motion
Vs   )   of the Deft by his attorny it is ordered by the
R. R. Leigue)   court that the clerk of this court notify Bird
)   S. Jones a witness on behalf of the Deft to
appear here at the next Term of this court to have his cost corrected in the above suit.

J. A. Rhea   )   Debt Motion to condemn Land in the matter of this
Vs   )   motion the following papers was Duly returned and
R. H. Dowell)   filed to wit - Warrant State of Tennessee Putnam
)   County to the Sheriff or any constable of said
County - I command you to summons R. H. Dowell to appear before me or some other Justice of said County to answer Rhea and Burton now to the use of J. A. Rhea in a plea of Debt for a sum under one hundred and seventy five Dollars - This 31st of October 1855.

                                                     R. D. Allison J. P.
(Seal)   for said County.

In the above case I give Judgment in favor of the plaintiff for one hundred and forty six Dollars and 45 cents this the 4 day of November 1854.

R. D. Allison J.P.

Executed and set for trial on the 4th of November 1854 before R. D. Allison Esquire my fee 50¢ .

J. M. Carr Const.

P-304   Tuesday December 11th 1855

Execution State of Tennessee Putnam County - To the Sheriff or any constable for said County - I command you that of the Goods and chattles Lands and Tenements of R. H. Dowell principle and Elias Green Stayor if to be found in your County - you make the sum of one hundred and forty six Dollars and 45 cents with Interest and cost to satisfy a Judgment that Rhea and Barton Recovered against R. H. Dowell to the use of J. A. Rhea before me on the 4th day of November 1854 and pay over the same as the Law Directs.

August the 27th 1855.   R. D. Allison   (Seal)
J. P. for sd. County

Indorsed Rhea and Burton to the use of J. A. Rhea Vs R. H. Dowell and Elias Green Debt $146.45 Wt. 10 serving warrant 50 Judgment 25 fifa 15.

No Goods and chattles found in my County - Levied upon one Tract of Land of the Defendants Lying in Putnam County Dist. No. 7 adjoining the Land of pff. Dyer and Simeon Greens on the North and on the East by Byers on the South Mark Mathews on the West R. F. Cooke on the South - One hundred acres this the 18th day of September 1855 J. M. Carr Const.

All of which being seen and heard by the court that the Land so Levied upon as aforesaid be and the same is hereby condemned and ordered to be sold to satisfy the pltff debt and cost and also the cost of this motion.

P-305   J. A. Ray   )   Debt Motion to condemn Land - The matter of
            Vs   )   this motion the following papers were re-
         R. H. Dowel   )   turned and duly filed to wit,

Warrant - State of Tennessee   )   To any Lawful officer of said County
           Putnam County   )   I command you to summons R. H. Dowel
)   to appear before me or some other Justice of said court to answer Ray and Burton now to the use of J. A. Ray in a plea of debt due of a sum of one Hundred Dollars this 31st day of October 1854 R. D. Allison J. P.

Putnam County - In this case I gave Judgment in favor of the plaintiff for seventy three Dollars and fifty one cents this 4th day November 1854.

R. D. Allison J. P.

Executed on and set for trial on the 4th Nov. 1855 before R. D. Allison Esqr. J. W. Carr Constable.

Execution-State of Tennessee) To the sheriff or any constable
Putnam County) of said County - I command out of
) the goods and chattles Lands and
Tenements if to be found in your county of R. H. Dowell principle and Elias Green stayor you make the sum of seventy three Dollars and 37 cents and the interest and cost to satisfy a Judgment that Ray & Burton recover against R. H. Dowell before me on the 4th day of November 1854 to the use J. A. Ray and pay over the same as the Law directs this 27th day of August 1855. R. D. Allison J. P. for Putnam Endorsed No. goods and chattles to be found in my County Levied upon a tract of Land of the defendants Lying in Putnam County in Dis. No. 7 adjoining the Land of I. A. Dyer and Simeon Green on the west by R. F. Cooke Estimated to contain one Hundred acres this 18th day of September 1855 my fee 50 J. W. Carr Const. Received on this fifa Ten Dollars 75/100 this 15th Sept. 1855.

P-306 Tuesday Dec. 11th 1855

All of which being seen and heard by the court on motion it is considered by the court that the Land so Levied upon as aforesaid be and the same is hereby condemned and ordered to be sold to satisfy the pltffs. debt and cost and also the cost of this motion and that an order of sale issue.

James D. Haws) Debt Motion to condemn Land In the matter of of
Vs) this motion the following papers were filed to
R. H. Dowel) wit:
Warrant State of Tennessee) To the Sher-
Jackson County) iff or any
) constable of
said County - I command you to summons R. H. Dowell to appear before me or some other Justice of said County to answer the complaint of James D. Haws in a plea of Debt due by acct a sum under Fifty Dollars this 10th July 1853.

John Terry (Seal) J.P.
for Jackson County

Endorsed Executed and set for trial the 30th July 1853 before John Grim at his house J. H. Moon Constable.

James D. Haws & Co. Vs R. H. Dowell - I give Judgment in this case for the plff against the deft for forty six Dollars and fifty seven cents and all costs for which Execution may issue this 30th July 1853.

John Grim (Seal) J.P.

Execution

State of Tennessee - Putnam County; to the Sheriff or any constable of said County - I command you of the goods and chattles Lands and Tenements of R. H. Dowel and George Swaringin his security for the stay of Execution if to be found in your county you make the sum of forty six Dollars and 57/100 with interest and all Lawful cost to satisfy a Judgment that James & Haws (p-307) obtained against them before John Grimm Esqr. on the 30th July 1853 and pay over the sum as the Law directs this 27th August 1855.

R. D. Allison J. P.
for Putnam County

Endorsed Judgment 30th July 1853 for $46 and 57 cents Received on this fifa Ten Dollars on the 19th Sept 1855 - No goods and chattles to be found in my County Levied upon a tract of Land of the Deft Lying in Putnam County in Dist. No. 7 adjoining the Land of Willis Pippin heirs on the north and on the East by Robert Judd and on the south by George Swaringin on the west by Jeffer Dyers and said to contain about one Hundred acres - This 18th Sept. 1855. My fee 50 ct. J. W. Carr constable all of which being seen and heard by the court on motion it is considered by the court that the Land be Levied upon as aforesaid be and the same is hereby considered and ordered to be sold to satisfy the debt and cost and also the cost of this motion and that an order of sale issue.

State	)	The grand Jury returned a bill of indictment against
Vs	)	the deft for assault and Battery Endorsed by their
Eliza Kinton	)	foreman a true Bill ordered that capias issue.

State	)	Presentments for Tipling - Ordered by court that
Vs	)	one Dollar in Each case disposed of at this Court
D. W. Sims	)	of the State against Deft.

Ordered that court be adjourned untill court in course.

John L. Goodall

p-308   State of Tennessee, Putnam County to wit- At a circuit Court of the fourth Judicial Circuit began and held in and for the County aforesaid at the court house in the town of Cookeville on the second Monday and it being the 14th day of April in the year of Our Lord Eighteen hundred and fifty six and of American Independance the 80th year Present the Honorable John L. Goodall Judge Presiding.

This day Pleasant Bohanon Sheriff, Returned into court a Writ of Venire Facias Delivered to him by the Clerk of the County Court of Putnam County showing that at the January Term thereof 1856 it being the first court held in this County after the Last term of this court. Said court had appointed the following persons being good and Lawful men of said County to serve as Jurors at the present Term of this court to wit: J. L. H. Huddleston, Daniel W. Hawes, Curtis Terry, David Nicholas, Thomas Bullock, Dudly Hunter, John Bohannon, Samuel Miller, Frank Goolsby, Henry Netherton, William Rippetoe, M. J. Gentry, Jesse Farley, William P. Campbell, Hezekiah Love, Thomas Scudder, Thomas J. Shaw, Kely Julien, Joseph Jarred, L. H. Draper, Ephraim Elrod, John Baulkman, Purteman Jones, Henry Roberts, Abraham Sims, Samuel Holliway, as Jurors Samuel Hughs and Jacob H. Henry as court officers to attend thereon - who being summonsed by the sheriff and the court proceeded to elect and empannelled a grand Jury when were Elected the said Joseph Jarred, Ephraim Elrod, Samuel Holliway, Thomas Bullock, Daniel W. Hawes, John Bohannon, Jesse Farley, J. L. H. Huddleston, Abraham Sims, Dudly Hunter, Prettiman Jones, David Nicholas and all good and lawful men out of whom the court appointed the said Daniel W. Hawes foreman and the said Grand Jury being empannelled sworn and charged to inquire for the body of the court aforesaid Retired to consider   (p-309)   of presentments and Indictments by Samuel Hughes a constable sworn to attend thereon.

C. F. Burton   )   Debt Motion to condemn Land – the following papers
Vs   )   to wit – Warrant State of Tennessee Putnam County
G. Anderson   )   to the sheriff or any constable of the County – I
J. Bartlett   )   command you to summons Gallant Anderson, Joshua
)   Bartlett to appear before me or some other Justice
of peace for said County to answer call to the use of F. C. Burton in the
place of Debt due by note under fifty dollars herein fail not.

Given under my hand and seal this 23 of January 1856.

J. W. McDaniel J.P.
for Putnam County

Endorsed thereon to wit – Executed and set for trial before R. G. Duke
Esqr. on the 21 day of February 1856.

A. Boyd Const.

Robert Hall Vs Gallant Anderson Joshua Bartlett to the use and benefit
of C. F. Burton I give Judgment in favor of the plaintiff for the sum of
twenty Dollars 60 cents and cost for which Execution may issue the 20
February 1855.

R. G. Duke J. P.

Execution State of Tennessee – Putnam County to the sheriff or constable
said County – I command you as I have heretofore of the goods and chattles
Lands and tenements of Gallant Anderson and Joshua Bartlett if to be found
in your County you make the sum of twenty Dollars and 60 cents and cost
amt. to sattisfy a Judgment that Robert Hale obtain against him to the
use of C. F. Burton before me on the second day of February 1856 and pay
over the sum as the Law Directs this 12 day of April 1856.

R. G. Duke J. P.

P-310   Levy finding no propperty to satisfy this Execution Levied on one
tract of land lying ___ Putnam County District No. 13 and with Lands of
E. Anderson and James Isbelle and Bird S. Jones and Hugh Wallace this the
13 April at 9 oclock, 1856.

A. Boyd Constable

All of which being seen and hereby the court on motion it is considered
by the court that the Land so Levied upon as aforesaid be and the same
is hereby condemned and ordered to be sold to sattisfy the plaintiff Debt
and cost also the cost of this motion and that an order of sale issue.

Edward Anderson   )   Debt Motion to condemn Land The following paper
Vs   )   to wit Warrant –
Gallant Anderson)   State of Tennessee Putnam County to the Sheriff
)   or any constable of said County – I command
you to summons Gallant Anderson to appear before me or some other Justice
of the peace for said County to answer the complaint of Edward Anderson
in a plea of Debt Due by note for the sum under fifty dollars herein fail
not.

Given under my hand and seal this the 9 day of April 1856.

R. G. Duke J.P.

Endorsed thereon to wit; for said County.

Acknowledged by Deft. E Anderson Vs G. Anderson - I give Judgment for the plaintiff and against for the sum of Eight Dollars and 75¢ and cost for which Execution may issue this 9 April 1856.

R. G. Duke J. P.

P-311   Execution State of Tennessee) To the sheriff or any constable of said County -
Putnam County) I command you of the goods and chattles Lands and tenements of Gallant Anderson if to be found in your County - You make the sum of Eight Dollars and 75¢ to sattisfy a Judgment Eward Anderson that I obtained against him before me on the 9 day of April 1856 and pay over to the same as the Law Directs this 12 day of April 1856.

R. G. Duke (Seal)
J. P. for Putnam County.

No good and chattles to be found in my County Levied upon a tract of Land of the Deft Lying in Putnam County Dist. No. 13 adjoining the Lands of Hugh Wallace on the East the Lands of P. S. Jones and James Isabell on the south Edward Anderson Lands on the west and north and said to contain two hundred acres more or less tenth day of April 1856.

C. Smith Const.

All of which being seen and heard by the court on motion it is considered by the court that the Land so Levied upon as aforesaid be and the same is hereby condemned and ordered to be sold to satisfy the plaintiff Debt cost and also the cost of motion and that order of sale issue.

C. F. Burton to the use of) Debt motion to consider Land the following papers were filed to wit-
E. Anderson) Warrant -
Vs) State of Tennessee) To the Sheriff
Gallant Anderson) Putnam County) or any constable of said County I command you (p-312) to summons Gallant Anderson to appear before me or some other Justice for said County to answer the complaint of C. F. Burton to the use and benefit Edward Anderson in a plea of Debt Due by note for a sum under five Hundred Dollars herein fail not.
Given under my hand and seal this 8 day of April 1856.

R. G. Duke (Seal)
J. P. for Putnam County

Endorsed hereon to wit -

Executed and set for trial on the 9th day of April 1856 before R. G. Duke Esqr. at his house this 9th day of April 1856.

C. Smith Const.

C. F. Burton Vs Gallant Anderson for the use of E. Anderson - I give Judgment for the plaintiff and against the Deft for the sum of one hundred and twelve and 76¢ and cost of suit for which Execution may issue this the 9th April 1856.

                         R. G. Duke (Seal)
                         J.P.

State of Tennessee) To the sheriff or any constable I command you
Putnam County) of the goods and chattels Lands and tenements
) of Gallant Anderson if to be found in your County you make the sum one hundred and twelve dollars and 75¢ and cost of suit to satisfy a Judgment that C. F. Burton obtained against him before me on the 9th April 1856 to the use of Edward Anderson and pay over the sum as the Law directs.

This 12th day of April 1856.   R. G. Duke (Seal)
                                     J.P. for Putnam County

P-313 Levy no goods and chattels to be found in County Levied upon a tract of Land of the Defts Lying in Putnam County in District No. 13 adjoining the Lands of Hughs on the East the Lands of B. S. Jones and James Isabell on the south the Lands of Edward Anderson on the west and north and said to contain two hundred acres more or less this the 12 day of April 1856.
                                          C. Smith Const.

All of which being seen and heard by the court on motion it is considered by the court that the Land so Levied upon as aforesaid be and the same is hereby condemned and ordered to be sold to satisfy the plaintiffs debt and cost and also the cost of this motion and that an order of sale issue.

Edward Anderson) Debt Motion to condemn Land - In this cause
       Vs) the following papers were filed to wit -
Gallant Anderson) Warrant -
                        State of Tennessee) To the Sheriff or
                        Putnam County) any constable for
) said County - I command you to summons Gallant Anderson to appear before me or some other Justice for said County to answer the complaint of Edward Anderson intered in a plea of Debt Due by note for a sum under one dollar herein fail not.

Given under my hand and seal this 9th day of April 1856.

                                      R. G. Duke (Seal)
                                      J. P. for Putnam County

Endorsed hereon to wit -

Acknowledged by the Defendant E. Anderson Vs Gallant Anderson (p-314) as true I give Judgment for plaintiff against the Defendant for a sum of forty two Dollars and 67 cents and cost for which Execution may this 9th of April.
                                            R. G. Duke J. P.

Execution

State of Tennessee) To the Sheriff or any constable for said
Putnam County) County I command you of the goods and chat-
) tles Lands and Tenements of Gallant Anderson
if to be found in your county you make the sum of forty two Dollars and
67 cents and cost of suit to satisfy a Judgment that Edward Anderson obtained against him before me on the 9 day of April 1856 and pay over the
sum as the Law Directs this 12 day of April 1856.

             R. G. Duke (Seal)
             J.P. for Putnam Co.

Endorsed hereon to wit - No goods and chattles to be found in my County
Levied on a tract of Land of the Defendant Lying in Putnam County in Dist.
No. 13 adjoining the Lands of Hugh Wallace on the East the Lands of B. S.
Jones and James Isabell on the south and the Land of Edward Anderson on
the west and north and said to contain two hundred acres more or less.
This the 12 day of April 1856.

             C. Smith Const.

 All of which being seen and heard by the court on motion it is considered by the court that the Land so Levied upon as aforesaid be and the
sum is hereby condemned and ordered to be sold to sattisfy the plaintiff
Debt and cost and also the cost of this motion and that an order of sale
issue.

P-315 Edward Anderson) Debt motion to condemn Land in this
    Vs   ) court - The following papers were
   Gallant Anderson) filed to wit: Warrant.

State of Tennessee) To the sheriff or any constable of the
Putnam County   ) County I command you to summons Gallant
) Anderson to appear before me or some
other Justice of the peace for said County to answer the complaint of Ed-
ward Anderson in a plea of Debt Due by note for a sum under five hundred
Dollars herein fail not - Given under my hand an seal this 8th day of
April 1856.

             R. G. Duke (Seal) J.P.
             for the County

Endorsed thereon to wit: Executed and set for on the 9th day of April
1856 before R. H. Duke Esqr. at his home this the 9th day of April 1856.

             C. Smith Const.

Edward Anderson Vs Gallant Anderson - I give Judgment for the plaintiff
against the Deft for the sum one one hundred and Eighty seven Dollars and
9¢ and cost of suit for which Execution may this _____ 9th April 1856.

             R. G. Duke J.P.

Execution

State of Tennessee)   To the Sheriff or any counstable for this County
Putnam County   )   I command you that of goods and chattles, Lands
)   and tenements of Gallant Anderson if to be
found in your County you make the sum of one hundred Eighty seven dollars
8 cents to settle by a payment that Edward Anderson obtained against him
before me on the 9th day of April 1856, (p-316) and pay over the sum
as the Law Directs this the 12 day of April 1856.

                                                                        R. Duke J. P. for
                                                                        said County

Endorsed thereon to wit for said County - No goods and chattles of the
Deft to be found in my County Levied upon a tract of Land of the Defts
Lying in Putnam County Dist. No. 13 adjoining the Lands of Hugh Wallace
on the East the Lands of B. S. Jones and James Isabell on the south and
the Lands of Edward Anderson on the west and north and said to contain
two hundred acres more or less this 12th day of April 1856.

                                                                        C. Smith Const.

All of which being seen and heard by the court on the motion it is considered by the court that the Land so Levied on as aforesaid be and the
same is hereby condemned and ordered to be sold to sattisfy the plaintiffs
Debt and cost also the cost of this motion and that an order of sale issue.

Sarah Richardson to the   )   Debt motion to condemn Land the follow-
use of Edward Anderson   )   ing papers were filed to wit.
         Vs   )   Warrant - State of Tennecsee   )   To the
Gallant Anderson   )   Putnam County   )   Sheriff
)   or any
constable of said County - I command you to summons Gallant Anderson to ap-
pear before me or some other Justice of the peace for said County to answer
Edward Anderson of a plea of Debt Due by note for a sum under one hundred
dollars herein fail not - Given under my hand and seal This the 8th day of
April 1856.

                                                                        R. G. Duke J. P.

Endorsed herein to wit, Executed and set for trial on the 9th day of April
1856 before R. G. Duke Esqr. at his home this the 9th April 1856.

                                                                     R.C. Smith Constable

Sarah Richardson Vs Gallant Anderson to the use of E. Anderson - I give
Judgment for the plaintiff against the Deft for the sum of sixty nine dollars and 37 cents and cost, for which Execution may issue this 9 of April
1856.
                                                                     R. G. Duke

Execution

State of Tennessee   )   To the sheriff or any constable of said County
Putnam County   )   I command you of the goods and chattles Lands
)   and tenements of Gallant Anderson if to be
found in your county you make the sum of sixty nine dollars and 37 cents

to sattisfy a Judgment that Sarah Richardson obtained against him to the ____ and benefit of E. Anderson before me on the 9th day of April 1856 and pay over the sum as the Law Directs.

This 12th April 1856.   R. G. Duke (Seal) J. P. for
                                     this County.

Endorsed thereon to wit- No goods and chattles to be found in my County Levied upon a tract of Land of the Defts Lying in Putnam County in Dist. No. 13 adjoining the Lands of Hugh Wallace on the East the lands of B. S. Jones and James Isabell on the south and the Lands of E. Anderson on the west and north said to contain two Hundred acres more or less this the 12th April 1856.
                                     Charles Smith Constable

P-318 All of which being seen and heard by the court on motion it is considered by the court that the Land so Levied upon as aforesaid be and the same is hereby condemned and ordered to be sold to sattisfy the plaintiffs Debt and cost and also the cost of this motion and that an order of sale issue.

S. M. and T. J. Madax to) Debt Motion to condemn Land in this
use of E. Anderson   ) case the following papers were filed
Vs   ) to wit - Warrant.
Gallant Anderson   ) State of Tennessee   ) To the Sher-
                           Putnam County   ) iff or any
) constable
of said County I command you to summons Gallant Anderson to appear before me or some other Justice of said County to answer the complaint of S. M. and T. J. Madax to the use and benefit of Edward Anderson in a plea Debt Due by note for a sum under one hundred dollars herein fail not.

Given under my hand and seal this 9th April 1856.

                                     R. G. Duke J. P.
                                     for said County

Endorsed herein to wit:
Executed and set for trial on the 9 of April 1856 before R. G. Duke Esqr. at this house this the 9 day of April 1856.
                                     C. Smith Constable

                        Judgment

S. H. and T. J. Madax Vs G. Anderson to the use of E. Anderson give Judgment for the plaintiff and against the Deft for the sum of fifty dollars and (p-319) 3 cents of suit for which Execution may issue this the 9th of April 1856.
                                     R. G. Duke J.P.

Execution

State of Tennessee) To the sheriff or any constable of said County
Putnam County   ) I command you that of the goods and chattles
) Lands and tenements of Gallant Anderson if to
be found in your county you make the sum of fifty three Dollars 3 cents

and cost of suit to sattisfy a Judgment that S. H. and T. J. Madux obtained against him to the use and benefit of E. Anderson before me on the 9th of April 1856 and pay over same as the Law directs. This 12th day of April 1856.

                R. G. Duke (Seal)
                J.P. for said County

No goods and chattles to be found in my county Levied upon a tract of Land of the Defts Lying in Putnam County in Dist. No. 13 adjoining the Lands of Hugh Wallace on the East the Lands of B. S. Jones and James Isabell on the south and Edward Anderson Lands on the west and morth and said to contain two hundred acres more or less this 12th day of April 1856.

                C. Smith Const.

All of which being seen and heard by the court on motion it is considered by the court that the Lands so Levied upon as aforesaid be and the same is hereby condemned and ordered to be sold to satisfy the plaintiffs Debt and cost and also the cost of this motion and that an order of sale issue.

P-320 Douglass and Ford) Debt motion to condemn land in this
       Vs   ) case the following papers were filed
     James Allcorn) to wit - Warrant -

State of Tennessee   ) To the sheriff or any constable I com-
Putnam County   ) mand you to summons James Allcorn to
) appear before me or some other acting
Justice of Peace for said County to answer E. F. Douglass and H. B. Ford known as a firm styled Douglass and Ford in a plea of debt due by note under fifty dollars herein Fail not.

Given under my hand and seal September 20th 1855.

                   J. W. McDaniel J.P.

Endorsed herein to wit: Executed and set for trial before J. W. McDaniel Esqr. on the 21st day of Nov. 1855.

                   A. Boyd Constable

Douglass and Ford Vs James Allcorn In this case I give Judgment against the Defendant for fifty one Dollars and 99 3/4 cents and all cost for which Execution may issue this the 12 day of Nov. 1855.

                   J. W. McDaniel J.P.

Execution - State of Tennessee) To the sheriff or any constable of
Putnam County   ) said County - I command you that
) of goods and chattles Lands and
tenements of James Allcorn if to be found in your County you make the sum of fifty one 99 3/4 cents with Enterest and cost to satisfy a Judgment that E. F. Douglass, C. R. Ford known as the name of Douglass & Ford obtained against him before me (p-321) on the 21st of November 1855 and pay over the same as the Law directs.

This 2 day of Feb. 1856.   J. W. McDaniel J.P.
                                 for said County

There being no personal property Exempt from Execution of said Allcorn. I Levy upon a tract of land Lying in Dist. No. 9 Putnam County containing fifty acres more or less bounded by the Lands of J. W. Amonett J. Bartlett and Thomas Cudders.

This the 22 March 1856.   A. Boyd Constable

All of which being seen and heard by the court on motion it is considered by the court that the Land so Levied upon as aforesaid be and the same is hereby condemned and ordered to be sold to satisfy the plaintiffs Debt and cost and also cost of this motion and that an order of sale issue.

A. M. Burton to the use) Debt motion to condemn Land Papers filed
of Edw. Anderson) in this cause to wit:
Vs) Warrant -
Gallant Anderson) State of Tennessee) To the Sher-
Putnam County) iff or any
) constable of
my County - I command you to summons Gallant to appear before me or some other Justice for said County to answer the complaint C. F. and A. M. Burton to the use and benefit of Edward Anderson for a sum under fifty Dollars due by note herein fail not (p-322) Given under my hand and seal this 8th day of April 1856.

R. G. Duke Esqr. at his home this 9 day of April 1856.

                                                C. Smith Const.

C. F. and A. M. Burton Vs Gallant Anderson to the use of Edward Anderson to the use of Edward Anderson I give Judgment for the plaintiff and against the Deft for the sum of nineteen dollars and 11 cents and cost of suit for which Execution may issue this the 9th day of April 1856.

                                                R. G. Duke J.P.

Execution -

State of Tennessee) To the sheriff or any constable of said County
Putnam County) I command you that of goods and chattles Lands
) and tenements of Gallant Anderson if to be
found in your county you make the sum of nineteen dollars and 11 cents and cost of suit to satisfy a Judgment C. F. and M. A. Burton obtained against him before me on the 9th day of April 1856.

                                                R. G. Duke (Seal)
                                                J.P. for Putnam
                                                County.

No goods and chattles to be found in my County, Levied upon a tract of Land of the Deft Lying in Putnam County Dist. No. 13 adjoining to Hugh Wallis on the (p-323) Lands of B. S. Jones, James Isbelle on the south and Edward Anderson Land on the West and North and said to contain two hundred acres more or less this 12th day of April 1856.

                                                C. Smith Constable

All of which being seen and hereby the court on motion it is considered by the court that the land so levied so levied upon as aforesaid be and the same is hereby condemned and ordered to be sold to satisfy the plaintiffs Debt and cost and also the cost of this motion and that an order of sale issue.

Allen Young)   Debt Appeal
Vs)   Motion for plaintiff to give security.
Willis and John Coggins)   On motion of the Deft ordered by the
)   court that the plaintiff give security
for the prosecution of this suit on or before the calling of the same for trial or the same shall stand Dismissed.

On affidavit of Hezekiah Love, L. H. Draper, Henry Roberts, T. J. Shaw, John Bankman, Kelly Julien ordered by the court they be released and Discharged at this term of the court as Jurors.

Joseph Mitchell & son)   Debt Appeal
Vs)   Came the plaintiff herein to open court
A. J. Wallace)   and Dismissed his suit and assinned all
)   costs herein - It is therefore ordered
by the court that the Deft go hence and Recover against the plaintiff all costs herein and that Execution issue.

P-324   State of Tennessee)   Indictment for an affray - Elly Bennett Pros. Came the attorney General
Vs)   for the State and the defendant in
John Cates)   proper person who being arraigned and
charged upon the above Indictment says he is Guilty as therein charged against him. It is therefore ordered by the court that said Deft for such his offence he pay a fine of two Dollars and the cost of this prosecution.
Whereupon came here into open court E. L. Thompson and confessed Judgment jointly with said Deft for said fine and cost this day adjudged against him. It is therefore considered by the court that the State of Tennessee Recover against John Cates and E. L. Thompson the sum of two Dollars the fine aforesaid and also all cost herein and that Execution issue etc.

James W. Brooks)   Slander
Vs)   Came the plaintiff by attorney and dismissed his
James Bartlett)   suit. It is therefore ordered by the court that
)   the Deft go hence and Recover against the plaintiff and Thomas T. Watson and Benjamin H. Watson his securities all the cost herein and that Execution issue.

Ordered that the court be adjourned untill tomorrow morning 8 oclock.

                                                            Jno. L. Goodall

Tuesday Morning April 15th A.D. 1856

Court met persuant to adjournment present the Honorable John L. Goodall Judge Presiding.

Elijah Brown	)	Ejectment
Vs	)	Came the parties by attornies (p-325) and on
Thomas Pullin	)	motion and affidavit of the plaintiff this cause
	)	is ordered to be continued until next Term of this

court upon the payment of all costs not heretofore adjudged in this cause by said plaintiff.

It is therefore considered by the court that the court Recover against the plaintiff all cost not heretofore assessed in this cause and that Execution issue.

John Farly	)	Ejectment
Vs	)	Came the parties by attornies and on motion of the
Jesse Farly	)	plaintiff. It is ordered by this court that this
	)	cause be continued untill the next Term of this

court upon the payment of the cost of this term by said plaintiff It is therefore considered by the court that the Deft Recover against said plaintiff the cost of this term and that Execution Issue - and it is also ordered by the court that the plaintiff have a survey of the Lands mentioned in this cause according to the title papers by Isaac Buck Surveyor of Putnam County and that he give the parties ten days notice of the time and place of the same and that he return two platts of the same on or before the next term of this court.

State of Tennessee	)	Indictment for Drunkness - On motion of the
Vs	)	attorney General an alias capias awarded
John Watson	)	against said defendant directed to the sher-
	)	iff of Dekalb County Returnable etc.

State of Tennessee	)	Indictment for A. & B. John Grider Prosecutor
Vs	)	(p-326) came the attorney General for the
James Bullington	)	State and the Deft in proper person - who
	)	being arraigned and charged upon said Indict-

ment says he is not guilty as therein against him is charged and for his trial puts himself upon the County and the Attorny General for the State doth the Like. Whereupon came a Jury of good and Lawful men to wit: Charles Crook, Benjamin H. Watson, Elijah Carr, Henry Netherton, William P. Campbell, Meridith P. Gentry, William Ripitoe, Curtis Terry, Thomas Scudder, Frank Goolsby, Ridley Draper, and Winchester P. Dowell, who being Elected tried and sworn the truth to speak upon the issue Joined upon their oath do say that said Deft is not guilty in manner and form as therein is charged.

It is therefore ordered by the court that said Deft be discharged and it appearing to the satisfaction of the court that the prosecution was frivolous and malicious.

It is therefore ordered by the court that John Grider the prosecutor in this cause be Taxed with all cost herein and that Execution issue for collection of the same.

Allen Young) Debt Appeal - Came the plaintiff
Vs) and came along with him John R.
Willis Coggins & John Coggins) Murry here in to open court and
) as security for said plaintiff
acknowledged himself to owe and stand indebted to the Defendants in this
suit in the sum of two hundred and fifty Dollars for the payment of all
costs in this suit should the same be adjudged against him (p-327)
upon a final hearing of the same.

State of Tennessee) Indictment for A. & B. Dabner Pennington
Vs) Pros. Came the attorney General for the
Claborn Stone) State and the Defendant in proper person
) who being arraigned and charged upon the
Indictment says he is Guilty in manner and form as there charged against
him. It is therefore ordered by the court that said Deft for such his
offence, he pay one Dollar a fine and the cost of this prosecution.
Whereupon came here into open court Robison Dyer and confessed Judgment
Jointly with said Deft for said fine and cost this day adjudged against
said Deft. It is therefore considered by the court that the State of
Tennessee Recover against said Deft and Robison Dyer the sum of one Dollar the fine aforesaid and also all cost herein and that Execution Issue.

Ordered by court that first Tuesday after the second Mondays of Circuit court be set apart as States day.

State of Tennessee) Indictment for Murder - Robert Brown Pros.
Vs) Came the attorny General for the State and
William Crabtree) the Defendant in proper person and on affi-
) davit of Robert Brown the (p-328) prose-
cutor in this cause is ordered to be continued until the next term of
this court whereupon came here into open court the Deft William Crabtree
together with William E. B. Jones, Isaac Crabtree and Ephraim Crabtree
and acknowledged themselves to owe and stand Indebted to the State of
Tennessee in the sum of Four Thousand Dollars to wit The Deft William
Crabtree in the sum of two Thousand Dollars and the said William E. B.
Jones, Isaac Crabtree and Ephraim Crabtree in the sum of two thousand
Dollars Jointly to be Levied of their proper Goods and chattles Lands and
Tenements to the use of the State of Tennessee to be rendered nevertheless
to be void on condition that the Deft William Crabtree make his personal
appearance before the Judge of the Circuit Court of Putnam County to be
held at the court house in the town of Cookeville on the second Monday
in August next on the Tuesday after the second Monday thereof to answer
the State of Tennessee upon a charge of Murder and then and there attend
untill Legally discharged.

State of Tennessee) Indictment for murder Robert Brown Prosecutor
Vs) This day came herein open court Robert Brown
William Crabtree) William Brown, Manuel Hatfield, Galeman Crag,
) and James Latham who severally acknowledged
themselves to owe and stand Indebted to the State of Tennessee the sum of
two hundred and fifty Dollars Each to be Levied of there proper Goods and
chattles Lands and tenements to the use of the State to be rendered never
the (p-329) less to be void on condition that they make their personal
appearance before the Judge of the Circuit Court of Putnam County to be

held at the court house in the Town of Cookeville on the first Tuesday after the second Monday in August next then and there the said Robert Brown to prosecute and give Evidence in behalf of the state and the other named witnesses to give Evidence in behalf of the State in the case now pending in this court against William Crabtree for murder in the 1st Degree and then and there attend until Legally Discharged.

State of Tennessee) Indictment for murder 1st Dg. Robert Brown
Vs) prosecutor - On motion and affidavit of the
William Crabtree) Defendant It is ordered by the court that an
) attachement issue against the Boddy of Jesse
Crabtree compelling him to appear here at the next Term of court to Give Evidence in behalf of the Deft directed to the sheriff of Fentress County returnable etc.

State of Tennessee) Indictment for murder 1st Degree Robert Brown
Vs) Prosr.
William Crabtree) This day came here into open court Permelia
) Crag, Isaac Crabtree, Ephraim Crabtree, Sherred Dolk, J. A. Croutch and Martin Croutch, who severally acknowledged themselves to owe and stand Indebted to the State of Tennessee in the sum of two hundred and fifty Dollars Each to the use of the State to be rendered but to be void on condition that they make their personal appearance before the Judge of the Circuit Court of Putnam County to be heard at the Court house in Town (p-330) of Cookeville on the first Tuesday after the second Monday in August next then and there to give Evidence in behalf of the Deft in the case of the State against Wm. Crabtree now pending in the court and then and there attend untill Legally discharged.

State of Tennessee) Indictment for an assault with intent to com-
Vs) mit a Rape - Nelly Looper Prosecutor Came the
Major Alias Nig) attorny General for the State and the Defend-
) ant Led to the bar of the court in custody of
the sheriff of Putnam County and on motion and affidavit of the Attorney General for the State. It is ordered by the court that this cause be discontinued untill the next Term of this court and there being no public Jail in the county of Putnam and the Deputy Sheriff of Overton County to wit, Jackson Hamilton being present in open court. It was ordered by the court that said Defendant be delivered up to him and that he fourthwith, with a sufficient Guard convey and Lodge said Defendant in the common Jail of Overton County Ten there to be safely and securely kept untill the next Term of the Circuit Court of Putnam County to be held at the Courthouse in the Town of Cookeville on the Tuesday after the second Monday in August next at which time the sheriff of Overton County is ordered to have him before said Court on motion of the Defendant supported by affidavit he moved the court to change the venire of this cause which motion was by the court continued over untill the next Term of this court. (p-331) This day the Grand Jury returned into open court the following Bills of Indictments to wit - State of Tennessee against John Watts for Larceny and State of Tennessee against Henry Ayres for murder both of which bills are Endorsed thereon to wit: Daniel W. Waws foreman of the Grand Jury and again retired to consider of presentments Indictments and etc. which Bill of Indictment against Henry Ayers is in words and figures following to wit:

State of Tennessee)   Circuit Court
Putnam County   )   April Term of said court In the Year of Our
)   Lord one Thousand Eight Hundred and fifty six
The Grand Jurors for the State of Tennessee Elected Empannelled sworn and
charged to enquire for the body of the County of Putnam in said State upon their oath present that Henry Ayres, Yeoman Late of said County and
State on the first day of April one Thousand Eight hundred and fifty six
not having the fear of God before his eyes and being moved and seduced
by the Instigation of the Devil with force and arms in the State and County
aforesaid in and upon one Samuel Ayers then and there being in the peace
of God and our said State feloniously, wickedly, wilfully deliberately
maliciously premediatedly and of mallis afore thought did make an assault
and that he the said Henry Ayres with a certain knife of the value of one
Dollar which the said Henry Ayres in his right hand then and there and
there had and held the said Samuel Ayres in and upon the Left side near
the nipple then and there feloniously wilfully, wickedly, deliberately
maliciously, premediatedly and of mallis of afore thought did strike and
thrust giving to him the said Samuel Ayres then and there with the knife
aforesaid in and upon the said Left side near the nipple of him the said
Samuel Ayres (p-332) one mortal wound of the breadth of two inches
and of the depth of seven inches of which said mortal wound the said Samuel Ayres then and there instantly died. The Jurors aforesaid upon their
oaths aforesaid do say that the said Henry Ayres him the said Samuel Ayres
in manner and by the means aforesaid feloniously wickedly wilfully deliberately maliciously premediately and of his mallis of fore thought did kill
and murder in the 1st Degree contrary to the form of the statutes in such
cases made and provided and against the peace and dignity of the State.

   Tim N. Williams Attorny General 4th Circuit which Bill of Indictment
is Endorsed to wit: Murder State Vs Indictment Henry Ayres - Shadrack
Moonyham prosecutor C. S. Pounds, Wm. McKee, S. Monnyham, Robert McKee
witness sworn in open court and sent before the Grand Jury to Give Evidence on this Bill of indictment.

   This 15th April 1856.   Curtis Mills Clerk

   A True Bill Daniel W. Haws foreman of the Grand Jury.

State   )   Indictment for Larceny - James M. Ledbetter Prosr.
 Vs   )   The following is a true copy of the Indictment in
John Watts   )   this cause to wit,

State of Tennessee)   Circuit Court for said County April Term for
Putnam County   )   said Court.
)   In the year of Our Lord one thousand eight
Hundred and fifty six - the Grand Jurors for the State of Tennessee, Elected
Empannelled sworn and charged to enquire for the Body of the County of Putnam (p-333) in said State upon their oath present that John Watts,
Yeoman, Late of said County and State on the first day of April one Thous-
and Eight Hundred and fifty six with force and arms in the County and State
aforesaid and pistole Commonly called revolver of the value of Five Dollars the personal goods and chattles of James M. Leadbetter then and there
in his possession being found feloniously did steal, take, and carry away
contrary to the form of the statute in such cases make and provide and
against the peace and dignity of the State 2nd count and the Jurors aforesaid upon their oaths aforesaid do f ther present that the said John Watts

Yeoman on the said first day of April one thousand Eight Hundred and fifty six with force and arms in the County and State aforesaid one small Gun commonly called a pistole of value of Five Dollars the personal Goods and chattles of one James M. Ledbetter then and there in his possession being found feloniously and wilfully did steal, take and carry away contrary to the form of the statute in such cases made and provided and against the peace and dignity of the State 3rd count and the Jurors aforesaid upon their oath aforesaid do further present that said John Watts Yeoman, on the said first day of April one thousand Eight hundred and fifty six with force and arms in the County and State aforesaid one small Gun commonly called a pistole of the value of five Dollars the personal goods and chattles of one James M. Leadbetter then and there in his possession being found feloniously, wilfully did steal take and carry away contrary to the form of the statute in such cases made and provided and against the peace and (p-334) dignity of the state.

            Tim. H. Williams
            Attorney General 4th
            Circuit.

Upon the Back of which Bill of Indictment are the following endorsement to wit: Larceny - State Vs John Watts Indictment James M. Leadbetter Prosecutor - James M. Leadbetter - William D. Officer and John H. Officer witnesses - sworn in open court and sent before the Grand Jury to give Evidence in this Bill of Indictment this 15th April 1856.

            Curtis Mills Clerk

A True Bill - Daniel W. Haws foreman of the Grand Jury.

Hezekiah Love) Motion to correct Taxation of cost - Came the
 Vs   ) parties by their attornies and the motion Entered
Rily R. Liegue) at the last Term of this court in this cause to
) correct Taxation of cost in this cause as to Bird
S. Jones a witness which being heard by the court and fully understood It is considered by the court that the motion be dismissed and that the Deft pay all cost of the same - It is therefore considered by the court that the plaintiff Recover against the Deft the cost of this motion and that Execution Issue.

State of Tennessee) Presentment for A. & B. Came the attorney
 Vs   ) General for the State and the Deft in proper
H. H. Bryant   ) person and he being arraigned and charged upon
) said presentment says he is not guilty in manner and form as there in against him is charged and for his trial puts himself upon the county and the attorny General for the State doth the Like (p-335) whereupon came a Jury of good and Lawful men to wit: Benjamin H. Watson, Elijah Carr, Henry Netherton, William C. Campbell, Meridith P. Gentry, William Ripitoe, Curtis Terry, Thomas Scudder, Frank Goolsby, William H. Gentry, Ridly Draper and Winchester P. Dowell who being Elected tried and sworn the truth to speak upon the issue of Traverse Joined upon there oath do say that Defendant is guilty in form and manner as therein against him is charged It is therefore ordered by the court that said Defendant for such his offence pay a fine of ten Dollars and the cost of this prosecution whereupon came here into open court Elmore

Carrington and confessed Judgment Jointly with said Deft for said fine and cost this day adjudged against him - It is therefore considered by the court that the State of Tennessee Recover against said Deft and Elmore Carrington the sum of ten Dollars the fine aforesaid and also all cost herein and that Execution issue.

F. N. Patterson to the use of Elijah Wheeler) Debt Motion to condemn Land in this cause the following papers were filed to wit:
Vs) Warrant -
Henry Roberts) State of Tennessee) To the Sheriff or any constable of said County - I command you to summons Henry Roberts personally to appear before me or some other Justice of the peace for said County to answer complaint of Felix N. Patterson to the sum and benefit of Elijah Wheeler in a plea of Debt Due by note in a sum under the Jurisdiction of a magistrate herein fail not and Return the warrant according to (p-336) Law this 20 March 1856.
Putnam County)

                 E. C. Crowell (Seal)
                 J.P. for said County

Endorsed thereon to wit:
 Executed and set for trial on the 22nd day of March 1856 before E. C. Crowell Esqr. at his house this the 21 March 1856.

                 C. S. Smith Const.

 F. N. Patterson Vs Henry Roberts in this case I give Judgment in favor of the plaintiff and against the Deft for Four Hundred and thirty six Dollars and fourteen cents principal with all lawful Interest and cost this 22nd of March 1856.
                 E. C. Crowell J.P.

Execution -

State of Tennessee) To the sheriff or any constable of said County I command you of the goods and chattles lands and tenements of Henry Roberts if to be found in your County - you make the sum of four Hundred and thirty six dollars 14 cents with all interest and the cost of suit to sattisfy a Judgment Feliz N. Paterson for the use and benefit of Elijah Wheeler obtained against him before me on the 22nd March 1856 and pay over the sum as the law Directs this 22nd March 1856.
Putnam County)

                 E. C. Crowell (Seal)
                 J.P. for Putnam County

Endorsed thereon to wit -
 Came to hand this 22nd March 1856 Levied upon a still and still cap and on one flake stand and <u>fourty five</u> still tubs 1 wagon - twenty three head of stock hogs Eleven head of sheep one Large Kettle not a sufficient quanity of goods and chattles to be found in my county to satisfy this fifa this March 22nd 1856.

                 C. Smith Const.

P-337 After <u>givin</u> legal notice sold the property Disclosed in the within

Levy to the highest bidder for one hundred and six dollars and 95 cents this 5th April 1856.

C. Smith Const.

Levied upon three tracts of land of the Defts lying in Putnam County Dist No. 13 adjoining the lands of the heirs of Joseph Roberts Decd. on the south and said to contain one hundred and ninety acres in all including the premise where the Deft now lives this 22 day of March 1856 and also upon one sheer of Land of the Defts Lying in Putnam County his interest in the land of Joseph Roberts Decd. this 22th March 1856 the said sheer was brought from Willis Lee.

Charles Smith Const.

All of which being seen and hereby the court on motion it is considered by the court that the land so levied on be and the same is hereby condemned and ordered to be sold to satisfy the plaintiffs debt and cost of this motion and that an order of sale issue.

F. Starnes to the use of Edward Anderson) Debt Motion to condemn Land the following paper were filed to wit : Warrant
Vs
Gallant Anderson)

State of Tennessee) To the Sher-
Putnam County) iff or any
) constable of
said County I command you to summons Gallant Anderson to appear before me or some other (p-338) of the peace for said County to answer the complainant F. Starnes to the use of Edward Anderson in a plea of Debt Due by note for a sum under fifty dollars herein fail not. Given under my hand and seal this the 8th day of April 1856.

R. G. Duke J. P. for said County

Endorsed herein to wit: Executed and set for trial on the 9th day of April 1856. Before R. G. Duke Esqr. at his house this the 9th day of April 1856.

C. Smith Constable

F. Starnes Vs G. Anderson to the use of Edward Anderson I give Judgment for the plaintiff and against the Deft for the sum of nine dollars and 65 cts. and cost of suit for which Execution may issue this 9 April 1856.

R. G. Duke J. P.

Execution

State of Tennessee) To the sheriff or any constable of said County
Putnam County) I command you that of the goods and chattles
) lands and tenements of Gallant Anderson if to
be found in your County you make the sum of nine dollars and 65 cents to sattisfy a Judgment that F. Starnes obtained against him before me to the use of Edward Anderson on the 9th of April 1856 and pay over to same as the law Directs this 12 day of April 1856.

R. G. Duke J.P. for P. C.

Endorsed thereon -

No goods and chattles to be found in my County - Levied upon a tract of Land of the Defendant lying (p-339) in Putnam County in Dist. No. 13 adjoining the lands of Hugh Wallace on the East and B. P. Jones and James Isbell lands on the south and Edward Anderson Lands on the west and north and said to contain two hundred acres more or less this the 12 day April 1856.

                                                C. Smith Constable

All of which being seen and heard by the court on motion it is considered that the land levied upon as aforesaid be and the same is hereby condemned and ordered to be sold to satisfy the plaintiffs Debt and cost and also cost of this motion and that an order of sale issue.

James Brown)   Trespass
  Vs   )   Came the parties by attorny and there came a
Elizabeth Franklin) Jury of good and lawful men to wit: Benjamin
) H. Watson, Henry Netherton, William Ripitoe, Curtis Terry, Thomas Scudder, Frank Goolsby, William M. Gentry, Ridly Draper, Winchester P. Dowell, Meridith P. Gentry, John Terry and Joseph Hester, who being Elected, tried and sworn the truth to speak upon the issue of Traverse Joined who after having heard all of the Evidence and the argument of counsel thereon and Received their charge from the Honorable court retired to consider of their verdict and again returned into court and upon their oaths declared they could not agree upon a verdict in this cause and there not being time this day to finish the trial of this cause they were permitted to disperse untill the meeting of the court tomorrow morning.

P-340   State   ) It appearing to the satisfaction of the
         Vs   ) court that the Defts is now confined in
    Henry Ayres and) the common Jail of White County It is
    John Watts   ) therefore ordered by the court that the
) sheriff of Putnam County fourth with
proceed to bring said Defts here into this court to answer the charge against them.

Ordered that court be adjourned untill tomorrow morning 15 after 7 oclock.

                                                    Jno. L. Goodall

                Wednesday Morning April 16th A. D. 1856

State of Tennessee) Indictment for Larceny - James M. Ledbetter Prosr.
     Vs   ) Came the attorny General for the State and the
John Watts   ) Deft and it appearing to the satisfaction of the
) court that the Deft is poor and wholly unable to
employ counsel to aid and defend him upon the trial of cause The court therefore appoints and assines James W. McHenry and C. S. Stone Esqrs. Gentlemen practising attos. in this court to aid and defend him upon the trial of this cause.

State of Tennessee   )   Indictment for Murder

Vs) Shadrach Monnyham Prosr. - Came the attorny
Henry Ayres) General for the State and the Deft in proper
) person and it appearing to the court that said
Deft was poor and wholly unable to Employ consel (p-341) to aid and
defend him upon the trial of this cause The court therefore appoints and
assigned Samuel Terry and William E. Nelson Esqrs. Gentlemen practising
attos. at Law in this court to aid and defend him upon trial of this
cause.

State of Tennessee) Indictment for A. & B. Elly Bennett Prosr.
Vs) Came the attorny General for the State and
Hickman Whitaker) the Defendant in proper person and on motion
) it is ordered that this cause be continued
untill the next Term of this court - Whereupon came here into open court
the Deft together with Hampton Ramsy, Austin Choat and acknowledged them
selves to owe and stand indebted to the State of Tennessee in the sum of
five Hundred Dollars to wit: the Defendant in the sum of two hundred
and fifty Dollars and the said Hampton Ramsey Austin Choat and Edward
Choat in the sum of two hundred and fifty Dollars Jointly to be Levied
of their proper goods and chattles Lands and Tenements to the use of the
State to be rendered but to be void on condition the Defendant makes his
personal appearance before the Judge of the Circuit Court of Putnam County
to be held at the courthouse in the town of Cookeville on the first Tuesday after the second Monday in August next then and there to answer the
State upon the above charge and attend untill Legally discharged.

John McGhee) Debt motion to condemn Land In the matter this
Vs) motion the following papers were duly returned
Gallant Anderson) and filed to wit -
Warrant

State of Tennessee)
Putnam County) (P-342) To the Sheriff or any constable of
) said County I command you to summons Gallant
Anderson to appear before me or some other Justice of Peace for said
County to answer the complaint of John McGhee to the use and benefit of
Edward Anderson in a plea of debt due by note for sum under fifty Dollars
Herein fail not - Given under my hand and seal this 8th day of April 1856.

R. G. Duke (Seal)
J. P. for Putnam County

Endorsed, Executed and set for trial on the 9th day of April 1856 C. Smith
Const. Const Smith for 50¢ - John McGhee Vs G. Anderson to the use of Edward Anderson - I give Judgment for plaintiff against the Defendant for
the sum of nineteen Dollars and thirty six cents and cost of suit for
which Execution may issue this 9th day April 1856.
R. G. Duke (Seal) J.P.

Execution

State of Tennessee) To the sheriff or any constable of said County
Putnam County) I command you of the Good and Chattles Lands
) and tenements of Gallant Anderson if to be
found in your county you make the sum of nineteen Dollars and 36 cents
and cost of suit to satisfied a Judgment that John McGhee against him to

the use of and benefit of Edward Anderson before me on the 9th day of April 1856 and pay over the same as the Law Directs this the 2 day of April 1856.

            R. G. Duke (Seal) J.P.
            for Putnam County

Endorsed - Debt $19.36 Warrant 50 J. P. Duke fee 60 Const Smith Levying fee 50¢. No goods and chattles to be found in my County Levied on a tract of Land (p-343) of the Defendant Lying in Putnam County in District No. 13 adjoining the Lands of Hugh Wallis on the East the Lands of B. S. Davis and James Isbell on the South and Edward Anderson Lands on the west and north and said to contain two Hundred acres this the 12th day of April 1856.

            C. Smith Const.

  All of which being seen and heard by the court on motion it is considered by the court that the Land so Levied upon as aforesaid be and the same is hereby condemned and ordered to be sold to satisfy the plaintiffs Debt and cost and also the cost of this motion, and that an order of Sale issue.

John Richardson and William Richardson Vs John Roland	Eject By consent of parties by attorny this cause is ordered to be continued untill the next Term of this court.

  This day the Grand Jury returned in to court following presentment to wit: State against William Carland for Drunkness signed by foreman and all the Ballance of the Grand Jurors also returned into court at the same time a Bill of Indictment of the State against Henry Roberts and Catharine Markham for Ludness Endorsed thereon by their foreman to wit: True Bill Daniel H. Haws foreman of the Grand Jury and again retired to consider of Prests. Indicts. etc.

State of Tennessee Vs John Watts	Indictment for Larceny James M. Ledbetter Prosr. Came the attorny General for the State and the Defendant in proper person and on affidavit of Defendant this cause is ordered

to be continued untill the (p-343) next Term of this court and said Defendant having failed to Enter into bond and security as required by Law. It is ordered by the court that said Defendant be remanded back to the Jail at Sparta Ten untill the next Term of this court.

Allin Young Vs Willis Coggin and John Coggins	Debt Appeal By consent of the parties by attornies this cause is ordered to be continued untill the next term of this court as on affidavit upon the payment of the cost of this term of court

by said plaintiff. It is therefore considered by the court that the Deft Recover against the plaintiff the cost of this term of the court and that Execution Issue etc.

Nancy Officer) Trespass on the Case - Came the parties by at-
Vs) tornys and there came a Jury of good and Law-
Preston Roberson) ful men to wit: John Carr, Thomas Nicholas
) John T. Graham, Meridith P. Gentry, William
H. Gentry, Ridly Draper, Curtis Terry, Winchester P. Dowell, William
Ripitoe, Henry Netherton, Thomas Scudder and Frank Goolsby who being
elected tried and sworn the truth to speak upon the issue of Traverse
Joined who after having heard all of the Evidence and part of the coun-
sel thereon and there not being time this day to finish the trial of this
cause the Jurors were permitted to disperse untill tomorrow morning the
meeting of this court.

P-345   Isaac Burton) Debt Appeal
Vs) Came the parties by their attornies
Thomas Lancaster) and agree that the case be submitted
) to the arbitrament of Harvy Carr and
Joseph Mitchell and that their award be the Judgment of the court in the
premises.

Wiley Night) Ejectment
Vs) Came the parties by attornies and it appearing to
William Bean) the court from the argument the parties in writing
) filed in this cause that they had agreed to Leave
all matters in Dispute in this case to the arbitration of Reubin Whitson
and Anderson Matheny and such others as said arbitrators may select and
that the award of the arbitrators be the Judgment of this court - Which
is so ordered by this court.

James C. Officer Admr.) Debt Appeal - Came the parties by their
of W. G. Sims Decd.) attornies and their came a Jury of good
Vs) and Lawful men to wit: Elijah Carr,
William Courton) William P. Campbell, Robert Mackie,
) Aaron Mackie, Jefferson Cole, Joshua
White, Hosa Maden, Anthany McBroom, James Carr, Tyra Bullington, A. S.
Ferrell and Mark Mathis who being Elected tried and sworn well and truly
to try the matters in controversy between the parties and who after having
heard of of the Evidence   (p-346)   and the argument of counsel thereon
and Received their charge from the Honorable court retired to consider
their verdict and again return into court and declared they could not agree
upon a verdict in this cause and there not being time this day to finish
the trial of this cause the Jurors were permitted to disperse untill the
meeting of this court tomorrow morning.

James Brown) Trespass
Vs) Came again the parties by their attornies
Elizabeth Franklin) and came also the same Jury, Elected, Em-
James White) pannelled, sworn and charged in this cause
John C. White) on yesterday and upon their oaths do say
) that they find the issue in favor of the
plaintiff and assess his Damage to the sum of ten cents. It is therefore considered by the court that the plaintiff Recover against said Defendant the sum of ten cents the Damages aforesaid by the Jury aforesaid

assessed and also all costs herein and that Execution issue and on motion of the Defendants by attorny it is ordered by the court that no witness on part of the plaintiff Except John Grider, Thomas Brown, Charlotte, T. White, Sidny Byres, Shadrack Stanly and the Depotsition of L. C. Byres be Taxed against the Defendants in this cause.

Grand Jury returned into court following presentments to wit: State Vs Edward Choat for nusance overseer of road and stand against Jefferson Cole for nusance as overseer of road again retired to consider of presentments Indictments etc.

P-347 C. F. Burton to the use of Edward Anderson Vs Gallant Anderson) Debt Motion to condemn land - The following papers were filed to wit: Warrant.

State of Tennessee) To the sheriff or any constable
Putnam County) of said County I command you to
) summons Gallant Anderson to appear before me or some other Justice for said County to answer the complaint of C. F. Burton to the use of Edward Anderson for a sum under one hundred Dollars herein fail not given under my hand and seal this 8th day of April 1856.

R. G. Duke (Seal)
J.P. for Putnam County

Endorsed herein to wit:

Executed and set for trial on the 9th day of April 1856 before R. G. Duke at his house this the 9th April 1856.

C. Smith Const.

C. F. Burton Vs Gallant Anderson I give Judgment for the plaintiff and against the Deft for the sum of twenty Dollars and 88 cents to the use of Edward Anderson for which Execution may issue this the 9th April 1856.

R. G. Duke (Seal) J.P.

Execution

State of Tennessee) To the sheriff or any constable of said
Putnam County) County I command you that of goods and
) chattles lands and tenements of Gallant
Anderson if to be found in your county you make the sum of twenty dollars and 88 cents to satisfy a Judgment that C. F. Burton obtained against him before me on the 9 of April 1856 to the (p-348) use of Edward Anderson and pay over the same as the law Directs this the 12th of April 1856.

R. G. Duke J.P.
for Putnam County

No goods and chattles to be found in my county - Levied upon a tract of Land of the Defendants Lying in Putnam County and district No; 13 adjoining the Lands of Hugh Wallis on the East the Lands of B. S. Jones and James

Isabell on the south and the Lands of Edward Anderson on the west and North and said to contain two hundred acres more or less. This the 12th day of April 1856.

C. Smith Const.

All of which being seen and heard by the court on motion it is considered by the court that the same is Levied upon as aforesaid be and the same is hereby condemned and ordered to be sold to satisfy the plaintiffs debt and cost and also the cost of this motion and that an order of <u>sail</u> issue.

Susan Cole Vs David G. Harris	By agreement of the parties by attornies the plaintiff asked and obtained Leave of the court to with Draw the Declaration in this cause and file another.

John Terry Vs Elias Green	In Debt Came the parties by attornies and on motion of the plaintiff - It is ordered by the court that the 2nd plea of the Defendant be stricken out.

Ordered that court be adjourned untill tomorrow morning ½ after 7 oclock.

Jno. S. Goodall

P-349 Thursday Morning April 17th A.D. 1856 - Court met pursuant to adjournment present the Honorable John L. Goodall presiding.

State of Tennessee Vs Henry Ayres	Indictment for murder Shadrach Monnyhan Prosr. Came the attorny General for the State and the Defendant in proper person and on affidavit of Shadrach Moonyham the prosecutor in this

cause. It is ordered by the court that this cause be continued untill the next Term of this court and it is ordered by the court that the Sheriff of Putnam County convey and deliver said Deft over to the Jailer of White County there to be safely and securely kept in said Jail untill the next term of this court and on motion and affidavit of the prosr. in this cause it is ordered that an attactment issue against the body of Pherly Mackie compelling her to attend here at the next term of this court a witness in the above cause on behalf of the State returnable here at the next Term of this court.

William H. Barons Admr. of Thos. Saylor Decd. Vs John Baron	Came the parties by their attornies and the matters of Law arrising upon the Demur of plaintiff to the Defendants plea pleaded in this cause being by the court heard and fully understood. It

was considered by the court that the Demur be <u>overuled</u> and on motion of plaintiff he have Leave to reply to said plea.

Charlotte T. White) Pet. for Divorce — On motion of Petitioner
Vs) and it appearing to the satisfaction of this
Joshua White) court (p-350) that copy petition and sub-
) poena to answer herein and be served upon
Defendant more than five days previous to the Last Term of this court and
that Defendant has failed to appear and answer complainants petition — It
is therefore ordered adjudged and Decreed by the court that Judgment for
confessed be entered against said Defendant and this cause set down for
hearing Expartee, and the petitioner by attorny asked and obtained Leave
of court to strike out of said petition the following word after the word
such to wit, alimony, which is accordingly done and by consent of the
parties by attornies this cause is continued untill the next Term of this
court.

Nancy Officer) Trespass on the case — Came again the parties
Vs) by their attornies and came also the same Jury
Preston Roberson) Elected Empannelled and sworn in this cause
) on yesterday and who after having heard the
Ballance of the argument of counsel thereon and received their charge
from the Honorable court retired to consider of their verdict and again
returned into court and upon their oaths do say that they find the issue
in favor of the plaintiff and assess her damage to the sum of Five thous-
and Dollars. It is therefore considered by the court that the plaintiff
Recover against said Defendant the sum of Five thousand Dollars the Damages aforesaid by the Jury aforesaid assessed and also all cost herein
and that Execution issue and the plaintiff by attorny came here in open
court and release the sum of four thousand Dollars of the above Judgment.

P-351 Grand Jury returned into court the following presentments to wit:

State against William Roberson for nusance as overseer of Road and State
against George McCormick for obstructing public road Both Endorsed thereon by the foreman of the Grand Jury and all the Ballance of the Grand Jurors
in due form of Law also returned at the same time the following Indictment
to wit — State of Tennessee against Wm. B. Rowland and Jane Bruce for Ludness Endorsed thereon by their foreman a true Bill Daniel W. Haws, foreman a true Bill Daniel W. Haws foreman of the Grand Jury and again retired
to consider of presentments Indictments and etc.

Margaret Irwin) Debt Appeal
Vs) Came the parties by their attornies and there
John B. Pointer) came a Jury of good and Lawful men to wit,
) Isaac Lollar, John E. Campbell, Samuel McCaleb
Benjamin H. Watson, Thomas T. Watson, William Peek, John Madewell, Shadrach Moonyhan, John C. Dyer, John B. Brown, Isaac Sadler, and Lincoln
Nicholass who being Elected tried and sworn well and truly to try the
matters in controversy Between the parties upon their oaths do say that
they find the same in favor of the Defendant — It is therefore considered
by the court that the Deft go hense and Recover against the plaintiff all
costs herein and that Execution issue.

William Austin) Debt Appeal — The parties failing to attend
Vs) and prosecute his suit. It is ordered by
Edward McGuffy) the court that this cause be stricken from

Docket as the plaintiff (p-352) cost. It is therefore considered by the court that the Deft Recover against the plaintiff the cost herein and Execution issue.

Thomas W. and W. H. Evans) Debt
of the firm of T. W. & W. H. Evans) Came the plaintiff by their
Vs) attorney and the Defendants
Charles Ford, Robert Allin and) being solemnly called to
V. H. Allin) come into court and defend
) this suit came not but made
default. It is therefore considered by the court that the plaintiff Recover of the Defendants the sum of four hundred and one Dollars and also all costs herein and that Execution issue and the plaintiff by attorney came here into open court and releases the sum of four hundred and one Dollars all Except the cost.

State of Tennessee) Indictment for murder Robert Brown Prosr.
Vs) Came the attorny Genl. for the State and
William Crabtree) the Deft in proper person and on motion and
) affidavit of Robert Brown the prosecutor in
this cause it is ordered by the court that attachments issue against the bodys of P. F. Laysdon, Berry Hatfield, Patsy Huff and Betsy Simpson witness directed to the Sheriff of Fentress County Ten Returnable here at the next Term of this court compelling them to attend here at the next Term of this court to give Evidence on the behalf of the State in the above cause - This entry should have appeared upon the minutes of Tuesday and is now for then.

P-353 James C. Officer Administrator) Debt Appeal
of W. G. Sims Decd.) Came again the parties by
Vs) their attornys and came
William Coureton) also the same Jury Elected
) tried and sworn and charged
in this cause as yesterday and upon their oaths declared they could not agree upon a verdict in this cause and by consent of the parties by attornys a mistrial is Entered and this cause is ordered by the court to be continued untill the next Term of this court.

Nancy Officer) Trespass on the case - Came the parties by
Vs) their attornies and the Defendant by attorny
Preston Roberson) moved the court for a new trial in this cause
) and in arrest of Judgment both of which was
overuled by the court from which several opinions of the court the Defendant prays an appeal in the nature of a writ of Error to the next term of supreme court at Nashville Ten and having Given bond with E. L. Gardenhire and J. D. Goodpasture his security said appeal is granted, and the Defendant tendered here into open court his bill of Exceptions which was signed and sealed by the court and ordered to be made a part of the Record in this cause.

Grand Jury returned into court the following presentments to wit, State Vs James B. Lowery for nusance as overseer of Road and State against John

Roberts for selling Liquor on Sunday both of which presentments are signed by the foreman of the Grand Jury and all (p-354) the Ballance of the Grand Jurors in due form of Law and the Grand and Traverse Jurors having no further business to perform in this Term of this court they are released and discharged as such from further attendance.

Court adjourned till court in course.

Jno. L. Goodall

State of Tennessee -

Pleas at a Circuit Court Began and held for the County of Putnam and State aforesaid in the court house in the Town of Cookeville on the second Monday it being the Eleventh day of August in the year of our Lord one Thousand Eight hundred and fifty six and in the the Eightith year of American Independance.

Present the Honorable John L. Goodall Judge of the fourth Judicial Circuit and assigned to hold the Circuit Courts in said State.

This day Robison Dyer, Sheriff of Putnam County returned here into court the States Writ of Venirafacious to him directed from the County Court of Putnam County it being the first Term of said Court after the last term of this court - May Term commanding him to summons the following named persons to attend this term of court as Jurors to wit: Eli Shipley, William H. Barons, Sr., Joshua Brown, Zebedee J. B. Dearing, Henry Whitaker, C. J. Bohanon, James J. Bohannon, Alexander Bohannon, John Jackson, William Walker, Thomas J. Poteet, Enoch H. Stone, Watson G. Dowell, John Stewart, Abraham Ditty, G. C. Maxwell, Alexander Durham, William B. Grogan, Alexander Montgomery, Joseph Evans Sr., Obadiah Evans Allen Mancar, James R. Wallis, William Wallis, Lewis Medley, A. J. Levisy Elijah W. Terry and John Phillips as Jurors and Hampton Ramsey and Alexander Boyd as constable to attend (p-353) thereon as court officers came to hand the same day issued and Executed in full this the 11 day of August 1856.

R. Dyer Sheriff

Out of which venirafacias and Jurors aforesaid the court proceeded to Elect and empannell a Grand Jury as the Act of the General Assembly in such case provides when the following named persons were drawn and Elected to wit: Obadiah Evans, William H. Barons Sr., William Walker, Henry Whitaker, Zebedee B. Dearing, Enoch H. Stone, William Wallis, James J. Bohannon, Abraham Ditty, C. J. Bohannon, Eli Shipley, John Phillips and John Jackson of whom the court appointed William H. Barons Foreman of this Grand Jury all of whom are good and Lawful men house holders or Free holders of the County of Putnam who being Elected Empannelled sworn and charged a Jury of Grand Inquest for the State of Tennessee to Enquire for the Boddy of the County of Putnam who retired to Enter upon their duties attended by Hampton Ramsey a constable sworn in due form to attend thereon.

On affidavit of James Wallace he is released and discharged from further attendance at this Term as a Juror.

L. L. and J. F. Colbert) Debt motion to condemn Land.

                    Vs   )   The following papers were filed to wit -
        John Roberts   )   Warrant.

State of Tennessee   )   To the Sheriff or any const of said County
Putnam County   )   I command you to summons John Roberts to
)   appear before me or some other Justice for
said County to answer J. L. and J. F. Colberts in a plea of Debt for a
sum under ten dollars this the 6th of Sept 1853.
                                        R. H. Dowell   (Seal)
                                        J.P. for Jackson County

    The following Endorsment to wit: Executed and set for trial on the
18 - Sept. 1853 (p-356) before E. C. Crowell Esqr. my fee 50¢ J. M.
Carr Const. Judgment J. L. Colvert Vs John Roberts in this case I give
Judgment in favor of the plaintiff and against the Deft for five dollars
and 43 cents and cost of suit for which Execution may Issue this 10th
Sept. 1853.
                                        E. C. Crowell J. P.

Execution

State of Tennessee   )   To the Sheriff or any constable I command you
Putnam County   )   that of the goods and chattles Lands and tene-
)   ments of John Roberts if to be found in your
County you make the sum of five dollars 43 cents with Interest and cost
to satisfy a Judgment that J. L. and T. J. Colbert obtained against him
before E. C. Crowell on the 10 Sept. 1853 and pay over the same as the
Law Directs this 20 June 1856.
                                        J. A. Jarred   (Seal)
                                        J.P. for said County

    The following Levy and Endorsement hereon to wit: No goods and chat-
tles to be found in my county Levied upon one tract of land of the Defts
in Putnam County in Dist. No. 13th adjoining the lands of John Carr on
the south and on the East by Vauns Lands and on the west by said Vauns
Land and said to contain one Hundred acres this 30 of June 1856 D.C.L.
Franklin Const. all of which being seen and heard by the court and on
motion It is considered by the court the Land so Levied upon as aforesaid
be and the same is hereby condemned and ordered to be sold to satisfy the
plaintiffs Debt and cost and also the cost of this motion and that an order of sale issue.

P-357   J. L. and J. F. Colbert   )   Debt motion to condemn
                Vs   )   Land - The following papers
        William Cronk and J. Roberts   )   were filed to wit: Warrant.

State of Tennessee   )   To the sheriff or any constable of said County
Jackson County   )   I command you to summons William Cronk and
)   John H. Roberts to appear before me or some
other Justice of said County to answer J. L. and J. F. Colbert in a plea
of Debt under ten dollars this 6 Sept. 1853.
                                        R. H. Dowell J.P.

    For said Count, the following Endorsements hereon to wit: Executed set
for trial on the 10 Sept. 1853 before E. C. Crowell Esqr. my fee $1.00

J. W. Carr, J. L. and J. F. Colbert Vs William Cronk and John Roberts in this case - I give Judgment in favor of the plaintiff and against the Deft for five dollars 65¢ and cost of suit for which Execution may issue this 10 Sept. 1853.

                 E. C. Crowell J.P.
                 Putnam County

Execution -

State of Tennessee) To the sheriff or any constable of said
Putnam County   ) County - I command you that of the goods
) chattles Lands and Tenements of Wm. Cronk
and John Roberts if to be found in your county you make the sum of five Dollars and 65 cents with interest and all cost to satisfy a Judgment that J. L. and J. F. Colbert obtained against them before E. C. Crowell on the 10th day of December 1853 and pay over the sum as the Law Directs this 15th July 1856.

                 M. A. Jarred for
                 said County

Wtt. The following Levy herein no goods and chattles to be found in my County Levied upon one tract of Land in Putnam County Dist. No. 13 ajoining the Lands of John R. Carr on the south and on the East by Vons land and on the West by the said Vons said to contain one Hundred acre this 30 of July 1856 my 100¢ Levied (p-358) all of which being seen and heard by the court It is considered by the court that Land Levied upon as aforesaid be and the same is hereby condemned and ordered to be sold to satisfy the plaintiff Debt and costs and all the cost of this motion and that an order of sale issue.

J. L. and J. F. Colbert) Debt motion to condemn Land - The follow-
    Vs   ) ing papers were filed to wit - Warrant.
John H. Roberts   )

State of Tennessee) To the sheriff or any constable of said
Jackson County   ) County - I command you to summons John
) Roberts to appear before me or some other
Justice of said County to answer J. L. and J. F. Colbert in a plea of Debt under ten dollars this the 6th of Sept. 1853 R. H. Dowel J. P. for said County Wtt. the following Endorsement hereto were Executed and set for trial on the 10th of Sept. 1853 before E. C. Crowell Esq. my fee 50¢ J. W. Carr Const. Judgment J. L. and J. F. Colbert Vs John Roberts In this case I give Judgment in favor of plaintiff and against the Debt for six dollars 96 cents and all cost for which Execution may issue this 10 Sept. 1853.

                 E. C. Crowell J.P.

Execution

State of Tennessee) To the Sheriff or any constable of County
Putnam County   ) I command you that of the goods and chattles
) Lands and tenements of John Roberts if to be
found in your county you make the sum of six Dollars and 96 with interest and cost to satisfy a Judgment that J. L. and J. F. Colbert obtained against him before E. C. Crowell on the 10th Sept. 1853 (p-359) Over the same as the Law this 22 June 1856/

                 M. A. Jarred J. P.
                 said County

Endorsed hereon to wit: No goods and chattles to be found in my County Levied upon a tract of land of the Deft in Putnam County in District No. 13 adjoining the Lands of John R. Carr on the south and on the west by Vons Land and said to contain one Hundred acres this 30 June 1856.

              David E. L. Franklin Const.

  All of which being seen and heard by the court. It is considered by the court that the Land Levied as aforesaid be and the same is hereby condemned and ordered to be sold to satisfy the plaintiffs Debt and cost and also the cost of his motion and that an order of sale issue.

J. L. and J. F. Colbert   ) Debt Motion to condemn Land - The
    Vs   ) following papers were filed to wit:
Wm. Cronk and John Roberts) Warrant -

State of Tennessee   ) To the sheriff or any constable of
Jackson County   ) said County - I command you to sum-
) mons Wm. Cronk and John Roberts to
appear before me or some other Justice of Peace to answer J. L. & J. F. Colbert in a plea of Debt for sum under ten dollars this the 6 of Sept. 1853.

                R. E. Dowell (Seal)
                J.P. for said County.

Witt the following Endorsement hereon to wit, Executed and set for trial on the tenth of Sept. 1853 before E. C. Crowell my fee 100 J. W. Carr. Const. Judgment J. L. and J. F. Colbert Vs Wm. Cronk and John Roberts in this case I give Judgment in favor of the plaintiff and against the Deft for three dollars and 22¢ and cost for which Execution may issue this 10th (p-360) Sept. 1856.

                E. C. Crowell J.P.

Execution -

State of Tennessee   ) To the sheriff or any constable of said County
Putnam County   ) I command you that of the Goods and chattles
) Lands and Tenements of Wm. Cronch and John
Roberts if to be found in your County you make the sum of three Dollars and 22 cents with Interest and cost to satisfy a Judgment that J. L. and J. F. Colbert obtained against them before E. C. Crowell on the 10th Sept. 1853 and pay over the same as the Law directs this June 20th 1856.

                M. A. Jarred (Seal)
                J. P. for said County.

Endorsed Judgment $3.22 Carr 1.00 Crowell 40 Jarred 65 Dowell 10¢ .

No good and chattles to be found in my County - Levied upon one Tract of Land of the Defendants in Putnam County in District No. 13 adjoining the Land of John R. Carr on the South and on the East by Vons Land and on the west by Vons Land and said to contain one Hundred acres this the 30th of June 1856. My fee $1.00.

              David E. L. Franklin Const.

  All of which being seen and heard by the court - On motion It is considered by the court that the Land so Levied upon as aforesaid be and the same is hereby condemned and ordered to be sold to satisfy the plaintiffs Debt and cost and also the cost of this motion and that an order of sale issue.

J. W. Carr and A. F. Carr Adm.) Debt Motion to condemn Land-
of William Carr Decd.) The following papers were
         Vs) filed to warrant -
Wm. Gibson, Wm. Evan & R. E. Fain)

State of Tennessee) To the sheriff or any constable I command you
Putnam County) to summons Wm. Gibson, William Evans and R. E.
) Fain to appear before me or some other Justice
for (p-361) said County to answer John W. Carr and A. F. Carr in a place of Debt Due by note in sum under _____. Warrant and _____ lien.

Make this 26 of December 1855.
                                                   R. D. Allison   (Seal)
                                                   J.P. for said County.

In the above case I give Judgment for the plaintiff for thirteen Dollars and ninety seven cents with Interest and cost this the 27 day of December 1855.
                                                   R. D. Allison J. P.
                                                   for said County.

Judgment confessed fifa issued the 10th of June 1856.

Execution -

State of Tennessee ,) To the sheriff or any constable of said County
Putnam County) I command you that of the Goods and chattles
) Lands and Tennessee of Wm. B. Gipson, Wm.
Evans, and R. E. Fain if to be found in your county you make thirteen Dollars and 97 cents with Interest and cost herein to satisfy a Judgment that A. J. and John Carr, Deceased, Recovered against them before me the 27th December 1855 and pay over the same as the Law Directs - This the 10th of June 1856.
                                                 R. D. Allison   (Seal)
                                                 J.P. for sd. County.

Endorsed Debt $13.97 cts. Wart. 10¢ Judgment 25 fifa 15 prs. fines hereon _____ R. D. Allison J. P.

No goods and chattles to be found in my County to ad. Levying to satisfy this fifa Land of Joseph - Levied upon a Tract Shaw and Wm. Evans of Land of the Rodgers and said Wm. Evan to contain Lying in Putnam one hundred County Dis. No. 10 acres be the same more or less on the waters of Martins Creek this the 12 of June 1856.
                                                 Joseph Shaw Const.
                                                 fee $1.00

All of which being seen and heard by the court on motion it is considered by the court that the Land so Levied upon as aforesaid be and the same is hereby condemned and ordered to be sold to satisfy the plaintiffs Debt and cost and all so the cost of this (p-362) motion and that an order of sale issue.

Ordered that _____ be adjourned untill tomorrow morning 8 oclock.

Jno. L. Goodall

Tuesday Morning August the 12th A. D. 1856 - Court met pursuant to adjournment Present the Honorable John Goodall Judge Presiding.

James C. Officer Admr) Debt Appeal
of W. G. Sims Decd) Came the parties by attornys and on affi-
Vs) davit of S. H. Colms attorny for the plain-
William Courton) tiff this cause is continued untill the
) next Term - upon the payment of the cost
of this Term by said plaintiff. It is therefore considered by the court that the Deft Recover of the plaintiff the cost of this Term of the court and that Execution issue.

State of Tennessee) Presentments for Drunkness - Came the at-
Vs) torney General for the State and the De-
William Carland) fendant in proper person They being arraigned
) and charged upon said presentments says he
is guilty in manner and form as therein charged against him. It is therefore ordered by the court that for such his offence he pay a fine of five Dollars and cost of this prosecution. It is therefore considered by the court that the State Recover against said Deft five Dollars the fine aforesaid and also all cost here in and that he be and remain in custody of the sheriff of Putnam County untill said fine and cost is paid or security Given for the same.

P-363 State of Tennessee) Presentment for nusance Came Attorny
Vs) General for the State and the Deft in
James B. Lowery) proper person and said Deft being ar-
) raigned and charged upon said present-
ment says he is guilty in manner and form as therein against him. It is therefore ordered by the court that said Deft for such his offence pay a fine of Five Dollars and the cost of this prosecution whereupon came here into open court Luther Clark and confessed Judgment Jointly with said Deft for said fine and cost this day adjudged against him. It is therefore considered by the court that the State of Tennessee Recover against said Deft and Luther Clark the sum of Five Dollars the fine aforesaid and also all cost herein and that Execution issue.

State of Tennessee) Indictment for murder - Robert Brown Prose-
Vs) cutor - Came the attorney General for the
William Crabtree) State and the Defendant in proper person and
) on affidavit of the Defendant this cause is
ordered to be continued untill the next Term of this court. Whereupon came the Defendant William Crabtree together Isaac Crabtree, Ephraim Crabtree, William E. B. Jones, Washington Crabtree, Galeman Craig, and Alfred Helms here into open court and acknowledged themselves to own and stand Indebted to the State of Tennessee in the sum of four Thousand Dollars to wit, the Defendant William Crabtree in the sum of Two Thousand Dollars and the said Isaac Crabtree, Ephraim Crabtree, William E. B. Jones Washington Crabtree, Galemon Craig and Alfred Helms Jointly and severally

in the sum of Two Thousand Dollars to be Levied of their proper goods and chattles Lands and Tenements to the use of the State of Tennessee to be remanded never the less to be void on condition (p-364) that the Defendant William Crabtree make his personal appearance before the Judge of Circuit Court of Putnam County to be held in the court house in the Town of Cookeville on the first Tuesday after the second Monday in December next then and there to answer the State upon the above Indictment and then and there attend untill Legally Discharged.

State of Tennessee) Indictment for murder Robert Brown Prosecutor
Vs) This day came here into open court Robert
William Crabtree) Brown, James Lathem, John Simpson, P. F.
) Laysdon, William Brown, Berry Hatfield, Manuel Hatfield, Washington Crabtree, James Wright, Augustine Allen, Galeman Craig, William Gilberth, Pleasant Miller and Alfred Helms and acknowledged themselves to owe and stand Indebted to the State of Tennessee in the sum of Two hundred and fifty Dollars Each to be Levied of there proper goods and chattles, Lands and Tennements to the use of State to be rendered never the less to be void on condition that they make their personal appearance before the Judge of the Circuit Court of Putnam County to be held at the courthouse in the Town of Cookeville on the first Tuesday after the second Monday in December next then and there the said Robert Brown to prosecute and Give Evidence in behalf of the State of Tennessee against William Crabtree and Ballance of said witnesses above named to give Evidence in behalf of the State against said Deft William Crabtree and then and there attend untill Legally Discharged.

State of Tennessee) Indictment for murder - Robert Brown Prose-
Vs) cutor - (p-365) Came into open court
William Crabtree) Ephraim Crabtree, James Niss, Jesse Crab-
) tree Jr., James M. Wright, Isaac Crabtree,
Martin Crautch, and acknowledged themselves to owe and stand indebted to the State of Tennessee in the sum of Two hundred and fifty Dollars each to be Levied of their proper Goods and chattles Lands and tenements to the use of the State to be remanded but to be void on condition that they make their personal appearance before the Judge of the Circuit Court for Putnam County to be held in the courthouse in the Town of Cookeville on the first Tuesday after the second Monday in December next then and there to testify and give Evidence in the behalf of the Deft in the above case and attend untill Legally Discharged.

State of Tennessee) Indictment for murder - Robert Brown Prose-
Vs) cutor - Came the attorney General for the
William Crabtree) State and the Deft in proper person and on
) affidavit of the prosecutor in this case
Robert Brown It is ordered by the court that an attachment issue against the Boddy of Fidelus Mason a witness in the cause Directed to the sheriff of Fentress County Ten - returnable here at the next term of this court compelling her to attend at the next term and Give Evidence in behalf of the state in the above cause.

E. W. Brown & Wife Alvira Brown) Ejeotment
Vs) Came the parties by attornies
Thomas Pullin) and on motion of Defendant by

attorny this cause is continued until the next term of this court upon the payment of the cost of this Term of this court by said Deft. It is therefore considered by the court that the plaintiff Recover against the Defendant the cost of this Term of the court and that Execution Issue.

P-366   On affidavit of Lewis Medly a Regular Traverse Juror at this Term of the court he being sick and not able to perform that duty as such. Ordered by the court that he be released and Discharged from further attendance.

James Bartlett and others   )   Ejectment
Vs   ) This day came the Defendant
Benjamin H. Watson and Lucy Watson) here in open court and came
) along with him Stephen H.
Colms and as security for said Defendants and acknowledged himself to owe and stand in debted to the plaintiff in this suit in the sum of Two Hundred and fifty Dollars for the payment of all costs in this suit should the same be adjudged against them upon a final hearing of the same.

State of Tennessee   ) Indictment for an assault with intent to com-
Vs   ) mit a Rape - Nelly Looper Prosecutor - Came
Major, Alias, Nig   ) the attorny General for the State and the
) Defendant in proper person by attorny having
heretofore at the last Term of this court moved the court to change the venire in this case - It is ordered by the court that the same be over ruled.

This day the Grand Jury returned into open court the following presentments to wit: State against John Dillon for Gaiming and State against John Dillon for Gaming - All of which is signed by the foreman of the of the Grand Jurors in Due form also at the same time returned and filed in court the following Bill of Indictment to wit: State against William Jones for an assault and Battery Endorsed thereon by their foreman. A True Bill, William H. Barons (p-367) Foreman of the Grand Jury and again retired to consider of the presentments Indictments and etc.

State of Tennessee   ) Indictment for an assault with intent to
Vs   ) commit a Rape - Nelly Looper Prosecutor.
Major, Alias, Nig   ) Came the attorny General for the State
) and the Defendant Lead to the bar in custody of the sheriff of Putnam County and said Defendant being arraigned and charged upon said bill of Indictment says he is not Guilty in manner and form as therein against him is charged, and for his trial puts himself upon the Country and the attorny General for the State Doth the Like. Whereupon came a Jury of good and Lawful men to wit, all house holders and free holders of the County of Putnam - James Brown, Shadrack Moonyham, Washington Cardwell, John R. Dun, John Farly, Mark Mathis, William Evans, Joseph Rodgers, Craven Shanks, Thomas Maddux, Armenias Lansford, and Johnathan Brown who being Elected tried and sworn well and truly to try and free deliverance to make Between the State of Tennessee and the Defendant at the Bar - who after having heard part of the Evidence in this

cause and there not being time this day to finish the trial of this cause, the Jurors were placed in charge of J. H. Moon Deputy sheriff of Putnam County, who was sworn to take them to some comfortable room and to keep them separate and apart from all other persons and to suffer no other persons to have any conversation with them that he would have none with them himself in relation to the trial of this cause and return again at the meeting of this court tomorrow morning.

F. N. Patterson) Debt Motion to condemn land - The following
Vs) papers were filed to wit, Warrant:
Edward McGuffy)

State of Tennessee) To the sheriff or
Putnam County) any lawful officer
) of said County. I
command you to summons Edward McGuffy to appear before me or some other Justice of peace for said (p-368) to F. N. Patterson in a plea of Debt to the use and Benefit of Gorden Shepherd Co. Due by note under fifty dollars herein fail not - given under my hand and seal January 17th 1855.

J. W. McDaniel (Seal)
for Putnam County

With the following Endorsements hereon to wit: Executed and set for trial before R. G. Duke Esq. This the 20th June 1855. A. Boyd Const. F. N. Patterson Vs Edward McGuffy - I give Judgment against Edward McGuffy and in favor of F. N. Patterson for the use of and Benefit of Gordon A. Shepard and Co. for the sum of forty six dollars and 78 and cost which Execution may issue this the 20 of January 1855 R. G. Duke for said County Execution.

State of Tennessee) To the sheriff or any constable for said
Putnam) County - I command of the goods and chattles
) Lands and Tenements for Edward McGuffy and
Silas McGuffy store if to be found in your County you make the sum of forty six dollars and 78 cents and cost to satisfy a Judgment that F. N. Patterson to the use of Gorden Shepard & Co. obtained against him before me on the 25 of June 1855 this the 30 of July 1856.

R. G. Duke (Seal)
J.P. for said County

Endorsed thereon to wit: finding no goods and chattles of the Deft. Levied on two hundred and twenty five acres of Land lying in Putnam County Dist. No. 13th to satisfy this Execution this Aug. 4th 1856.

A. Boyd Const.

This is Bounded with lands of J. M. Smelledge and Joseph Jarred - and Reubin Adams all of which being seen and heard by the court - It is considered by the court that the land Levied upon as aforesaid be and the same is hereby condemned and ordered to be sold to satisfy the plaintiffs Debt and cost (p-369) and also the cost of this motion and that an order of sale issue.

213

J. W. & A. F. Carr Adm. of William Carr Decd. Vs William Evans and H. H. Bryant	Debt Motion to condemn Land. The following papers were filed to wit: Warrant.

State of Tennessee Putnam County	To the sheriff or any constable of said County I command you to summons William Evans and H. H.

Bryant to appear before me or some other Justice of said County to answer John W. Carr and A. F. Carr Admr. of William Carr Decd. in a plea of debt Due by note for a sum under Warrant _____ this 26 December 1855.

R. D. Allison (Seal)
J.P. for said County

Endorsements thereon to wit: Judgment confesses in the above case - I give Judgment in favor of the plaintiff and against ____ for twelve and 56 ¢ with Interest and cost therein this 27 of December 1856.

R. D. Allison J.P.
for this County.

Execution -

State of Tennessee Putnam County	To the sheriff or any constable of said County I command you that of the goods, Lands and tenements of William Evans and H. H. Bryant if

to be found in your County you make twelve dollars and fifty to satisfy a judgment that A. F. Carr and John Carr adm. of William Carr Decd. against them before me on the 27 of December 1855 and pay over the same as the Law Directs this the 10 of Jan. 1856. R. D. Allison J. P. for Putnam County Endorsements thereon to wit: No goods and chattels to be found in my County to satisfy this fifa Levied upon a tract of Land of the said William Evans lying in Putnam County Dist. No. 10 on the waters of Martins Creek adjoining the lands of Joseph Shaw (p-370) and William Rogers and said to contain one Hundred acres be the same more or less - this the 12 of June 1856.

Joseph Shaw Const.

All of which being seen and heard by the court. It is considered by the court that the land Levied upon as aforesaid be and the same is hereby condemned and ordered to be sold to satisfy the plaintiffs Debt and cost and also the cost of this motion and that an order of sale issue.

Ordered that court be adjourned untill tomorrow morning ½ after 7 oclock.

Jno. L. Goodall

Wednesday Morning August 13th 1856

Court met persuant to adjournment - Present Hon. John L. Goodall Judge Presiding.

Wesley Harvy Vs J. W. Berry	Debt motion to condemn Land - The following papers were filed to wit: Motion It appearing to me that Judgment was Entered against Wesly Harvy - as security for J. W. Berry in favor of Gilbert Thompson

assinee of Green Crowder for sixty Eight dollars and twenty cents and the cost and that the said Wesly Harvy has paid the same it is therefore considered by me that the said Wesly Harvy Recover of the said J. W. Berry the said sum of sixty Eight dollars and twenty cents and all costs and that Execution issue for the same this 21 day of May 1856.

J. A. Baker J.P.

Execution -

State of Tennessee) To the sheriff or any constable of said County
Putnam County) I command you that of goods and chattles Lands
) and Tenements of J. W. Berry if to be found in your County you make the sum of sixty Eight Dollars and (p-371) twenty cents and all costs to satisfy that Wesly Harvy obtained against him before me on the 21st day of May 1856.

J. A. Baker J.P.
for Putnam County

Endorsed thereon to wit: No goods and chattles to be found in my County to satisfy this Execution of this fifa Levied upon a tract of Land of the said John W. Berry lying in Putnam County in the Dist. No. 8th on the waters of Cany fork adjoining the lands of Abraham Ditty and Peter Goolsby and to contain fifty acres by Estimation Be the same more or less this the 22 of May 1856.

A. S. Ferrell Const. fee 100 - All of which being seen & heard by the court It is considered by the court that the Land Levied upon as aforesaid be and the same is hereby condemned and ordered to be sold to satisfy the plaintiffs Debt and cost and also the costs of this motion and that an order of sale issue.

A. E. Hogin) Debt Motion to condemn Land - The following papers
Vs) were filed to wit: Warrant -
John W. Berry)

State of Tennessee) To the sheriff or any
Putnam County) constable of said County
) I command you to summons John W. Berry to appear before me or some other Justice of said County to answer A. J. Hogin in a plea of Debt due by note under fifty dollars herein fail not - Given under my hand and seal this the first day of June 1856.

John Lee (Seal)
J.P. for Putnam
County.

With the following Endorsements hereon to wit: Executed and set for trial before J. A. Baker Esq. on the 25th of this Instant this the 17 Aug. 1855. Joseph Shaw Const. fee 50¢ A. E. Hogin Vs John W. Berry.

In this case I give Judgment in favor of the plaintiff and against the Deft John W. Berry for twenty two Dollars and fifty two (p-372) cents and the cost for which Execution may issue this the 25 Aug. 1855.

J. A. Baker J.P.

Execution

State of Tennessee) To the sheriff or any constable of said County

Putnam County) I command you that of goods and chattles lands
) and tenements of J. W. Berry if to be found in
your County you make the sum of twenty six Dollars and fifty two cents
and all cost to satisfy a Judgment that A. E. Hogin obtained against him
before me on the 25th day of August 1855 and pay over the same as the law
Directs this 28th day of June 1856.

            J. A. Baker J. P. for
            said County.

Endorsed thereon to wit: No goods and chattles to be found in County Levied upon a tract of Land of the Deft Lying in Putnam County Dist. No. 8th on the waters of Cany fork adjoining the lines of Abraham Ditty and Peter Goolsby and said to contain fifty acres By estimation Be the same more or less this the 28 June 1856.

            Joseph Shaw Const.

All of which being seen and heard by the court It is considered by the court that the Land Levied upon as aforesaid be and the same is hereby condemned and ordered to be sold to satisfy the plaintiffs Debt and costs and also costs of this motion and that an order of sale issue.

State of Tennessee) Presentment for Drunkness came the Attorney
Vs) General for the State and the Deft in proper
William Carland) person whereupon came here into open court
) Washington G. Collier and confessed Judgment
Jointly with said Deft for the fine and cost adjudged against said Defendant on yesterday It is therefore considered by the court that the State of Tennessee Recover against said Deft and Washington G. Collier (p-373) the sum of Five Dollars the fine and also all cost herein and that Execution issue.

State) Indictment for murder in 1st Degree Shadrach Moony-
Vs) ham Prosecutor - Came the attorney General for the
Henry Ayres) State and the Deft in proper person and it appear-
) ing to the satisfaction of the court that Samuel
Turney Esqr who was appointed at the last Term of this court to aid and defend said Deft upon the trial of this cause being absent the court therefore appointes Stephen H. Colms attorny to aid and defend said Deft upon the trial of this cause he being poor and wholly unable to employ counsel.

Isam Smith)   Debt Appeal
Vs) Came the parties by attornies and on motion of
Edward Anderson) the Defendant It is ordered by the court that
) the plaintiff give security for the prosecution
of this suit on or before the calling of the same for trial or the same shall stand dismissed.

State of Tennessee) Indictment for assault to commit a Rape
Vs) Nelly Looper Prosecutor - Came again the at-
Major, Alias Nig) torny General for the State and the Defendant
) Led to the Bar of the court in custody of the
Sheriff of Putnam County and came also the same Jury Elected tried and sworn in this cause on yesterday in charge of J. H. Moon Deputy Sheriff of Putnam

County sworn to take charge of them, who after having heard the Ballance of the Evidence in this cause and the argument of counsel thereon and Received their charge from the Honorable court Retired to their room in charge of (p-374) J. H. Moon Deputy Sheriff to consider of their verdict and again Returned into court in charge of J. H. Moon Deputy Sheriff and upon their oath do say that said Defendant is Guilty in manner and form as in the Bill of Indictment is charged against him ordered that the Defendant be remanded to Jail.

State of Tennessee) Indictment for murder 1st Degree Shadrack
Vs) Moonyham Prosecutor - Came the attorny Gen-
Henry Ayres) eral for the State and the Defendant Lead
) to the Bar in custody of the sheriff of
Putnam County who being arraigned and charged upon said bill of Indictment says he is not Guilty in manner and form as therein is charged against him and for his trial puts himself upon the County and the attorney General for the State doth the Like whereupon came a Jury of good and lawful men to wit: William S. Saylor, Thomas Porter, Benjamin H. Watson, Samuel K. Wilkerson, Thomas J. Poteet, Gabrel Hearen , Harrison Green, Claborn Bohannon, Wiseman Hearen, J. W. Franklin, Gallant Anderson and Howard C. Martin all house holders or free holders of the County of Putnam, who being Elected tried and sworn well and truly to try and true deliverance to make Between the State of Tennessee and the Defendant at the Bar, and there not being time this day to further proceed with the trial of this cause the Jurors in charge of J. H. Moon Deputy Sheriff of Putnam County who was sworn to take them to some comfortable Room and to keep them separate and apart from all other persons and to suffer no person to have any conversation with them or himself in relation to the trial of this cause and return with them herein this (p-375) Court tomorrow morning ordered that the Defendant be remanded to Jail.

Isaac Burton) Debt Appeal
Vs) Came the parties by their attornies and the De-
Thomas Lancister) fendant by attorny objected to the arbitrators
) filed in this cause at this Term of the court
which objection was sustained by the court and by agrument of the parties by attornies - It is ordered by the court that the order made in this cause at the last Term of this court Refering arbitratment of this cause to Joseph Mitchell and Harvy Carr be revived.

State of Tennessee) Presentment for tipling - It appearing to the
Vs) satisfaction of the court that the Defendant
Drury W. Sims) was tried and convicted upon the above pre-
) sentment at the December Term of this court
1855 and that Judgment was rendered against him and James A. Mahan his security for the fine and cost and that Execution was regularly issued against them for the same and returned by the sheriff of Putnam County.

It is therefore considered by the court that Judgment be and the same is rendered against the State of Tennessee for the following bill of cost to wit: Atty. General T. H. Williams fee 2.50 Clk. Mills Taxing cost 25¢ for Judgment final 75¢ charging prisoner and his plea 50¢ capias 75¢ 2 spas for state 12½ each for this Judgment 75¢ Sheriff P. Bohannon fee Executing capias 100½ Bond 25¢ calling case 4¢ .   1.29

Ordered by court that the County of Putnam pay the above (p-376) bill of costs and that the sum be certified for allowance.

State of Tennessee) Presentment for Tipling - It appearing to the
Vs) satisfaction of the court that the Deft was
Drury W. Sims) tried and convicted upon the above present-
) ment at the December of this court 1855 and
that Judgment was Rendered him and James A. Mahan his security for the fine and cost and that Execution was regularly issued against said Debt and James A. Mahan his security for the same and Returned by the sheriff of Putnam, Nulla Bona It is therefore considered by the court that be and the same is Rendered against the State of Tennessee for the following bill of cost to wit Att. General T. H. Williams fee   2.50
Clk Mills for Taxing cost 25¢ Judgment   .75 ¢
Order remitting fine   .25 ¢
Charging and his plea   .50 ¢
issuing 1 spas   .12½ ¢
Capias   .75¢
1 security   .25¢
fifa   .37¢
for this Judgment   .75¢
Sheriff P. Bohannon Executing capias   1.00
Bond 25¢ calling case   -   -   -   .29

                    Making in all   7.79

Ordered by the court that the County of Putnam pay the above bill of cost and that the same be certified for allowance.

F. N. Paterson) Debt motion to condemn Land The following papers
Vs) were filed to wit: Warrant -
John Roberts)

        State of Tennessee) Debt motion to con-
        Vs) demn Land - The follow-
        John Roberts) ing paper were filed
) to wit: Warrant -

State of Tennessee) To the sheriff or any constable of said
Putnam County) County - I command you to summon John Roberts
) to appear before me or some other Justice
of the peace for said County (p-378) (Page 377 Left Out) to answer F. N. Paterson in a plea of Debt Due by note for a sum under fifty dollars herein fail not. Given under my hand and seal this the 23 of January 1855.

                                                  E. C. Crowell J. P.
                                                  for Putnam County

Endorsed hereon to wit: I acknowledge the service of the within warrant and agree that Judgment may be rendered against me for the same this 24 January 1855 John W. Roberts - I give Judgment in this case in favor of the plaintiff for twenty one dollars 85¢ and all Lawful cost January 24th 1855.

                                                  R. D. Allison (Seal)
                                                J.P. for Putnam County

Execution -

State of Tennessee) To the sheriff or any constable of said County
Putnam County) I command that of goods and chattles Lands and
) tenements of John Roberts and Marian Roberts
if to be found in your county you make the sum of twenty one dollars 86
cents besides Interest and all Lawful cost to satisfy a judgment that F.
N. Paterson obtained against them before me 22nd Feb. 1855 pay over the
sum as the Law Directs this the 29 May 1856.

                R. D. Allison (Seal)
                J.P. for Putnam County

Endorsed thereon to wit: No goods and chattles to be found in my County
Levied upon a tract of Land in Putnam Dist. No. 13 to ajoin the Lands of
John R. Carr on the south and on the East by Vons Land on the west by Vons
Land and said to contain one Hundred acres more or less this 4 June 1856.

                David E. L. Franklin
                Const.

 All of which being seen and heard by the court. It is considered by
the court that the land Levied upon as aforesaid be and the same is here
by condemned and ordered to be sold to satisfy the plaintiffs Debt and cost
and also the cost of this motion and that an order of sale issue.

P-379 J. A. Ray   ) Debt Motion to condemn Land - The
    Vs   ) following papers were filed to
   J. H. and F. M. Robert) wit: Warrant -

State of Tennessee) To the sheriff or any constable of said County
Putnam County) I command you to summons Joseph Roberts to
) appear before me or some other Justice of the
peace for said County to answer J. A. Ray in a plea of Debt for a sum under
ten Dollars this 20 June 1856.

                R. D. Allison J. P.
                for said County

Endorsed hereon to wit: Executed and set for trial on the 27 of June
1855 before E. C. Crowell Esq. J. W. Carr Const. Judgment for the plaintiff and against the Deft for nine dollars and 80 cents and all lawfull
cost for which Execution may issue this 24 June 1855.

                E. C. Crowell J.P.

Stayed by F. M. Roberts.

Execution -

State of Tennessee) To the sheriff or any constable of said County
Putnam County) I command you that of the goods and chattles
) Lands and tenements of John H. Roberts, F. M.
Roberts if to be found in your County make the sum of nine dollars and 80
cents principle besides all lawfull cost to satisfy a judgment that J. A.
Ray obtained against them before me on 27th June 1855.
 Given under my hand and seal this the 6 May 1856.

                E. C. Crowell (Seal)
                J.P.

Endorsed hereon to wit:

No goods and chattles to be found in my County - Levied upon a tract of land of the Deft lying in Putnam County Dist. 13 ajoining the lands of John R. Carr on the south and on the East by Vons Land and on the west by Vons land and said to contain one Hundred acres this 4 June 1856. My fee 100¢.

                David E. L. Franklin
                Const.

Page 380 All of which being seen and heard by the court - It is considered by the court that the land Levied upon as aforesaid be and the same is hereby condemned and order to be sold to satisfy the plaintiff debt and cost and also the cost of this motion and that an order of sale issue.

Susan Cole)   Trespass
 Vs) Came the plaintiff by hur attorny and moved the
David G. Harris) court for Judgment against Deft by Default and it
) appearing to the satisfaction of the court that the plaintiff in this suit had filed her Declaration in this cause on the 16th day of April 1856, which being the 3rd day of the Last Term of this court, and that the Deft had failed to plead to the same whereupon the Deft being solemnly called to come into court and defend this suit came not, but made default and because it does not appear to the court what Damages the plaintiff has sustained by reason of the premises - It is ordered by the court that a Jury come at the next term of court to assess the plaintiffs Damage - this Entry should have appeared upon the minits of this court of yestarday but is made now for then.

Susan Cole) Trespass and Damages came the parties by their
 Vs) attornys and on motion and affidavit of the Deft
David G. Harris) by attorny. It is ordered by the court that the
) Judgment Taken by Default against said Deft on yestarday be set aside and that the Defendant have Leave to plead to the plaintiff Declaration.

P-381 Ordered by court that Charles Hunter, William B. Grogan, J. T. Huston, Jefferson Dunagan they failing to attend when called as Tallismen Jurors It is ordered that Each of them pay a fine of one Dollar Each for their failure aforesaid.

State   ) Presentment for an assault and Battery - The
 Vs   ) Grand Jury returned into court a presentment
Elias Whitaker) against the Deft signed by the foreman of the
) Grand Jury and all the Ballance of the Grand Jury in due form and again retired to consider of presentments, Indictments and etc.

Ordered that Court be adjourned untill tomorrow morning half after 7 oclock.

                Jno. L. Goodall

      Thursday Morning August the 14th A.D. 1856

Court met pursuant to adjournment - Present the Honorable John L. Goodall Judge presiding and etc.

J. A. Ray   )   Debt Motion to condemn land - The following papers
  Vs   )   to wit: Warrant -
John Grider   )

State of Tennessee   )   To the sheriff or any constable of said County
Putnam County   )   I command you to summons John Grider to appear
)   before me or some other Justice of peace for
said County to answer the complaint of J. A. Ray in a plea of Debt Due by account herein fail not. Given under my hand and seal this 6th day of June 1856.

                  E. L. Thompson (Seal)
                  J.P. for said County

Endorsed hereon to wit: Executed and set for trial before E. L. Thompson Esq at his own house on the 14 day of June 1856 - J. Henry Const.

P-382   J. A. Ray   )   I give Judgment in this case for the plain-
           Vs   )   tiff and against the Deft for two Dollars
         John Grider   )   and forty two and ½ cents and cost for
)   which Execution may issue this 14th June
                             1856.
                  E.L. Thompson (Seal)

Execution

State of Tennessee   )   To the sheriff or any constable of said
Putnam County   )   County I command you that of goods and
)   chattles, lands and tenements of John
Grider if to ____ found in your County you make or cause to be made the sum of two dollars and forty two and ½ cents with interest thereon with all cost to satisfy a Judgment that J. A. Ray obtained against him before me on the 14th day of June 1856 and pay over the same as the Law directs this the 18th of June 1856.

                  E.L. Thompson (Seal)
                  J.P. for said County

Endorsed thereon to wit: Came to hand 18th June 1856 - No goods and chattles to be found in my county Levied upon a tract of Land of the Deft lying in Putnam County Dist. No. 1 adjoining the lands of Maragret Irvin and Permelia Pointer and William Crabtree and said to contain one Hundred acres this 18th day of June 1856.

                  J. Henry Constable

All of which being seen and heard by the court - It is considered by the court that the land Levied as aforesaid be and the same is hereby condemned and ordered to be sold to satisfy the plaintiffs Debt and cost also the cost of this motion and that an order of sale issue.

J. A. Ray   )   Debt Motion to condemn Land - The following papers
  Vs   )   were filed to wit, Warrant -
E. H. Bryant   )
John Grider

P-283   State of Tennessee) To the sheriff or any constable of
        Putnam County   ) said County - I command to summons
) Howel H. Bryant and John Grider to
appear before me or some other Justice for said County to answer the complaint of Jefferson Brown to the use of J. A. Ray in a plea of debt due by note in a sum under one Hundred dollars - Given under my hand and seal this 6th June 1856.

              E. L. Thompson J. P.
              (Seal)

Endorsed hereon to wit: Executed and set for trial before me E. L. Thompson Esq. at his own house on the 7th day of July 1856. J. Henry Const. Judgment J. A. Ray Vs H. H. Bryant and John Grider - I give Judgment in this case for the county and against the Deft for sixty five dollars and fifty two cents and cost of suit for which Execution may issue this 7th July 1856.

              E. L. Thompson J. P.

Execution

State of Tennessee   ) To the sheriff or any constable of said County.
Putnam County   ) I command you that of the goods and chattles
) Lands and Tenements of H. H. Bryant and John
Grider if to be found in your County you cause to be made the sum of sixty five dollars and fifty two cents with Interest thereon and all lawful cost to satisfy a Judgment that J. A. Ray obtained against them before me on the 7th day of July 1856 and pay over the same as the Law directs this 11 day of July 1856.

              E. L. Thompson J. P.
              for said County

Endorsed hereon to wit: Came to hand 11th day July 1856. No goods and chatles to be found in my County Levied upon a tract of land in Dist. No.1 adjoining the Lands of Permelia Pointer and William Crabtree and said to contain 100 acres this July 11th 1856 at the hour of Eleven morning.

              J. Henry Const.

All of which being (p-304) seen and heard by the court It is considered by the court that the land Levied upon as aforesaid be and the land is hereby condemned and ordered to be sold to satisfy the plaintiffs debt and cost and also the cost of this motion and that an order of sale issue.

J. A. Ray   ) Debt Motion to condemn Land - The following papers
Vs   ) were filed to wit: Warrant -
John Grider   )

      State of Tennessee   ) To the sheriff or any
      Putnam County   ) constable of said County
) I command you to summons
John Grider to appear before me or some other Justice of peace of said County to answer the complaint of J. A. Ray In a plea of debt and due by note under one Hundred dollars - Given under my hand and seal this 6 day of June 1856.

              E. L. Thompson (Seal)
              J. P. for said County

Endorsed thereon to wit: Executed and set for trial before me E. L. Thompson Esq. at his own house on the 14th day of June 1856.

J. Henry Constable

J. A. Ray Vs John Grider - I give Judgment in this case in favor of the plaintiff and against the Deft for sixty two dollars Eighty four and ½ cents and cost of suit for which Execution may issue this 14 June 1856.

E. L. Thompson J. P.

Execution -

State of Tennessee) To the sheriff or any lawful officer of said
Putnam County) County - I command that of goods and chatles
) Land and tenements of John Grider if to be
found in your county you make the sum of sixty two dollars and 84½ ¢ to satisfy a judgment that J. A. Ray obtained against him and pay ober the sum as the Law Directs this the 18th day of June 1856.

E. L. Thompson (Seal)
J.P. for said County

Endorsed thereon to wit: Came to hand 18th June 1856 No goods and chattles to be found in my (p-385) County Levied upon a tract of Land of the Deft lying in Putnam County, District No. 1 adjoining the lands of Margaret Irvin and Permelia Pointer and William Crabtree and said to contain one Hundred acres this the 18th day of June 1856.

J. Henry Const.

All of which being seen and herd by the court - It is therefore considered by the court that the land Levied upon as aforesaid be and the same is hereby condemned and ordered to be sold to satisfy the plaintiffs Debt and cost and also the cost of this motion and that an order of sale issue.

C. F. Burton) Debt Motion to condemn Land - The following
Vs) papers were filed to wit - Warrant -
Thomas J. Smith)

State of Tennessee) To any sheriff or
Putnam County) constable of said
) county - I command
you to summons Thomas J. Smith to appear before me or some other Justice of the peace for said County to answer the complaint of C. F. Burton in a plea of Debt Due by note under one Hundred dollars herein fail not.
Given under my hand and seal this the 5 day of June 1855.

J. W. McDaniell J. P.
for said County.

Endorsed hereon to wit: Executed and set for trial before E. C. Crowell on the 16th Feb. 1855.

A. Boyd Constable

C. F. Burton Vs T. J. Smith - I give Judgment for the plaintiff and against the Deft for ninety seven dollars and 72 cents with all lawfull cost and

Interest for which Execution may issue this 16th Feb. 1855.

                E. C. Crowell J. P.

Execution -

State of Tennessee) To the Sheriff or any constable of said County
Putnam   ) I command that of the goods and chattles, Lands
) and tenements of Thomas J. Smith and G. W.
Medly security for the same if to be found in your (p-386) County you make the sum of ninety seven dollars and 72 cents principal with all lawful Interest and cost to satisfy a judgment that Charles F. Burton obtained against the said Smith before me on the 16th Feb. 1855 - collect and pay over as the law directs.
 Given under my hand and seal this 8th of Aug. 1856.

                E. C. Crowell J. P.
                for said County

Endorsed thereon to wit: No goods and chattles to be found in my County Levied upon a tract of land of the Defts lying in Putnam County Dist. No. 13th and said to contain four Hundred acres adjoining the lands of Jonathan Smith this 8th August 1856.

                A. Boyd Constable

 All of which being seen and heard by the court it is considered by the court that the Lands Levied upon as aforesaid be and the same is hereby condemned and ordered to be sold to satisfy the plaintiffs Debt and cost and also the cost of this motion and that an order of sale issue.

J. H. Roberts   ) Debt Motion to condemn Land - The following paper
 Vs   ) were filed to wit, Warrant -
Linnsey Vickes)

         State of Tennessee) To the sheriff or
         Putnam County   ) any constable of
) said County I command you to summons Linsey Wickes to appear before me or some other Justice of peace for said County to answer John Roberts in a plea of Trespass on the case for taking two bee gums of his the said Roberts from the widow Roberts that he had bought and paid for to his damages fifty dollars and therefore he sues - Given under my hand and seal this 23 July 1855.

                E. C. Crowell J. P. for
                said County.

Endorsed hereon to wit: Executed and set for trial the 9 of Aug. 1856 before E. C. Crowell.

                J. W. Carr Constable

P-387 John Roberts Vs Lindley Vickes - It is considered by me that the Defendant is not guilty as charged in the warrant - I therefore give Judgment in favor of the Deft and against the plaintiff for all cost in this case accrued this 11th of August 1855.

                E. C. Crowell J. P.
                Stayed F. N. Patterson

Execution   )

State of Tennessee   )   To the sheriff or any constable of said Coun-
Putnam County   )   ty I command you that of the goods and chatles
)   lands and tenements of John Roberts and F. N.
Patterson for the stay of Execution.

State of Tennessee   )   To the sheriff or any constable of said County
Putnam County   )   I command you that of the goods and chatles
)   lands and tenements of John Roberts and F. N.
Patterson for the stay of Execution if to be found in your County you make
the sum of five dollars and seventy five cents with all lawful Interest
and cost that will be after to satisfy this fifa and Judgment Rendered
against the said Roberts for the cost of suit - wherein he was plaintiff
and Lindsley Vickes was Deft before me on the 9th day of Aug. 1856 fail
not - Given under my hand and seal this 9 June 1856.

                                        E. C. Crowell (Seal)
                                        J. P. for said County

Endorsed thereon to wit: No goods and chattles to be found in my County
Levied upon a tract of land of the Deft Lying in Putnam Dist. No. 13 adjoining the John R. Carr on the south and on the south and southeast Vons
and on the west by Vons containing one Hundred acres this 14 day of June
1856.
                                        David E. L. Franklin
                                        Constable

    All of which being seen and heard by the court - It is considered by
the court that the land Levied upon as aforesaid be and the same is here
by condemned and ordered to be sold to satisfy the plaintiffs Debt and
cost and also the cost of this motion and that an order of sale issue.

State of Tennessee   )   Indictment for an assault with intent to
        Vs   )   commit a Rape - Nelly Looper Prosecutor -
Major, Alias Nig   )   P-388 This day John E. Hamilton sheriff
)   and Jailer of Overton County produced and
read here in open court his account for keeping said Deft in the common
Jail of Overton County on a charge of Rape from the 14 of April 1856 up
to the 11 of Aug. 1856 making in all 119 days at 40 cents per day $47.60
April the 14th 1856 to 1 turnkey - -   .50
Aug. 10th to 1856 1   "   "   .50
To taking in Nig from Cookeville to Livingston by order of court at
April term 1856 - 44 mi 10¢.   4.40
Returning Nig to this Aug. Term of the court 1856 -22 miles 10¢   2.20
Mack Brown To two Guards Alexander Kendall   2.20   4.40
To Two men as a guard Alexander Kendall and Mack Brown 22 miles E. 2.20

                Making in all the sum $ 61.80

Which act. having been certified by the attorny General to be correct and
it appearing to the court there had been no Jail in Putnam County - It is
allowed by the court and ordered to be Taxed in the Bill of cost.

State of Tennessee   )   Peace Warrant Zilly Whitaker Prosecutor
        Vs   )   It appearing to the satisfaction of the
Elias Whitaker   )   court that the Deft was bound over to the

April Term of this court 1855 and that Zilly Whitaker the prosecutor in this cause was Taxed with the cost of the prosecution at the April Term of this court 1855 and that Judgment was rendered against her for the cost of the prosecution and that Execution had been Regularly issued against her for the same and Returned by the sheriff of Putnam County Nulla Bona - It is therefore   (p-389)   considered by the court that Judgment be and the same is hereby entered against the State of Tennessee for the following Bill of cost to wit: Atto. Genl. T. M. William Tax on $2.50. Clerk Mills Judgment for cost 25¢ Taxing Const 25¢ one continuance 37½¢ order, Discharging Deft 25¢ for this Judgment 75¢   1.87½
J. P. J. B. Clark issuing 1 spa. 10¢ issuing 2 spa 15¢ for issuing wrt. 25¢ for Judgment 75¢ - 1.25 const. Samuel Hughes serving warrant 50¢ summoning 2 witnesses 25¢ E.   1.00
Witness I. Whitaker before J. P.   .50
Making in all the sum of $7.12½

    Ordered by court that the County of Putnam pay the above Bill of cost and that the same is certified for allowance and etc.

State of Tennessee) Indictment for an assault with intent to com-
   Vs) mit Rape - Nelly Looper Prosr. - Came the
Major, Alias Nig) attorney General for the State and the Defend-
) ant in proper person, whereupon the Defendant by attorney moved the court for a new trial, whereupon the same was Granted ordered that Defendant be remanded to Jail.

State of Tennessee) Indictment for an assault - with intent to
   Vs) commit Rape - Nelly Looper Prosecutor - This
Major, Alias Nig) day came here into open court Nelly Looper
) Myra Looper, Granville Looper, Joel Looper
Fountain Sexton, W. L. Wright and Levi Clark and acknowledges themselves to owe and stand indebted to the State of Tennessee in the sum of Two hundred and fifty Dollars Each to be Levied of their Respective proper Goods and chattles Lands and Tenements to the use of the State to be rendered never the less to be void if they make their personal   (p-390) appearance before the Judge of the Circuit Court for Putnam County to be held for the County of Putnam in the court house in the Town of Cookeville on the first Tuesday after the second Monday in December next then and there the said Nelly Looper to prosecute and Give Evidence in behalf of the State of Tennessee against said Defendant and the Ballance of said witness above named to Give Evidence in behalf of the State of Ten - against said Defendant and not depart untill Legally Discharged.

William Mitchell) Debt Appeal
   Vs) Came the parties by attornies and on motion of
John Young) the Deft by attorny, It is ordered by the court
) that the plaintiff Give security for the prosecution of this suit on or before the calling of the same for trial or the same shall stand Dismissed.

State of Tennessee) Indictment for murder 1st Degree - Shadrach
   Vs) Moonyham Prosecutor - Came again the attor-
Henry Ayres) ney General for the State and the Defendant

Lead to the Bar of the court in custody of the shff of Putnam County and came also the same Jury Elected tried and sworn in this cause on yesterday in charge of J. H. Moore Deputy Sheriff of Putnam County sworn to take charge of them and who after having heard all of the Evidence in this cause and the argument of counsel thereon and Received their charge from the Honorable court Retired to consider of their verdict in charge of J. H. Moore Deputy Shff and again Returned into court and upon their oath do say that said Defendant is Guilty in manner and form as charged in the Bill of Indictment in this cause and the Jurors aforesaid upon their oath aforesaid to further say that said Defendant for such his offence be imprisoned in common Jail (p-391) and penitentiary house of the State of Tennessee for the Term of four years ordered by the court that the Deft be remanded to Jail.

State of Tennessee) Indictment for Pettit Larceny James M. Lead-
Vs) better Prosr. - Came the attorney General for
John Watts) the State and the Deft in proper person and
) it appearing to the satisfaction of the court
that the Deft was poor and wholly unable to Employ counsel to aid and defend him on the trial of this cause - Therefore the court appointe and assignes B. B. Washburn and L. T. Lowe Gentlemen practicing attornies in this court to aid said Deft upon the trial of this cause and thereupon entered upon their duties as such.

State of Tennessee) Indictment for Pettit Larceny - James M. Lead-
Vs) better prosecutor - Came the attorny General
John Watts) for the State and the Defendant Lead to the
) Bars of the court in custody of the sheriff
of Putnam County who being arraigned and charged upon the Bill of Indictment says he is not Guilty in manner and form as therein charged against him and for the trial puts himself upon the country and the attorny General for the State doth the Like whereupon came a Jury of good and Lawful men house holders or free holders of Putnam County - To Wit: Joseph Evans, Edward Choat, Jesse Elliott, John Stewart, Felix J. Carr, Carroll Dyer, Jesse Barons, Joshua Sherrell, John T. Graham, William J. Mills, James B. Bennett, Alexander Montgomery, who being Elected tried and sworn well and truly to try and True deliverance to make (p-392) Between the State of Tennessee and the Defendant at the bar - who after having heard all of the Evidence in this cause and the argument of counsel and received their charge from the Honorable court retired to consider of their verdict in charge of Alexander Boyd a constable of Putnam County sworn to take charge of them and again returned into court and declared they could not agree upon a verdict in this cause and there not being time this day to proceed further with the trial of this cause the Jurors were placed in charge of Alexander Boyd a constable sworn to take charge of them untill the meeting of this court to-morrow.

Ordered by the court that the Deft be remanded to Jail .

J. W. Richison) Ejectment - By consent of the parties by attor-
Vs) nies and there not being time at this Term of
John Roland and) court to try this cause the same is ordered to
Edward Vaughn) be continued untill the next Term of this court.

John Terry   )   Debt
   Vs   ) By consent of the parties by attorney and there not
Elias Green   ) being time at this Term of the court to try this
) cause. The same is ordered to be continued untill
the next Term of this court.

Allen Young   )   Debt Appeal
   Vs   ) By consent of the parties by attornies and there
John Coggins   ) not being time at this term of court to try this
Willis Coggins   ) cause the same is ordered to be continued untill
) the next Term of this court.

P-393 William W. Berry)   Debt
          Vs   ) By consent of parties by attornies and
       Robert E. Fain   ) there not being time at this term of
) court to try this cause the same is
ordered to be continued untill the next term of court.

George Bohannon)   Trespass
   Vs   ) By the consent of the parties by attornies and
John Slyger   ) there not being time at this Term of the court to
) try this cause the sum is ordered to be continued
untill the next Term of this court.

William Baker   )   Damage Appeal
   Vs   ) By consent of the parties by
W. H. Barnes and Jeremiah Whitson   ) attornies and there not being
) time at this Term of the court
to try this cause the same is ordered to be continued untill the next Term
of this court.

Thomas T. Murry)   Debt Appeal
   Vs   ) By consent of the parties by attornys and not being
K. M. Murphy   ) time at this Term of the Court to try this cause
) the same is ordered to be continued untill the next
Term of this court.

P-394 Patrick Brady   )   Damage Appeal
          Vs   ) By consent of the parties by attornys and
       John Jackson   ) there not being time at this Term of the
) court to try this cause the same is ordered
to be continued untill the next Term of this court.

Isam Smith   )   Debt Appeal
   Vs   ) By consent of the parties by attornies and there
Edward Anderson   ) not being time at this term of the court to try
) this cause the same is ordered to be continued
untill the next term of this court.

Daniel Brown   )   Debt Appeal
   Vs   )   By consent of the parties by attornies and there
R. G. Maddux   )   not being time of the court to try this cause the
)   same is ordered to be continued untill the next
Term of this court.

John Farley   )   Ejectment
   Vs   )   By consent of the parties by attor-
Jesse and Jefferson Farley)   nies and there not being time at
)   this Term of court to try this cause
the same is ordered to be continued untill the next Term of this court.

State of Tennessee)   Came the attorny Gen. for the State and
   Vs   )   the Deft in proper person and by consent
John H. Roberts   )   of attorny General this cause is ordered
)   to be continued untill the next - - Where
upon came here into open court the Defendant together with Edward Anderson, F. N. Patterson and Hugh Wallis and acknowledged themselves to owe
and stand indebted to the state   (p-395)   in the sum of five hundred
dollars to wit: The Deft in the sum of two Hundred and fifty dollars
and the said Edward Anderson, F. N. Patterson and Hugh Wallace in the sum
of two Hundred and fifty dollars, Jointly and severally to be levied of
their proper goods and chattles lands and tenements to the use of the State
to be rendered but to be void if the said John H. Roberts make his personal appearance before the Judge of the circuit for Putnam County to be held
at the court house in the town of Cookeville on the first Tuesday after
the second in December next then and there to answer the State upon the
above charge and attend untill legally Discharged.

Edward Vaughn   )   Ejectment
   Vs   )   Came the Deft and came along with him here into
John Roberts   )   open court F. N. Paterson and William B. Lee Sr.,
)   Joseph Lee and as security for the Deft acknow-
ledged themselves to owe and stand indebted to the plaintiffs in this
suit in the sum of two Hundred and fifty dollars for the payment of all
cost in this suit should the same be Judged against him upon the final
hearing of the same.

State of Tennessee   )   Indictment for Ludness John W.
   Vs   )   Maxwell, Prosecutor - Came the
Wm. B. Roland and Janie Bruce   )   Attorny General for the State
)   and with the assent of the court
says he will no further prosecute this suit against Wm. B. Roland one of
the above named Lefts - It is therefore ordered   (p-396)   by the court
that said Defts be Discharged and that the State of Ten - pay all cost on
part of the prosecution in this suit Expended as to him and that the same
be certified for allowance as the Law Directs This Entry should have appeared upon the minutes of yesterday but is made for then.

Josiah Webb   )   Decree
   Vs   )   Be it remembered that on the 14th day of August
Drucela Webb   )   1856 This cause came on to be heard before the

Honorable John L. Goodall Judge and upon the petition and order of publication when it appearing to the court that the Deft is a non resident of this state and that publication has been Regularly made in the herald of the times a news paper published in the town of Sparta Ten for more than four weeks warning Deft to appear and plead answer or demurr to complainants petition and that Deft has failed to enter her defence to said petition It is therefore ordered by the court that said petition be taken for confessed against Defendant and set for hearing Expartee at the present Term of this court when said cause came on again to be further heard upon the petition Judgment for confession and proof when it appeared to the court that complainant and Deft were married about seven years ago that they were citizens of Putnam County and in the teritory which now composes said County about five years that since their marriage Deft has been Guilty of Repeated acts of adultery an fornication - It is therefore ordered and adjudged and decreed and decided by the court that petitioner be Devorced from his wife and restored (p-397) to all rights of a single man and it is further ordered that petitioner pay the cost of this suit for which let fifa issue.

William H. Barons Jr. Admr of Thos. Saylor Decd Vs John Barnes	Debt Came the parties by attornies and the Question of Law arrising out of the Defendants Demur to the plaintiffs Replication, which being heard and

fully understood by the court It is considered by the court that the Demur be sustained - It is considered by the court the Defendant go hense and recover against the plaintiff the costs of this suit and that Execution issue.

Ordered that Court be adjourned untill tomorrow morning half after 7 oclock.

Jno. L. Goodall

Friday Morning August the 15th A.D. 1856

Court met pursuant to adjournment Present the Honorable John L. Goodall presiding & etc.

The reason appearing to the satisfaction of the court Thomas J. Poteet one of the Regular Traverse Jurors is released and Discharged from further attendance at this Term of the court as a Juror on act of sickness in his family this Entry should have appeared upon the minutes of this court on yesterday but is made now for then.

P-398 State of Tennessee Vs Janie Bruce	Indictment for Lewdness John W. Maxwell Prosr. Came the attorney General for the State and with the assent of the court enters a nole prosequi in

this cause against said Deft. It is therefore ordered by the court that said Deft be Discharged and that the State of Tennessee pay all cost on part of the prosecution in the cause Expended and that the same be certified for allowance as the Law directs.

State of Tennessee) Presentment for nuisance as overseer of Road.
Vs) Came the attorney General for the State and
William Robison) the Deft in proper person and on affidavit
) of the attorney General it is ordered by the
court that the cause be continued untill the next Term of this court
whereupon came the Defendant together with Stephen H. Colms here into
open court and acknowledged themselves to owe and stand indebted to the
State of Tennessee in the sum of Five hundred Dollars to wit - the Deft
William Robison in the sum of two hundred and fifty Dollars and the said
Stephen H. Colms in the sum of two hundred and fifty Dollars to be Levied
of their proper goods and chattles Lands and tenements to the use of the
State to be rendered but to be void if the said Deft W^m. Robison make his
personal appearance before the Judge of the circuit Court of Putnam County
to be held at the court house in the Town of Cookeville on the first Tuesday after the second Monday in December next then and there to answer the
State of Tennessee upon the above charge and then and there to attend untill Legally Discharged.

P-399 State of Tennessee) Presentments for nuisance - Came the
Vs) attorney General for the State and with
George McCormick) the assent of court enters a nolo Prose-
) qui in the cause against said Defendant.
It is therefore ordered by the court that said Defendant be discharged and
that the State of Tennessee pay all cost on part of the prosecution in
this cause Expended and that the same be certified for payment as the Law
Directs.

State of Tennessee) Indictment for an affray - Elly Bennett
Vs) Prosecutor - Came the attorny General for
Hickman Whitaker and) the State and Hickman Whitaker in proper
John Cates) person one of the above name Defendants
) who being arraigned and charged against him
self Indictment said Indictment says he is not Guilty as therein charged
against him, and for his trial puts himself upon the Country, and the attorny General for the State doth the Like, whereupon came a Jury of good
and Lawful me to wit: M. A. Jarred, E. W. Terry, Alexander Bohannon,
Joseph D. Hyder, Reubin Whitson, Absalem W. Sims, G. C. Maxwell, Alexander
Dunham, Watson G. Dowell, Allen Manear, Hosa Maden and Calvin Miller, who
being Elected tried and sworn the truth to speak upon the issue Joined
upon their oaths do say that said Defendant is Guilty in manner and form
as charged in the Bill of Indictment - It is therefore considered by the
court that said Deft for such his offense pay a fine of two Dollars and
the cost of this prosecution and that he be remain in custody of the shff.
of Putnam County untill the fine and cost is paid or security Given for
the same, whereupon the Defendant by attorny moved the court for a new
trial (p-400) in this cause, which was overuled by the court whereupon came here in to open court R. H. Dowell, William Carland and Moses
Conard and as security for said Deft confessed Judgment jointly with said
Deft Hickman Whitaker for said fine and cost this day adjudged against
said Deft. It is therefore considered by the court that the State of Ten.
Recover against said Deft Hickman Whitaker and William Carland, R. H.
Dowell, and Moses Conard the sum of two Dollars the fine aforesaid and
allso all cost herein and that Execution issue.

Wily Nights) Ejectment
Vs) This day came the parties by their attornies -
William Bean) When John A. Matheny, John R. Hancock, Reubin
) Whitson, Bird C. Kinslow, Curtis Terry and M. S.
Smith to whom the matters in constroversy was refered by argument of the parties filed in open court their award which is in the words and figures following to wit In this case unto whom the parties Refered the matter in constroversy after hearing all the Evidence on both sides find that the plaintiff is not entitled to the Land in his Declaration mentioned but that he is entitled to a small piece of improved Land which the said William Bean bought of John Garrison containing some two or three acres the Quanity and bounds of which are understood between the parties and we also find that Each party pay one half of the court cost and that the plaintiff pay the cost of arbitration of the Lower piece and that Defendant and pay the cost of the upper piece Given under our hands this 28th day of April 1856. John A. Matheny, John R. Hancock, Reubin Whitson, Bird C. Kinslow, Curtis Terry, Mat S. Smith. It is therefore considered by the court that the plaintiffs suit be Dismissed and that Each party Recover of the other and (p-401) half of the court cost and that plaintiff Recover of the Deft the cost in relation to the arbitration to the Lower piece and that the Deft Recover of the plaintiff the cost in relation to the upper piece and for all Execution issued - This entry should have appeared upon the minutes of this cause on Tuesday at this term but is made now for then.

Willis Coggin) Indictment for an assault and Battery prosecution.
Vs) Came the attorny General for the State and the
Allen Young) Deft in proper person and he being arraigned and
) charged upon said Bill of Indictment says he is
not guilty in manner and form as therein charged against him and for his trial puts himself upon the Country and the attorny General for the State doeth the Like whereupon came a Jury of good and lawful men to wit, Alexander Bohanon, W. G. Lowell, E. W. Terry, Wiseman Hearin, Noah Kerkendall Joseph Mills, Allen Manear, G. C. Maxwell, Alexander Dunham, Joseph Hester John Terry, and Calvin Miller who being Elected tried and sworn the truth to speak upon the issue of Traverse Joined upon their oaths do say that said Defendant for such his offence pay a fine of Five Dollars and the cost of this prosecution whereupon came here into open court Snodon Matticks (p-402) and as security for said Defendant confesses Judgment Jointly with said Defendant for said fine and cost this day adjudged against said Deft. It is therefore considered by the court that the State of Tennessee Recover against said Defendant and William James and Snoden Matticks the sum of five Dollars the fine aforesaid and also all cost here in and that Execution issue and etc.

State of Tennessee) Indictment for murder in 1st Degree - Shadrack
Vs) Moonyham - prosecutor - Came again the Attor-
Henry Ayres) ney General for the State and the Defendant
) Lead to the Bar of the Court in custody of
the sheriff of Putnam County. Whereupon the court ask the Defendant if he had anything further to say than he had already said why the Judgment of the Law should not be pronounced upon him and the Deft answering he had nothing further to say- Thereupon it is considered by the court that said Defendant for such his offence as found by the Jury in their verdict be imprisoned in the common Jail and penitentiary house of the State of

232

Tennessee for the space of Four years at hard Labor and that the Sheriff of Putnam County convey said Defendant and deliver him over to the keeper of penitintiary of the State of Tennessee imediatly after the adjournment of this court and that he have two men as a Guard to assist him in the same and that the State of Tennessee Recover against said Deft all cost herein and that Execution issue ordered by court that Defendant be remanded to Jail & etc.

State of Tennessee) Indictment for murder in 1st Degree – Shadrach
Vs) Moonyham, prosecutor – This day William L.
Henry Ayres) Bryant Jailer of White County produced and
) read here in open (p-403) court his account for keeping said Deft in the common Jail of White County on a charge of murder in 1st Degree from the 10th day of Feby 1856 up to the 10th day of August 1st 1856 making in all 179 days To Wit: 19 days at 37½ C. E.

$ 7.12½
159 days at 40 cents Each   63.00
Feby. 10th 1856
    To 1 Lawful Turnkey   50¢
April 15 1856
    To 1 Lawful Turnkey   50¢
"   17 1856
    To 1   "   "   50¢
Aug. 10 "
    To 1   "   "   50¢   2.00
                              Making in all the sum $ 72.12½

Which account having been Examined and certified by the attorny General to be correct is allowed by the court and ordered to be Taxed in the Bill of cost in this cause.

State of Tennessee) Indictment for Pettit Larceny – James M. Led-
Vs) better – This day William L. Bryant Jailer of
John Watts) the County of White produced and read herein
) open court his account for keeping said Defendant in common Jail of White County on a charge of Pettit Larceny from the 2nd day of Feby 1856 up to the 10th day of August, making in all 190 days.

To wit, 28 days at 37½ C. E. $ 10.50
and 161 days at 40 cents Each   64.40
2 Feby 1856 To 1 Lawful Turnkey   50¢
April 15 1856   1 "   "   50¢
"   17 1856   1 "   "   50¢
Aug. 10th 1856   1 "   "   50¢   2.00
                Making in all the sum of $ 76.90

Which account having been Examined by the attorny General and certified to be correct The same is allowed by the court and ordered to be Taxed in the Bill of cost in this cause.

233

State of Tennessee) Indictment for Pettit Larceny James M. Lead-
Vs) better Prosr. Came again the attorney Gen-
John Watts) eral for the State and the Defendant Lead to
) the Bar in custody of the Law and came also
the same Jury Elected empannelled sworn and charged in this cause on
yesterday in charge of J. H. Moore Deputy sheriff of Putnam County sworn
to take charge of them upon their oaths do say said Defendant is guilty
in manner and form as in the Bill of Indictment in this cause is charged
against him and the Jurors aforesaid upon their oaths do further say that
said Deft for such his offence be imprisoned in the common Jail and penitentiary house of the State of Tennessee for one year - whereupon the
court asked the Deft if he had anything further to say why the Judgment
of the Law should not be pronounced upon him and the Deft answering he
had nothing further to say - Thereupon it is considered by the court that
said Defendant for such his offence as found by the Jury in their verdict
be imprisoned in the common Jail and penitintiary house of the State of
Tennessee for Twelve months at hard labor and that he be Disqualified
from holding any office and from voting in any Election or from being
Examined as a witness and that the Sheriff of Putnam County convey said
Deft and deliver him over to the keeper of the penitentiary of the State
of Ten imediatly after the adjournment of this court and it is further
considered by the court that the State of Ten - Recover against said Deft
all cost herein and that Execution issue Ordered that the Defendant be remanded to Jail and etc.

State of Tennessee) Indictment for assault and Battery - (p-405)
Vs) Prosecution - Came the attorny General for
William James) the State and the Defendant in proper person
) and on motion of the Defendant - It is ordered
by the court that no witness on part of the State Except James Plunkett,
Thomas Maddux and Mrs. Webb be Taxed in the Bill of cost in this suit a-
gainst said Deft.

State of Tennessee) Presentment Nuisance Overseer of Road - Came
Vs) the attorny General for the State and the
N. J. Cole) Deft in proper person and the Defendant by
) attorny moved the court to quash the second
court in the presentments in this cause which was overruled by the court,
this Entry should have appeared upon the minutes of this court of yesterday but is made now for then.

State of Tennessee) Presentments for nuisance came the attorney
Vs) General for the State and the Defendant in
Edward Choat) proper person and he being arraigned and
) charged upon the presentments says he is not
guilty in manner and form as therein charged against him and for the trial
puts himself upon the Country and the attorny General for the State doth
the Like. Whereupon came a Jury of good and Lawful men to wit, William H.
Barons, M. A. Jarred, James Plunket, Corder Loller, Samuel K. Wilkerson,
Pleasant Hyder, James Lack, Alexander Montgomery, William Carlton, Lincoln Nicholas, Joseph Evans and Joseph D. Hyder, who being Elected tried
and sworn the truth to speak upon the issue of Traverse Joined upon their
oath do say that said Deft is not Guilty in manner and form as therein
charged against him. It is therefore ordered by the court that said Deft.

we (p-406) Discharged and that the State of Tennessee pay all cost on part of the prosecution in this cause Expended and that the same be certified for allowance and etc.

State of Tennessee) Presentments for nuisance overseer of Road.
Vs) Came the attorney General for the State and
N. J. Cole) the Defendant in proper person who being ar-
) raigned and charged upon the presentments for
plea says he is not guilty and for his trial puts himself upon the County and the attorney General doth the like – whereupon came a Jury of good and Lawful men to wit: Lincoln Nicholass, Syrous Kerkendall, Watson G. Dowell, P. M. Hyder, Thomas Martin, William H. Barons, Thomas Thompson, Alexander Dunham, G. C. Maxwell, E. W. Terry, Moses Conard and James Brown who being Elected tried and sworn the truth to speak upon the issue of traverse Joined upon their oaths do say that said Defendant is Guilty as charged in the second count in the presentment in this cause, whereupon the Defendant by attorney moved the court in arrest of Judgment and filed the following Reason to wit: first because there are two offences Joined in the second count in said presentments – second because there was no agreement of the time when the alledged offence was committed third an in sufficient Discription of the offence charged in the presentment 4th for the insufficiency of the presentment all of which being seen and fully understood by the court was overuled by the court – It is therefore considered by the court that said Deft for such his offence pay a fine of two Dollars and the cost of this prosecution from which opinion of the court in overuling the Defts motion in arrest of Judgment the Defendant prays an appeal in the nature of a writ of Errors to the next Term of the supreme court to be held in the citty of Nashville and the first (p-407) Monday in December, which to him is granted 1856. Whereupon came the Defendant together with Joseph Hester and Edward Choat into open court and acknowledged themselves to owe and stand indebted to the State of Tennessee in the sum of two Hundred and fifty dollars and the said Joseph Hester and Edward Choat in the sum of Two hundred and fifty dollars to be Levied of their proper goods and chatles Lands and tenements to the use of the State of Tennessee to be rendered never the less to be void on condition that the Defendant make his personal appearance before the Judge of the Circuit Court for Putnam County to be held in the Courthouse in the town of Cookeville Tennessee on the first Tuesday after the second Monday of April 1857 then and there to abide by and perform the Judgment of the supreme court of the State of Tennessee in the above causes and then and there attend untill Legally Discharged.

John Trousdale) Debt Motion to condemn Land The following papers
Vs) were filed to wit – Warrant:
H. H. Bryant)
State of Tennessee) To the sheriff or
Putnam County) any constable of said-
) I command you to sum-
mons Harvel H. Bryant to appear before me or some other Justice of said County to answer the complaint of John Trousdale in a plea of Debt Due by note under fifty dollars herein (p-408) fail not – Given under my hand and seal this the 23 of July 1855.

John Lee J. P.

Endorsed hereon to wit: Executed and set for trial before John Lee Esq.

the 24 1855 this the 23 June 1855.

Wm. McDonal Const.

John Trousdale) I give Judgment in this cause for the plain-
Vs) tiff against the Deft for fifteen dollars 27
Harvel H. Bryant) cents and cost for which Execution may issue
) this 24 Jany 1855.
Execution - John Lee J. P.

State of Tennessee) To the sheriff or any constable of said County
Putnam County) I command that of the goods and chatls Lands
) and tenements of H. H. Bryant and William Evans
his security for stay of Execution if to be found in your County you make
the sum of fifteen and twenty seven cents with all Lawfull costs and Interest of suit to satisfy a Judgment that John Trousdale obtained against
him before me on the 24 of Jany 1855 and pay over the same as the Law
Directs this April the 18th 1856 John Lee J. P. for Putnam County - Endorsed thereon to wit: No goods and chattles to be found in my ___ to
satisfy this fifa Levied upon a tract of Land of the said William Evans
lying in Putnam County on the waters of Martins Creek in Dist. No. 7 adjoining the ___ of Joseph Shaw and William Rogers and supposed to be one
Hundred acres be the same more or less.

A. S. Ferrell Const.

All of which being seen and heard by the court. It is considered by the
court that the Land Levied upon as aforesaid be and the same is hereby
condemned and ordered to be sold to satisfy the plaintiff Debt and cost
and also the cost of this motion and that an order of sale issue.

P-409 State of Tennessee) Presentments for nuisance - On motion
Vs) of defendant it is ordered that the
N. J. Cole) attendance of Absalom Sims, Curtis
) Terry, and Joseph Pearson witnesses
for State be taxed in the bill of cost in this cause against defendant
and none other of the states witnesses.

John Ramsey) Trespass on case - Came the parties by their
Vs) attornies and the question of law arising upon
Oswell H. Dillon) defendants demurer to the plaintiffs decla-
) ration being argued and by court fully under-
stood the court was of opinion that the matters of law were in favor of
the plaintiff. It is therefore considered by the court that said demurer
be overruled and on motion and for reasons appearing in defendants affidavit leave was given him to file his pleas of not guilty and the statute
of limitation which he tendered with his said affidavit to the plaintiffs
declaration.

Samuel K. Wilkerson) Slander
Vs) Came the parties by their attorneys and on
Newel Jackson) motion of plaintiff it is ordered the 2nd
) and 4th pleas of the defendant pleaded is
this cause be stricken out.

State   )   Indict for A and B - On motion of the attorney
Vs   )   General it is ordered that an alias capias issue
Elijah Keeton)   in this cause directed to the Sheriff of Rhea
)   County.

State of Tennessee)   Presentments for Drunkenness - On motion of
      Vs   )   the attorney General it is ordered that an
John Watson   )   alias capias issue in this cause to the
)   Sheriff of White County.

P-410   David K. Lee)   Trespass on the case - Came the parties by
           Vs   )   their attorney an on motion of the plain-
      Robert Smith)   tiff it is ordered that the 3rd plea of the
)   defendant to the plaintiffs declaration be
)   stricken out.

State of Tennessee)   Indictment for murder - In this case Will-
      Vs   )   iam Baker Inn keeper, produced here in open
Henry Ayres   )   court his account sworn to for Boarding the
)   Jury in this cause which is in the words and
)   figures to wit:

State of Tennessee - In account with William H. Baker Inn Keeper for Boarding while on the trial of this cause of the State of Tennessee against Henry Ayers on a charge of murder at the August Term of the Circuit Court of Putnam County 1856 for 12 Jurors 3 diets each wanting one at 25¢ each making in all the sum of $8.75 .

Sworn to and subscribed in open court,   William Baker
This 15 day Aug. 1856 .   C. Mills Clk.

    The attorney General having examined the above account and report the same correct - It is ordered by the court that the same be allowed and taxed in the bill of cost in this cause.

State of Tennessee)   Indictment for Petit Larceny - In this cause
      Vs   )   William Baker In Keeper produced here in open
John Watts   )   court his account sworn to for Bording the
)   Jury in this cause which is in words and figures
following to wit -

    In account with William Baker Inn Keeper for bording the Jury while on the trial of the State of Tennessee against John Watts on the charge of pettie Larceny at the August Term of Circuit Court 1856 for twelve Jurors two diets Each at 25¢ Each making in all   6.00

Sworn to and subscribed in open court this 15 Aug. (p-411)   1856.

                                                         Curtis Mills Clk.

    The attorny General having Examined the above account and report the same correct It is ordered by the court that the same be allowed and taxed in the bill of cost in this cause.

State of Tennessee	)	Indictment for assault with Intent to
Vs	)	commit a Rape - William Baker, Inn Keeper
Major, Alias Nig a slave	)	produced and read herein open court his
	)	account sworn to for Bording the Jury in

this _____ which is in words and figures following to wit -

State of Tennessee -

In account with William Baker InnKeeper for Bording the Jury in the case of the State of Tennessee against Major alias Nig, for an assault with intent to commit a Rape at the August Term of the Circuit Court of Putnam County 1856 for 12 Jurors 3 diets Each at 25¢ Each.
Making in all   9.00

Sworn to and subscribed in open court the 15th Aug. 1856.

C. Mills Clk.

The attorney General having Examined the above and report the same correct It is ordered by the court that the same be allowed and taxed in the bill of cost in this cause.

Willis Davis Expartee Petition to be Restored to citizenship -

Be it remembered that the above cause came this 15th day of August 1856 to be here before the Honorable John L. Goodall Judge and upon the petition and proof when it appearing to the court that the Defendant at July Term of Jackson County Circuit Court was convicted upon a charge (p-412) of Larceny by said Court sentenced to Imprisonment In the penitentiary for the Term of one year and rendered infamous and that he served out his term of imprisonment and returned to this County about July 1853 and has resided in said County sence that time Demeaned himself as an honest industrious upright man since his return from said confinement it is therefore ordered and adjudged by the court that said Petitioner be restored to all the rights which the free white citizens of State of Tennessee are now entitled and that he pay all cost herein and that Execution issue.

Rebecca Wiser	)	Debt motion to condemn Land - The following
Vs	)	papers were filed to wit: Warrant -
A. G. Finch and	)	
Joseph Huddleston	)	State of Tennessee - Putnam County

I command you to summon A. G. Finch and Joseph Huddleston to appear before me or some other Justice of said County to answer the complaint of Rebecca Wiser in a plea of Debt Due by note herein fail not - Given under my hand and seal this the 17th day of July 1856.
Joseph Hyder
Justice of Peace

Endorsed hereon to wit:
Executed and set for trial before me or some other Justice of this County to answer the complaint of Rebecca Wiser in a plea of Debt Due by note herein fail not - Given under my hand and seal this the 17th day of July 1856.
Joseph D. Hyder
Justice of the peace

238

Endorsed hereon to wit: Executed and set for trial before John Madewell Esq at his own house on the 22th day of July 1856.

J. Henry Constable

Rebecca Wiser Vs A. G. Finch and Joseph Huddleston in this case - I give Judgment in favor of plaintiff and against the Deft fourteen dollars Eight and two third cents and all lawful cost for which Execution may issue this 22th day of July 1856.

John Madewell
Justice of Peace
of said County

P-412 - (There are two P-412) Execution -

State of Tennessee) To the sheriff or any constable of said County
Putnam County,) I command you that of the goods and chattles
) Lands and tenements of A. G. Finch and Joseph Huddleston if to be found in your County you make or cause to be made the sum of Ten dollars and nine cents with Interest and all lawful cost to satisfy a judgment that Rebecca Wiser obtained against them before me on the 22 of July 1856 and pay over the same as the Law directs this 30 day of July 1856.

John Madewell
J. P. for said County

Came to hand the 30 July 1856.

No good and chatles to be found in my County Levied upon a tract of Land of A. T. Finch lying in Putnam County Dist. No 6 adjoining the Lands of Littleton Smith and Lewis T. Barnes and Samuel Madewell are said to contain 200 acres this 31 day of Aug. 1856.

J. Henry Constable

All of which being seen and heard by the court It is considered by the court that the Land Levied upon as aforesaid be and the same is hereby condemned and ordered to be sold to satisfy the plaintiffs Debt and cost and also the cost of this motion and that an order of sale issue.

State of Tennessee) Indictment Larceny This day Pleasant Bohanon
Vs) produced and read here in open court this act
John Watts) to convey said Deft to the common Jail of
) White County to wit: For conveying said Deft
36 miles at 10 c. Each . 3.60
One Guard 36 miles 6 Each 2.16
(p-413) the above account was sworn and subscribed in open court.

C. Mills Clerk
P. Bohannon Sheriff

The above account having been Examined by the attorny General and reported correct - It is ordered by the court the same be taxed in the bill of cost.

State of Tennessee) Indictment for murder - This day Pleasant Bo-
Vs) hannon Sheriff of Putnam County produced and
Henry Ayres) read herein open court his account convey said

239

Deft Henry Ayres to the common Jail of White County 28 miles at 10 C. E.
making.   2.80
Two Guards 28 miles at 6 C. E.   3.36
Making in all   6.46

Sworn to and subscribed in open court this 15 Aug. 1856 C. Mills Clk.
P. Bohannon Sheriff the same having been Examined by the attorney General
and reported correct the same is allowed and ordered to be taxed in bill
of cost.

J. M. and T. P. Goodbar) Debt Motion – In the case the
Vs) following papers were this day
Stephen Ford and William Johnson) filed in court.

State of Tennessee) To any lawful officer in said County – I com-
Putnam County) mand you to summons Stephen Ford – and William
) Johnson to appear before me or some other Jus-
tice of said County to answer J. M. and T. P. Goodbar assignee of A.
West in a plea of Debt due by note for a sum under one hundred dollars
herein fail not given under my hand and seal this June 19th 1856.

J. Clark J. P.
for Putnam County

Endorsed Executed and set for trial June 28th 1856 before James Clark Esq.
at his own house – this June 27th 1856.

T. J. Whitaker Const.

P-414 J. M. and T. P. Goodbar) I give judgment in
Vs) this case for the
Stephen Ford and William Johnson) plaintiff and against
) the defendants for
seventy five Dollars and forty eight cents interest and costs for which
Execution may issue this 28th of June 1856.

Jas. Clark J.P.

State of Tennessee) To the sheriff or any constable of said County
Putnam County) I command you that of goods and chattles, lands
) and Tenements of Stephen Ford and William John-
son if to be found in your county you make the sum of seventy five Dollars
with interest and costs thereon to satisfy a Judgment that J. M. & T. P.
Goodbar obtained against them before me on the 28th of June 1856.

Jas. Clark   (S)
J. P. for Putnam
County

Endorsed – Justice Clark for warrant Judgment and fifa   50 cents.
Const. Whittaker, serving warrant and. $1.50
    No property to be found in my County – I therefore levy this fifa on
all the rights tittles and claims of Stephen Ford to a tract of land containing six hundred acres more or less lying and being in the County of
Putnam in the State of Tennessee and district No. 14 on Cumberland Mountain on the waters of East fork of Obies River known by the name of the

240

saw mill land. This July the 29th 1856.   T. J. Whitaker Const.

All of which being seen by the court said land is ordered by the court to be condemned and sold in satisfaction of the plaintiffs debt and costs of Suit and also the cost of this motion and it is further ordered that an order of sale issue rendered to the Sheriff of Putnam County commanding him and etc.

Court adjourned untill tomorrow morning 8 Oclock.

John L. Goodall

P-415 Saturday Morning August 16th 1856. Court met pursuant to adjournment present the Honorable John L. Goodall.

Judge Presiding.

This day the Grand Jury returned and filed in open court the following Indictments and presentments to wit - State Vs Henry Carlisle Presentments for nuisance - State Vs Oswell H. Dillon Presentment for Profane swearing State Vs Elijah Carr for presentments for Drunkenness - State Vs Elijah Carlen presentment for Drunkenness - State Vs John Pointer Presentment for Drunkenness State Vs Thomas Bohannon son of George Bohannon presentment for Drunkenness - State Vs Patrick Brady presentment for Drunkness - State Vs Austin Choate presentment for nuisance - State Vs Z. B. Nicholas presentment for nuisance - State Vs Jno. B. Pointer presentment for profane swearing - State Vs James Ramsey presentment for nuisance - State Vs William Crowder presentment for Disturbing public Wp. State Vs William Shanks presentment for Disturbing public Wp. State Vs Julius Cartwell presentment for Disturbing pub. W. P. State Vs Joel Gabbard and James Douglass and Mack Hampton Indictment for an assault and Battery, Joseph Hester prosecutor - State Vs W. B. Roland and Jane Bruce Indictment for Lewdness - M. J. Gentry Prosecutor - State Vs William Grogan, Easton Thompson - Chunky Thompson - Henry Thompson - Rowland Thompson and Stokes Rowland Indictment for assault and Battery.

Thomas Alridge Prosecutor

Each of the above indictments endorsed by their foreman A True Bill except the one of the State Vs W. B. Rowland and Jane Bruce for Lewdness which is Endorsed by their foreman "not a True Bill".

Ordered that capias issue upon all the above named presentments and Indictments except upon the Indictment of State Vs W. B. Rowland and Jane Bruce.

P-416

State of Tennessee)	Indictment for A. & P. Joseph Hester
Vs)	Prosecutor - Came here into open
Joel Gabbard, James Douglass)	court the defendants Joel Gabbard
and Mack Hampton)	James Douglass together with William
)	H. Barnes and William H. Barnes Jr.

as their security and acknowledged themselves to owe and stand indebted to the State of Tennessee as follows - said defendants in the sum of two hundred and fifty Dollars each and the said William H. Barnes Sr. & William H. Barnes Jr. jointly in the sum of two hundred and fifty Dollars To

241

be levied on their respective goods and chattles lands and tenements to the use of the State to be rendered but to be void if said Defendant make their personal appearance before the Judge of the Circuit Court of Putnam County at the court house in the town of Cookeville on the first Tuesday after the second Monday in December next then and there to answer the State of Tennessee upon a charge of assault & Battery and not depart with out leave of the court first had and obtained.

State of Tennessee)   Presentment for nuisance - Came the Defendant
Vs   )   together with William H. Barnes Jr. herein
Henry Carlisle   )   open court and acknowledged themselves to owe
)   and stand indebted to the State of Tennessee
in the sum of five hundred Dollars that is to say said defendant in the sum of Two hundred and fifty Dollars and the said William H. Barnes Jr. in the sum of two hundred and fifty dollars - To be levied of their respective goods and chattles lands and tenements to the use of the State to be rendered but to be void if said Defendant shall make his personal appearance before the Judge of the Circuit Court of Putnam County at the Court house in the town of Cookeville on the 1st Tuesday after the second Monday in December next then and there to answer the State of Tennessee upon a charge of nuisance and not to depart until Legally Discharged.

Ordered that court adjourn untill court in course.

                                            Jno. L. Goodall

P-417   December 1856

State of Tennessee -   Please at a Circuit Court began and held for the County of Putnam and State aforesaid in the courthouse in the town of Cookeville on the second Monday it being the Eight day of December in the Year of Our Lord one Thousand Eight hundred and fifty six and in the Eighty first year of American Independance Present the Honorable John L. Goodall Judge of the fourth Judicial Circuit of the State of Tennessee Presiding and etc.

This day Robison Dpt. Sheriff of Putnam County returned here into open court the States Writ of Vinirafacias to him directed from County Court of Putnam County It being the first County Court of said County after the last Term of this Court commanding him to Summons the following named persons to attend this Term of the court as Jurors to wit - S. D. Burton, Carr Terry, William P. Stone, Robert Howard, William Daniel, John A. Brown, James Roberson, Albert G. Horn, W. H. Miller, Samuel K. Wilkerson, A. G. Finch, William M. Buck, R. D. Allison, Thomas Laycock, Grim Crowder Amon Jones, Joshua Bartlett, Anthony McBroom, Elmore Carrignton, James Carlen, O. P. Apple, W. F. Young, Henry Saddler, Bird S. Jones, A. H. Carnahan, E. H. Matheny, Lewis Barnes, Elijah S. Ellis, James M. McCaleb as Jurors and John W. Carr and A. S. Ferrell as constables to attend thereon as court officer indorsed - came to hand the same day issued and returned this venire Executed in full this the 8 of December 1856.

                                            R. Dyer Sheriff

    Out of which vinire facias and Jurors aforesaid the court proceeded
to   (p-418)   Elect and Empannell a Grand Jury as the act of the General

Assembly in such cases provides when the following named persons were drawn and Elected to wit: Thomas Laycocks, A. H. Carnahan, John A. Brown William M. Buck, R. D. Allison, James Roberson, Samuel K. Wilkerson, Carr Terry, Albert G. Horn, William Daniel, Robert Howard, James Carlen, Green Crowder of whom the court appointed R. D. Allison foreman of the Grand Jury all of whom are good and Lawful men house holders or free - holders of the County of Putnam who being Elected empannelled sworn and charged a Jury of Grand Inquest for County aforesaid to Inquire for the Body of the County of Putnam who Retired to their Rooms to consider of presentments and Indictments attended by John Carr a constable sworn to attend thereon.

Samuel K. Wilkerson) Trespass on the case - Came the parties by
Vs) attorneys and by consent this is ordered
Newel Jackson) to be continued untill the next Term of
) this court.

Thomas B. Murry) Debt Appeal
Vs) Came the parties by attornys and by consent
K. M. Murphee) this cause is continued until the next term
) of court.

P-419 Milton Draper) Eject
Vs) Came the parties by attornys and on affi-
James Kirklin) davit of the plaintiff this cause is
) ordered to be continued untill the next
term of this court upon the payment of the cost of this term of the court by the plaintiff - It is therefore considered by the court that the defendant Recover of the plaintiff the cost of this term of the court and that Execution issue and it is also ordered by the court that the plaintiff have a survey of the lands mentioned in the pleadings in this cause and that Isaac Buck surveyor of Putnam County be appointed to survey the same and that he return two platts of the same on or before the next Term of this court.

James Bartlett & others) Eject
Vs) Came the parties by attorneys
Benjamin H. Watson and Lucy Watson) and by consent this cause is
) ordered to be continued until
next Term of this court.

George Bohannon) Damage - Came the parties and the plaintiff by
Vs) attorney dismissed his suit and assumes all cost
John Slyger) It is ordered by the court that the Defendant go
) hence and recover against the plaintiff all cost
Expended and assumed as aforesaid and that Execution issue.

David M. Lee) Trespass on the case - Came the parties by at-
Vs) torneys and by consent this cause is ordered to
Robert Smith) be continued untill the next term of this court.

P-420 W. W. Berry and Demovel) Debt
Vs) Came the parties by attorneys
Robert E. Fain) and there came a Jury of good
) and Lawful men to wit: O. P.
Apple, W. F. Young, William P. Stone, Amon Jones, Henry Saddler, James
M. McCaleb, Elmore Carrington, Allen G. Finch, Wade H. Miller, Stephen
D. Burton, Anthony McBroom, and Joshua Bartlett, who being Elected,
tryed and sworn the truth to speak upon the issue Joined upon their oaths
do say they find the issue in favor of the plaintiff and that said defendant has not well and truly paid the Debt in the plaintiffs Declarations
mentioned as in pleadings he has aggreed and that the plaintiff hath sustained damages by reason of the Detention of the Debt in the Declaration
mentioned.

W. W. Berry) Debt
Vs) Came the parties by attornies and there came a
Robert E. Fain) Jury of good and Lawful men to wit: O. P. Apple,
) William F. Young, William P. Stone, Amon Jones,
Henry Saddler, James M. McCaleb, Elmore Carrington, Stephen Burton, Anthony McBroom, and Joshua Bartlett who being Elected tryed and sworn the
truth to speak   (p-421)   upon the issue Joined upon their oaths do say
they find the issue in favor of the plaintiff and that said Deft has not
well and truly paid the Debt in the plaintiffs declaration mentioned as
in pleadings he has alledged and that the plaintiff hath sustained damages
by reason of the detention of the Debt in the declaration mentioned to
the sum of forty four dollars Eighty five cents - It is therefore considered by the court that the plaintiff recover of the defendant the sum
of two Hundred and Eighty three dollars and thirty two cents and the Debt
in the Declaration mentioned together with the further sum of forty four
dollars Eighty five cents the damages aforesaid by the Jury aforesaid assessed and also all cost herein and that Execution issue.

State of Tennessee) Indictment for pettit Larceny - James M. Lead-
Vs) better prosecutor It appearing to the satis-
John Watts) faction of the court that the Defendant was
) convicted upon the above Indictment by the
Judgment of this court at its August Term thereon 1856 and that Judgment
was Rendered against him for the cost of prosecution and that Execution
had been regularly issued against him for the same and Returned by the
Sheriff of Putnam County Nulla Bona. It is therefore considered by the
court that the Judgment be and the same is hereby Rendered against the
State of Tennessee for the following Bill of cost To Wit:

Atto. General T. A. Williams tax fee	$10.00
Clerk Mills filing & docksting cause	75 c
Judgment finial	75 c
Copy of Bill of cost	25 c
for 1 continuance	25 c
Empannelling Jury Each	10 c
Copying Indictment on Record (p-422) 420 words	42 c
One order appointing consel for Deft. each	25 c
for 3 orders Remanding Deft to Jail each	25 c
3 orders to tax account in Bill of cost	25 c
for this Judgment against State	75 c
for Issuing fifa	40 c

Charging Deft this plea	25 c
Taking 6 witnesses affts. of State witnesses 5 cents each Enrolling cause 1000 word 100 cents.	7.52
Shff R. Dyer summoning Jury and calling cause .	15 c
Executing 3 Spas for the State 25 c. E.	.90
Shff. P. Bohannon arrest	.50
Executing 2 spa for the State	.25 C. E.
Carring Defendant to Jail when first committed 36 mi. 10 C. E.	4.60
To one man as a Guard 36 miles 6 C. Each .	$2.16
Justice J. D. Hyder issuing Wt.	.25
2 spas for State 15 cents	.40
Justice Thomas Cooper Judgment	.75 c
Docketing cause 15 cents for Bill of cost.	.50 c
for minutes	.50 c
for 3 Recognizance of State witnesses 50 cents Each.	2.95
Witnesses before Justice for State James M. Leadbetter - Wm. Officer and J. H. Officer 1 day each.	1.50
Witnesses for State in court James M. Leadbetter 6 days 100 Cts. Each 100 miles.	$ 10.00
John H. Officer 6 days 100 C.E. 72 mi.	$ 8.88
Wm. D. Officer " " 100 C.E. 72 mi.	$ 8.88

Wm. S. Bryan Jailer of White County his account for keeping said Defendant in the common Jail of White County on a charge of Pettit Larceny from the 2nd day of Feb. 1856 up to the 10th day of August 1856 making in all 190 days to wit:

for 28 days at 37½ cents Each.	10.50
161 days at 40 cents Each	64.40
Feby. 2nd 1856 To 1 Lawful Turnkey	.50
Apr. 15 " " 1 " "	.50
" 17 " " 1 " "	.50
Aug. 10 " " 1 " "	.50
	$ 76.90

William Baker Inn Keeper his account for Boarding the Jury while on the Trial of (p-423) the above cause at August Term 1856 for 12 Jurors 2 Diets Each   6.00

Making in all the sum of $139.19

Ordered by court that the same be certified to the Treasurer of Tennessee for payment as the Law directs.

State of Tennessee) Indictment for Murder Shadrack Moonyhan prose-
Vs) cutor - It appearing to the court that the
Henry Ayres) Defendant had been convicted upon the above
) Indictment by the Judgment of the court at its
August Term 1856 and that Judgment had been Rendered against him for the costs of prosecution and that Execution had been Regularly issued and Returned by the sheriff of Putnam County Nulla Bona. It is therefore considered by the court that Judgment be and the same is hereby rendered against the State of Tennessee for following Bill of cost to wit: Atto. Genl. T. H. Williams. Tax fee $10.00.

Clerk Mills charging Deft this plea 25 cents. fileing and docketing cause 75 cents. Judgment 75 cents. Taxing cost 25 cents. Taxing and copying

Bill of cost 25 cents. 2 orders remanding Deft to Jail 25 c. E.
One continuance 25 cents for 3 orders allowing accounts 25 cents Each.
Orders to issue attachment 25 cents issuing fifa 40 cents Enrolling
cause 1000 words 100 cents. $ 8.55
Shff. R. Dyer Executing 5 Spas. for State 25 C. E. Returning 1 Spa for
State not found 10 cents summoning Jury and calling cause 15 cents.
Executing attachment and Taking Bond States witness 125 cents $2.75
(p-424)   Shff P. Bohannon for arrest of Deft. 50 cents 21.30 Executing
5 spas for State before J. P. 25 cents Each - for conveying Deft to Jail
28 miles 10 C.E. 4.55 To 2 men as a Guard 28 miles Each 8 cents Each
4.48 Justice W. C. Bounds issuing Warrant 25 cents. Issuing 5 spas. for
State 35 c. .60 . L. R. Taylor for Judgment 75 cents for witnesses 50
cents for 3 Reconizance of States witnesses 50 cents E.   2.75
Witnesses for State before J. P. W. C. Bounds, William Macky and Shade
Moonyham, all one day Each at 50 cents Each.   1.50
Witnesses for State in court Shadrack Moonyham 7 days 75 c.E. 5.25
William Macky 7 days 75 cents each   5.25
Robert Macky   "   "   "   "   "   5.25
Sarah Elliott 1 "   "   "   "   "   .75
Shirley Macky 3 "   "   "   "   "   2.25

Inn Keeper, William Baker his account for Boarding the Jury while on the
Trial of the cause of the State against Henry Ayres on a charge of murder
at August Term 1856 for Twelve Jurors at 3 Diets Each at 25 cents Each
wanting one at 25 cents.   8.75
Jailer Wm. S. Bryan his account for keeping the Defendant in the common
Jail of White County Ten. On a charge of murder from the 10th of Feby.
1856 up to 10th August 1856 making in all 178 days to wit 19 days at 37½
cents per day.   7.12½
and 159 days at 40 cents   63.60
Feby 10th 1856 to 1 Lawful Turnkey   .50
April 15th 1856   1 "   "   .50
August 10   " " 1 "   "   .50
                                                           $ 72.72½

Making in all the sum of   135.40½

Ordered by the court that the same be (p-425) certified to the Treasurer of Tennessee for payment as the Law Directs.

State   )   This day the Grand Jury returned into court a
  Vs   )   Bill of Indictment against said Defendant for
Elias Whitaker   )   an assault and Battery Endorsed thereon by their
)   foreman a True Bill and again retired to consider
of presentments Indictments etc.

James B. Terry   )   Debt Motion to condemn land the following papers
  Vs   )   were filed to wit: Warrant -
James H. Brown   )
                     State of Tennessee)   To the Sheriff or any
                     Putnam County   )   constable of said Coun-
)   ty - I command you to
summon James H. Brown to appear for said County to answer the complaint
J. B. Terry in a plea of Debt Due by note under one Hundred Dollars Here

in fail not. Given under my hand and seal at office the 3rd day of September 1856.

             S. M. McCaleb (Seal)
             J.P. for Putnam County

Endorsed thereon to wit:

Executed and set for trial on 21 of October 1856 before J. M. McKinny my fee 50 c. J. W. Carr Const. Judgment-I give Judgment for plaintiff fee and all cost of. $ 52.62 c
This to 21 day of October 1856. James M. McKinny J. P. for Putnam Co. and all cost of suit, this the 21 day of October 1856.

             James M. McKinny J.P.
Execution -   for Putnam Co.

State of Tennessee) To the sheriff or any const. of said County
Putnam Co.   ) I command you that of goods and chattles,
) Lands and tenements of James Brown you make
the sum of fifty five dollars and fifty cents if to be found in your County. It being a Judgment that James B. Terry obtained Before me on the 21st day (p-426) of October 1856.

             James M. McKinny J.P.
Endorsed   for Putnam County.

No property to be found Levied on a lot in the town of Cookeville on Block No. 1 north west No. 2 this 3 day of Nov. 1856.
 My fee $100 John W. Carr const. all of which being seen and heard by the court It is considered by the court that the Lot Levied upon as aforesaid be and the same is hereby ordered to be sold to satisfy the plaintiffs Debt and cost and also the cost of this motion and that an order of sale issue.

Burton and Hawes) Debt Motion to condemn Land - The following
  Vs   ) papers were filed to wit -
Levi Sparks   )

       State of Tennessee) To the sheriff or
       Putnam County   ) any constable of
) said County I command you to summon Levi Sparks to appear before me or some other Justice of the peace for said County to answer the complaint of Burton and Hawes in a plea of Debt Due by note herein fail not. Given under my hand and seal this 12 day of Aug. 1856.

             John Lee (Seal)
             J.P. for Putnam County

Endorsed, Executed and set for trial before Wm. R. Hutcherson Esqr. at his house on the 13th day of August 1856.

             J. Henry Const.
             fee 50 c Judgment

Burton & Hawes) I give Judgment in this cause for the plaintiff
  Vs   ) and against the Defts for twenty two dollars and
Levi Sparks   ) nineteen cents and all cost for which Execution
) may issue .
 This 15th day of August 1856 W. R. Hutchirson J. P. for Putnam County.

P-427   Execution -

State of Tennessee   )   To the sheriff or any constable of said County
Putnam County   )   I command of you that of the goods and chattles
)   Land and tenements of Levi Sparks if to be in
your county you make the sum of twenty two Dollars and 44 cents and all
lawful cost to satisfy a Judgment that Burton and Hawes obtained before
me on the 13 day of August 1856 and pay over the same as the Law directs
this 16 day of Aug. 1856.

                  W. R. Hutchirson J.P.
                    for said County

Endorsed - Came to hand 21st August 1856 No good and chattles to be found
in my County Levied upon a tract of Land of the Defendants lying in Putnam County in List. No. 1 adjoining the Lands of James Kerby and Jefferson Cole and said to contain forty acres this 21st day of Aug. 1856.

                  J. Henry Const.

 All of which being seen and heard by the court It is considered by the court that the Land Levied upon as aforesaid be and the same is ordered to be sold to satisfy the plaintiffs Debt and costs and also the cost of this motion and that an order of sale issue.

T. S. Spivey   )   Debt motion to condemn Land - The following papers
Vs   )   were filed to wit: Warrant -
James D. Ford   )

     State of Tennessee   )   To the sheriff or any
     Putnam County   )   const of said County
)   I command you to summon James D. Ford to appear before me or some other Justice of said County
to answer the complaint T. S. Spivey in a plea of Debt Due by   (p-428)
and make Due return of this wright - given under my hand and seal as the
Law directs this 23rd day of January 1856.

                  W. C. Johnson J.P.
                    for said County

Endorsed, Executed and set for trial before W. C. Johnson Esqr. on the
5 day of Feb. 1856 at his house or office.

                  Wm. Vandever Const.

T. S. Spivey   )   I give judgment in favor of the plaintiff three
Vs   )   dollars and ninty cents Debt and all cost given
James D. Ford   )   under my hand and seal this the 5th day of Feb.
                      1856.
                  W. C. Johnson J.P.

Execution -   State of Tennessee   )
      Putnam County   )   To the sheriff or any constable
)   of said County I command you
that of the goods and chattles Lands and tenements, James D. Ford and
William Johnson his security for the stay of Execution if to be found in
your county you make the sum of three dollars and ninety cents with Interest with all lawful cost to satisfy a Judgment that Thomas S. Spivey
obtained before me on the 5 day of Feb. 1856 and pay over the same as the

Law directs this the 13 day of Oct. 1856.

W. C. Johnson   (Seal)
J.P. for said County

No property to be found in my County Levied upon a tract of Land of the Deft containing two hundred acres lying in Putnam County Dist. No. 12 adjoining the lands of Abraham Julius Elmore and others this the 25 day of October 1856.

Wm. Vandever

All of which being seen and heard by the court - It is considered by the court that the land Levied upon as aforesaid be and the same is ordered to be sold to satisfy the plaintiffs debt and cost and also the cost of this motion and that an order of sale issue.

P-429 Crutcher and Spivey) Debt Motion to condemn Land - The
              Vs   ) following papers were filed to wit:
        James D. Ford   ) Warrant -

State of Tennessee   ) To the sheriff or any constable of
Putnam County   ) said County - I command you to sum-
) mon James D. Ford to appear before
me or some other Justice of said County to answer the complaint of Crutcher and Spivey in a plea of Debt Due by note herein fail not and make Due return of this Writ. Given under my hand and seal this the 23 day of January 1856.

Wm. Johnson Justice of the Peace for Putnam County.

Executed and set for trial before W. C. Johnson on the 5 day of Feb. 1856 at his house or office.

William Vandever Const.

Crutcher and Spivey) I give Judgment in favor of the plaintiff and
         Vs   ) against the Deft for Eight dollars and 59
James D. Ford   ) cents Debt and all cost Given under my hand
) and seal this the 5 day of Feb. 1856.

William C. Johnson (Seal)
J.P. for said Cty.

Execution -

State of Tennessee) To the sheriff or any constable of said County
Putnam County   ) I command you that of the good and chattles
) Lands and tenements of James D. Ford and
William Johnson his security for the stay of Execution if to be found in your county you make the sum of Eight dollars and 59 cents Debt with interest and all Lawful cost to satisfy a Judgment that Crutcher and Spivey obtained before me on the 5th Feb. 1856 and pay over the sum as the Law directs this 13 day of October 1856.

Wm. C. Johnson
Justice of Peace

No property to be found by me Levied upon (p-430) one tract of Land lying in Putnam County in Dist. No. 12 on Cumberland Mountain Containing two hundred acres adjoining the lands of Abraham Ford, Julius Elmore and others - this 23 day of October 1856.

William Vandever Const.

All of which being seen and heard by the court - It is considered by the court that the land Levied upon as aforesaid be and the same is ordered to be sold to satisfy the plaintiffs Debt and cost and also cost of this motion and that an order of sale issue.

Ordered that Court be adjourned untill tomorrow morning 8 oclock.

Jno. L. Goodall

Thursday Morning December the 9th A.D. 1856

Court met pursuant to adjournment, present the Honorable John L. Goodall Judge presiding.

State of Tennessee) Indictment for murder Robert Brown prosecutor.
Vs) Came the attorney General for the State and
William Crabtree) the Defendant in proper person and on affi-
) davit of Defendant this cause is ordered to
be continued untill the next Term of this court whereupon came here into open court the Defendant William Crabtree, Galeman Craig, Hiram Crabtree, Washington Crabtree, Alfred Helms, Barthollett Lee and acknowledged themselves Indebted to the State of Tennessee in the sum of Four thousand Dollars (p-431) to wit, the Defendant, William Crabtree in the sum of Two Thousand Dollars and William E. B. Jones, Isaac Crabtree, Galeman Craig, Hiram Crabtree, Washington Crabtree, Alfred Helms and Bartholett Lee in the sum of Two Thousand Dollars Jointly and severally to be Levied of their proper goods and chattles, Lands and Tenements to the use of the State of Tennessee to be rendered but to be void if the said Deft William Crabtree makes his personal appearance before the Honorable Judge of Circuit court for Putnam County to be held at the court house in the Town of Cookeville the first Tuesday after the second Monday in April next then and there to answer the State upon the above Indictment and then and there attend untill Legally Discharged.

State of Tennessee) Indictment for murder - Robert Brown Prose-
Vs) cutor - This day came here into open
William Crabtree) Robert Brown, William Brown, Henry Hatfield
) Manuel Hatfield, James Wright, John W. Simpson, Robert Hatfield, Pleasant Miller, Fidelus Mason, Galeman Craig, James Hatfield, William Gilbrith and Washington Crabtree and acknowledge themselves to owe and stand Indebted to the State of Tennessee In the sum of Two Hundred and Fifty Dollars Each to be Levied of their proper goods and chattles Lands and Tenements to the use of the State of Tennessee to be remanded But to be void on condition that they make their personal appearance before the Judge of the Circuit Court of (p-432) Putnam County to be held at the Court house in the Town of Cookeville on the first Tuesday after the second Monday in April next then and there the said Robert Brown to prosecute and Give Evidence in behalf of the State of Tennessee against William Crabtree and the Ballance of the above named witnesses to Give Evidence in the behalf of the State against William Crabtree and then and there attend until Legally Discharged.

250

State of Tennessee) Indictment for murder Robert Brown Prosecutor
Vs) This day came into open court Isaac Crabtree
William Crabtree) James Kimp, Hiram Crabtree Jr., James Wright,
) Daniel Brown and Shirred Delk and acknowledged
themselves to owe and stand Indebted to the State of Tennessee in the sum
of Two hundred and fifty Dollars Each to be Levied of their proper Goods
and chattles Lands and Tenements to the use of the State to be remanded
But to be void if they made their personal appearance before the Judge
of the Circuit Court of Putnam County to be held at the courthouse in
the Town of Cookeville on the first Tuesday after the second Monday in
April next then and there to Testify and give Evidence in behalf of the
Deft in the case of State against William Crabtree the Deft and there
attend untill (p-433) Legally Discharged.

State of Tennessee) Presentment for Drunkness - Came the attorney
Vs) General for the State and the Deft in proper
William Carland) person and by consent this cause is continued
) untill the next Term of this court - Where-
upon came here into open court the Deft Wm. Carland together with Henry
Carlile and acknowledged themselves to owe and stand Indebted to the
State of Tennessee in the sum of Two hundred and fifty Dollars and the
said Henry Carlile in the sum of Two hundred and fifty Dollars to be
Levied of their proper Goods and chattles Lands and Tenements to the use
of the State of Tennessee to be rendered but to be void if the Deft William Carland makes his personal appearance before the Judge of the Circuit
Court to be held at the Courthouse in the Town of Cookeville on the first
Tuesday after the second Monday in April next then and there to answer
the State upon the above presentment and attend untill Legally Discharged.

State of Tennessee) Presentment for an assault and Battery - Came
Vs) the attorny General for the State and with
Elias Whitaker) the assent of the court Enters a nole prose-
) quey in this cause against said Deft. It is
therefore considered by the court that said Deft be Discharged and that
the State of Tennessee pay all cost on part of the prosecution in this
cause Expended and that the same be certified for allowance as the Law
Directs.

P-434   State of Tennessee) Indictment for an assault and Battery.
Vs) David Nicholas Prosecutor - Came the
Elias Whitaker) attorny General for the State and
) the Deft in proper person and It
appearing to the court that the Deft is poor and wholly unable to Employ
counsel to aid him upon the trial of this cause, whereupon the court appoints and assigns W. W. Goodpasture Esqr. attorney at Law to aid and
defend said Deft who being present Entered upon the discharge of that
duty.

State of Tennessee) Indictment for an assault & Battery -
Vs) Joseph Hester Prosecutor Came the attorney
James Douglass and) General for the State and the Defendant in
Joel Gabbard) proper person and they being arraigned and

charged upon said Indictment says they are not guilty as therein against them charged and for their trial puts themselves upon the Country and the attorney General for the State doth the like whereupon came a Jury of good and Lawful men to wit: Wade H. Miller, O. P. Apple, W. F. Young, William P. Stone, Amon Jones, Henry Saddler, Elmore Carrington, James M. McCaleb, Joshua Bartlett, Elijah S. Ellis, and E. H. Matheny who being Elected, tried and sworn the truth to speak upon the issue of Traverse Joined upon their oath do say that said Defendants are not Guilty in manner and form as in the Bill of Indictment is charged against them It is therefore ordered by the court that said Defendants be discharged and that the State of Tennessee pay all cost on part of the prosecution in this cause Expended and that the same be certified for allowance as the Law directs.

State of Tennessee) Indictment for an assault and Battery.
Vs) David Nicholass Prosecutor - Came the attor-
Elias Whitaker) ney General for the State and the Defendant
) in proper person who being arraigned and
charged upon said Indictment says he is not Guilty as therein charged against him and for his trial puts himself upon the country and the attorney General for the State doth the like. Whereupon came a Jury of Good and Lawful men to wit: O. P. Apple, W. F. Young, William P. Stone, Amon Jones, Henry Saddler, James M. McCaleb Elmore Carrington, Wade H. Miller, Anthony McBroom, Joshua Bartlett, Elijah S. Ellis and E. H. Matheny who being Elected tried and sworn the truth to speak upon their oaths do say that said Defendant is guilty in manner and form as therein against him is charged. It is therefore ordered by the court that said Defendant for such his offence pay a fine of five Dollars and the cost of this prosecution. It is therefore considered by the court that the State Recover against said Defendant the sum of five Dollars the fine aforesaid and also all cost herein and that he be and remain in custody of the Sheriff of Putnam County untill the fine and cost are paid or security Given for the same.

State of Tennessee) Presentment for Disturbing Public worship.
Vs) Came the attorney General for the State and
W. Shanks) the Defendant in proper person and on motion
) of the attorney General this cause is ordered
to be continued untill the next (p-436) Term of this court. Whereupon came here into open court the Deft W. Shanks together with Meridith P. Gentry and acknowledged themselves to owe and stand indebted to the State of Tennessee in the sum of five hundred Dollars to the Defendant in the sum of Two hundred and fifty Dollars to be Levied of their proper goods and chattles Lands and Tenements to the use of the State to be rendered but to be void if the Deft W. Shanks make his personal appearance before the Honorable Judge of the Circuit Court of Putnam County to be held in the court house in the Town of Cookeville on the first Tuesday after the second Monday in April next then and there to answer the State of Tennessee upon the above presentments and then and there attend untill Legally Discharged.

Susan Cole) Trespass
Vs) Came the parties by attornies and on motion & affi-
David G. Harris) davit of plaintiffs attorney this cause is ordered

to be continued untill the Term of this court upon the payment of the cost of this Term of the Court by said plaintiff. It is therefore considered by the court that the Defendant Recover against the plaintiff the cost of this Term of the court and that Execution issue.

State of Tennessee) Presentment for profane swearing – Came the
Vs) attorney General for the State and the De-
Henry Carlile) fendant in proper person (p-437) who
) being arraigned and charged upon said presentment says he is guilty as in the presentment is charged against him. It is therefore ordered by the court that said Defendant for such his offence pay a fine of two Dollars and cost of this prosecution. Whereupon came here into open court Ella Bennett and as security for said Deft confessed Judgment Jointly with said Deft for him & cost this day adjudged against said Deft. It is therefore considered by the court that the State of Tennessee Recover against Henry Carlile the Deft and Ella Bennett the sum of Two Dollars the fine aforesaid and <u>allso</u> cost herein and that Execution issue.

State of Tennessee) Presentments for profane swearing – Came the
Vs) attorney General for the State and the De-
Elijah Carr) fendant in proper person – who being arraigned
) and charged upon the presentment says he is guilty as therein charged against him. It is therefore ordered by the court that said Defendant for such his offence he pay a fine of five Dollars and cost of the prosecution – It is therefore considered by the court that the State of Tennessee Recover against said Deft the fine and cost aforesaid and that Execution issue and that he be and remain in custody of the sheriff of Putnam County untill said fine and cost are paid or security Given for same.

State of Tennessee) Presentment for profane swearing – Came the
Vs) attorney General for the State and the De-
Oswell H. Dillon) fendant in proper person who being arraigned
) and charged upon said presentments says he is not guilty in manner and form as therein charged against him & for his trial (p-438) puts himself upon <u>to</u> County and the attorney General for the State doth the Like. Whereupon came a Jury of good and Lawful men to wit – O. P. Apple, William F. Young, William P. Stone, Amon Jones, Henry Saddler, James M. McCaleb, Elmore Carrington, Elijah S. Ellis, Wade H. Miller, E. H. Matheny, Anthony McBroom, Joshua Bartlett, who being Elected tryed and sworn the truth to speak upon the issue of traverse Joined upon their oath do say that the defendant is guilty in manner and form as in the presentment is charged against him – It is therefore considered by the court that said Defendant for such his offence pay a fine of two dollars and the cost of this prosecution. It is therefore considered by the court that the State of Tennessee recover against the Defendant the fine and cost aforesaid whereupon came here into open court, John B. Pointer and confessed Judgment Jointly with said Defendant for the fine and cost this day adjudged against said Deft. It is therefore considered by the court that the State of Tennessee recover against the Defendant John P. Pointer the fine and cost aforesaid and that Execution issue.

State of Tennessee) Indictment for Lewdness Felix Patterson Pro-
 Vs) secutor - Came the attorney General for the
Henry Roberts and) State and Henry Roberts one of the above
Cathrine Markam) named Defendants in proper person and by
) consent this cause continued untill the next
Term of this court whereupon came here into open court Henry Roberts one
of the above named Deft. Henry Roberts (p-439) together with Hugh
Wallace, James Austin, Joseph R. Lee and Edward Anderson and acknowledged
themselves to owe and stand Indebted to the sum of five Hundred dollars
to wit: The Deft in the sum of two Hundred and fifty dollars and the
said Hugh Wallace - James Austin - Joseph R. Lee and Edward Anderson in
the sum of two hundred and fifty Dollars and severally and Jointly to be
Levied of their proper goods and chattles lands and tenements to the use
of the State of Tennessee to be rendered but to be void if the Deft Henry
Roberts make his personal appearance before the Judge of the Circuit Court
of Putnam County to be held at the court house in the town of Cookeville
on the first Tuesday after the second Monday in April next then and there
to answer the State upon the above Indictment and attend untill Legally
Discharged.

State of Tennessee) Presentment for nuisance overseer of Road.
 Vs) Came the attorney General for the State and
Z. B. Nicholas) the Defendant in proper person, who being
) arraigned and charged upon the presentment
says he is not guilty in manner and form as in the presentment is charged
against him and for the trial puts himself upon the County and the Attorney General for the State doth the Like - Whereupon came a Jury of Good
and Lawful men to wit: O. P. Apple, William F. Young, William P. Stone,
Amon Jones, Henry Saddler, James M. McCaleb, Elmore Carrington, Elijah
S. Ellis, Wade Miller, E. H. Matheny, Anthony McBroom and Joshua Bartlett
who being Elected Tried and sworn the Truth to speak upon the issue Joined
upon their oath do say that said Deft is not Guilty as in the presentment
is charged against (p-440) him - It is therefore ordered by the court
that Deft be Discharged and that the State of Tennessee pay all cost on
part of the prosecution in this cause Expended and that the same be certified for allowance as the Law Directs.

State) Presentment for Gaming - Came the attorny General
 Vs) for the State and on his motion an alias capias
John Dillon) is awarded against said Deft directed to the sher-
) iff of Overton County returnable & etc.

State) Indictment for Lewdness F. N. Patterson Pros.
 Vs) On motion of the attorney General an alias
Catharine Markam) Capias is awarded against Catharine Markam
and Henry Robert) of the above named Deft. Directed to the
) Sheriff of Putnam County returnable and etc.

William Turner and) Debt Appeal - Came the plaintiff by attorny
William Hanner) and dismisses their suit and the Defendants
 Vs) here in open court assumed all cost herein.
Allin Young and) It is therefore considered by the court that

John M. Young   )   the plaintiff Recover against said De-
James Carland and   )   fendants all cost here Expended and as-
John H. Ammonett   )   sumed aforesaid and that _____ Execution
                             issue.

James Pippin Adm of   )   Debt Motion to condemn Land - The follow-
Willis Pippin   )   ing papers were filed to wit: Warrant
Vs   )
F. M. Burk and   )   State of Tennessee   )   To the Sheriff
A. F. Carr   )   Putnam County   )   or any const.
)   of said County

(p-441) I command you to summon F. M. Burk and A. F. Carr to appear before me or some other Justice of said County to answer James Pippin Adm.
of Willis deceased in a plea of Debt for a sum under fifty dollars this
the 21 of January 1856.

                 Howel H. Bryant J. P.
                 for said County

Endorsed and Executed and set for trial on the 24th of January 1856 before H. H. Bryant Esqr. fee 100.

                 J. W. Carr Constable

James Pippin Vs F. M. Burk & A. F. Carr - In this case I give Judgment
in favor of the plaintiff and against the Deft for twenty three dollars
and Eighty five cents and cost for which Execution may issue this the 29th
day of January 1856.

                 Howel H. Bryant (Seal)
                 J.P. for Pttnam Co.

Execution - State of Tennessee   )   To the sheriff or any constable
    Putnam County   )   of said County I command you that
)   of the goods and chattles Lands
and Tenements of F. M. Burk and A. F. Carr, William Gipson their security
for the stay of Execution if to be found in your County you make the sum
of twenty three dollars and 45 cents together with Interest and all Lawfull cost of suit to satisfy a Judgment that James Pippin Decd obtained
against them before me on the 29 of January 1856 and pay over the sum as
the Law directs herein fail not - Given under my hand and seal this the
13 of Oct. 1856.

                 Howel H. Bryant (Seal)
                 J.P. for said County

Levy - No goods and chattles to be found in my County - Levied on tract
of Land of the Deft in District No. 10 and adjoining the Lands of Joseph
Allison on the East on the west by Robert Walker and said to contain twelve
acres this the 13 of Oct. 1856. My fee 100 c .

                 J. W. Carr Constable

P-442 All of which being seen and heard by the court - It is considered
by the court that the Land Levied upon as aforesaid be and the same is
ordered to be sold to satisfy the plaintiff Debt and cost and also the
cost of this motion and that an order of sale issue.

State of Tennessee) Forfeiture on Bond - Came the attorney Gen-
Vs) eral for the State and the Defendant Thomas
Thomas Bohannon) Bohannon being solemnly called to come into
) Court and answer the State of Tennessee on
a charge of Drunkenness according to the tenor of his Bond Entered into
before J. H. Hamilton Sheriff of Overton on the 13th day of September
1856 came not but make Default, and the said John H. Hamilton the security of the said Thomas Bohannon in the said Bond being solemnly called
to come into court and bring with him the Boddy of Thomas Bohannon to
answer the State of Tennessee on said Charge of Drunkness according to
the said tenor of said Bond, Brings him not, but makes default. Therefore it is considered by the court that the State of Tennessee Recover of
said Thomas Bohannon the sum of Two hundred and fifty Dollars according
to the tenor of this Bond unless they show sufficient reason for their
default at the next Term of this court and on motion of attorny General
a scirafacious is awarded against said Defendant etc.

P-443 Edward Anderson) Debt Appeal
Vs) Came the parties by attornies and the
John R. Jones) Defendant by attorny moved the court to
) dismiss the appeal in this cause, which
motion was overuled by the court.

Isam Smith) Debt Appeal
Vs) Came the parties by attornies and on motion
Edward Anderson) and affidavit of the plaintiff ordered by
) court that an attachment be awarded the plain-
tiff against the Body of Jacob Cooper a witness in behalf of the plaintiff in the above cause Returnable at the present Term of this court.

Robert Smith) Ejectment
Vs) Came the Defendant Gordon Maxwell and came a Long
Gordon Maxwell) with him here into open court Edward Anderson and
) as security for said Defendant acknowledged him
self to owe and stand indebted to Robert Smith the plaintiff in the sum
of two hundred and fifty Dollars for the payment of all cost in the suit
should the same be adjudged against said Deft upon a final hearing of the
same and the Deft by attorny pleads not Guilty of the trespass and Ejected
in the plaintiffs Declaration mentioned and agrees to rely upon the Title
only.

Isam Smith) Debt Appeal
Vs) This day came here into open court Hugh Smith and
Edward Anderson) Felix N. Patterson and as security for the plain-
) tiff acknowledged themselves to owe and stand indebted to the (p-444) said Deft Edward Anderson in the sum of Two
hundred and fifty Dollars for the payment of all cost in this suit should
the same be adjudged against said plaintiff upon a final hearing of the
same.

Levi M. Pistole Exr.) Debt motion to condemn Land -

of L. L. Murphy Decd.) The following papers were filed to wit:
      Vs) Warrant
Joseph Hester)

State of Tennessee) To the sheriff or any constable of said
Putnam County) County - I command you to summons Jos-
) eph Hester to appear before me or some
other Justice of said County to answer the complaint of Levi L. Pistole
admr. of L. L. Murphy Decd in a plea of Debt due by note herein fail not.
Given under my hand and seal this 15th August 1856.

                                  L. L. Thompson (Seal)
                                  J.P. for Putnam County

Executed and set for trial before James McKinny Esqr. on the 13th of September 1856.
                                  R. Dyer Sheriff

Judge - In this case I give judgment In favor of plaintiff for 130.02 cents
and all lawful cost of suit this 13 day Sept. 1856 for which Execution may
issue James M. McKinny J. P. for said County Putnam.

Execution -

State of Tennessee) To the sheriff or any constable of said County
Putnam County) Greetings, I command you that of the goods
) and chattles lands and tenements of Joseph
Hester if to be found in your county, you make or cause to be made the sum
of one Hundred and ninety dollars and two cents to satisfy a judgment that
L. M. Pistole and L. L. Murphee and Recover against (p-445) against
him before me on the 13 day of September 1856 and pay over the same as the
Law Directs. Given under my hand and seal this 24th day of September 1856.

                                  James McKinny (Seal)
                                  J.P. for said County

    No personal property of the Defendant to be found in my County I levy
this fifa on one tract of Land Lying in Dist. No. 15th on the waters of
Bear Creek containing one Hundred and ninety acres Bounded by the lands
of Holeman Curtis on the north and on the South by the land of Garrison
and west by the land of Gillom on the East Levi or the property of Joseph
Hester this the 27 day of September 1856.
                                  R. Dyer Shrff.

    All of which being seen and heard by the court that the Land Levied
upon as aforesaid be and the same is ordered to be sold to satisfy the
plaintiffs Debt and cost also the cost of this motion and that an order
of sale issue.

Levi M. Pistole Admr.) Debt Motion to condemn land - The fol-
  of L. L. Murphee Decd.) lowing papers were filed to wit: Warrant
      Vs)
Joseph Hester) State of Tennessee) To the Sher-
                           Putnam County) iff or any

constable of said County I command you to summon Joseph Hester to appear before me or some other Justice of said County to answer the complaint of Levi M. Pistole administrator L. L. Murphee Decd in a plea of Debt Due by note under two hundred dollars herein fail not.

Given under my hand and seal this the 24 day of November 1856.

P-446

W. R. Hutchison (Seal)
J.P. for Putnam County

Endorsed, Executed and set for trial before Wm. R. Hutchison Esqr. on the 29 day of November 1856.

R. Dyer Sheriff

Judgment - L. M. Pistole Admr. of Levi L. Murphee Decd Vs Joseph Hester I give Judgment for the plaintiff and against the Defendant for one Hundred and seventy nine dollars and 25 cents and the cost for which Execution may issue this 29 of Nov. 1856.

W. R. Hutchison (Seal)
J.P. for Putnam County

Execution - State of Tennessee) To the sheriff or any constable
Putnam County) Greentings, I command you that
) of the good and chattles lands
and tenements of Joseph Hester if to be found in your County, you make the sum of one Hundred and seventy nine dollars and twenty five cents with interest and all lawful cost to satisfy a judgment that Levi M. Pistole Admr. of L. L. Murphee Decd obtained before me on the 29 day of November 1856 W. R. Hutchison J. P. for said County, No personal property of the Defendant to be found in my County - I Levy this fifa on one tract of land in the fifteenth Dist. containing one Hundred and ninety acres Bound by the lands of William Curtis on the North Garrison on the South Gillium on the west Levied on as the property of Joseph Hester - this the 5th day of December 1856.

R. Dyer Sheriff

All of which being seen and heard by the court It is considered by the Court that the Land Levied upon as aforesaid be and the same is ordered to be sold to satisfy the plaintiffs Debt and cost and also the cost of this motion and that an order of sale issue.

P-447 Cleuborn Holaway) Debt Motion to condemn Land - The fol-
       Vs   ) lowing papers were filed to wit:
       James Ford and   ) Warrant -
       Abraham Ford   )

State of Tennessee) To the sheriff or any constable of said
Putnam County   ) County - I command you to summons James
) Ford and Abraham Ford to appear before
me or some other Justice of said County to answer the complaint of Clauborn Holaway in a plea of Debt due by note a summons under $100 dollars assignee by John Johnson and A. J. Lee hear in fail not. Given under my hand and seal this the 20th day of Oct. 1856.

James Clark (Seal)
J.P. for Putnam County

258

Judgment : Clawborn Holaway Vs James Ford and Abraham Ford I give Judgment in this cause for plaintiff against Deft for forty five dollars and five cents intrust and cost for which Execution may issue.

This Oct. the 20 day 1856.   James Clark, J. P. for
                                                              said County

Execution -

State of Tennessee   )   To the sheriff or any constable of said County
Putnam County   )   I command you that of the goods and chatles
)   Lands and tenements of James Ford & Abraham
if to be found in your county you make or cause to be made the sum of forty five dollars and cost to satisfy a Judgment that Claborn Holaway recover against them before me on the 20th day of October and pay over the sum as the Law directs.

This Oct. the 25th 1856.   James Clark J.P. for
                                                   Putnam County

Levy: No property found in my county I Levy this fifa on a tract of land of James D. Ford lying in Putnam County Dist. No. 14 of Putnam County and State of Tennessee on the East Fork of Obeeds river and below adjoining the Lands A. Ford and Julius Elmore known by the name of Crutell (P-448) Land.
                  This October the 27th 1856.
                                             J.J. Whitaker Const.

All of which being seen and heard by the court. It is considered by the court that the Land Levied upon as aforesaid be and the same is ordered to be sold to satisfy the plaintiffs Debt and cost and also the cost of this motion and that an order of sale issue.

Ordered that court be adjourned untill tomorrow morning half after 8 oclock.
                                   John L. Goodall

Wednesday morning December the 10th A. D. 1856 - Court met persuant to adjournment, present the Honorable John L. Goodall.

                                                        Judge Presiding & etc.

State of Tennessee   )   Indictment for an assault and Battery.
     Vs   )   Joseph Hester Prosecutor - Came the attor-
Mack Hampton   )   ney General for the State and with the
)   assent of the court Enters a nole prosequi
in this cause against said Defendant - It is therefore considered by the court that the Deft be discharged and that the State of Tennessee pay all cost on part of the prosecution in this cause and that the same be certified for allowance as the Law directs.

State of Tennessee   )   Indictment for an assault with intent to
     Vs   )   commit Rape - Nelly Looper Prosecutor.
Major, Alias Nig   )   Came the attorny General for the State
)   and the Defendant Lead to the Bar in cus-
tody of the sheriff of Putnam County and on affidavit of the Defendant

this cause is ordered to be continued untill the next Term of this court ordered that Defendant be remanded to Jail.

P-449 State of Tennessee) Forfeiture of Bond - Came the attor-
Vs) ney General for the State and the
Thomas Bohannon) Deft in proper person and on affi-
) davit of the Defendant It is ordered
by the court that the Forfeiture taken against said Deft in this cause on yesterday be set aside upon the payment of the cost of the same. It is therefore considered by the court that the State Recover against said Deft the cost in this case of Entering and setting aside the forfeiture and that Execution issue.

State of Tennessee) Presentment for Drunkness came the attorny
Vs) General for the State and the Defendant in
Thomas Bohannon) proper person, who being arraigned and
) charged upon said presentment - says he is
guilty as therein presentment charged against him. It is therefore or-
dered by the the court that said Deft for such his offence pay a fine of two Dollars and the cost of prosecution. Whereupon came here into open court Wilburn W. Goodpasture and as security for said Deft confessed Judgment Jointly with said Deft for the fine & cost this day adjudged against said Deft. It is therefore considered by the court that the State of Tennessee Recover against Thos. Bohannon the Deft and Wilburn W. Goodpasture and as security for said Deft confessed Judgment Jointly with said Deft for the fine and cost this day adjudged and against said Deft. It is therefore considered by the court that the State of Tennessee Recover a-gainst Thos. Bohannon the Deft and Wilburn W. Goodpasture the fine and cost aforesaid and that Execution issue etc.

State of Tennessee) Indictment for A. & B.
Vs) Thos. Alridge Pros.
William Grogan, Haston Thompson)
Plunky Thompson and Henry Thompson) P-450 Came the attor-
and Rowland Thompson and Stoke Rowland) ney General for the State
) and with the assent of
the court Enters a Nole Prosequi in this cause against said Defendants. It is therefore ordered by the court that Defendants be Discharged and that the State of Tennessee pay all cost on part of the prosecution in this cause Expended and that the same be certified for allowance.

State of Tennessee) Presentment for Disturbing Public Worship.
Vs) Came the attorney General for the State
William Crowder) and the Defendant in proper person and on
) motion of the attorny General this cause
is ordered to be continued untill the next Term of this court. Whereupon came here into open court the Deft William Crowder together with Green Crowder and acknowledged themselves to owe and stand Indebted to the State of Tennessee in the sum of five hundred Dollars to wit, the Debt in the sum of Two hundred and fifty Dollars and the said Green Crowder in the sum of Two hundred and fifty Dollars to be Levied of their proper Goods and chattles, Lands and Tenements to the use of the State of Tennessee to be rendered but to be void if the said Deft William Crowder makes his

personal appearance before the Judge of the Circuit Court of Putnam County to be held at the court house in the town of Cookeville on the first Tuesday after the second Monday in April next then and there to answer the State upon the above presentment and attend untill Legally Discharged.

P-451 Isam Smith) Debt Appeal
Vs) This day came here into open court Allen
Edward Anderson) Young - Hugh Smith and Felix N. Patter-
) son and as Security for the plaintiff
acknowledged themselves to owe and stand indebted to Edward Anderson the Defendant in this suit in the sum of Two hundred and fifty Dollars for payment of all cost in this suit should the same be adjudged against said plaintiff upon a final hearing of the same and on motion of the plaintiff by attorny It is ordered by the court that attachment awarded the plaintiff in this cause on yesterday be made returnable to the next Term of this court and by consent of parties this cause is continued untill the next Term of this court.

John Terry Executor & etc.) Debt
Vs) Came the parties and on an affidavit
Elias Green) of the plaintiff this cause is ordered
) to be continued untill the next Term
of this court.

State of Tennessee) Indictment for an assault with intent
Vs) to commit a Rape Nelly Looper Prosecutor.
Major, Alias Nig) This day came here into open court Gran-
) ville Looper, B. Lee, W. L. Wright,
Fountain Sexton, Levi Clark, Mira Looper, Nellie Looper and Joel Looper, and acknowledged themselves to owe and stand Indebted to the State of Tennessee in the sum of Two hundred and fifty Dollars Each to be Levied of their proper goods and chattles, Lands and Tenements to the use of the (p-452) State of Tennessee to be rendered but to be void if they make their personal appearance before the Judge of the Circuit Court of Putnam County to be held at the court house in the Town of Cookeville on the first Tuesday after the second Monday in April next then and there the said Nelly Looper to prosecute and Give Evidence in behalf of the State of Tennessee against Major Alias, Nig, the Deft and the Ballance of the above named witness to Testify and Give Evidence in behalf of the State against said Deft and then and there attend untill Legally Discharged.

State of Tennessee) Presentment for nuisance Overseer of Road.
Vs) Came the attorney General for the State and
James Ramsey) the Defendant in proper person, who being
) arraigned and charged upon the presentment
says he is not Guilty as therein charged against him and for his trial puts himself upon the Country, and the attorny General doth the Like. Whereupon came a Jury of Good and Lawful men to wit, Joseph S. Allison, Ridly Draper, John T. Graham, Calvin Miller, James Carr, Wilkerson Copeland, Elly Bennett, James B. Terry, Campbell Bohannon, Jordon Harris, Moses A. Jarred, and Isaac Brown who being Elected tried and sworn the truth to speak upon the issue of Traverse Joined upon their oaths do say that said Deftant is Guilty in manner and form as in the presentment is charged against him. It is therefore considered by the court that said

Deft for such his offence pay on a fine (p-453) of Two Dollars and the cost of this prosecution - Whereupon came here into open court - Wilkerson Copeland, and as security for said Defendant confessed Judgment Jointly with said Deft for the fine and cost this day adjudged against said Deft. It is therefore considered by the court that the State of Tennessee Recover against said Deft and Wilkerson Copeland the sum of Two Dollars the fine aforesaid and also all cost herein, and the Attorny General for the State agrees to stay the Execution four months.

John Farley) Ejectment
Vs) Came the parties and on affidavit of
Jesse and Jefferson Farley) the plaintiff this cause is ordered
) to be continued untill the next Term
of this court upon the payment of the cost of this Term by said plaintiff. It is therefore considered by the court that the Defendant Recover against the plaintiff the cost of this Term of the court and that Execution issue and etc.

Edward Vaughn) Ejectment
Vs) By consent of parties by attornies this cause is
John Roberts) continued untill the next Term of this court.

State of Tennessee) Presentment for Drunkness came the attorney
Vs) General for the State and the Deft in proper
Patrick Brady) person, who being arraigned and charged up-
) on said presentment says he is not Guilty
as therein charged against him (p-454) and for his trial puts himself upon the country and the attorny General for the State doth the Like whereupon came a Jury of good and Lawful men to wit: Meridith P. Gentry, James B. Terry, Robert Alcorn, Joseph S. Allison, T. W. Warly, Moses Conard, Moses A. Jarred, Ridly Apple, James Lack, William Crabtree, James Bullington and James Carr who being Elected tried and sworn the truth to speak upon the issue Joined upon their oath do say that said Deft is guilty as in the presentment is charged against him. It is therefore considered by the court that said Deft for such his offence pay a fine of five Dollars and the cost of this prosecution whereupon came here into open court Wilburn W. Goodpasture and as security for said Deft confessed Judgment Jointly with said Deft for said fine and cost this day adjudged against said Deft. It is therefore considered by the court the State of Tennessee Recover of the Defendant and Wilburn W. Goodpasture the sum of five Dollars the fine aforesaid and also all cost herein and that Execution issue.

State of Tennessee) Presentment for nuisance overseer of Road.
Vs) Came the attorney General for the State and
William Robison) the Defendant in proper person, who being
) arraigned and charged upon the presentment
says he is not Guilty as in the presentment is charged against him and for his trial puts himself upon the Country and the <u>attorny</u> General for the (p-455) State doth the Like. Whereupon came a Jury of Good and Lawful men To wit: James Bullington, O. P. Apple, William P. Young, Elijah S. Ellis, E. H. Matheny, Joshua Bartlett, Elmore Carrington, William P. Stone, Amon Jones, Henry Saddler, James M. McCaleb, Anthony McBroom who being Elected tried and sworn the truth to speak upon the issue of Traverse

Joined upon their oath do say that said Defendant is Guilty in manner and form as in the presentment is charged against him. It is therefore considered by the court that said Deft for such his offence pay a fine of Two Dollars and cost of this prosecution – Whereupon came here into open Court George McCormick and as security for said Deft for the fine and cost this day adjudged against said Deft. It is therefore considered by the court that the State of Tennessee Recover against said Defendant and George McComack the sum of Two Dollars the fine aforesaid and also all cost here and that Execution issue and etc.

Wily W. Harris) This day came here into open court Timothy M.
Vs) Williams and as Security for the Defendant David
David Maxwell) Maxwell acknowledged himself to owe and stand in-
) debted to Wily W. Harris the plaintiff in the sum
of Two hundred and fifty Dollars for the payment of all cost in this suit should the same be adjudged against said Defendant upon a final hearing of the same.

P-456 William Mitchell) Debt Appeal
Vs) Came the parties by attornies and motion
John Young) and as on affidavit of the plaintiff this
) cause is continued untill the next term
of this court upon the payment of the cost of this Term by said plaintiff It is therefore considered by the court that the Defendant Recover of the plaintiff the cost of this Term of the court and that Execution issue and that on motion of the Deft by atto. ordered by court that the plaintiff Give security for the prosecution of this suit on or before the first day after next Term of this court or the same shall stand Dismissed.

State of Tennessee) Presentment for profane swearing – Came the
Vs) attorny General for the State and the Deft
John B. Pointer) in proper person who being arraigned and
) charged upon said presentment says he is not
Guilty as therein against him is charged and for his trial puts himself upon the Country and the attorny General for the State doth the Like whereupon came a Jury of Good and Lawful men to wit, O. P. Apple, William F. Young, Wade H. Miller, Elijah S. Ellis, E. H. Matheny, Joshua Bartlett, Ellmore Carrington, William P. Stone, Amon Jones, Henry Saddler, James M. McCaleb, Anthony McBroom who being Elected tried and sworn the truth to speak upon the issue of Traverse Joined who after having heard all of the Evidence in this cause and the argument of counsel thereon and re-ceived their charge from the Honorable court and there not being time this day to finish the trial of this cause the Jurors were permitted to disperse untill the meeting of this court tomorrow morning ½ after 8 oclock, this Entry should have appeared upon the minutes of this court of yesterday but is made now for then.

P-457 State of Tennessee) Presentment for profane swearing.
Vs) Came again the attorny General for
John B. Pointer) the State and the Defendant in
) proper person and came also the
same Jury Elected tried and sworn and Received their charge in this cause on yesterday upon their oaths do say that said Defendant is Guilty as

charged in the presentment against him. It is therefore considered by
the court that said Defendant for such his offence pay a fine of ten
Dollars and the cost of the prosecution whereupon came here into open
court Oswell H. Dillon and as security for said Defendant for the fine
and cost this day adjudged against him confessed Judgment Jointly with
said Deft. It is therefore considered by the court that the State of
Tennessee Recover against said Defendant and Oswell H. Dillon the sum of
Ten Dollars the fine aforesaid and also all cost herein and that Execution
issue and the attorny General for the State agree to stay the Execution
four months.

State of Tennessee) Presentments for Drunkness came the attorny
Vs) General for the State and the Defendant in
John B. Pointer) proper person who being arraigned and charged
) upon the presentment says he is not Guilty
as therein charged against him and for his trial puts himself upon the
country (p-458) and the attorny General for the State doth the Like.
Whereupon came a Jury of good and Lawful men to wit: O. P. Apple, W. F.
Young, William P. Stone, Amon Jones, Henry Saddler, James M. McCaleb, Elmore Carington, Elijah S. Ellis, Anthony McBroom, Joshua Bartlett, E. H.
Matheny, and Wade H. Miller who being Elected tried and Sworn the Truth
to speak upon the issue of Traverse Joined - who after having heard all
of the Evidence and the argument thereon and Received their charge from
the Honorable court and there not being time this day to finish the trial
of this cause the Jurors were permitted to disperse untill the meeting
of this court tomorrow morning This Entry should appeared upon the minutes
of this court on yesterday but is made now for then.

State of Tennessee) Presentment for Drunkness - Came again the
Vs) Attorny General for the State and the Defend-
John B. Pointer) ant in proper person and came also the same
) Jury Elected tried and sworn and Received
their charge from the court on yesterday upon their oath do say that said
Deft is not Guilty in manner and form as in the presentment is charged
against him - It is therefore considered by the court that the Deft be
Discharged and that the State pay all cost on part of the prosecution in
this cause Expended and that the same be certified for allowance as the
Law Directs.

State of Tennessee) Presentment for nuisance - Came the attorny
Vs) General (p-459) for the State and Defend-
Austin Choat) ant in proper person - who being arraigned
) and charged upon said presentment says he is
not Guilty as therein charged against him and for his trial puts himself
upon the Country and the attorny General for the State doth the Like.
Whereupon came a Jury of Good and Lawful men to wit: Meridith R. Gentry
O. P. Apple, W. F. Young, Amon Jones, Henry Saddler, James M. McCaleb,
Elmore Carington, Elijah S. Ellis, Wade H. Miller, E. H. Matheny, Anthony McBroom and Joshua Bartlett who being Elected tried and sworn the
Truth to speak upon the issue of Traverse Joined upon their oaths do say
that said Deft is Guilty as in the presentment is charged against him -
It is therefore ordered by the court that said Deft for such his offence
pay a fine of Two Dollars and cost of this prosecution - Whereupon came
here into open court William H. Baron and as security for said Deft for

264

said fine and cost this day adjudged against said Defendant confesses Judgment Jointly with Said Deft for said Deft. It is therefore considered by the court that the State of Tennessee Recover against said Deft and William H. Barons the sum of Two Dollars the fine aforesaid and also all cost herein and that Execution issue and etc.

Elijah W. Brown) Eject
and Alvira Brown) Came the parties by their attornies and there
Vs) came a Jury of Good and Lawful men to wit, Allin
Thomas Pullin) Young, Meridith P. Gentry, Patrick Brady, John
) Haws, James Lack, John Stewart, Isaac Brown,

David L. Dow, Terry W. Warly, James W. McDaniel, Henry (p-460) Bullington and John Murphy who being Elected Tried and sworn the truth to speak upon the issue Joined who after having heard all of the Evidence in this cause and the argument of counsel thereon and Received their charge from the Honorable Court retired to consider of their verdict and again returned into court and upon their oath declared they had not agreed upon a verdict in this cause and there not being time to finish the trial of this cause, this day the Jurors were permitted to disperse untill the meeting of this court tomorrow morning.

State of Tennessee) Presentment for Tipling - Came the attorney
Vs) General for the State and the Defendant in
John Roberts) proper person who being arraigned and charged
) upon said presentment says he is not Guilty

as therein charged against him - and for his trial puts himself upon the Country and the attorney General for the State doth the Like. Whereupon came a Jury of Good and Lawful men To wit: O. P. Apple, W. F. Young, William P. Stone, Amon Jones, Henry Saddler, James M. McCaleb, Elmore Carington, Elijah S. Ellis, Wade H. Miller, E. H. Matheny, Anthony McBroom and Joshua Bartlett who being Elected tried and sworn the Truth to speak upon the issue of Traverse Joined upon their oaths do say that said Deft is not Guilty as therein is charged against him - It is therefore ordered by the court that said Deft be Discharged and that the State pay all cost on part (p-461) of the prosecution in this cause Expended and that the same be certified for allowance.

Edward Anderson) Debt Appeal
Vs) Came the parties by attornies and on motion of
John R. Jones) the plaintiff by attorny It is ordered by the
) court that the Defendant Give security for the

prosecution of this suit on or before the calling of the same for trial or the same shall stand Dismissed.

J. W. Huddleston) Debt Motion to condemn Land - the following
Vs) papers wear filed to wit: Warrant -
Shadrack Mooneyham)

State of Tennessee) To the Sheriff or any constable of said
Putnam County) County I command you to summon Shadrach
) Moonyham to appear before me or some other

Justice of peace of said County to answer J. W. Huddleston in a plea of Debt under sixty dollars this 12 th of November 1856.
                 James M. McKinny
                  (Seal)

Endorsed Executed and set for trial on the 27 of Sept. 1856 before Lee R. Taylor Esqr. My fee 50 c.

                 J. W. Carr Constable

Judgment J. W. Huddleston Vs Shadrach Mooneyham - In this case I give Judgment in favor of the plaintiff Vs the Defendant for forty six dollars and 24 cents Debt with all lawfull ____ for which Execution may issue this 27 day of Sept. 1856.

                 Lee B. Taylor (Seal)
Execution -   Justice of the peace

State of Tennessee) To the sheriff or any constable of said
Putnam County   ) County, I command you that of goods and
) chattles Lands and tenements of Shadrach
Moonyham if to be found in your county you make the sum of forty six dollars and twenty four cents Debt with all lawfull cost to satisfy a Judgment that J. W. Huddleston obtained against him before me on the 27 day of Sept. (p-462) 1856 and pay over the same as the law directs. Given under my hand and seal the first day of Oct. 1856.

                 Lee B. Taylor (Seal) J.P.
                 for said County

Levy: No goods and chattles to be found in my County - Levied upon a tract of land of the Left in Dist. No. 2 and adjoining the lands of Sarah Dyer the south and on the East by J. C. Dyer and on the north by P. Dearing on the west by Mansells Land and said to contain fifty acres this the 3 day of October 1856.

                 J. W. Carr Const.

 All of which being seen and heard by the court that the land Levied upon as aforesaid be and the same is hereby condemned and ordered to be sold to satisfy the plaintiffs Debt and cost and also the cost of this motion and that an order of sale issue.

 Court adjourned until 8½ oclock tomorrow morning.

                 Jno. L. Goodall

Thursday Morning December 11th 1856 A. D. 1856. Court met persuant to adjournment present the Honorable John L. Goodall Judge presiding This day the grand ____ returned and filed in open court the following bill of Indictments and presentment - State Vs John Madden - Indictment for Illegal voting - State Vs George W. Donley Indictment for assault & Battery. State Vs David L. McCaleb A. & B. not a true Bill. All signed by R. D. Allison a true bill foreman of the second Jury State Vs George Ramsey. Presentment for nuisance State Vs Claiborne Rodgers and Caroline Burks Presentment for Lewdness - State Vs James Plunkett - Presentment nuisance State Vs John W. Kerby - presentment for swearing. State Vs William Mills presentment for Tipling.

P-463 John Richardson and William Richardson   ) Ejectment
        Vs   ) Came the defendant
    John Roberts   ) by attorney and the
) plaintiffs failing
to appear and prosecute their suit after being solemnly called to come into court and prosecute the same. It was considered by the court that said

defendant go hence without day and recover against the plaintiff all costs herein and that Execution issue etc.

James Lack & wife) Trespass on the case - Came the parties in
Vs) proper person herein open court and the de-
Moses Kinnaird) fendant confessed Judgment in favor of the
) plaintiff in the sum of ten thousand dollars
and the plaintiff agree to set aside and release to defendant all of said sum of Ten thousand dollars except the sum of twenty dollars and the costs of this suit. It is therefore considered by the court that the plaintiff recover against the defendant said sum of twenty dollars and also all costs herein and that execution issue & etc.

James Lack & wife) In this case the plaintiff executed and acknow-
Vs) ledged herein open court the following transfer
Moses Kinnaird) to wit:

I hereby transfer to John P. Murray all the Judgment - I obtained in the suit of myself and wife against Moses Kinnaird for slander in Cookeville Circuit Court December 10th 1856.

Attest: A. F. Capps

              his
             James X Lax
              mark

James C. Officer Adm. of) Debt Appeal
W. G. Sims decd) Came the parties by their attorney and
Vs) came a jury of good and lawful men, to
William Cureton) wit: Jesse Elliot - John Terry - Will-
) iam F. Young, Truston Leach (p-464)
Oliver P. Apple, William P. Stone, Henry Saddler, Elmore Carrington, Elijah S. Ellis, Wade H. Miller, Elijah H. Matheny, Joshua Bartlett who being elected tried and sworn well and truly to try the matters in constroversy between the parties upon their oath do say they find the matters in controversy for the plaintiff and that the defendant owes the plaintiff the sum of fifty four dollars and eleven cents. It is therefore considered by the court that the plaintiff recover against the defendant the sum of fifty four dollars and eleven cents. It is therefore considered by the court that the plaintiff recover against the defendant the sum of fifty four dollars and 11 cents the debt aforesaid and also all cost herein and that execution issue and etc.

Allen Young) Debt Appeal came the parties by
Vs) attorney and came a Jury of good
Willis Coggins & John Coggin) and lawful men to wit: Jordon K.
) Harris, William C. Bounds, John C.
White, Z. Hopkins, William S. Saylor, John Harris, James White, James G. Early, Elly Bennett, Thomas Nicholas, James Bullington and Absalom Sims, who being elected tried and sworn well and truly to try the matters in constroversy between the parties upon their oaths do say they find the matters in constroversy in favor of the plff. and that the defendants owes the plaintiff the sum of forty two dollars and twelve cents - It is therefore considered by the court that the plaintiff Recover against the defendants the sum of forty two dollars and 12 cents the Debt aforesaid and also

all cost herein and that Execution issue and etc.

Isaac Burton)   Debt Appeal
Vs) Came the parties by attorny and by consent this
Thomas Lancaster) cause is ordered to be continued untill the
) next Term of this court.

Charlote White)   Pet. for Divorce
Vs) Came the parties (p-465) by attorny's and
Joshua White) on affidavit of the the plaintiff this cause
) is ordered to be continued untill next term of
this court.

Daniel Brown)   Debt Appeal
Vs) Came the parties by attorny and by consent this
Redman G. Maddux) cause is ordered to be continued untill the
) next Term of this court.

William Baker)   Damage Appeal
Vs) Came the parties by attorneys and came
William H. Barnes &) a Jury of good and Lawful men to wit:
Jeremiah Whitson) Amon Jones, William Daniels, Albert G.
) Horn, R. D. Allison, James Cureton, Green
Crowder, Tyra Bullington, Preston Stewart, Robert Howard, James M. Mc-
Caleb who being elected tried and sworn well and truly to try the matter
in controversy between the parties upon their oaths do say that they find
the same in favor of the Defendants. It is therefore considered by the
Court that the Defendants go hence without day and Recover against the
plaintiff all costs herein and that Execution issue.

State of Tennessee) Indictment for Pettit Larceny James M.
Vs) Ledbetter Prosecutor - This day William
John Watts) R. Hutchison, Jailer for Putnam County
) produced and read in open court his ac-
count sworn to for keeping John Watts in the common Jail of Putnam County
on charge of pettit Larceny from the 10th day of August 1856 up to the
20th day of August 1856 making in all 10 days at 40 c per day $ 4.00
Aug. 10th 1856 1 Lawful turnkey .50 c
(p-466) Aug. 13 to two Lawful turnkeys 50 c.E. 1.00
Aug. 14 " 1 " " 50 c.E. 1.00
Aug. 20 " " " .50

                            Making in all $ 7.00

Which account having been Examined and certified by the attorney General to be correct is allowed by the court and ordered to be taxed in the
bill of cost in this cause.

State of Tennessee) Indictment for murder - Shadrach Mooneyham
Vs) Pros. This day William R. Hutchison, Jailer
Henry Ayres) of Putnam County, produced and read in open

court his account for keeping Henry Ayres in the common Jail of Putnam
County on a charge of murder from the 10th day of August to the 20th of
August 1856 making in all 10 days at 40 c. E. per day. $ 4.00
August 10th 1856 to 1 lawful Turnkey   .50
"   12th "   " 2 "   "   1.00
"   13th "   " 2 "   "   1.00
"   14   "   " 2 "   "   1.00
"   20   "   " 1 "   "   .50

         Making in all   8.00

Sworn and subscribed to in   W. R. Hutchison Jailer
open court 11 Dec. 1856.   Test - G. Mills

 Which account having been Examined and certified by the attorney General to be correct in allowance by the court and ordered to be taxed in the bill of cost in this case.

Elijah W. Brown and wife)   Ejectment
    Vs   ) Come again the same Jury sworn in this
Thos. Butler   ) case on a former day of the Term who
) upon their oaths do say they have not
agreed who by consent of the parties are permitted to disperse to meet
again at the meeting of the court tomorrow morning.

P-467 Allen Young   )   Debt Appeal
    Vs   ) Came the attorneys and the defendants
  Willis and John Coggin) moved the court for a new trial in
) this court, which motion is contin-
ued for further considereation.

 Court adjourned until tomorrow morning 8½ oclock.

                   John L. Goodall

     Friday Morning December 12th A. D. 1856

 Court met pursuant to adjournment - present the Honorable John L. Goodall Judge presiding.

 The grand Jury this day returned into court a bill of Indictment against John W. Kerby for Larceny endorsed by their foreman a true bill.

State of Tennessee) Indictment for Larceny Joseph Randolph Prose-
  Vs   ) cutor - The following is a true copy of the
John W. Kerby   ) bill of Judgment in this case to wit:

State of Tennessee) December Term of said Court in the year of
Putnam County   ) our Lord one thousand eight hundred and fifty
) six - The grand Jurors for the State of Tenn-
essee Elected, empannelled sworn and charged to inquire for the body of
the County of Putnam in the State of Tennessee upon their oaths present
that John W. Kerby Yeoman on the twelfth day of December one thousand

eight hundred and fifty six with force and arms in the County of Putnam
and State aforesaid did unlawfully and feloniously did steale, take and
carry away one Jug of the value of fifty cents and one half gallon of
whiskey of the value of fifty cents the property of Hiram Brown then and
being in the possession of Hiram Brown being found against his will, contrary to the form of the statutes in such cases made and provided and
against the peace and dignity of the State.

          Tim. H. Williams
          Attorney General 4th Circuit

P-468 Endorsed - Joseph Randolf Prosecutor Hiram Brown Sr - Hiram Brown
Jr - No Trespass sworn in open court and sent before the Grand Jury to
give evidence on the bill of Indictment.
          C. Mills Clk.

A true bill Robert D. Allison Foreman of Grand Jury.

James Allison	)	Debt Motion to condemn land - The following
Vs	)	papers wear filed to wit:
Seborn Stewart and	)	
J. J. Campbell	)	State of Tennessee) To any lawful of-
S. M. McCaleb	)	Putnam County) ficer of said

)   County to execute
and Return - Now are hereby commanded to summons Seborn Stewart J. J.
Campbell, Samuel M. McCaleb to appear before some acting Justice of the
peace for said County to answer the complaint of James Allison Senr. in
a plea of debt due by note sum under-warrant herein fail not.
 Given under my hand and seal this March _____.
                    Isaac Lollar (Seal)
                    Justice of Peace

I. Lollars fee Judgment 10 cents - Endorsed, Executed and set for trial
before Isaac Lollar Esqr. on Saturday the 31st this Inst.

This March 29th 1855.   J. H. Early Const.
My fee $1.50
        Judgment -

James Allison	)	I give Judgment in favor of the plaintiff
Vs	)	against the defendants for twenty nine dol-
Seborn Stewart and	)	lars and ten cents debt with cost for which
T. J. Campbell and	)	execution may issue the 31st day of March
M. M. McCaleb security	)	1855.

                    Isaac Lollar (Seal)
                    Justice of Peace

Execution:

State of Tennessee	)	To the sheriff or any constable of said County
Putnam County	)	you are hereby command that of the goods and
	)	chattles lands and tenements of Seborn Stewart

Joseph J. Campbell and S. M. McCaleb their securities if to be found in
your county you make the sum of twenty nine dollars and ten cents debt with
interest and all lawful cost to satisfy a Judgment (p-469) which James
Allison Senr. obtained against them before me on the 31st day of March 1855.
Herein fail not - Given under my hand and seal the 13th Nov. 1856.
                   Isaac Lollar (Seal)

Levy: No goods and chattles to be found in my County - Levied upon a tract of Land the defendant in Dist. No. No. 1 and adjoining the lands of Kerbys on the south and on the west by Corder Lollar and on the north by the town of Cookeville and on the East by Ramseys land and said to contain _____ acres this 1st day of Decr. 1856. My fee $100 .

                 I. W. Carr Const.

 All of which being seen and heard by the court it is considered by the court that the land levied upon as aforesaid be and the same is ordered to be sold to satisfy the plaintiffs debt and cost and also the cost of this motion and that an order of sale issue.

State Vs Elijah Carr	Indictment for Drunkness - Ordered by the court that three Dollars of the five imposed upon the defendant on a former day of this Term be released.

State of Tenn Vs Patrich Brady	Indictment for Drunkness - Ordered by the court that three dollars of the five imposed on the defendant on a former day of this Term be released.

Jas. Bullington)   Debt Appeal
  Vs   ) Came the parties by attornies and came also
William R. Hutchison) a jury of good and lawful men to wit: Oliver
) P. Apple, Wm. T. Young, Wm. P. Stone, Amon
Jones, Henry Sadler, James M. McCaleb, Elmore Carrington, Elijah S. Ellis Wade H. Miller, Elijah H. Matheny, Anthony McBroon, Joshua Bartlett, who being Elected tried and (p-470) sworn the truth to speak and to well and truly try the matter of controversy between the parties upon their oath do say they find the matter in controversy in favor of the plaintiff and do assess his damages at twenty Eight Dollars six and two thirds cents.
 It is therefore considered by the court that the plaintiff recover of the defendant the sum of twenty Eight dollars six and two thirds cents the damages by the Jury assessed and all cost and that Execution issue for the collection of the same.

Levi M. Pistole Executor) Trespass Appeal - Came the parties by
of Levi S. Murphy Decd.) attornies and there came a Jury of good
   Vs   ) and lawful men to wit: Truston Leach,
John Watson   ) John Terry, John Harris, Jas. A. Mahan,
) Thomas Pullin, Ella Bennett, Mathew S.
Smith, Isaac Buck, James O. Hall, John Grider, John West and Robert Smith who being elected tried and sworn well and truly to try the matters in controversy between the parties joined upon their oaths do say they find the matters in controversy in favor of the plaintiff and do assess his damages at thirty seven dollars and twelve cents -
 It is therefore considered by the court that the plaintiff recover of the defendant and Patrich Brady his security in the appeal bond the said sum of thirty seven Dollars and twelve cents the damages by the Jury aforesaid assessed and also all cost and that execution issue for the collection of the same.

271

P-471 James Brown)   Case
              Vs) Came the parties by attornies and
       Elizabeth Franklin) there came a jury of good and lawful
       David E. L. Franklin) men to wit: Charles Crook, O. P.
       John C. White) Apple, William F. Young, William P.
       James White) Stone, Amon Jones, Henry Saddler,
) Elmore Carrington, Elijah S. Ellis,
Wade H. Miller, Elijah H. Matheny, Anthony McBroom and Joshua Bartlett, who being elected tried and sworn the truth to speak upon the issue joined after having heard the evidence in the case the argument of council and there not being time to go through with the trial of this cause on this day the Jurors by consent of the parties are permitted to disperse untill the meeting of court to-morrow morning.

Elijah W. Brown & wife) Ejectment - Came again the parties by at-
          Vs) tornies and came the same Jury sworn in
Thomas Pullin) this case on a former day of this term.
) Who upon their oaths do say they have not
agreed upon a verdict in this cause and by consent of the parties they are permitted to disperse to meet here again tomorrow morning to resum the further consideration of this cause.

    The Grand Jury this day returned and filed in open court the following presentments to wit -

State Vs Alfred Myatt for Illigal voting. State Vs James Bean for Illigal voting. State Vs Alexander Myatt for Illigal voting. State Vs John Jackson for Illigal voting. State Vs Lothery Childers for profane swearing. and also the following Indictment - to wit: State Vs Benj. H. Watson for Assault & Battery - State Vs Henry Whitaker for assault & Battery.

    Each of the above named Indictments endorsed by their foreman "A True Bill".

P-472 A. J. Wallace) Trespass - Appeal: By consent this
            Vs) cause is continued until next term
       Green B. Hamilton) of this court.

James Bullington) In this case the plaintiff acknow-
       Vs) ledged herein open court the execution
William Hutchison) of the following:
) I hereby transfer to Denton and Washburn Ten dollars of the judgment I have this day recovered in the Circuit Court of Putnam County against William R. Hutchison.

This 12 Dec. 1856.   James Bullington

State of Tennessee) Indictment for murder R. Dyer Sheriff of
       Vs) Putnam County This day produced in open
Henry Ayres) court his account sworn for conveying the
) defendant from Sparta Jail to Cookeville
Tenn as follows: At April Term 1856.

36 Miles going and returning at 10 c pr. mi.	$ 3.60
Also for Boarding Deft & two Guards	$ 1.75
Two Guards, Towns Watson & Taylor Huddleston 36 miles travel each at 5 c per mile.	3.60
Shrff. Dyer also at same Term for returning said Deft. from Cookeville to Sparta Jail - 36 miles travel at 10 c pr. mile	3.60
2 Guards Pinckerey Huddleston and Andrew Huddleston 36 miles travel each at 5 c per mile.	3.60
D. S. J. H. Moore and H. G. Huddleston and Claiborn Brown Guarding deft 1 day each at 50 c.	1.50
Also D.S. Moore for Bringing deft. from Sparta Jail to Cookeville at August Term 1856 36 miles travel at 10 c pr. mile.	3.60
John C. Dyer and Robert Mackie Guards 36 miles travel each at 5 c. per. mile.	3.60
Amounting in all	$ 24.85

And the Attorney General having Examined said account (p-413) report it correct - Ordered by the court that the same be allowed and taxed in the bill of cost in said cause.

State of Tennessee) Indictment for Larceny - This day R. Dyer
     Vs   ) Sheriff of Putnam County produced and read
John Watts   ) in open court this account sworn to for con-
) veying the defendant from Sparta Jail to Cooke-

ville Tenn as follows - At April Term 1856 36 miles going and Returning at 10 cents per mile.	3.60
Also for Boarding Deft and two Guards.	1.75
Two Guards, Towns Watson and Taylor Huddleston, 36 miles travel each at 5 ¢ per mile.	3.60
Shrff. Dyer, also at same Term for returning said Deft from Cookeville to Sparta Jail 36 miles travel at 10 ¢ pr. mile.	3.60
2 Guards Thompson Hughes and John Bradford 36 miles travel each at 5¢ per mile.	3.60
D. S. J. H. Moore and H. G. Huddleston and Claiborn Brown guarding deft 1 day each at 50 ¢	1.50
Also R. Dyer for Bringing deft. from Sparta Jail to Cookeville at August Term 1856 36 miles travel at 10 c. per mi.	3.60
Robert Mackie two guards at 50 c. E. pr. mile	3.60
	$ 25.10

And the attorney General having Examined said account report it correct ordered by the court that the same be allowed and taxed in a bill of cost in this cause.

State of Tennessee) Indictment for Rape - This day R. Dyers Sher-
     Vs   ) iff of Putnam County produced and read in open
Major, Alias, Nig) court his account sworn to for boarding Deft.
) 3 guards 1 day E. D. Shrff. McDonald - W. C.
Brown and Henry Whitaker.

	3.00
Also the same for guarding said Deft 1 day 50 c.	1.50
Making in all	$ 45.00

Patrich Brady) Debt Appeal
Vs)   Came the parties by their attorneys and there came
John Tucker)   a jury of good and lawful men to wit: Thomas A.
)   Porter, Tyra Bullington, John Grider, William H.
Barnes, James White, John C. White, M. W. Copeland, Z. Hopkins, John Terry, Peter Goodwin, James A. Mahan and James Z. Bohannon who being elected, tried and sworn well and truly to try the matter in constroversy between the parties upon their oaths do say they find the same in favor of the defendant - It is therefore considered by the court that the defendant go hence and recover of the plaintiff his cost about this suit in this behalf expended and that execution issue for collection of the same.

P-477   James Brown) Case
Vs)   Came the parties again by
Elizabeth Franklin and others)   their attorneys and came
)   again the same jury sworn
in this cause on yesterday, who after having received their charge from the court retired and again returned into court and upon their oath do say they find the issue in favor of the defendants. It is therefore considered by the court that defendants go hence and recover of the plaintiff their costs about their suit in this behalf expended and that execution issue for the collection of the same.

Elijah W. Brown and wife) Ejectment
Vs)   Came again the parties by attorneys and
Thomas Pullin)   came the same jury sworn in this cause
)   on a former day of this term, who say
they have not agreed upon a verdict in this cause, whereupon by consent of the parties a mistrial is entered and the case continued until next Term.

Patrich Brady) Debt Appeal
Vs)   Came the parties again by attornies and the defend-
John Jackson)   ant moved the court for a new trial in this cause
)   which motion by the court was overruled to which
action of the court the defendant excepts and prays an appeal to the next term of the supreme Court which is granted upon his Security as required by law which being done the defendant tendered his bill of exceptions which is signed sealed and ordered to be made a part of the record in this cause.

Samuel K. Wilkeson)   Trespass on the case - Came the parties by
Vs)   attorneys and by consent this order is ordered
Newel Jackson)   to be continued untill the next Term of this
)   Court.

Willis Coggins) Debt
Vs)   There not being time at this Term of the Court

P-474 The attorney General having Examined and certified the same to be correct - It is ordered by the court that the same be taxed in the bill of cost in this cause.

Ordered that the court adjourn untill tomorrow morning half past 8 oclock.
John S. Goodall

Thursday Morning December 13 1856

Court met persuant to adjournment present the Honorable John L. Goodall Judge presiding.

James C. Officer Etux.)   Debt Appeal
      Vs   )   This day came the parties by their attor-
William Cureton   )   neys and the defendant by attorney moved
)   the court to correct the taxation of the card in this case which motion being understood by the court: It is ordered that L. G. Fisk, Jesse Farley, John Grime, Joshua R. Stone and Presley Russel and none other of the plaintiffs witnesses be taxed against the defendant in this cause.

State of Tennessee   )   Tipling
      Vs   )   Came the attorney General and the defendant
William Milles   )   in proper person who being charged upon
)   the indictment for plea says he is guilty in manner and form as in the presentment is charged against him and puts himself upon the mercy of the court - It is therefore considered by the court that for such his offence he pay a fine of Two dollars and all cost of prosecution. Thereupon came here into open court William H. Barnes Jr. and acknowledged himself the defendants security for the fine and costs aforesaid and agreed that execution might issue against him Jointly with the defendant for the collection of the same - It is (p-475) further considered by the court that the State of Tennessee recover against the defendant and William H. Barnes the said sum of two dollars of this suit. Therefore came here into open court Alexander Madden and confessed Judgment Jointly with the defendant for the fine and cost aforesaid - It is therefore further considered by the court that the State of Tennessee recover against the defendant and Alexander Madden the fine and cost afore said and that Execution issue.

P-476 John Ramsey   )   Slander
        Vs   )   Came the parties by their attorneys and
Oswell H. Dillon   )   there came a Jury of good and lawful
)   men to wit: Oliver P. Apple, William F. Young, William P. Stone, Amon Jones, Henry Sadler, James M. McCaleb, Elmore Carrington, Elijah S. Ellis, Wade H. Miller, Elijah H. Matheny, Anthony McBroom and Joshua Bartlett who being Elected tried and sworn the truth to speak upon the issue Joined upon their oath do say they find the issue in favor of the plaintiff and assess his damages at one Thousand Dollars - It is therefore considered by the court that the plaintiff recover against the defendant the sum of one thousand Dollars the damages

Allen Young) to try this cause - It is ordered by the court that
) the same be continued untill the next term of this
court and by consent of the parties the demurer in this cause is also
continued untill next Term.

The Grand Jury this day returned and filed in open court the following presentments.

State Vs Philander D. Hughes for Betting on Election - State Vs Ferrel Maynor for Illegal voting, which presentments are signed by the foreman of the Grand Jury and all the balance of the jurors in due form of Law and the Grand and Traverse Jurors having no further Business to preform at this term of the court they are released and Discharged as such from further attendance.

John Ramsey) Slander.
Vs) Came the plaintiff here in open court and exe-
Oswell H. Dillon) cuted and acknowledged the following transfer
) to wit:

"For value received I assign the judgment I this day obtained against Oswell H. Dillon in the Circuit Court of Putnam County Ten. for one thousand dollars to William H. Botts, Holland Denton, Benjamin B. Washburn - this 13th Decr. 1856.
                                                              his
                                           John X Ramsey (Seal)
Test Josh R. Stone   mark
Roberson Dyer

P-478 Left out.

P-479 John Ramsey) Slander
Vs) In this case Wm. H. Boots, H. Denton, B.
Oswell A. Dillon) B. Washburn to whom the Judgment in this
) case was transferred here in open court
agree to release to defendant all of said Judgment of one thousand dollars except the sum of one hundred and thirty five dollars and costs of said suit.

Allen Young) Debt Appeal
Vs) Came the parties by attorneys and the defendants
John Coggins and) motion for a new trial in this cause being over
Willis Coggins) ruled the defts except and prays an appeal in
) the nature of a Writ of error in this cause which
is to be and is granted upon his giving bond and security as required by law.

Ordered that court be adjourned until court in course.

                                                               Jno. L. Goodall

THE END

PUTNAM COUNTY

CIRCUIT COURT MINUTES
1842-1856

ORIGINAL INDEX

Note: Page numbers in this index refer to those of the original volume from which this copy was made. These numbers are carried throughout the copy within parentheses.

A

Austen, William Vs Isom Smith
   159, 169, 173, 246
Anderson, Garland Vs E. Anderson 242, 284, 302
Allison, R. D. Vs Drury W. Sims
   285
Anderson, Edward Vs Gallant 10,
   13, 15
Awston, W. Vs McGuffy 351
Anderson, Edward Vs John R. Jones
   443, 461
Allison, James Vs Seborn Stewart
   468
Anderson, Green and Co. Vs John
   Johnson and others 40

B

Buck, Abraham Vs Gideon Anderson
   13, 28
Burton, Robert G. Vs Gideon Anderson 23
Bounds, William C. Vs William
   Kinnaird and Wiley Night 37
Bank of Tennessee Vs Thomas B.
   Johnson and others 40, 48
Bank of Tennessee Vs John Pott
   and others 40, 80
Bank of Tennessee Vs Henry B.
   Johnson and others 47, 53
Bank of Tennessee Vs Joseph L. B.
   Graham and others 48
Bank of Tennessee Vs John Bumbalough and others 49
Bank of Tennessee Vs Joseph Bartlett and others 49
Brown, Benjamin Vs Snowden H.
   Maddux 73
Bank of Tennessee Vs John Whitaker
   and others 96
Bank of Tennessee Vs David Bean
   and others 96
Bank of Tennessee Vs John B.
   Pointer and others 96

Bank of Tennessee Vs Adison Maddux and others 101
Bank of Tennessee Vs James Bartlett and others 102
Bartlett, James Vs Isaac Lollar
   102
Burton, R. G. and C. F. Vs George
   Apple 31
Burton, R. G. and C. F. Vs Samuel
   T. Vaden and John B. Conditt
   104
Bank of Tennessee Vs John B.
   Pointer and others 105
Bank of Tennessee Vs Thomas Welch
   and others 105
Bank of Tennessee Vs John Officer
   and others 106
Bank of Tennessee Vs William Scaborough and others 107
Bank of Tennessee Vs Joseph Bartlett and others 107
Bank of Tennessee Vs L. H. Maddux and others 107, 121
Bank of Tennessee Vs S. T. Vaden
   and others 108
Bank of Tennessee Vs H. D. Marchbanks and others 108
Bank of Tennessee Vs Lawson Clark
   and others 108
Brown, Benjamin Vs Charles Smith
   121
Bradford, W. K. Vs Samuel Mansel
   128
Buck, Isaac Chairman Vs B. M.
   Draper & others 131
Bank of Tennessee Vs Robert Allcorn and others 132
Bartlett, John S. and others Vs
   Benjamin Watson and Lucy 152
Brown, Eliajh W. and wife Vs
   Thomas Pullin 154, 259, 324,
   365, 459, 471, 477
Bounds, Thomas Vs Jesse B. Terry
   154, 234, 275
Brooks, James Vs James Bartlett
   168

Brooks, James Vs George Henry 168
Burton, R. G. Vs Stephen Ward 170
Burton and Haws Vs Benjamin Watson 178, 179, 180
Burton, R. G. Vs Anderson Cole 182
Bounds, Thomas Vs Jesse B. Terry 234
Burton, Isaac Vs Thomas Lancaster 243, 375
Buren, S. D. Vs John B. Pointer 244
Brooks, James W. Vs James Bartlett 250, 259, 324
Burks, James W. Vs George Henry 250, 264
Bohannon, Campbell Vs Levi Phillips 261
Burton, R. G. Vs Walker Brown 293
Brown, James Vs E. Franklin & others 270, 339, 346
Barnes, W. H. Vs John Barnes 774, 339, 346
Barnes, W. H. Vs John Barnes 274, 349, 397
Burton, Isaac Vs Thomas Lancaster 280, 345
Brown, J. Vs William Rogers 289, 290
Burton, C. H. Vs Gallant Anderson 309, 11, 46,
Burton, A. N. Vs Gallant Anderson 321
James, Bartlett Vs B. H. Watson and Lucy Watson 366, 419
Berry, W. W. Vs Robert Faine 393, 420
Baker, William Vs Whitson and Barnes 393, 465
Bohannon, George Vs John Slyger 393, 419
Brady, Patrick Vs John Jackson 394, 476
Brown, Daniel Vs R. G. Maddux 394, 465
Burton, Isaac Vs Thos. Lancaster 464
Bullington, James Vs W. R. Hutchison 469
Brown, James Vs E. Franklin 471 477

C

Carlin, William for the use of Hugh Wallace Vs Jesse Pollard 13
Conway, Jesse Vs Charles & David Phillips 14
Camron, Elisha Vs Harrison Whitson 16
Conger, John to the use & etc Vs Mark Harper 41, 84
Carlin, Hugh W. Vs William Jared 74
Clendemon, Isaac Vs Henry L. McDaniel 87
Cassety, Sampson Vs Sarah Kinnaird 95
Carlin, Hugh W. Vs William Jared 127
Clark, Lawson Vs Wesley Harvey 128
Clark, Lawson Vs Mathew Cowen 128
Clark, Lawson Vs Mathew Cowen 129
Clark, Lawson Vs E. S. T. Anderson 133
Cassaty, Sampson Vs Sarah Kinniard 133
Clark, Isaac Vs Duddley Hunter 153
Clark, Isaac Vs Dudley 155
Dunavin, Ephraim Vs Restored to Citizenship 167
Coggin, Jeremiah Vs William C. Mitchel 169, 176, 178, 266
Cole, Susan Vs D. G. Harris 348, 380, 436
Colbert, J. F. and J. L. Vs John Robert 355, 357, 378, 359
Carr, J. W. & A. F. Vs Wm. Gipson and William Evans and R. E. Faine 360, 369
Coggin, Willis Vs Allen Young 401 478

D

Dearing, Zebedee P. Vs Joseph Bartlett 91, 99
Dearing, Sims admr. of Joshua Fox Deed Vs John Robinson & others 34, 99, 116
Dearing, Zebedee Vs Joseph Bartlett 100
Draper, Brice M. and others Vs Chairman of Putnam County Court 99
December Term of Circuit 1854
Davidson Judge 142
Douglass and Ford Vs James Allcorn 320
Draper, Milton Vs James Kirklin 419

E

England, Mathew Vs John
    Johnson 13
Evans, Joseph Vs Charles Smith
    77, 95, 109
Evans, Morris Vs Charles Ford
    352

F

Ferrell, Isaac E. Vs Lawson Clark
    71
Farris, James Vs Amos Maxwell
    91, 100, 117
Ford and Douglass Vs A. H. Harget 194
Farley, John Vs Jefferson, Jesse
    285, 325, 394, 453

G

Glover, Elizabeth Vs Henry Glover
    13, 35, 46
Grant, Moses Vs Joseph Bartlett
    29
Gentry, Green Vs William Wilmoth 54, 87, 99
Gardenhire, Adam Vs Hiram K.
    Hodges 60
Gardenhire, Adam Admr. of Sarah
    Rawson deceased Expartee
    74, 85
Grogan, Andrew Vs H. H. Briant
    and Milton Stanton 154,
    172
Hellam, Hiram Vs R. G. Duke
    183
Grogan, A. J. Vs George W. Harper 290
This day the Grand Jury Returned
    into court 306
Goodbar, J. M. and T. P. Vs
Stephen Ford and William Johnson 413

H

Hogin, Simon Admr. Vs Lawson
    Clark 6, 7
Harpole, Henry Admr. of Jacob
    Harpole Vs Amos Maxwell 29
Hughes, William Q Vs Samuel
    Mansell 40, 73
Hughes, John Vs Peter McDonald
    57
Hogin, Simon Vs Peter McDonald 63

Hughes, James T. Vs Lewis R.
    71, 75
Harper, Mark Vs Amos Maxwell
    73, 87
Hollaman, James Vs John Simmons
    74
Henley, Julian Vs Mirah Henley 81
Hunter, Braxton D. Vs Joseph L. B.
    Graham and others 82
Hughes, John Vs James Land 81,
    127
Hunter, Braxton D. Vs Henry Bohannon 96
Hunter, Dudley Vs Thomas T. Nicholas
    97
Hall, William A. Admr. Vs Henry
    and Nancy Patton 29, 50,
    97
Hogan, Simon Admr. of Hogan Vs
    Thomas Holliday 109, 115, 121
Hughes, John Vs Needham Apple 117,
    119
Humble, John Vs Moses N. Scatlett
    130
Hail, Jesse Vs M. H. Presly 168
Haws, Daniel Assine of Samuel
    Madewell Vs Benjamin B. Watson
    185
High, James T. Vs Joseph Johnson
    198
Haws, Daniel W. Vs Benjamin H. Watson 188
Haws, J. O. Vs D. W. Sims 246
High, James T. Vs Joseph Johnson
    292
Haws, James Vs R. H. Dowell 306
Harvy, Wesly Vs J. W. Berry 370
    371
Holoway, C. Vs Ford 446
Harris, Willy Vs David Maxwell 455
Huddleston, J. W. Vs Shade Moonyham 461

I

Irwin, Washington H. Vs John Barnes
    30, 54
Irwin, Margaret Vs John B. Pointer
    351
James, John R. Vs Robert Lindsey
    and James Allison 35
Johnson, Robert G. Vs Mark Harper
    71
Jared, William Vs Hugh W. Carlin
    71
Johnson, Richard Vs Expartee 134
Johnson, Absalom Vs Ingrim Bussell
    191

K

Kuykendall, Peter Vs Gideon Anderson 19
Kerby, Nancy Vs Absalom Sims 44

L

Lee, Baronet Vs William Q. Hughes 53, 78
Lynn, Joel Vs Sarah Kinniard 34, 99
Lee, John Vs Alfred Jones and others 95, 116
Love and Null Vs R. G. Duke 190
Love, H. Vs Riley R. Liegue 241 267, 273, 275, 303, 334
Lee, David M. Vs Robert Smith 419
Luck, James and wife Moses Kinniard 463

M

McKee, Benjamin Vs John L. H. Huddleston 13, 32, 70
Marchbanks, E. R. and T. Vs Alfred Jones and others 16
McDaniel, Anna Vs the heirs of Riley McDaniel 37, 75
McDaniel, Henry L. Vs Eliajah C. Crowell 44
Marchbanks, E. R. & T. Vs Alfred Jones and others 53, 78, 120
Maddux, Snowder H. Vs Mark Harper 72
McNichols, A. B. Vs Lewis R. Vance 86, 115, 122
Maddux, Snowder H. Vs Mark Harper and Josiah Whitefield 93
Martin, George W. assinee & ect Vs William R. Vance and others 28, 53, 78, 92, 93, 101
McNichols, A. B. Vs Lewis R. Vance and R. G. Benson 115, 122
McNichols A. B. Vs Thomas Smith 115
Maddux, S. H. Vs Mark Harper 129
Mills, Curtis certified for Election 142
Mills, Curtis to bond 143, 4, 5, 6, 7
Mills, Curtis to oath of office 147
Mitchel, Joseph Vs A. T. Wallace 240, 284, 323

Maxwell, Samuel Vs A. Boyd 295, 296
Medly, Polly Vs Draper 296
Maddux, S. H. & T. J. Vs Gallant Anderson 318
McGee, John Vs Gallant Anderson 341
Mitchel, William Vs John Young 390, 456
Thomas T. Murry Vs Keziriah M. Murphy 393

N

Nicholes, Thomas Admr. of John Allison Expartee 7, 45, 47
Nicholes, Thomas T. Vs Dudley Hunter 92
Nichol, David H. Vs Joseph T. McGlee 136
Nichol, David H. Vs Jno. Verble 137
Nichol, David H. Vs Hiram Hallim 137
Nichol, David H. Vs Samuel Simpkin 137
Nichol, David H. Vs Archibald Hallim 137
Nichol, David H. Vs James Sutton 137
Nichol, David H. Vs Almarine Sutton 137
Nichol, David H. Vs Joseph Evans 138
Nichol, David K. Vs Paskal Hunt 138
Nancy, Norris Vs Wm. Bean 285 345, 400

O

Owens, A. H. to use of John Watson Vs Jesse B. Terry 63
Owens, A. H. to use of John Watson Sr. Vs Jesse B. Terry 67
Officer, James Admr. of W. G. Sims Vs William Crouton 269, 463, 474
Officer, Nancy Vs Preston Robinson 344

P

Price, Shadrach Vs Joseph Terry 7
Pippin, Redin Vs Samuel Mansell 16
Pointer, John B. Vs Hardy Chitty 72

Pearson, Joseph Vs Samuel Cole and others 83
Pointer, T. T. Vs John C. Boyd 287, 289
Pucket, G. W. Vs Y. W. Crabtree 297
Patterson, D. N. Vs Henry Roberts 335, 337
Patterson, F. N. Vs Edward McGuffy 367
Patterson, F. N. Vs John Roberts 376
Pippin, James Vs F. M. Burks and A. F. Carr 440
Pistole, L. M. Vs Joseph Hester 444, 445
Pistole, L. M. Vs John Watson 470

Q

Quarles, William H. Vs James Bartlett 31

R

Roberts, Henry Vs Calib Richardson 73
Ray, John Vs Samuel V. Carrick and others 80
Robison, Leah Vs Robert Officer and others 93, 94, 101, 126
Richardson, William and other Vs John Roberts, E. Vaughn 241 343
Ray, J. A. Vs G. W. Crabtree 258
Ray, Joseph Vs R. E. Dowell 303, 305
Richardson, Sarah Vs Gallant Anderson 316
Ray, J. A. Vs John Grider 381, 382, 384
Roberts, John Vs Linsey Viches 386
Richardson, J. Wm. Vs Edwin Vaughn and J. Roberts 392, 463
Ramsey, John Vs O. H. Dillon 409, 76, 89

S

Snodgrass, James Vs William Scarborough and William Kinniard 8
Snodgrass Vs Harrison Whitson 9

Snodgrass, James Vs James Scarborough 11
Snodgrass, James Vs Jeremiah Whitson 22
Snodgrass, James Vs Jeremiah Whitson 23
State, Vs Daniel Bartlett & Joseph Bartlett 12
State Vs Lawson Clark 28, 56
State Vs Hiram K. Hodges 28, 49
State Vs Jesse Pollard 28, 49
Smith, Robert S. Vs Mark Harper 31, 71
State Vs Hardy Chitty 32
State Vs Robert G. Hughes 32, 34, 43, 44, 51
State Vs Asa Herald 33, 43, 56
State Vs Matthias Welch 34, 42
State Vs Snowden Maddux 33, 56
State Vs William H. Quarles 40
State Vs Daniel W. Hawes 41, 69
State Vs George and Henry Hughes 41, 44, 52
State, Vs Jerry B. Terry 41
State Vs James Hayns 42
State Vs Edward Anderson 43, 70
State, Vs Samuel T. Vaden 44, 70
State Vs Hugh W. Carlin 51
State Vs Dudley Hunter 52
State Vs Thomas Welch 82
State Vs Baldwin Rowland 88, 39, 90, 91, 95, 101, 124, 125, 126
State Vs William H. Car 100
State Vs Spencer Phillips 81, 111, 114, 129, 130, 138
State Vs George Medly 109
State Vs Thomas Sailors 110
State Vs Hugh Owen 110
State Vs Nathaniel Whiteaker 110, 112, 113
State Vs James Jackson 111, 129
State Vs Joseph D. Huder 112, 129
State Vs Joseph S. Henry 112
State Vs James Brook 112
State Vs James Whitaker 113
State Vs H. W. Saddler 113
State Vs Asa Herald 114
State Vs Samuel P. Paren 114, 122
State Vs Thomas Cates 114
State Vs Thomas Pointer 114
State Vs Zechariah Sullens 114
State Vs Henry Arys 114
State Vs Jesse A. Bounds 114
State Vs Thomas Watts 114
State Vs John Sutton 114

State Vs Hampton Petillo 122
State Vs Bethel Bowman 122, 123
State Vs Peter McDonald 122, 131
State Vs James and Alex Brewington 123
State Vs Quinto Lowe 130
State Vs William McDonald & others 131, 133
State Vs Bennett Watts 132, 133
State Vs Elias Whiteaker 149
State Vs Isam 150
State Vs Joseph Floyd and Elizabeth Floyd 150
State Vs William Austen 153
State Vs William J. Taylor 145, 240, 253, 264
State Vs William Crabtree and Isaac Crabtree 146, 159, 160, 161, 162, 173, 175, 176, 237, 238, 239, 245, 253, 456, 260, 265, 277
Stone, Samuel B. and Terry Suttle Vs John 190
State Vs Elias Whiteaker
State Vs Major Nig a slave 201
Bill Exception 202, 203, 208, 212
State Vs George Dillard 252
State Vs James Lowery G. W. Collier 251, 300
State Vs Louisa Bright, Mary Bright and others 253, 269, 274
State Vs John Watson 280, 325, 410
State Vs James Bullington 280, 325
State Vs Robert Jackie 281
State Vs Drury Sims 281, 282, 372, 376
State Vs N. J. Brook 283, 299, 307
State Vs John Bohannon 283, 299
State Vs Elija Kinton 307, 327, 310
State Vs John Cates 324
State of Tennessee Claiborn Stone 327
State Vs John Watts 332, 340, 343, 391, 403, 404, 410, 412, 421, 465, 474
State Vs H. H. Bryant 334
State Vs Henry Ayers 340, 475, 390, 402, 410, 413, 423, 465, 472
State Vs J. H. Wheeler 341, 399

State Vs William Carlin 362, 372, 433
State Vs J. B. Lowery 363
State Vs William Crabtree 363, 364, 365, 430, 431, 432
State Vs Major Alias Nig 366, 367
Smith, Isam Vs Edward Anderson 375, 443, 451
Elis, Whitaker 381, 388, 425, 433, 435
John Roberts 394, 460
William, Roland Jane Bruce 395, 398
George McCormick 399
William James 401
H. J. Cole 405, 406, 409
Joel Gabbart, J. M. Douglass 416
Henry Carlile 416
Spivey, Thomas Vs Ford 427, 9
J. M. Douglass, Joel Gabbart 434
W. Shanks 435
William Crowell 450
Henry Carlile 436
Elijah Carr 437
D. K. Dillin 437
Y. P. Nicholas 439
Thomas Bohannon 442
Smith, Robert Gorden Maxwell 443
William Grogan & others 449
Ross Kerby 457
W. J. Mills 474
Henry Whitaker 475
John Maddin 475
William Robinson 454
John P. Pointer 456
Austin Choat 458, 220, 222, 223, 227, 242, 252, 253, 260, 270, 271, 272, 273, 267
State Vs James Lowe, Jasper Lowe 235
State Vs William Austin Ire Car 235
State Vs Henry Bohannon 242
State Vs A. J. Groggan 249, 250, 267, 268
Shoat, John to the use of Vs Daniel Kerby 294
Suten A. Vs William Whitefield 298
Smith, James & others Vs James W. McDonald, F. Burton 300

T

Terry, Jesse B. Vs Joseph L. B. Graham 96, 127
Terry, Curtis Vs Thomas Pullin 172

Terry, John Vs Elias Green 348, 392, 451
Trousdale, John Vs. H. H. Bryant 407
Terry, J. B. Vs James Brown 425
Turner and Hanner Vs Allen Young and other 440

V

Vaughn, Edward Vs John Roberts 395, 453

W

Wallace, Laban Vs Samuel and David Ansell 28, 30
Whitefield, Carter Vs John Simmons 29
Watson, Thompson T. Vs Zechariah Goss 115
Watson, John Sr. Vs Jesse W. L. Graham 122, 127
Whitten, Martin Vs Jackson Maxwell 172, 270
Watson, Benjamin H. Vs Samuel Madewell 185, 276
Winchester, Thursey Vs R. G. Duke 248, 270
White, C. F. Vs Joshua White 349, 464
Webb, Josiah Vs Ducilla Webb 396
Wilkinson, S. K. Vs Newel Jackson 409, 418
Wiser, Rebecca Vs A. G. Finch, J. Huddleston, 412, 478
Willis, Davis Expartee 411

Y

Young, Allen Vs Willis and John Coggin 323, 443, 401

THE END

PUTNAM COUNTY

CIRCUIT COURT MINUTES
1842-1856

NEW INDEX

Note: Page numbers in this index refer to those of the original volume from which this copy was made. These numbers are carried throughout the copy within parentheses.

A

Acres, James 205
Adams, Duro 212
Adams, Reubin 368
Albertson, Samuel 201, 202
Alcorn, James 169, 170, 236, 320
Alcorn, R. S. 236
Alcorn, Robert 120, 132, 169, 236, 242, 284, 302, 454
Alcorn, W. M. 236
Alexander, E. 205
Alexander, Ebenezer 211
Allcorn, John 275
Allcorn, R. S. 169
Allcorn, Robert 275
Allen, Augustine 304
Allen, Mary 189
Allen, (Allin) Robert 352
Allen, (Allin) V. H. 352
Allens Ferry 44
Allison, James 35, 468, 469
Allison, John 47
Allison, Joseph 27, 441, 452, 454
Allison, R. C. 118
Allison, R. D. 148, 258, 285, 286, 303, 304, 305, 307, 361, 365, 369, 378, 379, 379, 417, 418, 462
Allison, Robert D. 468
Alridge, Thomas 415
Alridge, Thompson 450
Ammonett, John H. 440
Amonett, J. W. 321
Amonett, John M. 284
Anderson, Albert 125
Anderson, E. R. 197
Anderson, Edward 43, 45, 46, 70, 71, 72, 120, 133, 242, 299, 310, 311, 313, 13 315, 316, 318, 321, 322, 337, 338, 342, 347, 348, 373, 394, 395, 439, 443, 444, 451, 461

Anderson, Frazier 285
Anderson, Galant 120
Anderson, Gallant 132, 175, 309, 310, 311, 312, 314, 315, 316, 318, 319, 321, 322, 337, 338, 342, 347, 374
Anderson, Gideon 12, 19, 20, 21, 22, 23
Anderson, Peter 12, 41, 42
Anderson, Thomas 111, 133, 233, 234, 298, 299
Anderson, V. W. 242, 284, 302
Anderson, William 157, 158
Andrea, Ada 142
Andrea, Agness 142
Andrea, Caroline 142
Andrea, Clara 142
Andrea, Edward E. 142
Andrea, Fanny 142
Andrea, Maximillian 142
Apple, G. W. 148, 150, 252, 269
Apple, George 31, 111
Apple, M. S. 148
Apple, Neadham 118, 119
Apple, Needham 117, 119
Apple, O. P. 417, 420, 434, 435, 438, 439, 455, 458, 459, 460, 471
Apple, Oliver P. 464, 469, 476
Apple, Ridly 45, 51, 54, 55, 56, 70, 71, 454
Austin, Godfrey 123
Austin, James 439
Austin, William 149, 150, 151, 153, 169, 173, 236, 246, 250, 351
Ayres, Choate 245
Ayres, Henry 114, 331, 332, 340, 348, 366, 373, 374, 390, 402, 410, 413, 423, 424, 472
Ayres, Samuel 332

B

Badger, Felix A. 125

Baken, James 283, 284
Baker, J. A. 370, 371, 372
Baker, William 393, 410, 411, 422, 424
Balaim, Robert H. 232
Ballwin, Wesley 212
Bankman, John 323
Banks, F. M. 280
Banks, Floyd M. 278
Bar, Jacob 193
Barnes, John 22, 27, 30, 54, 103, 105, 106, 107, 108, 110, 132, 133, 137, 143, 144, 145, 146, 147, 397
Barnes, Lewis 148, 417
Barnes, Lewis T. 412
Barnes, W. H. 393
Barnes, William H. 1, 2, 3, 45, 46, 71, 72, 93, 416, 476
Barnes, William H. Jr. 474, 475
Barnes, William S. 465
Barnes, Wm. H. 143, 144, 145, 147
Barnes, Wm. Jr. 416
Barnett, (Negro) 85
Barns, John 284
Baron, W. H. 281, 286, 301
Baron, William N. 172
Barons, Jesse 391
Barons, John 349
Barons, Lewis 148
Barons, Lewis T. 278
Barons, W. H. Jr. 274
Barons, William H. 185, 187, 348, 366, 405, 406, 459
Barons, William H. Jr. 252, 269, 274, 397
Barons, William H. Sr. 354, 355
Barry, W. H. 146
Bartlett, Daniel 12, 48, 96, 152
Bartlett, James 5, 27, 32, 36, 45, 66, 68, 69, 76, 77, 102, 143, 145, 146, 147, 152, 168, 259, 366, 419
Bartlett, Jane 152
Bartlett, Jesse 152
Bartlett, John S. 152
Bartlett, Joseph 12, 48, 49, 82, 83, 90, 98, 100, 105, 107, 324
Bartlett, Joshua 111, 233, 234, 309, 417, 420, 434, 435, 438, 439, 455, 456, 458, 459, 460, 464, 469, 471, 476
Bartlett, Nathan 152

Bartlett, William 99, 100
Baulkman, John 308
Bean, James 471
Bean, William 285, 400
Bear, Creek 445
Beaty, George 201
Beaty, William R. 157
Beech, Benjamin 157
Been, (Bean) David R. 96
Bell, Joseph 88
Bennet, Ella 437
Bennett, Ella 470
Bennett, Elly 324, 341, 399, 452
Bennett, James 173
Bennett, James B. 391
Bennett, Ray 134
Bennett, William 240
Benson, R. G. 115, 122
Berry, John W. 370, 371
Berry, W. W. 420
Derry, William W. 393
Bill, Joseph W. 86
Blackburn fork Creek 38
Bledsaw, Marian B. 219, 230, 232
Bledsoe, M. B. 163
Board Valley 17
Bohannon, Alexander 354, 399, 401
Bohannon, Campbell 107, 233, 236, 237, 240, 243, 250, 252, 261, 262, 267, 268, 452
Bohannon, George 393, 415, 419
Bohannon, Henry 242, 243
Bohannon, James J. 148, 150, 355
Bohannon, James Z. 476
Bohannon, John 251, 283, 298, 299, 308
Bohannon, Joshua 82
Bohannon, Lewis 45, 46, 71, 72, 87
Bohannon, Thomas 415, 442, 449
Bohannon, P. 148, 152, 177, 180, 375, 422, 424
Bohannon, Pleasant 142, 151, 233, 264, 265, 277, 308, 412, 413
Bohannon, Henry 96
Bolin, Andrew 205, 206
Boman, Bethel 122
Botts, William H. 234, 478, 479
Bounds, C. S. 332

Bounds, H. C. 143
Bounds, J. P. 287
Bounds, Jesse A. 114
Bounds, Thomas 154, 234, 275
Bounds, W. C. 424
Bounds, William 37, 38
Bounds, William C. 77, 80, 88, 100, 143, 145, 146, 147
Bounds, Wm. C. 48, 286, 287, 289
Bowen, John W. 89
Bowman, Bethel 123
Bowman, Bethel 124
Boyd, A. 196, 197
Boyd, A. L. 191
Boyd, Alexander 103, 104, 151, 295, 296, 392
Boyd, Bradford 190, 199, 289, 293
Boyd, J. W. 288
Boyd, John 190
Boyd, John C. 191, 287, 288, 289, 290
Bradford, David 103, 104
Bradford, John 473
Bradford, John A. 46, 51, 55, 56, 70, 71
Bradford, William K. 77, 80, 87, 90, 121
Bradford, Wm. K. 66, 68, 128
Bradly, John 135
Bradly, Nancy 135
Brady, Patrick 278, 394, 415, 453, 459, 469, 470, 476, 477
Bray, Joseph 240
Brewington, Alexander 123
Brewster, Jesse 201, 202
Briant, Howell H. 148
Briant, John H. 215
Bright, Francis 253
Bright, Francis Jr. 253
Bright, Louisa 253
Bright, Mary 253
Brook, N. I. 251, 299
Brook, James 264
Brooks, James 112, 113, 168, 259
Brooks, James M. 148
Brooks, James W. 247, 250, 324
Brown, Alvira 247, 250, 459
Brown, Benjamin 79, 98
Brown, Claburn 256
Brown, Daniel 394, 432, 465
Brown, E. W. 365
Brown, Elijah 154, 259, 459

Brown, Elijah W. 366, 471, 474
Brown, Enoch 219
Brown, Ephraim 159, 160
Brown, Henry 211, 212
Brown, Hiram 185, 467
Brown, Isaac 453, 459
Brown, James 270, 339, 346, 367, 406, 425, 471, 477
Brown, James H. 425
Brown, James J. 42, 51, 71, 80
Brown, James Jr. 88
Brown, Jefferson 383
Brown, John 1, 2, 3, 45, 46, 71, 72
Brown, John A. 417
Brown, John B. 351
Brown, Johnathan 367
Brown, Joseph 146, 147, 295
Brown, Joshua 177, 179, 181, 186, 189, 354
Brown, Josiah 298, 299
Brown, M. C. 266
Brown, Mack 388
Brown, Mary A. 185
Brown, Robert 158, 160, 161, 162, 164, 166, 173, 175, 176, 237, 239, 245, 253, 254, 256, 261, 265, 277, 327, 328, 329, 352, 364, 365, 430, 431, 432
Brown, Thomas 346
Brown, W. C. 473
Brown, Walker 263, 264
Brown, William 165, 175, 431
Brown, Wm. 161, 354
Bruce, Jane 200, 351
Bruce, Janie 251, 395, 398, 415
Bryan, H. H. 154
Bryan, Wm. S. 422, 424
Bryant, H. H. 172, 334, 369, 382, 383
Bryant, Harvel H. 407, 408
Bryant, Howel H. 441
Bryant, Howell 193, 194
Bryant, William L. 402, 403
Buck, Abraham 13, 28
Buck, Anderson 21
Buck, Betheul 103, 104, 105, 106, 107, 108, 110, 120, 121, 132, 133, 136, 137
Buck, E. I. 275
Buck, Isaac 27, 52, 60, 61, 62, 77, 79, 90, 131, 140, 325, 470
Buck, Isaam 419
Buck, William 237, 239

Buck, William Z. 264
Buck, Wm. M. 417, 418
Buckhannon, Robert 8, 9, 10, 11, 16, 17, 52
Buckner, William 284
Buggs, George 16
Bullard, Lian 85
Bullington, Henry 460
Bullington, James 34, 251, 280, 325, 454, 455, 472
Bullington, Jas. 469
Bullington, Tyre 345, 365, 476
Bullock, Joseph 100
Bullock, Thomas 67, 69, 308
Bullock, William 100
Bumbalough, Isaac 49
Bumbalough, John 49, 107
Burgess, Joel 46, 278
Burgess, Washington 233, 236, 237, 250, 264, 267
Burgis, Joel 33, 45
Burk, F. M. 440, 441
Burks, Caroline 462
Burton, A. M. 321, 322
Burton, C. F. 104, 300, 309, 311, 312, 322, 347
Burton, Charles F. 31, 385, 386
Burton, Isaac 243, 267, 275, 280, 345, 375
Burton, R. G. 170, 171, 182
Burton, Robert G. 23, 31, 104, 170, 263, 417
Burton, S. D. 294, 417
Burton, Stephen 420
Burton, Stephen D. 12, 40, 85, 86, 244
Burton, William 59, 75
Burtram, 210
Burtram, Baily 232
Burtram, James 205
Burtram, William 205, 206
Bustle, Ingram 191, 192, 193, 194
Butler, J. M. 276
Butler, Thos. 366
Byres, Sidney 346
Byrne, Alexander 58, 59
Byrne, Lawrence 5, 57, 58, 59, 63, 64, 65, 70, 72, 77, 80, 87, 90, 102, 117, 118

C

Cain, Creed 36
Cain, Lenard C. 205, 206
Cain, Wm. C. 208

Calvin, John 219
Campbell, Daniel 46, 51, 54, 55, 56, 70, 71
Campbell, J. J. 468
Campbell, John B. 148, 351
Campbell, William B. 109
Campbell, William C. 335
Campbell, William P. 308, 326, 345
Canard, Moses 172
Cany Fork 371
Capps, A. F. 463
Car, Elijah 1, 2, 3, 5
Car, Elijah (Carr) 77, 80, 87, 90
Car, William 90
Car, or Carr, William 77, 79, 87
Cardwell, Washington 367
Carick, Samuel V. 79
Carland, William 342
Carland, (Carlen) Wm. 13
Carlen, Hugh H. 51, 77
Carlen, Hugh W. 54, 55, 74
Carlen, (Carland) James 417, 418, 440
Carlen, William 415
Carlen, (Carland) William 362, 372
Carlen (Carland) Wm. 400, 433
Carlet, Moses 245
Carlile, Henry 433, 436, 437
Carlin, Hugh 127
Carlin, William 72
Carlisle, Henry 415, 416
Carlisle, Waddy 111
Carlisle, William 102, 104, 105, 106, 107, 108, 110, 120, 121, 136, 137
Carlton, John H. 71
Carlton, John W. 46, 54, 55, 56, 71
Carlton, William 405
Carnahan, A. H. 417, 418
Carr, A. F. 360, 361, 369, 440, 441
Carr, Elijah 31, 33, 41, 42, 77, 151, 152, 243, 326, 335, 345, 415, 437, 469
Carr, Felix J. 391
Carr, Harvy 345
Carr, I. W. 469
Carr, Ira 169, 236
Carr, J. H. 192
Carr, J. M. 304
Carr, J. N. 193, 194
Carr, J. W. 258, 259, 305, 307,

356, 358, 360, 369, 386, 425, 426, 441, 461, 462
Carr, James 264, 386, 452, 454
Carr, James R. 284
Carr, John 278, 344, 356, 369
Carr, John R. 172, 357, 378, 379
Carr, John W. 148, 425
Carr, Joseph 375
Carr, Terry 1, 2, 3, 7
Carr, W. H. 74, 87, 90, 98, 139, 141
Carr, William 77, 125, 360, 369
Carr, William H. 1, 2, 3, 7
Carr, William H. (or Car) 100
Carr, Wm. 35, 132
Carr, Wm. H. 39, 154
Carrington, Elmore 240, 335, 417, 420, 434, 435, 438, 439, 455, 456, 458, 459, 460, 464, 469, 471, 476
Carter, James 125
Cartwell, Julius 415
Caruthers, A. B. 7, 26, 27, 103
Caruthers, Ab. 29, 36, 37, 45, 46, 50, 60, 74, 75, 76, 77, 85, 90, 99, 109, 117, 126, 135, 139
Caruthers, Abraham 1, 2, 3, 5, 6, 77, 91, 97
Carwlthers, Robert L. 223
Cassitty, Sampson L. 95
Cassitty, Sampson W. 133
Cates, John 31, 85, 295, 324, 399
Cates, Thomas 114, 141
Caulk, Elbert 213
Caulk, Ethoert 212
Central Gazette (News Paper) 14
Chambers, Sheriff 210
Childers, Lothery 471
Chiles, Henry 212
Chitty, Harden 12
Chitty, Hardy 32, 72
Chitwood, James L. 205
Chitwood, William 205
Choat, Austin 341, 458
Choat, Edward 341, 391, 405, 407
Choate, Austin 415
Choate, John 85
Choate, Thomas 15, 71, 72
Clark, Calvin 93
Clark, I. B. 185, 186
Clark, Isaac 149, 153, 155

Clark, J. B. 185, 246, 247, 388, 389
Clark, James 27, 447
Clark, James J. P. 413, 414
Clark, James C. 31, 33, 34
Clark, James P. 227
Clark, Jesse B. 52
Clark, Lawson 27, 28, 56, 71, 93, 108, 126, 132, 133, 140, 141
Clark, Levi 389, 451
Clark, Luther 233, 363
Clark, William 155
Clark, Wm. 154
Clendennon, Isaac 87
Clinton, George W. 42
Clinton, J. C. 301
Coale, (Cole) Anderson 83, 84, 85
Coale,(or Cole) Sameul 83, 84
Cobb, Jesse 157, 158
Coggins, Jeremiah 169, 266, 278
Coggins, John 323, 326, 392, 464, 467, 479
Coggins, Willis 169, 243, 323, 326, 367, 392, 401, 464, 478, 479
Colbert, J. F. 355, 356, 358, 359
Colbert, J. L. 355, 356, 358, 359
Cole, Anderson 182
Cole, Jefferson 183, 301, 345, 346, 426, 427
Cole, N. J. 404, 406, 409
Cole, Susan 348, 380, 436
Collier, G. W. 251, 274, 300
Collier, Joseph 274
Collier, Washington G. 372
Collins, John 279
Collon, Alvin 36
Colms, S. H. 362
Colms, Stephen 373, 398
Colms, Stephen H. 366
Conard, (Kinniard) Moses 400, 406, 454
Conaster, Phillip 201, 202
Conger, John 41, 73
Conger, John 93
Conway, Jesse 14
Conway, Thomas 103, 104, 105, 106, 107, 108, 121, 132, 133, 136, 137
Cook, John 212
Cooke, R. F. 33, 41, 42, 47, 304, 305
Cooke, Richard 31
Cooke, Richard F. 27

Cooper, Jacob 443
Cooper, Thomas J. P. 422
Copeland, Wilkerson 452, 453
Cotten, J. W. 148, 150
Courton, William 269, 270, 345, 362
Cowen, Mathew 125, 128, 129
Cowen, W. W. 278
Cox, Elijah 90
Cox, Peter G. 190
Crabtree, Ephram 164, 166, 174
Crabtree, Ephriam 176, 327, 328, 330, 363
Crabtree, G. W. 176, 297
Crabtree, George W. 258
Crabtree, Hiram 163, 164, 166, 174, 176, 257, 420, 431, 432
Crabtree, Isaac 156, 158, 159, 160, 161, 162, 163, 164, 165, 167, 173, 174, 175, 176, 237, 238, 239, 245, 246, 253, 255, 257, 261, 266, 327, 328, 330, 363, 431, 432
Crabtree, James 164, 166, 175, 176
Crabtree, Jesse 329, 365
Crabtree, Nancy 164
Crabtree, Samuel 164, 166, 174, 175, 257
Crabtree, Washington 303, 364, 430, 431
Crabtree, William 237, 238, 239, 245, 246, 253, 254, 255, 257, 261, 265, 266, 277, 327, 328, 329, 330, 352, 363, 364, 365, 382, 383, 385, 430, 431, 432, 454
Crabtree, Wm. 156, 158, 159, 160, 161, 162, 164, 165, 167, 173, 174, 175, 176
Crag, Galeman 328
Crag, Permelia 329
Craig, Galeman 175, 363, 364, 430, 431
Craig, Goldmon, 164, 165
Craig, Permelia 176
Craig, Permila 165
Craigg, Goldman 164
Crautch, Martin 365
Crockett, James 157, 158
Cronk, William 357, 358, 359
Crook, Charles, 7, 284, 326, 471
Crook, Isaac 7
Cross, A. Wm. 205, 206

Cross, Caswell 205
Crouch, Martin 164, 165
Crowder, Green 365, 418, 450
Crowder, Grim 417
Crowder, James 193, 194
Crowder, William 415, 450
Crowel, Elijah 283
Crowel, Elijah C. 44
Crowell, E. C. 194, 195, 196, 197, 248, 249, 297, 298, 336, 356, 357, 358, 360, 378, 379, 385, 387
Crowell, E. G. 184
Crowell, Elijah 33
Crowell, Elijah C. 107, 121
Cudders, Thomas 321
Culaer, John 165
Cumberland River 118
Cummings, David H. 208
Cureton, (Coureton) 474
Cureton, James 365
Cureton, William 463
Cureton, (Coureton) William 353
Curtis, Holeman 445
Curtis, William 446

D

Daniel, William 417, 418
Daniels, William 365
Daugherty, F. E. 254
Davidson, H. L. 142, 148, 151, 202, 219, 220
Davidson, H.J. 212
Davidson, Pearson 219
Davidson, Wm. 190
Davis, Albert G. 243
Davis, B. S. 342
Davis, Henry 1, 2, 3
Davis, Jesse 157, 158
Davis, Thomas H. 211
Davis, Willis 411
Dawson, Isaac A. 157
Dearing, Sims 99, 116
Dearing, Z. B. P. 100
Dearing, Zebedee 27, 41, 42, 354
Dearing, Zebedee B. 355
Dearing, Zebedee P. 99, 100
Dearing B. Zebidee 33
Dearing, Joseph 41
Deering, Zebedee 31
Deering, Zebedee P. 90
Delk, (or Dilk) Henry 175
Delk, Minnie 176
Delk, Shered 175, 176

Delk, Sherred 3, 29
Delk, Sherrill 164, 167
Delk, Shirred 432
Denton, Holland 241, 478
Dibrell, Anthony 96
Dibrell, Joseph B. 10
Dilk, Henry 166
Dilk, Minny 164, 166
Dilk, Perandy 166
Dilk, Sherill 164, 166
Dillard, George 172, 252, 269
Dillon, Oswell, 397, 409, 437, 440, 476
Dillon, Oswell H. 415, 457, 478, 479
Ditty, Abraham 5, 354, 355, 371, 372
Ditty, John 27
Donley, George W. 462
Douglass, E. F. 195, 320
Douglass, James 415, 416, 434
Dow, David L. 459
Dowell, John M. 77, 79
Dowell, Martin 173
Dowell, R. M. 243, 285, 286, 303, 304, 305, 306, 355, 357, 358, 359, 400
Dowell, R. M. 192
Dowell, Reubin 152
Dowell, Reubin H. 151
Dowell, Watson, G. 399, 401, 406
Dowell, Winchester P. 326, 335, 339, 344
Downs, Edward 201, 202
Draper, Brice 131
Draper, Brion A. 99, 123
Draper, Edward 131
Draper, L. H. 308, 323
Draper, Milton 419
Draper, Prior M. 93
Draper, Ridly 252, 269, 285, 326, 335, 339, 344, 452
Dribel, Joseph B. 23
Duggor, Henry 103, 104
Duke, John 124
Duke, R. U. 193, 195, 196, 197, 248, 309, 311, 312, 313, 314, 315, 316, 317, 318, 321, 322, 337, 338, 342, 347, 348, 368
Duke, William 184
Dukes, R. U. 183, 184
Dun, John R. 367
Dunavin, Ephraim 167

Dunavin, Samuel 36
Duncan, John 157
Dunham, Alexander 354, 399, 401, 406
Dunn, Hezekiah 125
Duval, William 133
Dyer, Carrell 391
Dyer, J. C. 462
Dyer, Jefferson 307
Dyer, John C. 123, 351, 472, 473
Dyer, R. 148, 152, 417, 422, 423,
Dyer, Roberson 187
Dyer, Robison 143, 144, 145, 146, 185, 187, 238, 239, 240, 244, 245, 252, 256, 264, 265, 287, 288, 290, 327, 354, 478

E

Early, J. H. 468
Edward, Anderson 43, 394
Edward, Julian 233, 234
Edward, William A. 219
Elliot, Sarah 424
Elliott, Jesse 42, 240, 391, 463
Ellis, Elijah S. 417, 434, 435, 438, 439, 455, 456, 458, 459, 460, 464, 469, 471, 476
Ellison, John 7
Elmore, Julius 251, 428, 430, 447
Elmore, Thomas A. 212
Elms, Edward 46, 47, 51, 53, 54, 55, 56, 70, 71, 103, 104
Elms, T. S. 8, 9, 10, 11, 12, 17, 18, 19, 23
Elms, Thomas S. 76, 103
Elrod, Ephraim 45, 51, 54, 55, 56, 70, 71, 308
Elrod, William 125
England, Austin 81
England, James S. 48, 102
England, James T. 40, 79, 102
England, Mathew 13
Enson, William A. 148
Enson, Wm. 191
Ensor, Wm. 199
Ervin, K. D. 275
Evans, Alexander 162
Evans, Joseph 77, 95, 109, 137, 138, 391, 405
Evans, Obadiah 131, 355
Evans, T. W. 352
Evans, W. H. 352
Evans, William 367, 369, 408
Evans, Wm. 350, 361
Exum, K. D. 243

F

Fain, (Fane) R. E. 360, 361
Fain, Robert E. 420
Faine, Robert E. 393
Falling Water 287
Farley, Jefferson 285, 394, 453
Farley, Jesse 285, 301, 308, 325, 394, 453, 474
Farley, John 285, 325, 394, 453
Farly, John 367
Farmer, Enoch 212
Farris, James 90, 100
Farris, R. E. 191
Ferrell, A. S. 345, 371, 408, 417
Ferrell, I. E. 291, 292, 293
Ferrell, Isaac E. 71
Ferrell, J. E. 198
Ferrell, Joseph 98
Field, William A. 211
Field, Wm. A. 212
Finch, A. G. 412, 417
Finch, Allen, G. 420
Findly, Rufus 52
Fisk, L. G. 474
Fletcher, Joseph 233, 234
Floyd, Elizabeth 150
Floyd, Joseph 150
Ford, Abraham 287, 430, 447
Ford, Charles 352
Ford, Charles R. 195
Ford, H. B. 320
Ford, James 447
Ford, James D. 42, 427, 428, 429
Ford, Stephen 413, 414
Fountain, Sexton 231, 232
Fowler, Jonathan 27, 52, 77, 79, 111
Franklin, D. B. L. 357
Franklin, David E. B. 471
Franklin, David E. L. 358, 359, 360, 378, 379, 387
Franklin, E. L. 356
Franklin, Elizabeth 270, 339, 471, 477
Franklin, J. W. 374
Freeman, Andrew 82
Frogg, James 162

G

Gabbard, Benjamin 295
Gabbard, Joel 415, 416, 434
Gainer, John 196

Galeman, Craig 176
Gammon, William 12
Gardenhire, A. 85
Gardenhire, Adam 60, 61, 74, 85, 86
Gardenhire, E. L. 353
Gardenhire, Erasmus L. 160
Garrison, John 400
Gass, Zechariah 115
Gateswood, Henry 167
Gentry, Green W. 54, 87, 99, 100
Gentry, M. J. 283, 284, 308, 415
Gentry, Meridith 436
Gentry, Meridith P. 326, 335, 339, 344, 454, 459
Gentry, Silas W. 103, 104, 105, 106, 107, 108, 110, 120, 121, 132, 133, 136, 137
Gentry, William 101, 155, 173, 233, 234, 335, 339, 344
Gibson, Wm. 300
Gilbreath, William 364
Gilbrith, William 431
Gilreath, William A. 219
Gipson, William 151, 155, 240, 252, 269, 441
Goodall Jno. L. 184, 185, 249, 259, 272, 277, 324, 340, 354, 362, 370, 381, 397, 416, 417, 430, 462, 473, 474
Goodall, John L. 142, 157, 158, 161, 162, 167, 168, 200, 201, 222, 230, 238, 239, 266, 268, 296, 307, 308, 340, 396, 411, 415, 448, 467, 479
Goodbar, J. M. 134, 413, 414
Goodbar, T. P. 413, 414
Goodpasture, J. D. 353
Goodpasture, John 151
Goodpasture, John L. 227, 228
Goodpasture, W. W. 434
Goodpasture, Wilburn 148
Goodpasture Wilburn W. 449, 454
Goodwin, Peter 476
Goolsby, Frank 308, 326, 335, 339, 344
Goolsby, Peter 36, 371, 372
Graham, Daniel 134
Graham, David 39, 133
Graham, Jas. L. B. 49, 52
Graham, Jesse W. S. 82, 83, 122, 127
Graham, John G. 151
Graham, John S. 152

Graham, John T. 27, 103, 104, 344, 391, 452
Graham, Joseph 105
Graham, Joseph B. 48, 107
Graham, Joseph L. B. 67, 68, 82, 83, 96, 111, 127
Grain, John 173, 250
Grant, Moses 29, 40
Green, David 227, 229
Green, Elias 264, 304, 305, 348, 392, 451
Green, Harrison 374
Green, Hugh 172
Green, Simeon 304
Greer, David 201
Grider, John 155, 236, 237, 250, 264, 267, 280, 299, 325, 326, 346, 381, 382, 383, 470, 476
Griffin, Joseph 219
Grim, John 306, 307
Grime, John 45, 46, 233, 474
Grimes, John 283, 284
Grissom, William 173
Grogan, A. J. 249, 268
Grogan, Andrew 200
Grogan, Andrew J. 154, 172, 290, 291
Grogan, William 415, 449
Grogan, William B. 381
Grogan, Wm. 154
Grover, Elizabeth 13, 35, 46
Grover, Henry 13, 35, 46
Gwinn, Granville 201, 202

H

Hagin, Simon 7
Hale, Jesse 168
Hale, John D. 201
Hall, James O. 470
Hall, Robert 309
Hall, Thomas 190
Hall, William A. 29, 97, 98
Hall, Wm. A. 50
Hallum, Archibald 137
Hallum, Hiram 137
Hamby, Joel 205, 206
Hamilton, Green B. 472
Hamilton, J. H. 442
Hamilton, John 228
Hamilton, John H. 253, 254, 388
Hampton, Mack 415, 416, 448
Hancock, John R. 400
Hanner, William 440
Harget, Holden 31
Hargis, Margaret 135

Hargis, Washington G. 134
Hargret, A. W. 194
Harper, Clark 31
Harper, George H. 233
Harper, George W. 290, 291, 292
Harper, Mark 31, 41, 71, 87, 93, 123, 128
Harpole, Henry 29, 93
Harpole, Jacob 29, 37, 38
Harpoole, (widow) 263, 264
Harris, David 348, 380
Harris, David G. 436
Harris, George A. 161
Harris, John 470
Harris, Jordon 452
Harris, Jordon K. 464
Harris, Wily W. 455
Harrison, Whitson 9, 10
Harvy, Wesley 128, 129, 370, 371
Hatfield, Berry 161, 352, 364
Hatfield, Henry 164, 431
Hatfield, James 431
Hatfield, Mancell 175
Hatfield, Manuel 164, 166, 167, 328, 364, 431
Hatfield, Park 165
Hatfield, Perry 161
Hatfield, Robert 167, 431
Hatfields, Berry 166
Hawes, D. W. 57, 60, 64
Hawes, Daniel 43, 44, 56, 59
Hawes, Daniel W. 21, 22, 32, 41, 69, 102, 123, 308, 332, 334, 351
Hawes, J. O. 246, 247
Hawes, John 459
Haws, James D. 306
Haws, John 301
Haws, W. D. 294
Hawse, Benton 176
Hawse or Hawes, Daniel 185
Haynes, James 12, 32, 39, 42, 55
Heildrith, Clerk R. T. 165, 167
Heildrith, Reece, T. 166
Hellum, Hiram 183, 184
Helm, Alfred 164, 165, 167, 175
Helm, R. 276
Helms, Alfred 363, 364, 430, 431
Henley, Julian 81
Henley, Ninah 81
Henry, Andrew 106
Henry, George 42, 106, 151, 173, 250, 264
Henry, I. R. 212
Henry, Jacob 233, 262

Henry, Jacob H. 308
Henry, John 9, 95
Henry, Joseph S. 112
Henry, Vinet 17, 18
Herald, Asa 12, 32, 39, 43,
   44, 55, 114
Herren (Hearen) Gabrel 374
Herren, Wiseman 374
Hester, Joseph 81, 250, 251, 339,
   401, 407, 415, 416, 434, 444,
   445, 446, 448
Hicky, Elijah 156
Hider, Pleasant 284
High, James J. 198, 192, 293
Hildreth, R. T. 158, 161, 220,
   222, 228
Hildreth, Reece T. 232
Hill, William S. 229
Hodges, Hiram 27
Hodges, Hiram K. 28, 49, 60,
   61, 63
Hogan, Anthony 109, 115, 121
Hogan, Simon 109, 121
Hogan, Simon(Or Hogin) 64, 65,
   115
Hogin, or Hagin, A. E. 371, 372
Hogin, Simon 63
Holaman, James 74
Holeford, Elizabeth 118, 119
Holeford, Jonathan 118, 119
Holiday, (Holladay) John 27,
   41, 42
Holiday, Thomas 115
Holladay, John 31, 33
Hollaway, Claborn 447
Hollaway, Claborn 447
Holliway, Samuel 308
Holloway, Joseph 237, 239
Hollyday, John 103, 104
Hollyday, Thomas 109, 121
Honeycutt, Daniel 212
Honeycutt, David 212
Hooten, Pleasant 125
Hoover, John 201
Hopkins, Z. 476
Horn, A. V. 278
Horn, Albert 417, 418
Horn, Albert G. 365
Horn, Albert V. 135
Horn, Jane 135
Horn, Nathaniel 212
Howard, Robert 365, 417, 418
Huddleston, Andrew 472
Huddleston, H. G. 143, 144,
   145, 146, 147, 472, 473
Huddleston, Hugh. G. 27, 51,
   110, 120

Huddleston, I. A. 67, 69
Huddleston, Isaac A. 1, 2, 3, 42,
   46, 77, 79, 104, 151, 152
Huddleston, J. A. 61, 62, 63
Huddleston, J. L. H. 22, 38, 70,
   85, 117, 118, 119, 143, 144,
   145, 146, 147, 308
Huddleston, J. S. H. 26
Huddleston, J. W. 461
Huddleston, James 172
Huddleston, James A. 201, 202, 227,
   229
Huddleston, John L. 1, 2, 3, 33,
   42, 55, 56
Huddleston, John L. H. 1, 2, 3, 13,
   14, 15, 32, 42, 52, 70
Huddleston, Joseph 412
Huddleston, Lenard C. 157, 158
Huddleston, Lewis 142, 143, 144,
   266
Huddleston, Pinckerey 472
Huddleston, Snowden 32
Huddleston, Taylor 472
Huddleston, Wm. M. 289, 290
Hudgens, Dudley 31, 33
Hudgens, William 72
Hudgin, William 236, 237
Hudgins, Dudly 41, 42, 103, 104
Hudgins, William 42, 233, 243,
   251, 252, 267, 268
Huff, Patsy 352
Hugh, Robert G. 12
Hughes, George 32, 41, 52, 53
Hughes, Harry 32, 41, 52
Hughes, Henry T. 240
Hughes, James I. 51
Hughes, James T. 71, 75
Hughes, John 57, 58, 90, 117, 119,
   127
Hughes, Philander D. 478
Hughes, Robert G. 40, 43, 51
Hughes, Robert T. 42
Hughes, S. 247, 286
Hughes, Samuel 148, 149, 172, 265,
   388, 389, 475
Hughes, Thompson 473
Hughes, William 40
Hughes, William Q. 73, 78
Hughes, Wm. Q. 53
Hughs, John 291
Hughs, Robert G. 44
Hughs, Robert S. 32
Hughs, Samuel 308
Human, Hansley 211
Humble, John A. 130
Hunt, Paschal 138
Hunter, Braxton 82, 83, 96

Hunter, Charlie 148, 381
Hunter, Dudley 52, 77, 149, 153, 154, 237, 239, 308
Hunter, Dudly 77, 79, 90, 93, 97, 155
Hunter, John 45, 46, 237, 239
Huston, J. T. 381
Hutcherson, Wm. R. 426
Hutchison, W. R. 426
Hutchison, William 472
Hutchison, William R. 365, 366, 446, 469
Hyder, J. D. 189, 276, 422
Hyder, Jacob 46, 51, 54, 55, 56, 70, 71
Hyder, John L. 93
Hyder, Joseph 112, 399, 412
Hyder, Joseph P. 1, 129, 138, 177, 178, 180, 181, 185, 187, 284, 286, 405, 409
Hyder, P. M. 406
Hyder, Pleasant 405

I

Indian Creek 59, 60, 118, 119
Insor, William 284
Irwin, Margaret 296, 351, 382, 385
Irwin, Washington H. 30, 54
Isam, Charles 234, 275
Isbell, James 103, 104, 105, 106, 107, 108, 132, 133, 136, 137, 310, 313, 323, 338, 342, 348
Ivie, William P. 96
Ivy, Josiah 205

J

Jackson, Andrew 77, 80, 87, 88, 90
Jackson, Hamilton 330
Jackson, James 27, 35, 49, 66, 68, 77, 78, 111, 123, 129, 130, 138
Jackson, John 32, 240, 261, 262, 278, 284, 354, 355, 394, 471, 477
Jackson, Newel 409, 418, 478
James, John R. 35, 36
James, William 402
Jared, John 151, 155, 173
Jared, Joseph 105, 106, 107, 108, 110, 120, 121, 132, 136
Jared, M. A. 184, 190, 191, 197, 264, 267

Jared, Martin 93
Jared, Mathew R. 28, 78, 90, 101
Jared, Moses A. 172, 236, 237
Jared, N. A. 196
Jared, William 74, 77, 78, 90, 93, 101, 127
Jarred, John 283, 284
Jarred, Joseph 27, 103, 104, 308, 368
Jarred, Josiah 287, 288, 289, 290
Jarred, M. A. 249, 250, 288, 290, 297, 356, 357, 358, 359, 360, 399, 405
Jarred, Moses A. 452, 454
Johnson, Absalom 191, 192
Johnson, Asa 164, 166, 174, 175
Johnson, Henry 135
Johnson, Henry B. 47, 53
Johnson, James M. 79
Johnson, John 13, 40, 47, 53, 135, 148, 233, 236, 237, 243, 251, 252, 267, 268, 447
Johnson, Joseph 135, 190, 191, 198, 292, 293
Johnson, Richard 134
Johnson, Robert G. 71
Johnson, Samuel 135
Johnson, Thomas B. 48, 102
Johnson, W. C. 42
Johnson, William 413, 414
Johnson, William C. 428, 429
Johnson, Winie 135
Johnson, Wm. C. 135
Jones, Alfred 16, 30, 52, 53, 54, 78, 95, 116, 119, 132
Jones, Ammon 284
Jones Amon, 237, 239, 417, 420, 434, 435, 438, 439, 455, 456, 458, 459, 460, 469, 471, 476
Jones, B. S. 316, 317, 319, 334, 348
Jones, Bird 95
Jones, Bird I. 123
Jones Birds 55, 56, 116, 119, 132, 148, 237, 239, 310, 313, 314
Jones, Birds 417
Jones, Birds S. 284
Jones, Edward 61
Jones, James (Gov.) 53, 120
Jones, James C. 1, 2, 78
Jones, John R. 461
Jones, L. J. 237, 239
Jones, McClellan 71, 72, 105,

106, 107, 108, 110, 117,
  119, 121
Jones, McClelland 45, 46, 103,
  104
Jones, P. 197
Jones, Prettiman 236, 308
Jones, Pretty man 132, 183
Jones, Putnam 95
Jones, W. E. B. 257
Jones, William 366
Jones, William E. B. 327, 328,
  431
Jones, Wm. E. B. 363
Judd, Jacob 245
Judd, Robert 307
Julien, Kelly 308, 323
Julin, James 298

K

Kaip, James 167
Keeton, Elijah 409
Kendall, Alexander 388
Kerby (Kirby) James 42
Kerby, John W. 467
Kerby, Nancy 90
Kimp, James 176, 432
King, Mathew 38
King, Robert 157, 158
King, William 162
Kinnaird, Moses 463
Kinnaird, Sarah 95, 133
Kinnard, William 3
Kinniard, Wm. 37, 38
Kinslow, Bird C. 400
Kinton, Eliza 307
Kirby, Columbus 183
Kirby, Daniel 294, 295
Kirby, John 242
Kirby (Kerby) John W. 462
Kirby, Nancy 44
Kirklin, James 419
Knight, Wiley 285
Kuykendall, Mathew 38
Kuykendall, Noah 27, 31, 33,
  41, 42, 233
Kuykendall, Peter 19, 20, 21
Kuykendall, (Kerkendall) Syrous
  406

L

Lack, James 240, 405, 454, 459,
  463
Lacock, Joseph 130
Lancaster, Thomas 243, 345, 464
Lancister, Thomas 280, 375
Land, James 90, 127
Lansford, Armenias 367
Latham, James V. 164
Lathan, James 328
Lathan, James C. 164, 175, 176
Lathem, James 364
Lawson, Clark 7
Lawson, Jacob 205, 206
Lax (Lack) James 463
Laycock, Thomas 417, 418
Laysdon, P. F. 352
Laysdon, P. S. 364
Leach, Truston 463, 470
Ledbetter, James 332, 333, 334
Ledbetter, James M. 340, 365,
  391, 403, 421
Lee, A. B. 197
Lee, Augustine 77, 79
Lee, Barnet 78
Lee, Barnett 40, 53
Lee, Barthaelet 163
Lee, Bartholett 430, 431
Lee, David K. 410
Lee, David M. 419
Lee, Jackson 233, 236, 237, 250,
  264, 267
Lee, John 77, 79, 95, 116, 125,
  130, 151, 152, 237, 239, 371,
  408, 426
Lee, Joseph 395
Lee, Joseph R. 439
Lee, Lawson 123, 131
Lee, S. B. 231
Lee, William B. Sr. 395
Lee, Willis 337
Lee, Zachariah 278, 283, 284
Leigue, R. M. 303
Leigue, Riley R. 241, 273, 275
Lewellon, Emanuel 205
Lewellon, John 205, 232
Lewis, Allen 35, 82
Lewis, Ephram P. 229
Lewis, Jesse Alvis 35
Lewis, John H. 35
Leigue, Riely R. 267
Liegue, Rily 334
Liew, Larkin B. 211, 212
Lindsey, Robert 35, 36, 70, 102
Lindsy, John W. 136
Livingston, Thomas 157, 158
Lollar, Corder 405, 469
Lollar, Isaac 102, 192, 193, 194,
  258, 302, 351, 468, 469
Long, Riley 204, 216
Looper, Granville 209, 210, 213,
  214, 218, 222, 230, 231, 233,
  389, 451

Looper, Joel 209, 210, 213, 214, 389, 451
Looper, John 231
Looper, Mira 214, 217, 451
Looper, Mirah 203, 204, 207, 209, 218, 222, 224, 230, 231, 233
Looper, Myra 389
Looper, Nelly 204, 207, 209, 210, 213, 216, 217, 219, 222, 227, 229, 231, 232, 243, 252, 254, 270, 271, 272, 276, 277, 367, 373, 387, 388, 390, 448, 451, 452
Loosdon, Phillip 164
Love, Hezikiah 241, 255, 273, 275, 303, 308, 323, 334
Love, N. 196
Lowe, James 172, 234
Lowe, Jasper 172
Lowe, L. J. 391
Lowe, Phillips 205, 206
Lowe, Quinton 88, 90, 93, 125, 130
Lowery, James B. 151, 152, 156, 240, 251, 253, 254, 274, 353, 363
Lowery, T. B. 300

M

Mackie, Aaron 345
Mackie, Benjamin 12
Mackie, Pherly 349
Mackie, Robert 345, 472, 473
Macky, Robert 237, 239, 281, 424
Macky, Shirley 424
Macky, William 424
Madden, Alexander 1, 2, 3, 4, 475
Madden, Hosa 345, 399
Madden, John 462, 475
Maddux, Adison A. 102
Maddux, Craven 90, 102, 130
Maddux, R. G. 148, 394
Maddux, Redman G. 465
Maddux, S. H. 264, 318
Maddux, (Matticks) Snowden 33, 56, 72, 73, 107, 110, 121, 128, 275, 401
Maddux, Snowden H. 79, 88, 93
Maddux, T. J. 318, 319
Maddux, Thomas 367, 404

Madewell, John 77, 79, 151, 155, 173, 285, 286, 351, 412
Madewell, Samuel 185, 186, 189, 276
Mahan, James 240, 301, 375, 376
Mahan, James A. 282, 476
Mahan, Jas. A. 470
Major (Negro slave) 201
Major, (Alisa) Nig 219, 220, 222, 227, 229, 243, 252, 254, 260, 270, 271, 272, 276, 277, 303, 367, 373, 387, 388, 389, 411, 448, 451, 452, 473
Malone, Theophalus 233, 236, 237, 250, 251, 267
Malone, Theopholus 264
Manear, Allen 399, 401
Maneer, Allen 151, 152
Mansel, David 148, 150
Mansel, Samuel 73, 128
Mansell, Batey 125
Mansell, Land 40
Mansell, Sam 16
Mansell, Samuel 28, 30, 42, 93, 103, 104
Marchbank, Burton 27, 31, 41, 42, 77, 80, 87, 90
Marchbanks, H. D. 51, 53, 54, 55, 56, 71, 75, 90
Marchbanks, H. I. 70
Marchbanks, H. R. 16, 120
Marchbanks, H. T. 78
Marchbanks, Herald 46, 78, 108
Marchbanks, James C. 42, 52
Marchbanks, R. 78
Marchbanks, Russell 108
Marchbanks, William 44, 105, 106, 107, 108
Marchbanks, William M. 77, 80, 87, 90, 105, 233, 251, 274, 275
Marchbanks, Wm. M. 104, 233, 234
Markam, Catharine 438, 440
Martin, George W. 28, 52, 78, 90, 101
Martin, Howard C. 374
Martin, Samuel 101
Martin, Sanders 90
Martin, Thomas 406
Martin, Thomas C. 285
Martins, Creek 292, 361, 408
Mason, F. 164

Mason, Fidelus 365, 431
Mason, Fidley 166
Mason, Fridley 167
Mason, Sidney 164
Masson, Andrew 173
Masters, Mark 90
Matheny, E. H. 417, 434, 435, 438, 439, 455, 456, 458, 459, 460
Matheny, Elijah E. 464, 469, 471, 476
Matheny, John A. 400
Matheny, Samuel 46, 51, 70, 71, 345
Matheny, Thomas R. 252, 269
Mathews, Mark, 55, 56, 90, 304
Mathis, Mark 345, 367
Maxwell, Amos 29, 73, 81, 90, 100, 101
Maxwell, C. M. 228
Maxwell, Charles 228
Maxwell, David 455
Maxwell, G. C. 354, 399, 401, 406
Maxwell, Gordon 443
Maxwell, J. J. 276
Maxwell, Jackson 110, 120, 132, 133, 136, 172, 235, 253, 270
Maxwell, John W. 395, 398
Maxwell, S. H. 251
Maxwell, S. P. 170, 300
Maxwell, S. P. W. 250, 275
Maxwell, Samuel 68, 90, 98, 117, 260, 295, 296
Maynor, Ferrell 478
McAdoo, Wm. S. 207
McBride, Thomas J. 42
McBroom, Anthony 345, 417, 420, 435, 438, 439, 455, 456, 458, 459, 460, 469, 471, 476
McBroom, James 122
McCabe, Samuel 287, 296
McCabe, Samuel M. 54
McCaleb, David L. 462
McCaleb, James 476
McCaleb, James M. 365, 417, 420, 434, 438, 439, 455, 456, 458, 459, 460, 469
McCaleb, S. M. 278, 425, 468
McCaleb, Samuel 47, 148, 252, 351
McClellan, Jones 5, 7
McCormack, George 9, 116
McCormack, or McCormich, George 77, 79
McCormich, George 99, 350
McCormick 17, 18, 399
McCormick, George 278, 455

McCowen, Mathew 212
McCoy, John 212
McCulley, George 155
McCully, George 151
McCurly, George W. 173
McCurt, Pleasant 212
McDaniel, Amy 75
McDaniel, Anna 39
McDaniel, Elizabeth 118, 119
McDaniel, H. H. 276
McDaniel, Henry L. 12, 44, 87, 90
McDaniel, J. M. 252
McDaniel, James 173, 300
McDaniel, James M. 155
McDaniel, James P. 60
McDaniel, J. W. 269, 275, 286, 309, 320, 368, 385
McDaniel, James W. 301, 459
McDaniel, Peter 57, 58, 59, 63, 64, 65
McDaniel, Riley 39, 75
McDaniel, William 123, 175, 291, 292, 293
McDaniel, Wilson 133, 134
McDaniel, Wilson M. 233
McDaniel, Wm. 133
McDonald, George 210
McDonald, Henry 140
McDonald, James 131, 139
McDonald, Middleton 131, 139, 140
McDonald, Nicholas 12
McDonald, Peter 122, 133, 139
McDonald, William 131
McDonald, Wilson 131
McDonald, Wm. 139, 140, 198, 199
McGhee, John 341, 342
McGhue, Joel J. 163
McGhu, John R. 163
McGinnis, Wm. 196
McGuffin, Lilly 197
McGuffy, Edward 299, 351, 367, 368
McGuffy, Silas 368
McHenry, James W. 340
McKee, Benjamin 32, 70
McKee, Joseph 136, 137
McKee, Joseph Y. 110
McKee, Robert 332
McKee, Wm. 332
McKinley, F. B. 7
McKinney, James 143, 144, 145, 146
McKinney, James M. 172
McKinney, Robert 223

McKinny, James 185, 187
McKinny, James M. 263, 425, 426, 444, 445, 461
McNichols, Ab. 122
McNichols, Alex. B. 32
McMinnville 14
McWhirter, George 98
Medley, George 32, 109, 123
Medly, G. W. 385
Medly, George 296
Medly, Lewis 366
Medly, Patty 296
Merett, John 243
Merit, John 275
Meritt, John 233, 236, 237, 275, 267, 268
Mill Creek 12
Milledgeville 7
Miller, Armstead 219, 230
Miller, Calvin 399, 401, 452
Miller, Pleasant 219, 232, 354, 431
Miller, Samuel 308
Miller, W. H. 233, 417
Miller, Wade 439
Miller, Wade H. 438, 464, 469, 471, 476
Miller, Ward H. 234
Millidgeville 47
Mills, Curtis 142, 143, 144, 145, 146, 147, 332, 334, 411, 468
Mills, Henry 156
Mills, William J. 391
Mills, William 463, 474
Millsap, Hiram 167
Minnin, John A. 88
Mitchel, Sally 135
Mitchell, James C. 77, 79
Mitchell, Joseph 151, 240, 243, 323, 345, 375
Mitchell, William 275, 390, 456
Mitchell, William C. 266
Mitchell, Wm. 153, 169
Montgomery, Alexander 98, 391, 405
Montgomery, John 233
Montgomery, Robert 98
Moody, Michael 219
Moon, J. H. 256, 265, 266, 278, 367
Moon (or Moore) J. H. 373, 374
Moonyham, Shadrach 332, 340, 348, 351, 366, 367, 402
Moonyham, Shadrack 373, 374, 390, 423, 424, 461
Moore, J. H. 142, 143, 145, 146, 147, 244, 245, 472, 473

Moore, Jonathan 171
Moore, Russel 142
Moore, Russell 255, 256
Morgan, Amy 164, 166
Morris, William 55
Mott, Amos 148, 150, 193
Murphee, Kim 418
Murphree, Levi L. 41, 43
Murphy, Andrew 165, 270
Murphy, John 460
Murphy, K. M. 393
Murphy, (Murphee) L. L. 444, 445, 446
Murphy, Levi L. 186, 187
Murphy, Levi S. 470
Murphy, Robert 270
Murry, John P. 326, 463
Murry, Thomas B. 219, 302, 418
Murry, Thomas 148
Murry, Thomas T. 393
Myatt, Alexander 471
Myatt, Alfred 471

N

Nelson, William E. 341
Netherton, Henry 107, 308, 326, 335, 339, 344
Netherton, James 95
Newport, B. S. 205
Nicholas, A. B. 115
Nicholas, David 46, 308, 434, 435
Nicholas, Jonathan 120
Nicholas, Lincoln 405, 406
Nicholas, Thomas 7, 45, 47, 52, 62, 71, 151, 155, 173, 344
Nicholas, Thomas B. 90
Nicholas, Thomas T. 55, 56, 97
Nicholas, William 52
Nicholas, Z. B. 415
Nicholas, Lincoln 351
Nicholes, David H. 111
Nicholls, David H. 136, 137, 138
Nichols, David 45, 72, 143, 145, 146, 147
Nichols, David H. 136, 137
Nichols, Thomas 97, 132
Night, Wiley 37, 38, 400
Niss, James 365
Noland, Elijah 157
Norris, Nancy 153, 260, 272
Norris, Soloman 157
Norris, William 111, 260, 272
Norris, William R. 153
Null, John M. 196

O

Officer, Alexander 106
Officer, James 93, 101, 103, 104, 126, 463
Officer, James C. 269, 345, 353, 362, 474
Officer, John 45, 46, 103, 104, 151, 152
Officer, John H. 334, 422
Officer, Nancy 344, 350, 353
Officer, Robert 45, 46, 71, 72, 87, 93, 101, 106, 126
Officer, William 106
Officer, William D. 334
Officer, Wm. 422
Oldham, Nicholas 66, 67, 68, 69
Owen, A. H. 65, 67, 68
Owen, Albert H. 66
Owen, Hugh 12, 110, 113

P

Parson, James 35, 36
Patterson, F. N. 335, 367, 368, 375, 376, 378, 394, 395
Patterson, Felix 438, 440, 443
Patterson, Felix N. 241, 335, 336, 451
Patterson, N. A. 208
Pattom, Samuel 29, 31, 33, 50, 98
Patton, David 1, 2, 3, 47, 87, 90, 117
Patton, Henry 29, 50, 97, 98
Patton, Nancy 29, 50, 97, 98
Peak, William 237, 239
Pearin, Samuel P. 55
Pearson, Joseph 42, 83, 84, 103, 104, 141, 199, 200
Peek, James K. 250
Peek, Robert 41, 42
Peek, William 250, 351
Peek, William W. 281, 283
Peek, Wm. 148, 150
Pemberton, Henderson 203, 204
Pemberton, Stewart 205
Pennington, Dabner 278
Pennington, John 233, 234
Perkins, Jourdon 260, 261
Perrin, Samuel P. 114, 122
Perrington, Dabner 227
Pharris, James 117
Pharris, John 171
Phillips, Charles 14, 15
Phillips, David 14, 15
Phillips, James 15

Phillips, John 205, 206, 355
Phillips, Levi 261, 262, 287
Phillips, Spencer 81, 111, 112, 114, 129, 130, 148, 155, 261, 262, 284
Pile, Wm (or Pill) 201, 202
Pippin, James 440, 441
Pippin, Kirchin 285
Pippin, Reddin 16
Pippin, Willis 307, 440
Pistole, Levi M. 443, 444, 445, 446, 470
Pittito, Hampton 122
Plunket, James 405
Plunkett, James 462
Pointer, Jno. B. 415
Pointer, John B. 5, 72, 78, 96, 105, 244, 245, 296, 351, 415, 438, 456, 458
Pointer, Permelia 382, 383, 385
Pointer, Thomas 287, 288, 289, 290
Pointer, Thomas T. 244, 245
Polard, Jesse 72
Pollard, Jesse 13, 27, 28, 49
Porter, E. R. 170
Porter, Thomas 374
Porter, Thomas A. 476
Poteet, Thomas J. 354, 374, 397
Pott, John 79
Potts, John 40
Prestley, M. N. 168
Price, John 201
Price, Shadrach 7
Prichard, Mansel 219
Prickett, Benjamin 259
Prock, N. J. 283
Pryer, Wm. 83
Puckett, G. W. 297
Pullin, Thomas 154, 172, 259, 325, 365, 459, 470, 471, 477

Q

Quarles, William H. 31, 32, 40, 41, 120
Quarles, Wm. H. 27

R.

Rains, James 157
Ramsey, George 462
Ramsey, H. 171, 266
Ramsey, Hampton 151, 152, 171, 295, 301, 341, 355
Ramsey, James 415, 452

Ramsey, John 397, 409, 476, 478, 479
Ramsey, Robert 201
Randolf, Pleasant 41, 42, 247
Randolph, Joseph 467, 468
Raney, Delila 89, 90
Ranson, Sarah 85, 86
Rasson, Sarah 74
Rawson, Sarah 86
Ray, J. A. 258, 305, 379, 381, 382, 383, 384
Ray, John 79
Ray, Joseph A. 23
Ray, Richard 148
Read, James 219
Reagan, Charles 201, 202
Rector, Owen B. 278
Reed, C. C. (or Read) 205
Rhea, Birds (or Ray) 86
Rhea, J. A. 193, 194, 303, 304
Rich, Jesse 157
Rich, Whitlsy 205, 206
Richard, Caleb 73
Richard, John 201
Richards, William H. 28
Richardson, Jeffry N. 161, 167
Richardson, John 240, 241, 285, 342, 463
Richardson, Sarah 316, 317
Richardson, William 240, 285, 342, 463
Richardson, William B. 88
Richardson, William H. 89
Richardson, Wm. H. 27
Richerson, Barnett 243
Richison (Richardson) J. W. 392
Right, Jeremiah 162
Riley, John F. 201, 202
Riley, Thomas 157, 158, 161
Ripitoe, William 326, 335, 339, 344
Robards, John 241
Roberson, Alexander C. 40
Roberson, E. M. 157
Roberson, James 417, 418
Roberson, James R. 220
Roberson, Preston 344, 350, 353
Roberson, William 350
Robert, Henry 73
Robert, John 285, 375, 376, 378
Roberts, Evan 205
Roberts, F. M. 379
Roberts, Henry 308, 323, 335, 336, 342, 438, 439, 440
Roberts, J. H. 379, 386

Roberts, James R. 222
Roberts, John 354, 355, 356, 357, 358, 359, 360, 387, 453, 460, 463
Roberts, John A. 151, 152
Roberts, John H. 394, 395
Roberts, Joseph 258, 298, 336
Roberts, Leah 126
Roberts, Marian 378
Robertson, Charles V. 247
Robinson, Alexander 48
Robinson, Alexander C. 79, 102
Robinson, James 148, 150
Robinson, John 48, 102, 116
Robison, Leah 93, 101
Robison, William 398, 454
Rockholt, Robert 52
Rock Spring Valley 288, 290
Rodgers, Claiborne 462
Rodgers, Jesse 27
Rodgers, John 75, 108
Rodgers, Joseph 367
Rodgers, Mathew 59, 60
Rogers, William 103, 104, 133, 298, 299, 370, 403
Roland, Jefferson 299
Roland, John 34, 392
Roland, N. B. 415
Roland, Wm. B. 395
Rollin, Jefferson 278
Rowland, Baldwin 88, 90, 95, 100, 124, 125, 126
Rowland, Louisa Jane 95
Rowland, Stokes 415, 449
Rowland, William 93
Rowland, Wm. B. 351
Russel, Presley 474
Ryan, Joel 205

S

Saddler, Henry 417, 420, 434, 435, 438, 439, 455, 458, 460, 464
Sadler, Garrett 118, 119
Sadler, Henry 131, 139, 151, 469, 471, 476
Sadler, Henry M. 156
Sadler, Henry W. 5, 113, 152
Sadler, Isaac 351
Sadler, John K. 27, 148
Sadler, Washington 118, 119, 120
Sadler, William 118, 119
Sanders, Martin 90, 93
Satwood, Pemberton 212
Savage, John H. 33
Savage, John K. 90

Saylor, Thomas 274, 349, 397
Saylor, William 374
Saylors, Thomas 55, 110
Scarborough, James 11
Scarborough, William 8, 9, 107
Scarborough, Wm. 49
Scarlett, Moses 130
Scarlett, Moses N. 111
Schooler, James B. 211
Schooler, Wm. L. 211
Scott, George 229
Scroggins, Samuel 219
Scudder, Thomas 308, 326, 335, 339, 344
Sells, George 125
Sexton, Amanda 214
Sexton, Bird 275, 276
Sexton, Fountain 209, 210, 213, 214, 222, 230, 389, 451
Sexton, Manda 222
Shanks, Craven 367
Shanks, W. 435
Shanks, William 415
Sharpman, John 205
Shaw, Joseph 292, 361, 369, 371, 392
Shaw, T. J. 323
Shaw, Thomas J. 308
Shepherd (Shepard) Gorden 368
Shepherd, Levi 201
Sherrell, Joshua 391
Shipley, Eli 354, 355
Shoat, Austin 301
Shoat, Austin 301
Shoat, (Or Choate) Edward 183
Shoat, John 5, 294
Simmons, John 29, 74, 75
Simpkin, Samuel 137
Simpkins, Samuel 123
Simpson, Betsy 352
Simpson, J. W. 175, 431
Simpson, John G. 270
Simpson, John M. 166
Simpson, John N. 164, 167
Sims, A. 71
Sims, Abraham 27, 44, 308
Sims, Absalem 155
Sims, Absalom 151, 409
Sims, Absalom A. 104
Sims, Absolem W. 399
Sims, Absolom 77, 80, 125, 173, 284
Sims, D. W. 262, 275, 301, 307
Sims, Drury 151, 152, 246, 247, 375, 376
Sims, Drury W. 282
Sims, Dury 285, 286

Sims, Martin 103, 104, 105, 106, 107, 108, 121, 132, 133, 136, 137
Sims, N. D. 287
Sims, W. G. 269, 345, 353, 362, 463
Sylger, (Sliger) John 393, 419
Smellage, Joseph 368
Smith, Alexander 74
Smith, Charles 77, 95, 109, 337
Smith, George 157, 158
Smith, Gideon 300
Smith, H. L. 276, 300
Smith, Hugh 443, 451
Smith, Isam 149, 150, 153, 169, 173, 236, 246, 250, 373, 394, 443, 451
Smith, J. L. 207
Smith, J. R. 300
Smith, James H. 300
Smith, John 37, 196
Smith, Jonathan 386
Smith, Leroy B. 191
Smith, Littleton 412
Smith, M. S. 300, 400
Smith Mathew 260
Smith, Mathews 278, 470
Smith, Mathis 283, 284
Smith, M. E. J. 300
Smith, N. I. A. 300
Smith, Robert 31, 151, 152, 410, 419, 443, 470
Smith, Robert S. 71
Smith, Samuel 74
Smith, T. F. 210, 211
Smith, Thomas 103, 104, 115
Smith, Thomas J. 385
Smith, Wm. 201, 202
Snodgrass, James 8, 9, 10, 11, 17, 18, 22, 23
Snowden, Maddux 111
Sparks, Levi 426
Sparta 7, 47, 136
Sparta Gazette 29, 34
Spears, Joseph 98
Spencer, Phillips 138
Spivey, T. S. 426, 427, 428
Stamps, Edmond 16, 17, 18, 77, 80, 87, 88, 90
Stamps, William 46, 71, 72
Stamps, Wm. 45
Stanly, Shadrack 346
Stanton, Champ 125
Stanton, Garland 148
Stanton, Jesse 82
Stanton, Milton 154, 172, 291

Stars, Eli 162
Stephen, Wilson 90
Stephens, James 14
Stephens, Martin 247
Stephens, W. G. 170
Stephens, William 123
Stephens, William W. 125
Stephenson, Caleb 164
Stepp, John 157
Stevens, Caleb 166, 175
Stewart, John 354, 391, 459
Stewart, Preston 251, 365
Stewart, Reece C. 27
Stewart, Seborn 468
Stone, Claibourne 32
Stone, Enoch H. 354, 355
Stone, Josh R. 478
Stone, Joshua 474
Stone, S. C. 191, 340
Stone, Samuel 190
Stone, William P. 455, 456, 458, 460, 464, 471, 474
Stone, Wm. P. 417, 420, 434, 435, 438, 439, 469
Sullens, Zechareal 114
Summer, Levi 211
Suttle, Leroy 190
Sutton, Abraham 298
Sutton, Almarine 137
Sutton, James 137
Sutton, James H. 123
Sutton, John 114
Swaraingin, George 306, 307

T

Talton, A. N. O. 223
Taylor, L. R. 424
Taylor, Lee B. 460, 462
Taylor, Lee R. 185, 261, 262
Taylor, W. J. 199
Taylor, William T. 240, 253, 254, 255, 264, 265
Taylor, Wm. J. 155, 156
Terry, Bob 38
Terry, Carr 38, 42, 417, 418
Terry, Curtis 172, 308, 326, 335, 339, 344, 400, 409
Terry, E. W. 399, 401, 406
Terry, James 77, 80, 88, 90, 183, 272
Terry, James B. 264, 294, 425, 452, 454
Terry, Jesse 65, 67, 96
Terry, Jesse B. 12, 32, 41, 66, 67, 68, 69, 127, 133, 145, 234, 275

Terry, John 1, 2, 3, 5, 21, 83, 84, 182, 183, 244, 245, 264, 284, 306, 339, 348, 392, 401, 451, 463, 470, 476
Terry, Joseph 7
Terry, Samuel 341
Terry, Vincent M. 285
Thomas, Abner, 205, 206
Thomas, Nicholas 54
Thomas, Pointer 114
Thompson, Chunky 415
Thompson, E. L. 170, 171, 294, 295, 324, 381, 382, 383, 384, 444
Thompson, Gilbert 370
Thompson, Hasten 415
Thompson, Haston 449
Thompson, Henry 415, 449
Thompson, Plunky 449
Thompson, Rayburn 205, 206
Thompson, Rowland 415, 449
Thompson, Thomas 406
Tilly, Henderson 278, 280
Tousdale, John 407, 408
Travis, Davis C. 158
Tucker, John 476
Turner, Sterling T. 220, 222
Turner, William 440
Turny, Samuel 373

U

Upchurch, George 201
Upchurch, S. M. 175
Upchurch, S. N. 166
Upchurch, Washington 164

V

Vaden, John 27
Vaden, Samuel 2, 27
Vaden, Samuel T. 27, 44, 55, 70, 75, 77, 80, 87, 101, 104, 108
Vance, Lewis R. 31, 54, 71, 75, 86, 115, 122
Vance, William 28
Vance, William R. 54, 78, 90, 93, 101, 125
Vance, Wm. R. 53, 108
Vandever, Wm. 428, 429, 430
Vaughn, Edward 241, 285, 392, 395, 453
Vick, Nathan 38
Vickes, Linnsey 386, 387

W

Walker, Evander 161
Walker, Robert 441
Walker, William 354, 355
Wallace, A. J. 240, 284, 323, 472
Wallace, Hugh 14, 72, 184, 249, 283, 300, 310, 311, 314, 316, 317, 319, 322, 338, 348, 355, 394, 439
Wallace, Jackson 233, 234
Wallace, Laban 30
Wallace, Mathew 33
Wallace, Mathew H. 105
Wallace (Wallis) William 355
Wallis, Hugh 278
Wallis, (or Wallace) Hugh 197
Wallis, Laban 28
Ward, Nelly 103, 104
Ward, Stepehn 170, 171
Warly, T. W. 454
Warly, Perry W. 459
Washburn, D. B. 142, 391
Washburn, Benjamin B. 478
Wassum, Andrew 1, 2, 3
Waters, Joseph 205
Watson, B. H. 177, 178, 179, 180, 185, 256, 265
Watson, B. W. 185
Watson, Benj. H. 471
Watson, Benjamin 185, 186, 187, 267, 276, 324, 419
Watson, Benjamin F. 152, 176, 260, 325, 326, 339, 351, 366, 374
Watson, Dowell J. 354
Watson, Jabers 70
Watson, Jno. 186
Watson, John 60, 66, 83, 123, 127, 187, 251, 280, 325, 409, 470
Watson, John S. 151, 155, 173, 237, 239
Watson, Lucy 152, 366, 419
Watson, Thomas 114, 115
Watson, Thomas F. 52
Watson, Thomas J. 155, 173
Watson, Thomas L. 151
Watson, Thomas T. 150, 186, 187, 324, 351
Watson, Towns 472, 473
Watt, John 403, 404
Watts, Bennet 132, 133, 140
Watts, John 331, 333, 334, 340, 365, 391, 410, 412, 420, 473
Watts, Mason 132, 140
Watts, Thomas 77, 79, 140
Webb, Austin 103, 104, 105, 106, 107, 108, 121, 132, 133, 136, 137

Webb, Ducela 396
Webb, John 136, 137
Webb, Josiah 395
Webb, William 148, 150, 236, 237, 240, 250, 264, 267
Welch, George 90, 103, 104, 105, 106, 107, 108, 110, 120, 121, 124, 132, 133, 136, 137
Welch, John 12, 14, 15, 22, 26, 28, 37, 38, 124
Welch, Mathias 34, 35, 42
Welch, Thomas 41, 42, 48, 49, 82, 96, 105
West, Anderson 233, 236, 237, 264, 267
West, John 1, 45, 46, 71, 72, 148, 150, 250, 251, 252, 269, 470
West, Reubin 205, 206
Wheeler, Elijah 335
Whitacre, David 283, 284
Whitacre, Henry 152
Whitaker, David 278
Whitaker, Elias 199, 381, 388, 425, 433, 434, 435
Whitaker, Henry 189, 276, 354, 455, 471, 473, 475
Whitaker, Hickman 295, 341, 399, 400
Whitaker, Isaac 85, 233, 236, 237, 250, 251, 265, 267
Whitaker, J. J. 448
Whitaker, John 82, 83
Whitaker, Robert 278
Whitaker, T. J. 414
Whitaker, Zilly 199, 388
White, Charlotte 464
White, Charlotte 346, 349
White, James 346, 371, 476
White, John C. 346, 471, 476
White, Joshua 264, 275, 301, 345, 349, 464
Whiteacre, Elias 149
Whiteacre, John 42, 93, 96
Whiteacre, William 42
Whiteaker, Nathaniel 112, 113
Whited, Robert 157
Whitefield, Carter 29
Whitefield, Carter B. 278
Whitefield, John 191
Whitefield, Josiah 233, 234
Whitefield, William 298
White Plains 1, 2, 7, 14, 27, 29, 43, 44, 50, 76, 85, 86, 103, 131, 134, 141
Whitson, Jeremiah 10, 22, 365, 393

Whitson, Hamson 49
Whitson, Harrison 16, 17
Whitson, John 151, 152
Whitson, Reubin 150, 345, 399, 400
Whitson, Ruebin 283, 284
Whitten, Martin 172
Whitton, Marton 270
Wiering, Eliese 142
Wiering, Emma 142
Wilkerson, Esther 98
Wilkerson, Samuel K. 237, 374, 405, 409, 418, 478
Williams, Alfred 201, 202
Williams, John 158, 161, 163, 164
Williams, Samuel H. 95
Williams, T. A. 421
Williams, T. H. 234, 375, 376, 388, 389, 423
Williams, Theopholis 157, 158
Williams, Tim. H. 156, 332, 334, 467
Williams, Timothy H. 455
Williams, W. F. 83
Williams, Washington 125
Williams, Washington F. 27
Williams, Wilburn 164, 166, 175
Williams, William 212
Williams, William M. 212
Williams, Wm. M. 211
Williamson, Wm. B. 201
Willmoth, William 54, 87, 99
Wilmoth, Wilson 284
Wilson, Jonathan 219
Winchester, Thersay 248
Wisor, Rebecca 412
Wnoe, Benjamin F. 13, 67, 69, 77, 80, 82, 83, 87
Wright, Isaac 165
Wright, James 364, 431, 432
Wright, James M. 164, 166, 175

Wright, James W. 176
Wright, Jo. Mitchell 230, 232
Wright, Maxwell 231
Wright, Mitchell 163, 253
Wright, W. D. 270
Wright, W. L. 222, 389, 451
Wright, Wilson, L. 157, 165, 201, 230

Y

Yoman, Baldwin Rowland 88, 89, 90
York, Elijah 229
Young, Allen 73, 75, 87, 107, 118, 119, 120, 121, 243, 268, 323, 326, 367, 392, 401, 451, 459, 464, 478, 479
Young, Allin 440
Young, Berdine 157, 158
Young, James 77, 79
Young, John 390, 456
Young, John Jr. 212
Young, John H. 120, 278
Young, John M. 440
Young, Parker, 201, 202
Young, Robert 164, 174, 175, 176, 201
Young, Samuel 60
Young, W. F. 417, 420, 434, 435, 438
Young, William 93, 201
Young, William F. 439, 455, 456, 458, 459, 460, 463, 471, 476
Young, Wm. F. 65
Young, Wm. T. 469

THE END

www.ingramcontent.com/pod-product-compliance
Lightning Source LLC
Chambersburg PA
CBHW020641300426
44112CB00007B/203